D1000883

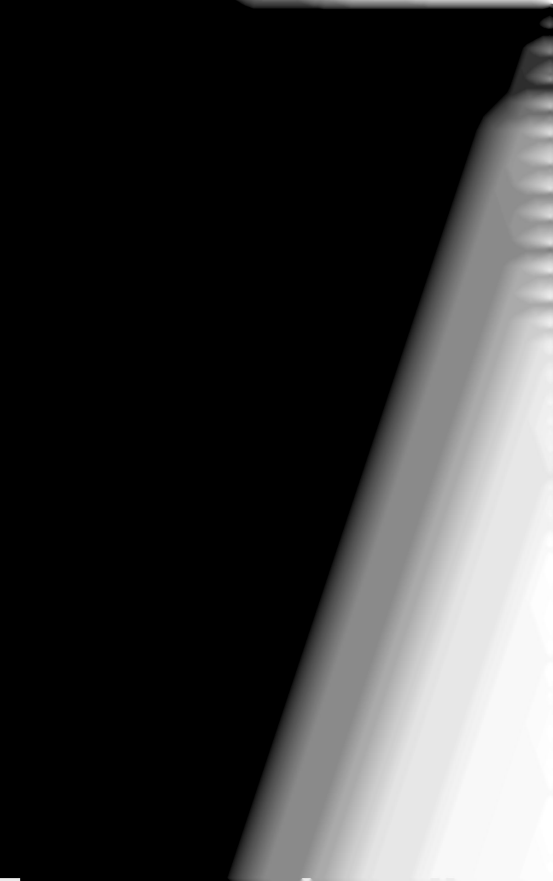

# PLANES OF COMPOSITION
*Dance, Theory and the Global*

Edited by André Lepecki and Jenn Joy

LONDON NEW YORK CALCUTTA

**Seagull Books 2009**

© Individual authors 2008

ISBN-13   978 1 9064 9 724 8

ISSN      1751 0864

**British Library Cataloguing-in-Publication Data**

A catalogue record for this book is available from the British Library

Typeset by Seagull Books, Calcutta, India
Printed and bound by Spectra Graphics, Calcutta, India

CONTENTS

## PREFACE

ANDRÉ LEPECKI AND JENN JOY

When thinking about dance, dancing, theorizing dance and how these practices respond, move with and are moved by our current political, economic
and discursive predicament of a globalized planet, an insight from one of the
contributors to this volume, the German philosopher Peter Sloterdijk, is of
particular relevance: 'The current implementation of networks encircling the
entire Earth—along with all its virtual excrescences—does not represent so
much, from a structural point of view, a globalization, than a foamization
[écumisation]' (2002: 80).

By displacing the emphasis from the figure of the globe as metaphor for
the planetary condition, and replacing it with the bubbling dynamic of foam,
Sloterdijk is identifying the demise of all narratives that insist on 'a unique
integrating hypersphere' (ibid.: 80). Rather, our current condition, where a
hyper-mobilization of the planet is under way, primarily fuelled by well-
tested colonialist and capitalist policies and dynamics, demands the creation
of a political phenomenology of heterogeneities—a theory that acknowledges
the reality of the irregular, the proliferation of dynamic eccentricities, and
thus challenges the very notion of centre upon which colonial and postcolonial melancholic and neoliberal kineticism gain their organizational and
hegemonic forces.

As market imperatives propel the circulation of bodies, commodities, capital and bytes across ever more controlled borders, the question of mobilization, so central to the project of critical dance studies (as Randy Martin so accurately proposed [1998]), remains the question for performance and dance theory to tackle.

How to choreograph, or how to improvise, a mobilization of limbs and of thinking (never in opposition to each other, but always already chiasmatically coupled in generative assemblages) that does not fall prey to other forces of mobilization at the service of market acceleration and neo-imperial dislocations? How to dance and how to theorize dancing that explicitly addresses the fact that its grounds are heterogeneous, dynamic, bumpy, bubbling, treacherous, violent, resonant, vibrant and always inventive political terrains? These questions not only challenge dancers and choreographers to reconsider the premises under which they create their dance practices, but they also challenge dance theorists to rethink what may be the adequate analytical and critical tools for these dances.

In this challenge, what needs to be activated is the capacity for discourse to always escape itself, to decentre itself, to misbehave and flee in order to find and forge words, concepts, sites and sentences whose heterogeneity would inform a renewed critical-kinetic effort to revitalize well-established, properly poised theoretical positions. In order for critical dance studies to enter into a dialogue with the political dynamics of the current planetary mobilization, it must hear what the particularities of postcolonial critiques, what the heterogeneous voices of decentred positions and subjectivities, what the forces of critical and neo-Marxist theories, and what the forces animating any philosophical project that replaces ethics for ontology (and that, moreover, ties that ethics to a resisting biopolitics that relaunches, in a pragmatic, empirical way, Spinoza's call to experimentally know 'what a body can do') have to add to our understanding of dance today. This is not yet another call for interdisciplinarity but rather a call for the activation of a slightly chaotic, slightly uncontrollable, theoretical foaming, exact and rigorous, poetic and political, dynamic and concrete, as a way to allow for these heterogeneities to become critical imperatives.

But, if it is about imperatives, these should never become absolute sovereigns, totalitarian choreographers enacting a reinscription of origin as the sole qualifier for a critical position. If postcolonial theory, dance studies, philosophy and performance studies are the four major fields invoked in the essays gathered in this book, the worst that could happen would be to see the first as belonging only to third and fourth worlds; the second as belonging only to dance; the third as belonging primarily to Euro-American contexts; and the fourth as belonging only to performance art.

To use a concept advanced by another contributor to this anthology, Anurima Banerji, any politically informed theory is already a theory attuned to the concrete performance practices bubbling out of the quotidian and the aesthetic realms. Her neologism 'paratopia' describes such theory as a performative force running along and beyond the placedness of place, fully participating in the dynamics of movement that promotes change by (choreographically) carving for itself an agential suturing between actions, gestures, steps, moves and dance styles with thought, concept, theory, critique and biopolitics. Banerji's notion of the paratopic complicates the notion of site and place as the location of cultural resistance and political action. Thus, by necessity, it complicates notions of dance. Again, the dynamics of foaming, the force of heterogeneities, demand a particular alliance between phenomenology and politics, between movement and concept, and between critical dance theories and dance practices understood as critical forces. The question is how and when and where to activate these forces—which is basically a choreographic question.

Perhaps for this reason, Richard Schechner in 2006 generously accepted an unusual proposal for the journal he has edited for many years: to have a short series, guest-edited by André Lepecki, spread out in three issues of *The Drama Review* (*TDR*), on 'Dance and Philosophy'.[1] The opening essays for the series already indicated that the philosophy being invoked by the series was one explicitly related to dance and to kinetics and was also profoundly embedded in a 'practical philosophy' with direct political drives. Indeed, given the current performative turn in choreographic creation, a turn where conceptualism and critical theory are central, it is not a surprise to find out that many of the choreographers discussed in the essays for that series were drawing from philosophy, from postcolonial theory, from neurosciences, from psychoanalysis, from queer and feminist theories, from critical race studies, and from performance studies (in sum, from *theory*) to further experiment with moving, with embodying, with gesturing, with dancing.

The *TDR* series 'dance composes philosophy composes dance' is thus the heterogeneous ground from which the current book took shape. In expanding the series into a book, we decided to make explicit the imperative of theory in the creation of a multilingual, decentred and planetary discussion on dance. Thus, the 18 essays animate the many planes of composition that arise from these hybrid theoretical and performative formations—compositions between everyday kinetics and philosophical considerations of political modernity; compositions between particular choreographic works and particular formations of race in the postcolonial context; compositions between body practices and theoretical practices.

We invited a diverse team of eminent scholars, artists and choreographers, as well as new critical voices coming from different continents and countries (from the United States to Portugal, from Belgium to Brazil), and from different disciplines (from political philosophy to performance studies, from postcolonial theory to aesthetics), to address a variety of topics: these ranged from racialization and urbanity in globalization (from Hong Kong to India) to the ethics of dance in contemporaneity (finding this ethics in unexpected places and characters, like Walter Carter, co-creating a true paratopia with choreographer, writer and visual artist Ralph Lemon in the US Deep South); from the kinetics of the private political body discussed by Jeroen Peeters to Victoria Anderson Davies' meditation on the ethics of faciality in contemporary choreography.

'The Stop and Go of Postmodernity' titles this anthology's first section and begins with German philosopher Peter Sloterdijk's critique of critical theory that points to modernity's imperative toward movement and extends to the particularities of gesture arising in response to these cultural and political imperatives. Against the hyper-legibility of the violent act, Jenn Joy discusses the spasm's disruption through sensual address in the work of Jeremy Wade and Bill Durgin. The politics of postcolonial or neocolonial identity is addressed by SanSan Kwan through the work of Hong Kong's City Dance Company during the moment of Hong Kong's handover from British to Chinese rule. Royona Mitra negotiates the ambivalent spaces of postcoloniality through the relationship between diasporic identity and classical dance in the work of Akram Khan.

The encounter between philosophies of perception and economies of movement explored in the second section of this anthology ('Assembling

Relations') opens with José Gil's meditation on the paradoxical body; Noémie Solomon stages the meeting of French choreographer Mathilde Monnier and philosopher Jean-Luc Nancy; Erin Manning extends the problem of affective relationality to tango; Paula Caspão describes economies of movement and language as stuttering fields; Frédéric Pouillaude considers time—as a constantly morphing present, as a trace on the edge of disappearance, as polemical affiliation between modernity and postmodernity through contemporary French choreographic works.

The final section, 'Expanding Choreography', examines contemporary works by artists and choreographers including South African Robin Rhode, Iranian-Norwegian Hooman Sharifi, Indian Chandralekha and Brazilian Marta Soares to articulate how dance itself acts as a radical political discourse, a new philosophical mode. This section also explores specific choreographic techniques—André Lepecki addresses athleticism in the work of visual artist Robin Rhode; Gerald Siegmund examines the containment of the spectator in the work of Boris Charmatz; Danielle Goldman questions the function of improvisation through the choreography of Deborah Hay; Christine Greiner aligns the anthropological with cognitive science to argue for a political conception of self through dance; Myriam Van Imschoot translates gesture as simultaneously a philosophical and corporeal mode that resists language and representation—to foreground the production of new subjectivities through physicality. This section also includes a new graphic and textual piece by Ralph Lemon juxtaposing drawings and notes from his project *Come Home Charley Patton* and tracing the interstitial relationships between memory, geography and race.

Shifting between critical theory and the dancing body, philosophies of movement and choreographic motion, *Planes of Composition: Dance, Theory and the Global* asks how the mutual interrogation of dance and philosophy might recompose another agency for both disciplines.

*Note*

1   The guest editor of the series was André Lepecki, based on his proposal to *TDR*. Jenn Joy became the assistant editor assigned to the series. Both Jenn and André are extremely grateful not only to Richard Schechner for his

generosity in hosting a series that went slightly against the general editorial project of *TDR*, but also to Mariellen Sandford for her unflinching support of the series, and for her unwavering professionalism and commitment to the project. Thank you also to T. Nikki Cesare.

*References*

Martin, Randy. 1998. *Critical Moves: Dance Studies in Theory and Politics*. Durham: Duke University Press.

Sloterdijk, Peter. 2002. *Sphéres I. Bulles. Microsphérologie* (Olivier Mannoni trans.). Paris: Fayard.

# PART I

## THE STOP AND GO OF POSTMODERNITY

# MOBILIZATION OF THE PLANET FROM THE SPIRIT OF SELF-INTENSIFICATION

PETER SLOTERDIJK

In this essay,[1] the interpretation of the present is based on a philosophical kinetics originating from three axioms. First, that we are moving in a world that is moving itself; second, that the self-movements of the world include our own self-movements and affect them; and third, that in modernity, the self-movements of the world originate from our self-movements, which are cumulatively added to world movement. From these axioms, it is possible to more or less entirely develop a relationship between an old world, a modern world and a postmodern world.

If we want to show the world in its motion as pregnant with catastrophes, we have to assume that today's world process has received its dynamics from the initiatives accumulated over the past centuries. Thus, a perception of the present that claims to be at the level of real events presupposes something that has hitherto been successfully rejected by intellectual conscience: a physics of freedom, a kinetics of moral initiatives. Let's say it openly: this is the end of aestheticism in cultural theory. The seemingly most empty, the most external, the most mechanical movement (which had been left to the physicists and sports medicine doctors to research) penetrates the humanities and at once turns out to be the cardinal category, even of the moral and social sphere.

As an expression of movement, the ethical-political adventures of the human mind become a branch of physics. While all over the West ethics commissions gather for seminars, while everywhere people with good intentions sacrifice their weekends to discuss the principles of new morals in idyllic sites of evangelical academies and political study centres, the best-guarded secret of modernity seeps from the hermetic studios of fundamental philosophical research into the world. What nobody wanted to know became unambiguously evident. What nobody wanted to understand, angrily and stridently forced its way into our thought. Once it has been spoken out loud, the revealed secret evokes the question: why hasn't this most obvious thing been given attention long ago? Some urbanists and a few military theorists who were willing to speculate knew it first; dubious philosophers who distrusted modernity thought about it; schizos in intellectual circles in big cities followed the urbanists' example and got really into it; swanky art and literature sections in newspapers started talking about the matter—soon there will be many of them who say that they always knew it. Knew what? Well, the trivial fact that kinetics is the ethics of modernity.

What is worrisome or even obscene about this can only be diminished by referring to the old doctrines of progress that we are very familiar with. There, the relationship of morals and kinetics seemed still to be controlled morally. As a matter of fact, modernity has also defined itself from the beginning in kinetic terms because it determined its mode of realization and existence as advancing and progressive. Progress is the expression of movement in which the ethical-kinetic self-awareness of modern times expresses itself most powerfully yet at the same time is heavily disguised. If we mention progress we mean the kinetic and kinetic-aesthetic fundamental motive of modernity, which has as its only goal the elimination of the limits of human self-movement. At the beginning of progress there was the presumption, whether right or wrong, of a 'moral' initiative that cannot rest until the better has become the real. It belongs to the experience of real progress that a valuable human initiative comes 'out of itself', that it tears apart the old limits of mobility, that it broadens its work spectrum, and that it asserts itself with a good conscience against inner inhibitions and outer resistance.

In the political, technological and historical-philosophical doctrines of progress, the ongoing epoch declared its kinetic self-evidence. However, what it did not admit loudly was its secret inclination to take the moral motives seriously only to the extent that they serve as engines of outer movements. It is part of the essence of a progressive process to begin with ethical initiatives in order to continue its kinetic self-movements. It remains one of the great secrets of 'progress': how was it able at its initial spark to meld together morality and physics, motives and movements into an active unit? This secret leads us into the centre of what modern philosophy calls subjectivity. Its essence is inseparable from the mysterious initial force that expresses itself as the ability to ignite new chains of movement, which we call 'actions'. If something like progress does exist as a matter of fact it is because movements originating from subjectivity do undeniably take place. Kinetically they are the material that modernity is made of. When a subject gets to the point of carrying out the thought 'progress', then within him a self-igniter introduces progress-like self-movements. Whoever really knows what progress is already is moving toward what has been conceived; he knows it because he has progressed and is progressing further. Those who understand what modernity is can only understand it based on the self-igniting self-movement without which modernity would not exist. He must have made a step forward in his self-creation—the step that remains the kinetic element of further progress. Progress is initiated by this step toward the step that at first introduces itself, by itself, in order to run over itself. Therefore, the term 'progress' does not mean a simple change of position where an agent advances from A to B. In its essence, the only 'step' that is progressive is the one that leads to an increase in the 'ability to step'. Thus, the formula of modernizing processes is as follows: progress is movement toward movement, movement toward increased movement, movement toward an increased mobility.

Only because of the validity of this formula are ethics an immediate result of kinetics in modernity. Ethical imperatives of the modern type that are not at the same time kinetic impulses no longer exist. The categorical impulse of modernity is: in order to be continuously active as progressive beings man should overcome all the conditions where his movement is reduced, where he has come to a halt, where he lost his freedom and where he is pitifully fixed.[2]

To the same degree as we modern subjects understand freedom a priori as freedom of movement, progress is only thinkable for us as the kind of movement that leads to a higher degree of mobility. In a physical sense, movements toward freedom are always steps toward freedom of movement. We always mean self-movement even if we talk about self-determination. Before any differentiation between 'being' and 'having to be doing', the meaning of 'being' in modernity is understood as 'having to be' and 'wanting to be' more mobile. Ontologically, modernity is a pure 'being-toward-movement'. This interpretation of being is valid *for us* due to the fact that it becomes irresistibly real through us. It is irresistible because it cannot be reached by any countermovements and because the resistance leads to a moral ruin. It becomes real because it is executed by us in a mode of spontaneous will that does not allow criticism. In 'being-toward-movement', these circulating motives seem to come from the innermost of what we ourselves want and have to want. If the fundamental process of modernity promotes itself as a 'human movement to free oneself', then it is a process that we absolutely do not want and a movement that it is impossible for us not to make. It seems that there is a moral kinetic automatism working that 'condemns us not only to freedom' but also to a constant movement toward freedom.

If we realize the great changes of the modern world within ourselves, we immediately notice in our steps toward a higher mobility a deep contradiction. It is true that we have achieved an enormous range in numerous areas through the movement progress of modern generations, and what members of the modern bourgeoisie and middle class have achieved in the course of less than two centuries in the fields of politics, economics, language, information, traffic, expression and sex can almost be considered a miracle. There is the evidence of a kinetic 'tradition in modernity', no matter how suspicious the continuation of this tradition may be. However, in order to teach the agents of modernity a kind of astute mobility, most steps toward progress have also led to new types of forced movements that wrestle with the suffocating endings of premodern times regarding unknown forces and miserable energy.[3]

Modern 'dynamism' has made a contribution toward preserving the mindless rigour among super-mobile forms. Whoever wants to know what this means in detail has to find the right answer to the question 'What do machines, industrial companies and executive staff have in common with politics and economics?'—and to discover that these three agents contain an exemplary kinetic lesson for the citizens of modernity since they demonstrate effectively what self-movement wants and does: to start operations in order to be operating, to start up in order to keep running at any cost. This is the art of automation, which does not make any fundamental distinctions between intelligent machines and human agents. When the kinetic self-starts operations and takes the initiative, it becomes the central agency of the self-operated operation by its 'own' power.

This self-initiating subject is the miller of the 'mill of modern times that is grinding itself'—as the poet Novalis, in his 1799 essay on Europe,[4] referred to the principal course of the human–nature factory that started its operations at the time, and which gained impetus through prosaic self-motivating entrepreneur types, Protestants, Brits, Prussians and professors. At the same time, Novalis was the first to bring up the concept of the kinetic utopia of modernity by thinking of the subject and the machine together in the image of the 'mill itself', 'the real perpetuum mobile driven by the stream of coincidence and swimming in it', combining both kinds of movement (endogenous self-movement and exogenous external movement) into common motion—a motion, of course, where that which is dynamic is equally miserable, a drift driven by the I into mindlessness, catastrophe, loss of inhibition, death.

The diagnostic power of Novalis' formulations was not comprehensible to us in its full extent until today. In the meantime, we know without a breath of romantic irony *what* the self is able to achieve in *its* machine even if it is not quite a self-grinding mill. At least one of its utopian plans has been accomplished by modern society: the plan of complete automobilization—a circumstance in which every adult self moves itself at the wheel of its self-moving machine. Since in modernity the thought of the self without *its* movement is impossible, the I and its automobile belong together metaphysically like the soul and body of one and the same movement unit. The automobile is the technical double of the always active transcendental subject.

Therefore, the automobile is the sanctum of modernity; it is the cultural centre of a kinetic world religion; it is the rolling sacrament that makes us participate in something faster than ourselves. Whoever is driving an automobile is approaching the divine; he feels how his diminutive I is expanding into a higher self that offers us the whole world of highways as a home and that makes us realize that we are predestined to a life beyond the animal-like life of pedestrians.

From the view of motorists, we lived for a while in the Messianic time, in the fulfilled time where two-stroke vehicles were parked peacefully next to two-cylinder vehicles. The low-emission Messiah ruled in his celestial empire; with electronic ignition and ABS, with a controlled catalytic converter and turbo charger he lifted up his people to a celestial ride. But not all contemporaries let themselves be convinced that this ultimate automobile empire was paradise on earth. The antagonist had a finger in the pie and made sure that general self-movement turned occasionally into general immobility. In such moments we become aware, although we want to deny it, that we have already been chased out of the paradise of modernity, and that, in the future, we will have to learn the postmodern stop-and-go by the sweat of our brow. Therefore, the endless traffic jams each summer on Central Europe's highways (and the legendary power blackouts in New York, which make us feel nostalgic) are a phenomenon of historical-philosophical or even religious-historical importance. Such situations represent the failure of fake modernity, the end of an illusion—like a kinetic Good Friday when all hope for redemption by acceleration is lost. On these glowing hot afternoons in the funnel in Lyon, in the hellish Rhine valley near Cologne, or caught in Irschenberg, Europe's longest parking lot, in a 30-mile-long caravan of immobile and hot steaming steel, dark thoughts rise into the air just like black exhaust fumes; drivers gain historical-philosophical insight; critical words for civilization pronounced in glossolalia escape their lips; the obituaries of modernity blow out of the side windows; whatever school degree the drivers have, they come to the conclusion that it cannot go on like this for much longer: a foreshadowing of another 'era'. Even those who have never heard of the term 'postmodernity' are already familiar with the thing itself on such afternoons in a traffic jam. And, in fact, this can be formulated in terms of cultural theory: where unleashed self-movement leads to a halt or a whirl, the beginning of a transitional experience emerges in which the modern active changes to the postmodern passive.

Can we gain a serious theory of the present from these flickering observations? They do their job well enough if they help to create suggestions for our next step, which consists in applying the term 'mobilization' to describe and explain the basic process of modernity. First, let us ignore any premature consideration regarding the unavoidable shock over such a word choice and its inherent consequences and concentrate on strengthening the evidence that in kinetics, modernizations always have the character of *mobilizations*. Of course, we could also proceed inductively and discretely, and apply, so to speak, a method of infantry, and in the slow course of hearing evidence we could gather innumerable descriptions of the current *status lapsus quo* of the processes in the spheres of biology and noology: the number of billionaires is multiplying; the butterflies of our childhood are no longer around; tourism to faraway destinations and armament budgets are rising significantly; the populations in modernizing countries are exploding while those in modernized countries are stagnating; holes in the ozone layer over the poles are expanding rapidly; the sneaker business is flourishing while the one for surfboards is dropping; the trees of low mountain ranges are changing colour and growing only short brush-like crowns; there is South African fruit in Bavarian weekly markets; the flight time of nuclear missiles from the Ural Mountains to Bad Godesberg would take 420 seconds; and so on. However, the endlessness of such statements only makes sense if they have found their common denominator in the concept of mobilization, which at the same time makes a statement about the essence of the many separate processes; essentially, what is happening today is mobilization. Through the variety of different interpretations, modernity as a process has been shaped as a kinetic pattern that can be identified as the pattern of mobilization.

Whoever takes offence at the military connotation of the term has the right initial instinct. Mobilization is a category of a world of wars. It includes the critical processes by which combat potentials at rest reach the point of operation. It is not acceptable that the repugnance toward this idea, and even more the disgust for the actual deed, makes us blind to the circumstance that the fundamental kinetic pattern of this process—as self-actualization through the mission—is not at all specifically military, but rather that it expresses the fundamental principle of all modern undertakings of self-movement. The aesthetic shudder from the word could easily seduce us to turn away from the only concept that gave a name to the dynamic pattern of modernization.

In this context, we cannot ignore some notorious works by Ernst Jünger[5] who, as we know, in the early 1930s was already divorcing the phenomenon of mobilization from its specific military context in order to apply it to the process of modern society as a whole. From the point of view of the history of ideas, his affirmations have been wasted for half a century—they have not been used, but scandalized; not been accepted, but mainly, they have not been examined—hated rather than disproved, discriminated against rather than declared outdated. As a matter of fact, there is a reason for the general reticence against Jünger's reflections, which have raised suspicions of fascism. Whoever only wanted to apply his evil and cold optics in the analysis of the late-modern processes would run the risk of reviving Damascus in a historical-philosophical sense. Far beyond Jünger's intention, the category of mobilization can liberate intuitions that are not compatible with the Sleep of the Just in the project of modernity. The ominous formula 'total mobilization' prepares for the still scandalous, almost unbearable recognition that in the modern world there is a fundamental political-kinetic process that neutralizes the de facto morally important difference between war and work, a process that increasingly abrogates the former difference between rest and action. This precisely is the uncanny mobilization process that brings all the reserves of power to the 'front' and that pushes forward all potential toward realization. From the dubious time-diagnostic exercises by Jünger—the evil man who we would only cite from a great distance, but never without respect for his perceptiveness[6]—finally the definitions of modern technology emerged, not yet realized, as the 'mobilization of the planet by the Gestalt of the Worker'; the latter, of course, does not refer to the Marxist subject of history, the proletariat, but the planetary subject of mobilization, trembling from working out, hardened from pain, the neo-objective high-performance type in his decided mission for the action system that is exalting itself, arming itself, throwing itself to the front, also called the progressive action system (whether we mean a firm, class, people, nation, block or state of the world is irrelevant on this level of action).

If we now want to try again, under very modified constellations, to make the concept of mobilization fertile for a theory of modernity (of course, on a different path than Officer Jünger, decorated with Merit), our attempt will only remain promising as long as we are aware of the discomfort of the concept and use it for a critical perspective. This concept keeps the memory of the violent core of scientific, military and industrial leading-edge processes alive—especially in a time when these enter a smart phase where violence becomes informational, cool, procedural and analgesic. (What is the code of the new phase?—Change from heavy industry to fast information? Change from working society to learning society? The former was probably somewhat dirty whereas the latter will be as clean as a bathroom on a Swiss highway service area.) Particularly because the concept of mobilization—due to its uncanny, even devastating connotations (Jünger's highly unnerving attempt in this direction cannot be repeated)—resists a complete positivization, it is more apt than any other to describe a 'civilizational' mechanism that uses all the modern advances in ability and knowledge, mobility, precision and effectiveness for the strengthening and destructive processes, for armament, expansion, self-empowerment and mutilation of cohesion. Mobilization as a fundamental autogenous process of modernity leads to the provision of constantly growing movement potential in order to keep positions that turn out to be impossible as positions and become unsustainable through the conditions and effects of these provisions. This is where the vast area of kinetic paradoxes opens itself up to an alternative critique of modernity. Thus, criticism of society becomes criticism of a false mobility. If, after the debacle of Marxism and after the ambiguous fading away of the Frankfurt School, there is the possibility of a third version of an ambitious critical theory, it will probably only be in the form of a critical theory of movement. Its therapeutic criterion would be the differentiation, if it is possible to make it precisely, between real mobility and false mobilization. Its claim for truth would be based on the idea that the kinetic realm contains a spectrum that reaches from the physiological to the political. Through a critical theory of mobilization, the gap between the thinking process and what really happens with basic principles would be bridged—thinking 'outside' would no longer exist; a theorist would have to be asked with every sentence whether what he is doing is a sacrifice to the false god of mobilization or whether what he is doing is clearly different from this—because a theory can only be critical, no matter what critical semantics it transports, if it annuls in the worst of all possible directions its kinetic complicity with the movement of the world processes. Therefore, it remains an open question whether such a 'third' critical theory can exist only as a nominal value or if it can still be executed. If it were possible, it would establish itself from the very start as a pre-school of demobilization. Only as a tranquil theory of movement, only as a quiet theory of loud mobilization can a critique of modernity be different from that which is criticized—everything else is a rational make-up of complicity, giving the train that is already running a push, consciously or unconsciously, mimesis of the basic process in the process of reflection.

Such a 'tranquil' critique, however, cannot possibly produce its own beginning by itself, its own arising from the urge to make it different. The fact that it cannot do that is one of the enigmas that is concealed in the omnipresent chit-chat about postmodernism. Because whatever wanted to be *after* modernity would have experienced and brought to an end such a modernity—nobody can claim that this was the case in any essential regard. All that can be said is that we had experiences with the so-called postmodern passive and that it does not take much more to admit that we, especially in the prospective view, have come to the suffering side of modernity. In this case the following formula is valid: the more modern, the more postmodern. For the style of a 'third' or postmodern critical theory, this is of great significance because in order to know what it talks about it must have unreservedly been involved with the postmodern melee—otherwise it would never turn to the other side of things. But it will first have to explain to us, or rather demonstrate to us, how it will find its way out of the *Tempodrom* to something truly different. The question of the possibility of a truly different 'third' critical theory is thus reduced to the classic enigma of how it will be possible for beings who are through-and-through condemned to act to be still in the midst of the storm.[7]

It is now understood what the memory of movement brings to us: the approach to the epistemologically inscrutable point where a theory without wisdom is not even useful as a theory. Why should it precisely, out of all things, be kinetics that should become the school of calmness? It is hard to imagine what physics and metaphysics will have to say to it. But whatever objections they have shall be the beginning of an investigation into the progress of the process on the passive side of stronger self-mobilizations that is running *through us on top of us*. In the face of what happened, we ask ourselves what it was that turned out to be so different. It turned out differently than it had been thought, but how should we have thought it?

*Translated by Heidi Ziegler*

*Notes*

1   'Mobilization of the Planet from the Spirit of Self-Intensification' was originally published as 'Die Mobilisierung des Planeten aus dem Geist der Selbstintensivierung', in *Eurotaoismus: zur Kritik der politischen Kinetik* (Frankfurt am Main: Suhrkamp, 1989).

2   Marx was the first who saw through the moral mystification of kinetics. He found that the kinetic 'moral law' did not truly enter the interiority of a conscience of duty but that the conscience itself can be mobilized as a duty to make revolution. The kinetic imperative is therefore less an ethical, but rather a kinetic maxim; it does not so much express what you should do, but what you have to overthrow in order to do it, namely all conditions that inhibit kinetic potential.

3   Traditionally, the spirit has a precarious relationship with movement, except that it supposedly blows where it wants (which may be understood as a compliment to those who are inspired and which should in addition explain that it is not our fault if there is no wind in our spirit). If we want to understand this relationship positively, it could tentatively be characterized by five criteria: contextuality (spirit understands what is happening outside it); self-perception (it guesses how it is doing); self-limitation (it is aware when it is enough); reversibility (it has 'Spiel', it can do what it can do, back and forth); and spontaneity (not only can it go on as in the past, but it can also make a new start; if necessary it can even surprise itself). These criteria only guarantee an intelligent effect if they appear together—if separated from each other they guarantee intelligent stupidities (for example, our life as it is). [Spiel could be translated as play, meaning to have play or flexibility, elasticity or play as in a game, but it also means to play by heart, as in to know something very well.—Eds]

4   Sloterdijk refers to Novalis' 'Europe-Essay', also titled 'Europa' or 'Die Christenheit oder Europe', a lecture presented in 1799, later published in 1826. In this text, Novalis critiques the use made of philosophy after the Reformation as a rejection not only of religion, but also of the past and imagination which places man in the highest position within a 'perpetuum mobile'—a mill grinding itself.—Eds

5   Ernst Jünger's 1932 essay *'Der Arbeiter'* (The Worker) describes a totalizing conception of society as the complete mobilization of the worker. It was Jünger's

reactionary and conservative views that gave his works the 'notoriety' that Sloterdijk invokes.—Eds

6   The short text written by Jacob Taubes, *Ad Carl Schmitt—Gegenstrebige Fügung* (Berlin, 1879), published posthumously, might serve as an example of the free interaction with another evil man of our century, Carl Schmitt, who conceived of the civil war of the world.

7   The German idiom *die Stille im Sturm* describes the experience of a war going on outside and a calm in relation to it. The alliteration and the notion of calm fall out in the translation.—Eds

# JAGGED PRESENCE IN THE LIQUID CITY: CHOREOGRAPHING HONG KONG'S HANDOVER[1]

SANSAN KWAN

A man and a woman roll around centre stage. In fits and starts they jolt upright, throw out an arm or leg, toss their heads or shift positions—as if experiencing a restless night. A glaring television screen hangs just upstage and every so often the couple scrambles up to reach for it. Meanwhile, even further upstage, five women in Beijing opera make-up and long white robes move in and out of darkness, juxtaposing delicate Beijing opera gestures with fashion-model poses.

This is the opening to Helen Lai's *Revolutionary Pekinese Opera (Millennium Mix)*, choreographed for Hong Kong's City Contemporary Dance Company (CCDC),[2] an eclectic and jangling multimedia work that draws upon images of Beijing opera, as well as a mix of abruptly contrasting movement styles and a (sometimes screeching) sound collage. It premiered on 30 May 1997, exactly one month before the Hong Kong 'handover', when the colony reverted to Chinese rule after 99 years under the British, and is an explicit commentary on this major transitional moment in Hong Kong's history. Beyond its overt message about Hong Kongers' handover anxieties, however, I argue that the dance also offers a kinesthetic effect on the viewer that makes insistently material the bodies that occupy Hong Kong space at this moment of postcolonial identity crisis—a moment when Hong Kong was an object to be 'handed over' and it seemed that individual bodies might not, in the end, matter.

More largely, this essay considers the interrelationships of movement, space, history and community identity. I am interested in how corporeal movement through specific places at precise historical moments can illuminate those places and those moments, as well as the bodies that move through them. In this essay, then, I take up a case study to examine how choreography is constitutive and reflective of a particular, and particularly fraught, time and place. That is, what is it like to move through Hong Kong space in 1997 and what does the quality of this mobility reveal about Hong Kong and its inhabitants? In order to explore this question I draw information from two different kinds of choreographies: a staged dance about Hong Kong at the moment of the handover and the choreography of the city itself as a moving body. I am interested in how these two choreographies, both set in Hong Kong, both influenced by and influential to the space they occupy, relate to one another and reveal something about this postcolonial city. More specifically, I will argue that in the case of *Revolutionary Pekinese Opera* dance serves as a critique of the forces of neoliberal flow that can motivate the everyday choreography of the streets of Hong Kong. At the moment of the handover, dance strives to make material the bodies handed over through this transfer of sovereignty. I am hoping that, by placing the kinesthetic experience of Hong Kong in dialogue with a study of concert dance there, I can theorize more generally about the ways in which choreography, broadly conceived, is productively intertwined with processes of space, time and community formation.

I am assisted in this project by the idea of habitus famously developed by Pierre Bourdieu. A term with a long history in Western thought, 'habitus' generally refers to bodily habits, dispositions, styles, postures, gestures and mannerisms that are socially learned and culturally shared within a specific group (Wacquant 2005: 315–19). The idea of habitus as cultural behaviour that is non-discursive and that is anchored in the body is useful for my project on how Hong Kong moves. I draw on the notion that habitus is a set of relations produced through the body, and particularly to a community, that can be both observed and kinesthetically experienced in order to reveal information about that community.

Bourdieu extends the idea of habitus by explaining the complex ways in which people in communities interact with one another through corporeal practices that are simultaneously structurally determined and improvised without strategic intention: 'collectively orchestrated without being the product of the orchestrating action of a conductor' (Bourdieu 1977: 72). While habitus is more than motivated by pre-set social rules—there is an element of creativity and generativity—it is also not directed by individual agents. In other words, Bourdieu is interested in the middle ground between mechanistic, structuralist views of the ways societies operate and subjectivist ideals of individual free will. Habitus, then, becomes a socially acquired set of ways of acting in a group that, at the same time, is open to 'regulated improvisations' (ibid.: 78). This simultaneity of regulation and improvisation, structure and creativity, is key to understanding how habitus relates to history: 'In practice, it is the habitus, history turned to nature, i.e. denied as such, which accomplishes practically the relating of these two systems of relations, in and through the production of practice' (ibid.: 78). Individual and group histories bear upon the cultural practices of a community, which in turn incorporates that history into itself so that it becomes forgotten, that is, perceived as natural rather than conditioned. Habitus is produced and it is second nature. For my purposes, then, I cite habitus as a set of bodily practices that can be studied in order to understand both the history that produces those practices and the ways in which a community creatively responds to those objective conditions. Looking at Hong Kong, choreography can reveal Hong Kong as product and process—as a community determined by its time and place and as a group of individuals actively shaping its community.

But how do we study habitus? How do we perceive the collective movement practices of an entire community? When I describe movement in a certain city, can I rely on just my own somatic perception as information? In others words, is my body enough? I should be clear. This project is not an ethnography of the everyday movement of people in Hong Kong. Instead, it is a kind of auto-ethnographic choreography, an examination of my own movement through Hong Kong space in 1997. I pair this reflexive work with more traditional research: that is, close reading and analysis of concert dance.

FIGURE 1. Flyover in Hong Kong's Central District, 1997. Photograph by Kenneth Speirs.

FIGURE 2. Central to Mid-level escalator, Hong Kong, 1997. Photograph by Kenneth Speirs.

While I am convinced of the value of studying movement as a way of studying place, I am wary of the usefulness of watching other bodies move through a place and theorizing on general characteristics of that place through such an investigation. The idiosyncratic movement styles of individual bodies would be difficult to ignore. Would the bodies of my informants move perceptibly differently if transplanted to New York or to Paris? Furthermore, developing theories about the way Hong Kongers move would put me in danger of essentializing Hong Kong bodies. Nevertheless, I acknowledge that bodies and space do mutually transform each other and thus I am optimistic that by studying one we learn about the other. It is just that I am only comfortable with my using my own body as informant. How can I be convinced that my one body can fully account for Hong Kong space? It cannot, but I am still interested in charting its somatic experiences in Hong Kong as some, albeit partial, form of knowing. Doesn't my body also have its own idiosyncrasies that I carry from place to place? It does; nevertheless, it is the only lens through which I know the world around me.

Theorist José Gil, in the essay published in this volume, 'Paradoxical Body', develops an idea about 'the space of the body', which helps me to think through this question of whether one body is enough (see Gil 2006: 21). Speaking most specifically about dancers, but also about any affective engagement with the body in space, he explains that the space of the body is both interior and exterior. It becomes, through dance, that which is enveloped by the interior energy of the dancer as she moves through it and, at the same time, that which itself incorporates the body of the dancer who has exteriorized herself into it. (This paradoxicality is sounding a lot like Bourdieu describing habitus.) Gil describes the space of the body as a kind of 'secretion' or 'reversal' of the inner body to the outer. It is a space that extends the body beyond itself into virtuality and, what's more, into potentiality. The idea that a body and space mutually become one another helps me to argue for the kind of auto-ethnographic choreography I practise as a way of studying space. In other words, by moving through a particular space I engage in a dialogic relationship where I ingest that space as it enfolds me—dancing becomes a way of knowing geography, even if we must acknowledge that that geography is immediately made subjective the moment we enter it. There are echoes here of Bourdieu, who, over and against structuralism, calls for 'an experimental science of the dialectic of the *internalization of externality and the externalization of internality*, or, more simply, of incorporation and objectification' (1977: 72).

FIGURE 3. Helen Lai, *Revolutionary Pekinese Opera* (*Millennium Mix*), choreographed for City Contemporary Dance Company, Hong Kong, 1997. Photograph by Ringo Chan.

FIGURE 4. Escalators in the Hong Kong China Ferry Terminal, Hong Kong, 1997. Photograph by Kenneth Speirs.

Similarly, one of the central concepts developed by Bourdieu is that of the subjective–objective nature of social research. (He was responding to the work of structuralist anthropologists like Claude Lévi-Strauss.) In ethnographic work, there is a kind of doubling of the participant-observer who simultaneously objectifies her research material while also reflexively analysing her own responses as a social actor in her field site. The ethnographer cannot help but transform the site she studies. In a related way, the study of movement is always simultaneously objective and subjective, exterior and interior. Gil affirms this doubling notion through his idea of the 'paradoxical body' of the dancer who, when she moves, both senses herself moving internally, proprioceptively, and externally 'watches' herself dancing from afar. In this way, she engenders a kind of virtual double of herself with which she dances. So the double body of the dancer is akin to the double body of the ethnographer—both of whom subjectively sense while objectively watching. My project seeks to highlight the ways in which the duality of kinesthetics informs the duality of ethnographic work.

Interestingly, Gil goes on to discuss the phenomenon of dancing duos, where a couple of dancers execute the same choreography not through a mimetic process of copying each other but through collectively imagining a virtual body sharing the same rhythm and energy. This duo then easily becomes a series of bodies all contributing to the becoming of a virtual dancing body, all feeding it and in turn feeding off of it to create ensemble choreography:

> The partners in a duo do not enter into any mirroring mimetic relation; they do not 'copy' forms or gestures from each other. Instead, both enter into the same rhythm, while marking within it their own differences. This rhythm surpasses both partners, given that the difference perceived in one of the partners bounces back and resonates on the movement of the other reciprocally. Thus a plane of movement [reference is to Gilles Deleuze and Félix Guattari] is formed that overflows the individual movements of each dancer and acts as a nucleus of stimulation for both. The two partners will actualize other virtual bodies and so on. A duo is an arrangement for building multiplicities of dancing bodies (Gil 2006: 25).

Dancers often refer to this group phenomenon as 'feeling each other', an attention to, and often the effort to synchronize with, the collective movements of the group that draws not upon the sense of sight but upon the ability to perceive shared energy. For example, when performing a section of ensemble choreography either in silence or to an arrhythmic score, and spaced such that one dancer cannot see another, dancers who have rehearsed together long enough rely upon an ability to sense the energy of the group in order to move in harmony, an indefinable skill that dancers nonetheless manage to acquire. It is this ability to 'feel each other' that I wish to draw on as an ethnographer of urban space. Rather than analysing the movement of others through observation, I attempt to know space through a sensation of collective motion.

Deidre Sklar has coined the term 'empathic kinesthetic perception' as an ethnographic process of 'feeling oneself to be in the other's body, moving' (2001: 32). This process holds such that when watching others move I can experience their sensations by imagining their movement in my own body, playing it out internally as a way to comprehend it. Sklar tentatively cites empathic kinesthetic perception as a way for dance ethnographers to 'bridge subjectivities' (ibid.: 32), while also warning that such a temporary bridging does not produce a merger, but instead an articulation of the differences between bodies. Saidiya Hartman (1997) has challenged the idea that we can ever really empathize with another body, especially across the unequal divide of race with all the history that bears upon those separate corporealities. I am inclined to agree with her. And so I do not presume to inhabit, know or even 'read' the other bodies in the Chinese cities of my study. Instead, I offer the experiences of only my own body as a way to apprehend space.

Perhaps the 'feel(ing) each other' sensation can provide something of a way to study collective movement without presuming to fully sympathize with another's corporeal experience. Perhaps if I can tap into my 'paradoxical body', that which both proprioceptively and objectively sees itself, and, furthermore, that which can sense a shared energy not through imitation or sympathy but through a kind of virtual contribution to a mutual 'nucleus of stimulation', I can attempt to describe what it feels like to move in/with— even as—Hong Kong. I can be one dancer among a multitude all contributing energy toward a collective choreography of the city. In other words, my study of movement in the city draws upon my training as a dancer, and thus my particularly honed skills of kinesthetic perception, of 'feeling each other'. I approach Hong Kong, then, as a choreography I am learning and embodying.

And what will this collective choreography tell me about Hong Kong? I mention above that I wish to put alongside a study of my own movement

through the city an analysis of staged dance in Hong Kong—with the anticipation that the two choreographies will speak to each other and will reveal
a sort of Hong Kong habitus that helps me to depict Hong Kong and Hong
Kongers in 1997. In order to get to that mobile conversation I want first to
emplace and to historicize Hong Kong, describing its geographical, cultural
and political contours in 1997. I then depict my movement experience of
Hong Kong in 1997, kinesthetically sensing its energy as a way to apprehend
it. As a global city and thus a vital node on the circuits of global capital, Hong
Kong moves with incredible fluidity and speed, in accordance with the demands of world markets. Finally, I discuss a dance piece that choreographically responds to Hong Kong's kinetics at a time of postcolonial transition.
As a city poised at a moment of political uncertainty, I show that other kinetic
forces, dance in particular, can also work to inject blips and stutters into a
habitus otherwise dominated by free flow.

*Emplacing Hong Kong*

I lived in Hong Kong during the summer of 1997, just before and after the 30
June transition. In what follows, I depict how Hong Kong moves at this restive
moment in its history.

Hong Kong is like an amoeba. As a place through which people, goods
and information from every direction cross and recross, it has no fixed centre.
It sometimes feels like a place without any actual land—just an intricate network of transit systems in kinetic suspension. On the streets, double-decker
buses, minibuses, taxicabs, trucks and trams compete with Benzes and Hon-
das, bikes and bipeds, for road space. Meanwhile, trains teeming with passengers whisk in from the outer territories, the funicular lifts tourists up to
Victoria Peak, ferries chug to and fro, hydrofoils skim the surface of the harbour and an 800-metre-long escalator carries workaday commuters from
Central (Hong Kong's commercial heart) to the Mid-levels (a residential area)
and back. Hong Kong transports multitudes—quickly, efficiently and
via countless forms. Over the streets stretches a system of pedestrian flyovers
connecting one building complex to another in an endless string. At rush
hour, people stream through these passageways like water flowing to fill any
available channel. Underneath this frenetic tangle, Hong Kong's extensive
subway system glides noiselessly along its electric rails, disgorging a flood of
passengers at each station. Still deeper, underwater tunnels join island to

FIGURE 5. Helen Lai, *Revolutionary Pekinese Opera* (*Millennium Mix*), choreographed for City Contemporary Dance Company, Hong Kong, 1997. Photograph by Ringo Chan.

mainland and, overhead, planes touch down upon newly reclaimed earth on Lantau Island. A high-speed train zips passengers from the airport, across the water and into Central in just 23 minutes. Hong Kong seems composed entirely of crisscrossing arteries and veins pumping at an intense speed.

Situated at the mouth of the Pearl River, which wends its way through southern China, Hong Kong encompasses 530 square miles of mainland territory as well as 160 square miles' worth of small islands in the Pearl River Delta. Geographically, Hong Kong is an interstitial place, a place at the borders of other places. Lying at the western edge of East Asia, the northern edge of Southeast Asia and facing the open seas expanding westward, Hong Kong is literally, to borrow a term from Ackbar Abbas, 'inter-national' (1997: 74). Additionally, because it boasts one of the deepest natural harbours in the world, Hong Kong can count itself as the ninth largest trading port on the globe. Partly as a result of its geographical privilege, Hong Kong is also the third most competitive economy worldwide. The territory's strategic location in a time zone that bridges the gap between Asia and Europe allows for 24-hour international stock market trading (Information Services Department 1999: 43). Essentially, Hong Kong is a hub—a bustling centre of arrival and departure. As one magazine phrases it, Hong Kong is 'a city of permanent rootlessness, where inhabitants identify themselves, even after decades, as expatriates and refugees' (*The New Yorker* 2002: 77). Hong Kong is not only a port but a portal, a doorway, a space of transit through which people, products, data and money pass on their way to other end points. Hong Kong is a global conduit.

### Historicizing Hong Kong

On 30 June 1997, the former British colony of Hong Kong was returned to the control of mainland China. The handover upset conventional models of postcolonialism in that, unlike most ex-colonies, the territory was restored not to its own sovereignty but to rule by another authority. Such a predicament, orchestrated over the heads of Hong Kong denizens by the two reigning powers, left many in Hong Kong feeling powerless over their own destiny and self-definition. Additionally, as originally home to only a few fishermen before the British claimed the island in 1898, Hong Kong has no precolonial history to speak of. So, in effect, Hong Kong has only ever really known itself as a colony. While most of its inhabitants claim roots in China, Hong Kong itself tends to maintain a haughty cultural distance from its mainland neighbour. Like an adopted child returning to unfamiliar birth parents, the worldly and prosperous territory of Hong Kong was ambivalent about the return to its estranged mother country. After 99 years of Western laissez-faire rule, government by an entrenched communist dictatorship was daunting to many Hong Kong citizens. At the same time, other Hong Kongers cherished the return to their native land and did not wholly mourn the end of colonial rule.

Hong Kong's absence of a precolonial history makes the handover particularly fraught with questions of social, political and cultural identity. What becomes of Hong Kong at the point that the British sail out and the Chinese march in? Does the island territory instantly, seamlessly, become Chinese? If not, then what kind of sovereign identity, an identity not inextricably tied to British influence, can Hong Kong claim? Alternatively, before the territory is absorbed into the motherland, how can Hong Kong also distinguish itself from mainland traditions and define a distinct culture of its own? How does it recognize the traditions it has been inventing and living with as its own?

The 1960s and 1970s marked a cultural turning point for Hong Kong. This was the era in which the first generation of native Hong Kong colonials came of age. These were people who, having been born and raised entirely under colonial rule, had no ties to the mainland. Unlike their parents, they were not refugees or expatriates longing to reconcile with China, nor did they defer to mainland customs as a way of rounding out their sense of identity. Prosperous and well-educated, this new generation of Hong Kongers worked to establish a local collective consciousness (Yau 1994: 185). Rejecting both the imagined community of the Middle Kingdom, as well as that of the long-dead British empire, where 'the sun never set', they imagined their own Hong Kong community. They staged protests and incited riots demanding political representation from their British colonizers. This generation eventually built Hong Kong into a capitalist powerhouse more productive than Britain itself. As the first group to consider Hong Kong a home and not a way station, they were instrumental in establishing and sustaining a unique Hong Kong culture (Li 1994: 165). This local culture, distinct from that of both China and the West, had a life of about 20 years before 1982, when the handover agreement between Margaret Thatcher and Deng Xiaoping was finalized.

The Sino-British Joint Declaration, which set 30 June 1997 as the official date of reversion to mainland rule, bruised the confidence and halted the progress of Hong Kong's burgeoning local culture. Just as Hong Kongers began to build a sense of identity in spite of colonial rule, just as they felt the first flush of cultural recognition, the Joint Declaration forced Hong Kongers to confront the uncertainty of new rulers and new rules. Would China accept Hong Kong on its own terms, or would the communist leadership want to bend Hong Kong—by censorship or even force—to Chinese ways? The imminent return to the motherland brought into stark relief questions about the allegiances of Hong Kongers. Were they irreversibly defined by the influence of the British? Were they fundamentally Chinese? Were they distinctively 'Hong Kongese', and, if so, in what ways? 'Hong Kong identity' became a buzzword in the territory as people searched for a way to define Hong Kong's uniqueness in the face of ever-pervasive 'East–West' rhetoric. The dance I will be discussing represents one of the ways that Hong Kongers attempted to remind us of the people—the bodies—who were handed over as a result of the Joint Declaration.

### Disappearance and Lack

Hong Kong has always been an elusive space, a space whose most salient feature is its 'in-betweenness'. As a territory situated linguistically between Cantonese, English and Mandarin, politically between British imperialism and Chinese paternalism, morally between Confucian values and capitalist drives, Hong Kong is a borderland. As a result of its seemingly indeterminate character, it is often mistakenly characterized as a 'cultural desert'—as if it were simply a wasteland between the presumably more complete traditions of the East and the West. Abbas claims that the stereotypical designation of Hong Kong as a place where 'East meets West' occludes Hong Kong's distinctive cultural identity; it relegates the city to a phenomenon of what he calls 'disappearance' (1997). As such, Hong Kong recedes in the comparison between East and West and, transitively, between tradition and modernity, communism and capitalism, the exotic and the real. Such a binary logic dispossesses Hong Kong of its own space betwixt the two opposing—and necessarily essentialist—poles. In the years leading up to the handover, this 'culture of disappearance' took on another valence: a fear pervaded the city that whatever distinct culture and way of life Hong Kong did have was about to evaporate. The imminence of disappearance seemed palpable.

In conjunction with the culture of disappearance, Hong Kong is plagued by a similar—and mutually amplifying—trope of lack. As one tourist guide-book phrases it, 'For most Hong Kongers, business takes precedence over all other issues . . .' (Alexander and Lockhart 2001: 5). Hong Kong is widely re-garded as an economic and not a political city (See Ho 2002; Yeung 1996). The general view is that Hong Kong thrives economically precisely because it has never enjoyed political autonomy or self-determination. Hong Kongers are, and can afford to be, politically apathetic because while they have had no po-litical representation, at the same time capitalism has been allowed to reign free and unchecked in the city. This trope of lack was intensified by Britain's move to give Hong Kong citizens a few elected offices in the years just after the Joint Declaration was signed. By offering a taste of democracy just before it would be taken away in the return to China, the colonials made certain that Hong Kong's postcolonial experience would similarly be inscribed with a sense of lack and loss.

As Rey Chow describes it, Hong Kong's 'economism' is read as 'a com-pensation for a fundamental lack' (1998: 170). Chow even cites Abbas as falling into this rhetoric:

> One of the effects of a very efficient colonial administration is that it provides almost no outlet for political idealism (until perhaps quite recently); as a result, most of the energy is directed toward the economic sphere. Historical imagination, the citizens' belief that they might have a hand in shaping their own history, gets replaced by speculation on the property or stock markets, or by an obsession with fashion or consumerism. If you cannot choose your political leaders, you can at least choose your own clothes (quoted in ibid.).

Chow maintains that for writers like Abbas 'it is because the people in Hong Kong are lacking in something essential—political power—that they have to turn their energies elsewhere, economics' (ibid.: 171). Chow goes on to cri-tique what she sees as a false binary opposition between compensation and lack where economic success is merely a compensatory door prize and true value lies in political power. For Chow this is a masculinist position that serves to represent Hong Kong as the degraded feminine, involved in the frivolous pursuit of shopping as compensation for its lack of the phallus. Hong Kong's trope of lack is based on prevailing prejudices that idealize stability, tradition and origin. In fact, Chow wishes to recuperate the instability, the uncertainty, the temporariness and, yes, the materialism of Hong Kong as not that which makes Hong Kong inferior or lacking but as that which actually resists Western hegemony's heroic vision of itself and, in fact, invests Hong Kong with the value of the possible, the mutable, the portable. Hong Kong, for all its speed and fluidity, is not lacking but decidedly corporeal, and as such is in a constant state of growth and flux.

*Liquid City*

Often described as a 'floating city', Hong Kong sometimes seems less a solid piece of peopled earth, and more a perfect mechanism of global capitalist flow. Looking at Victoria Island from the Kowloon, or mainland side, the crowded skyline, with its overlapping skyscrapers, makes the city appear to float on the harbour. Additionally, since the beginnings of the colony, Hong Kong land reclamation projects have halved the original width of Victoria Harbour (Gutierrez and Portefaix 2000: 2–9); thus, much of central Hong Kong is actually floating. Land reclamation—the artificial establishment of land upon what was previously ocean—allows man-made space to run in any direction, desanctifying the boundaries of earth and sea, according to the demands of capitalist flow. A city on reclaimed land unsettles the lines between rootedness and fluidity, stasis and flux, history and the ephemeral. Again, Chow remarks: 'If land and space are what inspire visions of greatness and give rise to a heroic sense of history, land and space mean very different things in Hong Kong' (1998: 169). Hong Kong is a space ungrounded, where different times and speeds intersect and where ease of motion is the supreme ideal.

The liquid quality of the city manifests itself in many ways: in the interlocking transportation networks of highways, subways, train tracks, tunnels, bridges and runways; in the labyrinthine corridors running through the city's seemingly porous concrete structures, burrowing underneath buildings and moving fluidly through one to the next to the next in an endless maze; in the 'floating way' (Gutierrez and Portefaix 2000: 4–6) of pedestrian flyovers connecting building to building to building in mile-long circuits; and in the continuously climbing and falling escalators everywhere, outside buildings and inside them. Truly, Hong Kong is a 'fluid machine' (ibid.: 0–16).

The way to live in Hong Kong is to keep up with it. It is as if to stand still would be effectively to drop out—with nowhere to land. Like riding a bicycle, momentum is crucial. Hopping on to the escalators that transport me up the hills of the city, I must gauge my entering and exiting speed to match that of the moving stairway. If momentum is the defining element of Hong Kong, though, if the city is merely a highly efficient, fluid portal through which products and information pass, then what defines citizenship in Hong Kong? The new airport on Lantau Island is a feat of planning and engineering. It is a 'city within a city, but a city without citizens, a semiotic or informational city populated by travelers and service personnel' (Abbas 1997: 4). Like the airport, Hong Kong sometimes feels as if it exists only as an intricate maze of circuits. As I ride along the escalators, however, I notice the people sitting on the concrete stairway to the right, resting mid-ascent among the commotion. The tropical heat in this city makes it impossible not to sense one's own body: the dripping sweat, the heaviness in the limbs, the searing feeling on the surface of the skin. The air-conditioned machines of Hong Kong—the elevators, the flyovers, the underground passageways, the malls that serve as community hubs—all are attempts to protect the body from Hong Kong's weather. If the object is to *apprehend* the city, in both senses of the word—to understand it and to grasp it—then rhetorics of flow can only go so far. There persists a danger of relegating the discussion of Hong Kong's identity to continual indeterminacy. Narratives of Hong Kong as all flux must not be confused with a lack of situatedness. It may seem as if Hong Kong exists only as an ensemble of vectors of direction and velocity, but these vectors do converge at a particular *place*—a place the latitude and longitude of which make it muggy and hot in the summer, damp and chilly in the winter, a verdant place with celebrated cuisine and flashy pop stars, where locals speak a colourful version of Cantonese. To dismiss the city as merely a transit port is to allow it to be overshadowed by the seeming political stolidity of Britain and China, not to mention the homogenizing force of global capitalism.

Even as Chow wants to critique the overvaluation of the political as the heroic and instead celebrates Hong Kong as what she terms 'common/place' (1998: 175), May Joseph writes incisively about the complexities of citizenship in an era of increasing transnational capital flow. She explains that metaphors of heightened mobility, however seductive, are often advanced at the expense of the political and thus compromise local identities. Significantly, she cites the live body as central to anxieties over citizenship: 'At the centre of these anxieties is the live body and its unmediated struggle to achieve democratic participation in the city' (1999: 8). Joseph's work provides the link between the choreographics of Hong Kong space and the work of CCDC. If Hong Kong is a space of unmitigated flows, *Revolutionary Pekinese Opera* represents part of the struggle to stem those flows and call attention to Hong Kong bodies. Joseph asks us to recognize performance, as both a conceptual tool and a social practice, as integral to citizenship formation in the global city. Citizenship, in other words, is a performative process of self-invention that tempers the homogenizing effects of rapidly circulating commodities and consumers across transnational spaces.

### Revolutionary Pekinese Opera (Millennium Mix)

Choreographer Helen Lai was born and bred in Hong Kong and represents one of that first generation of Hong Kong natives of the 1960s and 1970s. She is a resident choreographer for CCDC, itself a Hong Kong native whose inception in 1979 was key in the early development of local culture in the territory. The company's press material currently boasts that CCDC is 'the artistic soul of Hong Kong'. Thus, both Lai and CCDC might be agents for representing that elusive, contested but much discussed notion of 'Hong Kong identity'.

*Revolutionary Pekinese Opera*[3] is a piece for 12 dancers that is structured in 11 sections with distinctively different sets, lighting and costume changes for each section. The music, composed by self-styled 'noise terrorist' Otomo Yoshihide, is a sound collage mixing contemporary popular culture sound bites with screeching voices and the clamour of Beijing opera (Cheng 1997b: 11). While not a narrative dance, the piece does draw heavily on gesture, quotidian movement, props and everyday clothing, as well as easily recognizable movement practices like cheerleading and martial arts (Lai 1997).

At one level, *Revolutionary Pekinese Opera* is very clearly about the handover. Many aspects of the dance lend themselves quite easily to a semiotic analysis: the array of systematized movement vocabularies (Beijing opera, the model operas of the Cultural Revolution, ballet, postmodern dance, jazz and tango); the wide use of gesture (shoulder shrugs, defiant fists in the air, arms crossed over the chest, head in hands, fists pounded on a table); the various costumes and props (kung-fu pants, wacky wigs, televisions, red ribbons, microphones); and the Beijing opera make-up that remains on the faces of some of the dancers. These all suggest the multiple cultural influences that bear on Hong Kong residents in 1997. Lai's work remarks on the seemingly hollow celebrations staged to mark the transition, the ambivalence Hong Kongers felt, and the looming presence of China. At another level, however, a less semiotic and more somatically attuned approach to the piece reveals a kinesthetic impression that I argue provides another kind of response to Hong Kong circa 1997.[4]

Aside from displaying so many different movement languages, the manic way that they are choreographed together deliberately emphasizes the materiality of the dancers' bodies. *Revolutionary Pekinese Opera* does not hide the physical effort required in so much code switching. And in fact the non-stop pace of the intercuts, the thrashing, spasmodic movement, the erratic breaks in rhythm and the repeated falling act as a visceral assault on the viewer too. The kinesthetic sensation of watching Lai's piece is one of gripping and tension. We do not experience any easy pleasure watching flowing, seamless movement. Bodies jerk and flail and bang to the floor in this dance and we physically wince as we watch.

In the section following the opening described at the beginning of this article, a group of dancers in various costumes—white robes, neon-coloured satin martial arts uniforms, black briefs with bare chests and legs—moves frantically from one spot on the stage to the next. Run, pose, run, pose. They grind their hips at one moment, raise their fists like Red Guards the next, throw in a few Beijing opera phrases, kick and tumble like kung-fu artists, 'vogue' and shimmy. Over time, their cohesion as a group breaks down into mass confusion and they begin running in all directions. At one point, a dancer dashes madly back and forth, looking for a group to belong to.

Later in the piece, dancers run up to rolled strips of Astroturf, balance hesitantly, then fall, then run again. Falling, breaking down, moving from unison to jaggedness, become recurring motifs in this dance. In the penultimate section, the full cast bursts on stage tossing red ribbons in the air. At first, it seems to replicate the traditional ribbon dance of so many Chinese celebrations. But its glee dissipates as dancers begin to fall out of rhythm, jumping and tossing erratically, smiling like automatons. As one journalist describes it, they are 'going through the motions of celebration' (Cheng 1997a: 9) in this handover moment. Eventually, each dancer succumbs to gravity, their bodies still hiccupping as they gradually flounder to the floor.

The freneticism of the choreography and repeated breakdowns create a sort of insistent, jagged presence. We cannot forget the labouring bodies in motion in this dance whose jarring existence is underlined by the score. Cutting sound bites of Japanese newscasts, communist propaganda and Cantonese television with screeching electronica, Beijing opera gongs, Chinese strings, shouting and yelping: the result is ear-splitting. Lai aims for discomfort here. In a review of the piece, she claims that she means to portray the 'confusion' Hong Kongers feel about the transfer of power. She wants to depict what she feels about Hong Kong: 'a very quick-moving, constantly changing society with a lot of mixed cultural influences' (ibid.: 9).

In my mind, however, the cacophony, the jerkiness, the reckless intercutting of forms not only represent Hong Kong's quick-paced life but also resist it. Recall my earlier depiction of the liquidity of movement on the city's streets. At one level, Hong Kong is, to cite Manuel Castells, a 'space of flows' (2000: 407–59). Movement flows according to the neoliberal demands of global capitalism. Writing in 2000, Castells predicts that the Pearl River Delta region, of which Hong Kong is a key node, is a mega-city in the making: 'It is this distinctive feature of being globally connected and locally disconnected, physically and socially, that makes mega-cities a new urban form' (ibid.: 436). As I discuss above, Hong Kong is characterized by tropes of lack and disappearance; Hong Kong space feels 'locally disconnected', fluid and ungrounded because it is built, and operates, as a space of in-betweenness, an 'international' space that facilitates the efficient exchange of global capital. In this space of global capital flow, of speed that becomes disappearance, *Revolutionary Pekinese Opera* presents some obstacles.

Of course, these terms, presence and disappearance, have a well-known history in performance studies and dance studies. Much has been written about dance as an ephemeral art form, one whose very presence is predicated on a process of continual disappearance: that is, the dance vanishes as soon as it is performed. There are no traces of it that remain except as memory. If presence in dance is immediately also disappearance, then how can I argue that the dance piece *Revolutionary Pekinese Opera* insists on the presence of

Hong Kong bodies over and against the neoliberal imperatives of flow that seek to obliterate localness at the time of the handover? How does this dance make those bodies stay?

I argue that two qualities in the choreography of this piece—its deliberate jaggedness and, in the finale, its deliberately sparse repetition—work to localize moving bodies. Brian Massumi, in his book *Parables for the Virtual: Movement, Affect, Sensation*, discusses a jerk of the body as a 'bifurcation point' (2002: 41). The momentary interruption of a jerk is an intersection, a moment of potential at which anything might happen next. 'At each jerk, at each cut into the movement, the potential is there for the movement to veer off in another direction, to become a different movement' (ibid.: 40). And, as an interruption, it breaks into the continual disappearance that is motion: 'Each jerk suspends the continuity of movement, for just a flash, too quick really to perceive but decisively enough to suggest a veer. This compresses into the movement underway potential movements that are in some way made present without being actualized' (ibid.: 40–1). In other words, the potentiality inherent in a jerk makes possible a flash of virtuality that resists a definition of movement as disappearance in favour of movement as multiple possibility. Following this logic, perhaps the jerkiness of *Revolutionary Pekinese Opera* serves to interrupt a narrative of Hong Kong as symbol of fluidity and instead attempts to inject bodies that remain present, or at least carry the promise of future actualizations. The extreme physicality of the choreography, where we are meant to see the labour involved in the abrupt cuts between movements, allows us to see these bifurcation points where movement does not seamlessly flow but instead stutters in a moment of potentiality—much the way a stutterer requires the listener to wait and perhaps to insert their own imagined thought in that space of anticipation.

Paula Caspão, in her article for this collection, helps me to explain another way that *Revolutionary Pekinese Opera* insists on its presence. In seeking an alternative to the ontology of dance as disappearance, she posits a way of considering contradictory levels of reality at once. We only see dance as vanishing present bodies because we have fixed and mutually exclusive notions of presence versus absence and because we view dance 'displayed on the very grounding grounds of a measurable Euclidean space and with-*in* a perception of time as a flowing linear line' (Caspão 2007: 136). In other words, conventional models of time and space require a distinct boundary between presence and absence that is inadequate to the possibilities of dance as having some futurity. Caspão, borrowing from Massumi, suggests, however, that if we could sense '"resonating levels" of emergence', 'bifurcation paths', or affect as a 'critical point' (ibid.: 143) at which intermingle multiple relational modes of sensory experience, then perhaps dance might last. In other words, affect is a synthesis of several sensations operating at once. The idea that the body and the mind, in putting sensory experience together, experience multiple, contradictory, not always synchronized or 'appropriate' levels of reality and spatiotemporal organizations at once, helps us to see dance not as vanishing but as constantly becoming in overlapping modes of potentiality. Dance, as an affective experience, hits us at a multitude of levels, not all logical nor linear nor even reconcilable. Caspão also speaks for this kind of multiplicity of affect as having critical, political possibilities:

> As operative modes of affect, resonance and bifurcation are the conditions for the becoming critical of perception at large. This means affect brings about a multitude of openings for more senses, more thought, more action, more whatever, that leads perception to its becoming critical of what is right now, of what was or has just been, or of what will possibly be (ibid.: 144).

The final section of *Revolutionary Pekinese Opera* makes me think about how Caspão deploys Massumi's ideas regarding synesthetic perception to talk about dance as potentially transformative. In the final section, dancers slowly, one by one, walk onstage and sit in chairs facing the audience. Once onstage, in contrast to the earlier sections of the dance, they do very little. Every so often they shift positions in their chairs: one props her head up by an elbow, one sits back and stretches his legs in front of him, one slumps to the side, one perches at the edge of her chair. They are watching a film that is in turn being projected onto them from the back of the theatre. Some dancers fight off sleep, one stands and shakes his fist, one slaps her thigh and laughs hysterically, one crosses and uncrosses her legs. All of this occurs over 12 long minutes and primarily in silence. The minimalism of the choreography is laborious to watch. Like the dancers themselves, the audience might begin to feel restless, too. About this section, Lai has said 'I just want to make [the audience] feel uncomfortable' (in Cheng 1997b: 11). It is a decidedly unsatisfactory way to end a dance. There is no clean closure, no final burst of energy to mark the boundary between the performance and everyday life, movement and stasis, presence and absence. Instead, the dancers continue 'going through the motions' over and over again in sometimes coinciding moments between sometimes empty moments. After observing for some minutes, it becomes evident that each dancer is, over quite a sustained period of time, drawing upon a collection of patterns—we see the same set of gestures in one dancer and a few minutes later it recurs in another. I think this is Caspão's idea of resonating levels of emergence. The dance keeps repeating in over-lapping reverberations. Time spreads out and space drifts. In the surreality of these long minutes, sensory experience becomes synesthetic, open to mul-tiple levels of perception. This section resists the ease of dance as linear in time and thus as perpetual self-erasure by seeming not to announce its pres-ence nor to fully come to an end. The dance just keeps recurring seemingly interminably. Eventually, the dancers leave one by one until one dancer is left repeating her patterns. Echoes and recurrences drizzle off.

*Revolutionary Pekinese Opera* makes insistent the presence of bodies in Hong Kong in 1997: first, through its extreme corporeality, its jerking and screeching and flinging and falling, and later, through the painstakingly slow, reverberating repetitions in the finale. If one facet of Hong Kong habitus in-vokes metaphors of fluidity (in the service of capital), then Lai's work strug-gles against that flow that would threaten to condemn Hong Kong to constant oblivion. Contradictions are co-present here. My analysis of city movement in Hong Kong detects a kind of amnesia of constant motion. Dance as disap-pearance. Continual flow as lack. In many ways, this depiction suffers the same delusions that Chow and Abbas want to challenge. In fact, when we con-sider the droves of Filipino service workers who, out of lack of a place to go on their day off, jam the public spaces of the city on Sundays, laying out blan-kets along the pedestrian flyovers, cooking from portable stoves in the public plazas, we remember that global capitalism has very material—sometimes paralysing—effects on people's bodies. Neoliberalism does not grace everyone with mobility. People live in Hong Kong. Some are born there, some work, some produce, some buy, some sell, some create, some marry, some procreate, some die there. Of course, they have complex histories: they come from all over the globe, they own joint citizenships, they study abroad, they conduct business internationally, they are often on their way to somewhere else. Despite Hong Kong's role in the forces of global capital flow, however, people were materially affected by Hong Kong's transfer from Britain to China. It is crucial to consider Hong Kong at this particular postcolonial moment, to choreograph its motion and to reflect upon the various ways that bodies, movement and space converge to determine the social, political and cultural subjectivity of its citizens.

## Notes

1   A portion of this article has been published in another form in my article: 'Hong Kong In-corporated: Falun Gong and the Choreography of Stillness', *Performance Research* 8(4) (2003): 11–20.

2   I gratefully acknowledge City Contemporary Dance Company for sharing press material and recordings from their repertory.

3   Choreographed by Helen Lai. Performed by City Contemporary Dance Company. Hong Kong Cultural Centre, Hong Kong, 1 June 1997.

4   Methodologically speaking, I am thinking here about combining methods of semiotic analysis with phenomenological analysis. Bert O. States (1992) argues that such a combination is not only very productive and appropriate to the study of performance, but that scholars, even when they feel they are working only semiotically or only phenomenologically, can often be found to be integrating both methods. The phenomenological—the seductiveness of presence—always creeps into analysis. Alternatively, even in focusing only on the sensory we are always engaged in the significative work of making meaning.

## References

ABBAS, Ackbar. 1997. *Hong Kong: Culture and the Politics of Disappearance*. Minneapolis: University of Minnesota Press.

ALEXANDER, Jan and Saul Lockhart. 2001. 'From China to China', in Amy Karafin, Laura M. Kidder and William Travis (eds), *Fodor's Hong Kong 2001*. New York: Random House, Inc., pp. 2–7.

BOURDIEU, Pierre. 1977. *Outline of a Theory of Practice* (Richard Nice trans.). London: Cambridge University Press.

CASPÃO, Paula. 2007. 'Stroboscopic Stutter: On the Not-Yet-Captured Ontological Condition of Limit-Attractions'. *TDR* 51(2) (T194): 136–56.

CASTELLS, Manuel. 2000. *The Rise of the Network Society*, 2nd edn. Malden: Blackwell Publishers, Inc., pp. 407–59.

CHENG, Scarlet. 1997a. 'An Artist's Skeptical View of Hong Kong's Transition'. *The Asian Wall Street Journal*, 13–14 June, p. 9.

——. 1997b. 'Throwing Everything into the Mix'. *Asia Times*, 26 June, p. 11.

CHOW, Rey. 1998. *Ethics after Idealism: Theory, Culture, Ethnicity, Reading*. Bloomington: Indiana University Press.

GIL, José. 2006. 'Paradoxical Body' (André Lepecki trans.). *TDR* 50(4) (T192): 21–35.

GUTIERREZ, Laurent and Valérie Portefaix. 2000. *Mapping Hong Kong*. Hong Kong: Map Book.

HARTMAN, Saidiya. 1997. *Scenes of Subjection: Terror, Slavery, and Self-Making in Nineteenth-Century America*. Oxford: Oxford University Press.

HO, Denny Kwok-leung. 2002. *Polite Politics: A Sociological Analysis of an Urban Protest in Hong Kong*. Aldershot: Ashgate.

INFORMATION SERVICES DEPARTMENT. 1999. *Hong Kong 1999*. Hong Kong: Information Services Department of the Hong Kong SAR Government.

JOSEPH, May. 1999. *Nomadic Identities: The Performance of Citizenship*. Minneapolis: University of Minneapolis Press.

LAI, Helen. 1997. *Revolutionary Pekinese Opera (Millennium Mix)*. Choreographed by Helen Lai. Performed by City Contemporary Dance Company. DVD recording.

LI, Cheuk-to. 1994. 'The Return of the Father: Hong Kong New Wave and Its Chinese Context in the 1980s', in Nick Browne, Paul G. Pickowicz, Vivian Sobchack and Esther Yau (eds), *New Chinese Cinemas: Forms, Identities, Politics*. New York: Cambridge University Press, pp. 160–79.

MASSUMI, Brian. 2002. *Parables for the Virtual: Movement, Affect, Sensation*. Durham, NC: Duke University Press.

SKLAR, Deidre. 2001. 'Five Premises for a Culturally Sensitive Approach to Dance', in Ann Dils and Ann Cooper Albright (eds), *Moving History, Dancing Cultures: A Dance History Reader*. Middletown, CT: Wesleyan University Press, pp. 30–2.

STATES, Bert O. 1992. 'The Phenomenological Attitude', in Janelle G. Reinelt and Joseph R. Roach (eds), *Critical Theory and Performance*. Ann Arbor: University of Michigan Press, pp. 369–80.

*The New Yorker*. 2002. 'Briefly Noted'. *The New Yorker* (5 August): 77.

Wacquant, Loïc. 2005. 'Habitus', in Jens Beckert and Milan Zafirovski (eds), *International Encyclopedia of Economic Sociology*. London: Routledge, pp. 315–19.

Yau, Esther. 1994. 'Border Crossing: Mainland China's Presence in Hong Kong Cinema', in Nick Browne, Paul G. Pickowicz, Vivian Sobchack and Esther Yau (eds), *New Chinese Cinemas: Forms, Identities, Politics*. New York: Cambridge University Press, pp. 180–201.

Yeung, Chris. 1996. 'Our Islands of Protest', *South China Morning Post*. Available at: archive.scmp.com (accessed 8 September 1996).

DANCING EMBODIMENT, THEORIZING SPACE:
EXPLORING THE 'THIRD SPACE' IN AKRAM KHAN'S *ZERO DEGREES*

ROYONA MITRA

This paper attempts to theorize the performative embodiment of diasporic identity within the work of Akram Khan, a contemporary, cutting-edge British Asian dancer and choreographer, whose practice is often referred to simplistically as 'contemporary Kathak' (Sanders 2007). I rest my analysis on one of Khan's recent and seminal performances: *zero degrees* (2005b), an explosive collaboration between Khan's Kathak[1] and the contemporary dance-theatre training of the Moroccan-Flemish dancer/choreographer Sidi Larbi Cherkaoui. The piece is a formal and narrative exploration of the politics of border spaces as a metaphor for diasporic identity. In the programme notes, Khan explains that 'zero degrees' symbolizes the liminal rite of passage between life and death, belonging and non-belonging and, most importantly, identity and the lack thereof. I propose that this is a seminal piece within British Asian dance for the following key reasons. Firstly, it marks a departure in Khan's own repertoire from his hitherto solo and group choreographic ventures to his first duet partnership with a European dance-theatre artist. Lorna Sanders reiterates this view and observes that '*zero degrees* has begun a period where the exchange of information is significant in artist-to-artist collaboration' (2007). Secondly, the piece embodies Khan's artistic vision of deconstruction of the Indian classical lexis in order to articulate both the dynamism and the paradox that characterize his diasporic identity in twenty-first-century Britain. Finally, it testifies that, unlike many of his contemporary British Asian colleagues who are in search of a stable creative formula with which to contemporize tradition, Khan's artistic endeavours mirror his transient diasporic identity and refuse to be categorized. To summarize, *zero degrees* encourages the celebration of rupture, rejects a formulaic approach and focuses on an articulation of a 'self' that is ephemeral, fragmented and volatile.

At this stage, a summary of the history of British Asian dance is crucial to contextualize Khan's place within it. Historically, dance in the British Asian diaspora has paralleled and promulgated the Indian nationalist project of preservation of the home culture as ancient, authentic and intrinsically Hindu through upholding these parameters of Indianness as advocated in the classical art forms transplanted in Britain from India. Mandakranta Bose, Alessandra Lopez y Royo, Avanthi Meduri, Janet O'Shea, Anannya Chatterjea and many others claim that the notion of Indian classical dance in itself is only as old as the nationalist project and directly linked to it. Lopez y Royo comments on this strategic relationship and says that, 'The re-making of Indian "classical dance" has been part of a wider project aimed at the re-making and re-shaping of Indian culture, which coincided with establishing the post-independence Indian nation and new ideas of Indianness' (2003: 157). Lopez y Royo substantiates her views further by paraphrasing Mandakranta Bose's argument (2001: 101), saying that 'the re-discovery of the classical tradition was linked with the nationalist project of reclaiming India's past [. . .] and that the cultural validation and cultivation of Indian dance as exotic art was facilitated by western romanticization of the Orient' (2003: 157).

Consequently, first-generation Indian migrants in Britain facilitated the proliferation of this exoticized India in an attempt to preserve and hold on to the newly conceived post-independent Indianness they had left behind. Floya Anthias summarizes this immigrant tendency to preserve the home culture as a process of 'ghettoization and enclavization', making the immigrant experience exist 'in a "timewarp", [through] a mythologizing of tradition' (2001: 626). Consequently, immigrants tend to 'reify their culture' (Ram

2005: 123) in an attempt to create a home away from home. By promoting Indian classical dance as one of the indicators of conserved tradition and heritage, the identity of Indian dance in Britain was conceived. In the decades
that followed, strategic and political categorizations of cultural traditions in
Britain witnessed the emergence of a new term—British Asian dance. This
new term is meant to reflect the assumed dual cultural heritage of these diasporic artists. 'British because it is made in Britain' and because the artists
are themselves British citizens (Lopez y Royo 2004); and 'Asian' to mark an
attempted homogenization of the multicultural and multinational ethnic
groups from India, Pakistan and Bangladesh, Sri Lanka, Nepal (to name a few
who comprise these artists) and to indicate the root of the performance traditions represented within the genre as belonging simplistically to Asia.[2]

In consequence, the practice of classical dance traditions within the
British Asian diaspora largely encourages adherence to tradition and preservation of authenticity. The most popular of the Indian classical dance idioms
represented in Britain are Bharatanatyam, Kathak and, to a lesser extent,
Odissi. Purist audiences and exponents of the forms alike disapprove of any
kinds of experimentation with and adulteration of the home culture. Despite
the initial secularization of the Indian nation and culture under Nehru's leadership, it is important to note that, within a matter of decades, Indianness,
both in India and in the diaspora, became entwined with a process of Hinduization and all indicators of Indian culture promulgated an essentially
Hindu identity. In Britain, the purist practice of these classical dance forms
in both community and high art settings reiterate the constructed relationship between these art forms and Hinduism explicitly.[3] It is somehow deemed
to validate their authenticity and links to Indianness in India with more
rigour.

But for some contemporary British Asian dancers, caught up in the dichotomy of the local and the global, sharing tenuous links with a concept of
'home', the prescriptive language of Hinduized classicism clashes with their
current secular lives.[4] It is at this point that British Asian dance witnesses the
birth of another phase in its identity, a phase that marks the acknowledgement of a hybridized existence and enables progression, creativity and artistic ownership to surface in the art. Much is owed in this discourse to
Shobhana Jeyasingh, a UK-based Bharatanatyam dancer who trained in India
and Malaysia, who is perhaps one of the first prominent British Asian dancers

to question the significance of classicism in her life and to deconstruct it in practice. Parm Kaur articulates the tension that took over Jeyasingh's artistic vision as she began to rationalize the place for the prescriptive language of Bharatanatyam, and summarizes:

> It was impossible for Jeyasingh to use her known language of Bharatha Natyam, as she was occupying a different physical, social, political and aesthetic space. i.e. Britain and her position in Britain as a post-colonial subject, within the context of stylistic changes in contemporary dance scene happening around her, as well as her own fascination for the intellectualism of dance (N. D.).

Jeyasingh herself states that subsequently her art has come to explore 'this tension between classical and personal styles, alternating between the precision of *Bharatanatyam* and more waywardly idiosyncratic movement' (in Kothari 2003: 160). Lopez y Royo observes this growing tension in the practice of many contemporary British Asian dancers and choreographers who, like Jeyasingh, have started to question the role of classicism in their current globalized existences. She claims, thus, that some contemporary diasporic artists are consciously embracing Western models of neoclassicism within their practice after a period of engagement with (and for some alongside) postmodern features of rupture and hybridity in order to look for ways to 'reclaim their artistic freedom and integrity and actively participate as interlocutors in British dance discourse' (Lopez y Royo 2004: 157). Nahid Sidiqqi (who has now returned to Pakistan), Mavin Khoo, Sonia Sabri, Anurekha Ghosh and Jayachandran Palazhy (partly based in Bangalore, India, as the Artistic Director of the Attakkalari Institute of Performing Arts) are only some of the influential practitioners in the British Asian realm whose creative vision and practice align themselves with Lopez y Royo's description above. However, I would like to propose that the subject of my analysis, Akram Khan and his relatively young repertoire, marks a seminal point of simultaneous departure and arrival in contemporary British Asian dance discourse. On one hand, it departs from the convention-bound practice and exoticized perception of the Indian classical lexis, while on the other it simultaneously enables British Asian dance to arrive at and make a significant contribution to the world of British dance.

Akram Khan, a second-generation British Asian, was born in London to Bangladeshi parents.[5] From a very young age, his mother introduced him to

Bengali folk music and dance in community settings. At the age of seven, Khan became a student of Sri Pratap Pawar, the celebrated Kathak maestro, and began his prolonged training under him. In parallel to his dance training, his passion for theatre was inculcated and enhanced by two professional acting roles: the first at the age of 10 in *The Adventures of Mowgli*, and the second, and perhaps more significant role, was of Ekalavya in Sir Peter Brook's *Mahabharata*. Khan claims that the world tour with Brook singlehandedly influenced his views on performance and performance-making. Thus, with substantial experiential knowledge, in 1994 Khan stepped into the world of British higher education and enrolled in a BA in Performing Arts at De Montfort University in Leicester. Two years later, he transferred to the Northern School of Contemporary Dance in Leeds. During the time spent on his degree programme, Khan expanded his skills beyond Kathak to include, 'classical ballet, Graham, Cunningham, Alexander, release-based techniques, contact improvisation and physical theatre' (Khan 2005a). Since graduating and launching a solo career, Khan also engaged in some influential artistic collaborations and laboratory projects with the British choreographer Jonathan Burrows in London and the X-Group Project in Brussels. These projects enabled him to expand his European dance-theatre training and made apparent to him the ways in which his Kathak training and his European dance training were coexisting in his body, creating tensions and vibrations that could be accessed to create powerful work to reflect this duality and dichotomy simultaneously. Thus, under the vision of producer and creative collaborator Farooq Chaudhry, was conceived the now thriving and ethnically diverse Akram Khan Dance Company, of which Khan says:

> To bring together a Company of such diverse cultures, experiences and voices is a blessing for me and to the work. It is a reflection of what I am today, which is to be in a state of 'confusion': where boundaries are broken, languages of origin are left behind and instead, individual experiences are pushed forward to create new boundaries (ibid.).

Since then, a successful repertoire of performances[6] followed rapidly, accompanied by Khan's steady and consistent rise to fame and recognition.[7]

Khan is thus undoubtedly a product of his environment and the work he creates is a clear extension of his multilayered, lived and learnt experience.

It would be fair to observe that while a contemporary and recurrent trend in British Asian performance is to trace this hybrid reality by 'contemporizing classicism', not all such endeavours are successful. Commonly termed as 'fusion', such experiments reinforce the existence of classicism alongside contemporary systems and often lack deliberation and depth. These primarily formal experiments do not pursue in depth the sociological issues at stake. The result is often superficial, representing a world where different language systems coexist without the potential to penetrate each other. For many, the point of collisions between tradition and postmodernity remain just so. Collisions: never attaining mutual growth and remaining irreconcilable. I propose that for such endeavours to succeed, an intellectual understanding of the corporeal and cerebral embodiment of diaspora must accompany any formalist experimentation. Khan's work is characterized by this quality and is an intersection of cutting-edge form and evocative intellect and content. Embodying Susan Leigh Foster's notions of 'corporeality' (1996), the body for Khan is both the source of narrative *and* the primary medium of communication that transcends technique. And his expression lies in his artistic articulation of diaspora as not 'fusion' but 'confusion'—a condition that he deems as empowering, transient, evolving and positively embracing multiplicity. This has little or no traces whatsoever of the pain and nostalgia of diaspora of the past.

By removing the diasporic experience from race- or nation-specific tropes and by working with global artists who are not bound to national or cultural borders, Khan constructs a multiplicity of identities as empowered existences in today's global world and urges classicists and purists to reject the notions of authenticity and homogeneity and recognize them as obsolete concepts. This intellectual statement is embodied in Khan's choreographic vision in *zero degrees*, where no singular movement tradition exists as authentic and pure. Khan celebrates rupture and fragmentation of his own body as he allows it to come in contact with movement styles that challenge his physiological condition. From Kathak's upright verticality, he is forced to embrace a horizontal and more risqué relationship to gravity. He learns to put pressure on a different part of his foot, while his spine negotiates a distinct and curvaceous language with the space around him and with his co-artist's corporeality. Khan celebrates this 'confusion' and uses it artistically to articulate this 'self', instead of lamenting about his hybrid condition.

Sanders (2007) speaks of Khan's engagement with diasporic multiplicity and calls for a need to find a new system with which to analyse his work distinct from pre-existent frameworks. She seems to suggest therefore that Khan's practice is a challenge not only to artistic norms but also to theoretical models for finding more appropriate language systems with which to discuss his expression of hybridity. In other words, if his work is multilayered, its language of analysis must also respond to its inherent intertextuality. Sanders says: 'a sophisticated complexity has reigned within the hybridity of his Contemporary Kathak approach which breaks apart the boundaries between genres typically considered to be polar opposites; [. . .] the type of multiplicity which Khan's work implies needs a shift in analytical perspectives' (in Khan 2005a).

While I agree with Sanders' acknowledgement of Khan's artistic celebration of multiplicity as a contemporary reality, a critique of the term 'Contemporary Kathak' is vital here. I find it simplistic in its implied binary opposition between classical Kathak on one hand and Western contemporary dance on the other, and believe it does not do justice to or capture Khan's sophisticated aesthetic vision and its interdisciplinarity and embodiment of intertextuality. If Sanders uses the term 'contemporary' in its literal sense to mean 'belonging to the present' then, too, it becomes rather one-dimensional in its implication that Khan's practice is Kathak as it belongs to the present in its denial of his European dance-theatre training. Indeed Khan himself repeatedly refuses to acknowledge and accept such a categorization as appropriate to his own artistic project. However, beyond the obvious logocentric trap that Sanders falls into, she appropriately rejects any formalist mode of analysis for *zero degrees* because she suggests that such frameworks generally problematize heterogeneity instead of seeing it as a productive and creative quality in art. She continues to provide instead examples of theoretical models that support plurality, embrace multiplicity and value the condition of hybridity as an influential and powerful one.

Once again Bhabha's literary concept of the 'third space' becomes a useful lens through which to study Khan's work, and its 'double consciousness' (Dayal 1996) becomes apparent to an informed audience. Bhabha argues that:

> [t]he borderline work of culture demands an encounter with 'newness' that is not part of the continuum of past and present. It creates

a sense of the new as an insurgent act of cultural translation. Such art does not merely recall the past as social cause or aesthetic precedent; it renews the past, refiguring it as a contingent 'in-between' space, that innovates, and interrupts the performance of the present. The 'past-present' becomes part of the necessity, not the nostalgia, of living (1994: 7).

Khan's ability to 'refigure' the past as a penetrative present reality in terms of 'newness' situates his work in Bhabha's dynamic, volatile and liminal 'third space'. Khan is not only empowered to influence the transmutation of the dual cultures of which he is a product, but, more importantly, he is able to radically transform the way in which the European dance-theatre genre on one hand, and Kathak performances on the other, can continue to develop, mutate and remain progressive in their modes of representation and reception in Britain. *zero degrees*, then, undoubtedly stands apart as a significant vehicle in this project.

In 2005, Khan began a collaboration with Sidi Larbi Cherkaoui to explore Kathak's power of storytelling and to extend his own repertoire beyond the comfort zones of classicism and contemporary dance, into the unpredictable realms of dance-theatre. The result was the critically acclaimed *zero degrees*. Khan and Larbi Cherkaoui's emotive vocal and corporeal storytelling coupled their captivating, agile and powerful physical lexicon throughout the piece. These elements came together beautifully to suggest that although the artists may have started at opposite extremes with their respective artistic training and aesthetic vision, through the collaboration they were able to have a dialogue and communicate an 'in-between' space that their bodies had comfortably negotiated through their prolonged encounter. Key characteristics of choreographic strategies used in *zero degrees* include duets between Khan and Larbi Cherkaoui where both the physicality and the text are delivered in perfect unison, retaining their sense of individuality while forging a way to merge into each other's bodies and identities. Movement vocabulary ranged from iconic Western pedestrian gestures familiar to the audience, to stylized pure Kathak solos by Khan, to erratic and provocative manipulation of the human body into inhuman imagery in the solo by Larbi Cherkaoui. The grounded, floor-oriented physicality of Larbi Cherkaoui was juxtaposed against the ethereal verticality of Khan's body as the artists played consistently with the space 'in-between' the vertical and the horizontal planes of their corporeal training and existence. The bodies moved from highly rhythmic and fluid compositions to extreme erratic convulsion and uncanny stillness.

At the very heart of the piece is the issue of in-betweenness. In content, it explores the in-betweenness of life and death, belonging and non-belonging, identity and its lack. In form, it explores the in-betweenness of autobiography and fiction, the process of reliving the past and recounting the past in the present, temporality and spatiality, communication via text and via movement, to mention but a few. At the heart of the collaboration, Khan and Larbi Cherkaoui approached the work from divergent aesthetics and disciplines of dance and theatre respectively, but were intrigued by the space that lay in wait for them in-between. Of their process, Khan recounts: 'Working together has taken us both a long time. He starts from theatre and moves toward dance, I start from dance and move toward theatre and we meet in the middle' (in Sanders 2007). In this liminal 'third space', *zero degrees* was conceived. Exploring Khan's autobiographical account of a journey across the border between Bangladesh and India, the piece itself unfolds along this figurative, political and geographical border space that is the land of complex Bengali identity.[8] Through effective and measured naturalistic delivery of text that recounts his own memories at border control, Khan acknowledges that in the current climate of globalized identities a passport is the only true form of identification; he says, 'I watched my passport pass through the hands of all the guards and I didn't let it out of my sight, because although it's just a piece of paper, without it you have no identity' (2005a).

Issues of identity and belonging surface throughout the piece and become potent when Khan recounts the painful memory of a particular point in this journey. To his traumatized bewilderment, Khan finds himself unable to help a dying man on the train and is asked to ignore the repeated requests of his wife for assistance. Against Khan's will, his cousin and travel companion advises him not to get involved, in order to avoid bureaucratic hassle, as he is a 'foreign' witness. Khan's choreography emphasizes the irony of dying identity-less in one's own country, witnessed by a helpless foreigner, a British person of Bangladeshi descent, who is unable to help because of being separated from his homeland and its people, by the burden of non-belonging and mindless political bureaucracy. He expresses with irony that the very same document, his red British passport, which endows him with a secure identity, also separates him harshly from the people of his homeland by virtue of their green passports and the consequent perceived difference of him. The painful narrative presents itself in fragments throughout the piece, interspersed with corporeal translation of the text between Khan and Larbi Cherkaoui. It is Khan's narrative that unfolds but Larbi Cherkaoui's corporeal place in the narrative re-emphasizes the issues of difference, sameness, duality and dichotomy. Khan's and Larbi Cherkaoui's movement vocabularies transcend technique as they communicate embodiment of lived history and situate *zero degrees* in the realms of dance-theatre. The audience gets a glimpse of the shared experience of the artists that goes beyond technique or even the common artistic process with which they arrived at *zero degrees*. More profoundly, the artists along with the programme provide glimpses of the immediacy of their common lived experience of growing up in Europe, learning the same prayers and Islamic rituals as immigrant Muslims, away from their respective homelands: in so many ways the same and yet marked by such distinct differences. Similarly, the formal exchange between Khan's Kathak training and Larbi Cherkaoui's contemporary dance vocabulary seem seamless as they blur into each other's systems while keeping their individuality alive but fluid. Khan's body works in athletic straight lines, while Larbi Cherkaoui's elasticity works in curvatures. Khan's vulnerable verbal recollection of the narrative of non-belonging contrasts with the visual and physical power with which he commands the space. His erect spinal alignment of Kathak allows him a confidence and security in his own skin, enabling him to recount his traumatic journey through the borderlands with elan. But then, suddenly, this false sense of security crumbles before us. Through the use of pure Kathak *abhinaya* (a Sanskrit term from the *Natyashastra* that means theatricality associated with characterization), and danced to the Urdu lyrics of a young bride mourning the loss of her lover, Khan's physicality becomes feminine, submissive and soft as his character is juxtaposed against his memory of the wife of the dying man on the train crying for help, in vain. The postmodern intertextuality of the song cuts deep into the heart of Khan's narrative, proving that tradition and postmodernity can indeed be in creative dialogue in an organic and moving way. The liminality of Khan's and Larbi Cherkaoui's hybrid identities at times melt into each other and at other times stand distinctly apart through the vehicle of volatile, ruptured and fragmented corporeality.

*zero degrees* is a postmodern creation with constant reference to the blurring and erasure of identities in relation to geographical and political space. Anthony Gormley's scenographic collaboration contributes two mannequin dummies that accompany Khan and Larbi Cherkaoui on stage as co-performers. They are clones of the artists, moulded out of their own shapes and representing at times each other, and at other times, the sameness of humanity. This further emphasizes the 'presence–absence' phenomenon that *zero degrees* touches on. The dummies stand for the anonymity of appearances, on one hand, while simultaneously entering the volatile discourse of reproduction of identity and cloning, on the other. They raise questions about the simulacrum of authenticity and originality of identity, most importantly that of humanity. Sanders theorizes Gormley's modelling process of the dummies as resembling the Baudrillardian concept of 'the death of the original and the end of representation' (2007). The relational positioning of the mannequin replicas of Khan and Larbi Cherkaoui presented the artists' identities in a state of simulacrum. Sanders suggests therefore that the interaction between the artists and the dummy replicas of themselves, and the latter's use and manipulation in the piece, makes her question the essence of humanity in asking, '[. . .] what is within us, or perhaps is there anything within us, that is authentic, essential unreproducible, our own?' (ibid.). Using the dummies to stand for self and other simultaneously, Khan aligns the diasporic experience of in-betweenness with erasure, transience, transmutance and growth. Sanders continues to analyse the significance of the word 'zero' or numeric '0' in the title, concluding that it simultaneously suggests both the absence of any numeric value and the presence of a symbol to stand for this absence, thus embodying erasure and growth at the very same moment. Similarly then, while diasporic identity may historically have been made to feel absent from the discourse of presence, the very acknowledgement of this absence makes the dancers' presence a significant aspect of the discourse in both temporal and spatial terms. Thus, yet again, the liminality of Bhabha's 'third space' emerges as a strong catalyst in the form and subject matter of *zero degrees*.

The volatility of the 'third space' is further fuelled in the piece by Peggy Phelan's theorization of 'liveness' (1993), the late twentieth-century Performance Studies discourse that advocates an audience's experience of the immediacy of a performer's corporeality in the moment of practice. Phelan's discourse of liveness constructs the performer and his/her body as the narrative and does not seek in addition a conventional story within the action. The lived history and experience of the performer sharing an intimate time and space with the audience becomes the premise of a shared experience. Applying the model of 'liveness' to the delivery and reception of *zero degrees*, Khan goes beyond the audience expectation of formalist experimentations between classicism and contemporary language. In placing his body and lived experience at the heart of both the form and the content of *zero degrees*, in making an offering of his corporeality, in overriding the tendency of classical dancers to enter the economy of repetition and reproduction, in allowing spontaneity, vulnerability and rupture to penetrate his physicality, Khan is upholding the 'ontology of live performance and providing the potential for ideological resistance' (Mock 2000: 4). The following statement by Colin Counsel substantiates the erratic and transgressive nature of Khan's live body in interaction with Larbi Cherkaoui's: 'The body of live performance is unique in that [...] the live performer's emphatic physical presence has the capacity to remind viewers of the outside of the fiction, juxtaposing the body which is signified, performed, with the real, signifying body of the performer' (in Counsel and Wolf 2001: 125).

What is unusual about the presence of liveness within *zero degrees* is the very fact that the signifying, real bodies of Larbi Cherkaoui and Khan coincide with the signified and performed bodies of the characters they embody in the space, suggesting that in this instance reality and fiction are one and the same. Khan is deliberately rewriting the technical virtuoso of the dancer and replacing it with the narration of his lived self. Every time he performs *zero degrees* and recalls the traumatic train journey across the border from Bangladesh to India, he occupies simultaneously the past and the present, both of which are realities that reside in and are expressed through his body. In his choreographic practice, negotiations between hybridity, intellect, corporeality and proxemics are occurring live as an articulation of what it means to occupy the 'third space' in Britain today. In this respect, Khan can be distinguished significantly from his British Asian dance colleagues, many of whose choreographic structures are mostly bound by the rigid lexis of 'reified' classicism. Instead, he can be aligned with the 'maniacally charged present' (Phelan, in Lepecki 1999: 130) and volatile unpredictability of the dancing body inhabiting the European dance-theatre genre. Lepecki argues that '[it] is within this reconfiguration of the boundaries of choreography, where choreography is recast as a theorization of embodiment, that one can start to understand the contours and aims of a radical innovation of contemporary theatrical dance' (in ibid.).

The liminality of the 'third space' allows its occupants empowerment and enables them to influence both sides of the fence with equal significance. Khan, therefore, is not only empowered to influence the transmutation of the dual cultures of which he is a product, but, more importantly, he is able to radically transform the way in which the European dance-theatre genre on one hand, and Kathak performances on the other, can continue to develop, mutate and remain progressive in their modes of representation and reception in Britain. Khan's influential position is further heightened by the fact that he is a male dancer constructing a new masculinity in British and Indian dance simultaneously. This must be understood within the dual contexts of a British Asian dance world that is primarily driven by female artists (as dance as a profession is not considered masculine enough) and the historicity of European dance-theatre with its associated expression of sexualized masculinity. I wish to propose that one of the specific ways in which Khan's art claims Bhabha's dynamic and liminal 'third space' and engages in 'cutting edge translation' and 'negotiation' is through challenging the iconography of the male dancer in both Indian and European dance in *zero degrees.*

The historicity of the male dancer in Western theatre dance is a long-contested zone of problematized masculinity. Prejudices that have linked male dancers to homosexuality for the last century continue to exist in contemporary Western society and have further percolated into the psyche of postcolonial cultural ideologies. Patriarchal control and monitoring of male behaviour have historically denied men 'a secure autonomy', requiring them to continually 'adjust and redefine the meanings attributed to sexual differences in order to maintain dominance in the face of changing social circumstances' (Burt 1995: 12). Through the first half of the twentieth century, Western theatre dance struggled against the problematized concept of 'the appearance of the dancing male body as spectacle' (ibid.). Through the latter half of the twentieth century, however, with emerging critical discourse on gender studies and a closer examination of masculinity in repressed crisis, male dancers and choreographers took to the stage to deliberately and politically expose the male body as desirable, erotic and sexual; not just as an object of spectacle, but as a subject demanding expression and articulation of the male condition in relation to both women and other men. Burt uses the term 'Post Men' with irony, as the name of a chapter in *The Male Dancer* that discusses the emergence of a new masculinity under the influence of the postmodern agenda. The chapter theorizes the emergence of this dynamic and sexualized masculinity as represented in the works of European artists like Lloyd Newson, Wim Vandekaybus, Liam Steele and Pina Bausch, to name a few, summarizing that suddenly masculinity in Western dance-theatre took centre stage in its most volatile, sexual and erotic forms. It is significant to note that Khan would have encountered the work of these practitioners and their erotic and volatile masculinity during his academic studies at De Montfort University and that Burt was one of Khan's lecturers at the same institution. Thus Khan's experience and understanding of representations of masculinity in Western dance was deeply influenced by this 'post men'[9] syndrome. However, equally, his associations of masculinity in dance were also defined by another set of rules through his Kathak training.

The male dancer in the history of Indian classical dance is an equally fascinating entity. Historically, having acquired and maintained the position of authority in the development, tutoring and rendition of the dance forms, the guru–*shishya* tradition of the patriarchal hierarchy of men as tutors and women as pupils was a dominant model of male supremacy. Male supremacy was thus written into the hierarchical structures in the transmission of Indian dance. This mirrored the mythological beginnings of Indian dance as an art form created by God Shiva and transmitted to his female consort Goddess Parvati. Thus, Indian dance was gendered from its celestial roots to its earthly practice. Mandakranta Bose substantiates this and states: 'The dancers were women [. . .] while the dance teachers and theorists were men [. . .] The balance of artistic autonomy and social agency was thereby titled decisively away from the performers themselves to their male mentors and guides' (1998: 51).

This hierarchical male dominance implied two things. Firstly, that the men, holding authoritative positions from behind the scenes, were therefore not objectified by the gaze. Thus exhibitionism of the male body within Indian dance traditions was an unfamiliar concept. Secondly, with the construction of the Indian nation, postcolonial values of a Victorian sensibility of morality and proper gendered social roles problematized the association of masculinity with dance, even in positions of authority. Thus, while female dancers gradually took centre stage and acquired authority as choreographers and subjects of their art, male dancers found themselves pushed more and more to the margins of acceptability. Consequently, first- and second-generation Indian immigrants in Britain mirrored this trend while living away from their nation. So while it was acceptable for women to engage with classical dance and thereby uphold the respectable signifiers of home culture within their host nation, it was unthinkable for men to enter the profession for the fear of not being 'man' enough. Thus, even among second- or third-generation British Asians, the male dancer is a rare phenomenon. And Khan is one such rarity. However, what is interesting about Khan's representation of his male body is that it simultaneously rewrites both Indian and Western treatment of masculinity as a male dancer. On one hand, he chooses to be perceived by a large percentage of the British Asian community as 'not man enough' and is feminized by sheer association with the profession of dance. He is simultaneously exoticized by the other segment of his white middle-class audience, who perceive his otherness in Orientalist terms and subsequently feminize the artist. On the other hand, he does not feel it necessary to mirror his European dance-theatre colleagues in their representation of masculinity as erotic and sexualized. He is therefore negotiating and 'writing' the male dancer's body in a way that does not feel the need to adhere to any models of pre-existent practice. His negotiation of masculinity cannot be divorced and analysed separately from the complexities of his diasporic identity. In fact, as a male dancer in the British Asian community, having found a place in mainstream British dance, his gendered identity is at the core of his performative embodiment of the diasporic experience.

In *zero degrees*, Khan constructs the visual impact of the male body on stage through structured and minimalist costumes that accentuate the contours and alignments of the masculine form. He and Larbi Cherkaoui appear in loose-fitted trousers made of floaty fabrics and tight-fitted T-shirts. While this at first projects a sinewy and sensual masculine form, the fluidity and speed with which they move across the space and within the fabric de-eroti-cizes them almost immediately. One catches a tantalizing glimpse of Lloyd Newson's 'post men' from *Enter Achilles* (1995) or *Strange Fish* (1992) before the alluring sensuality is replaced by virtuoso technique, and the minimalist structure of their clothes emphasizes this beautifully. The liminal masculinity that Khan constructs in *zero degrees* is kinesthetically present beneath the layer of fabrics within the torso itself. In fact, I would say it rests on an analysis of his use of the spinal column that is emphasized further when we are reminded of its culturally specific use in the traditionally solo form of Kathak. Inherent within his Kathak training, and therefore almost unconsciously inscribed into his corporeal lexis, is the alignment of his spine in clear vertical straight lines. In a previous article, I described the Kathak dancer's spine in the following manner: 'The spinal column of the *Kathak dancer* is upright and the use of the extended arms marks out a very clear personal space which is never invaded. This demarcation of physical space, this deliberate denial of physical contact reflects the post-colonial conditioning of India [. . .] and constructs the dancer as pure and abstinent' (2005: 170–1). Embodying such a distinct sense of demarcated reality that negates touch or contact with other bodies in the space, Khan moves against Larbi Cherkaoui's elasticity and permeability, and marks out clear boundaries of physical and metaphoric space between Larbi Cherkaoui's body and his own. These physical boundaries prevent their bodies from making intimate encounters, as, even when they come close together, inches of empty space prohibit their torsos from making full contact. In the moments of their interactions together, where each attempts to merge into the other's vocabulary, there is a clear and articulated use of the spine and the head. Khan's spine mostly remains vertical but fluid, except for allowing curvatures to make contact with the floor, from which he springs back into the vertical almost immediately. His head is always in control. The contact made between the performers is largely choreographic and rarely instinctual, leaving little room for ambiguities. Khan's practice visibly engenders a representation of masculinity that is sensual yet uneroticized, vulnerable yet unfeminized, powerful yet unaggressive as it constructs itself in the ontology of live performance. Khan's spinal articulation suggests to me that it has become the fulcrum at which the various tensions of his lived experience are played out, and it becomes the tool that negotiates between the contrasting ideologies of culture, gender, identity and politics that shape him. Khan's and Larbi Cherkaoui's choreographed bodies therefore never fully unify into a singular entity. Instead, they leave many openings and many unoccupied spaces that harbour a liminal masculinity that is in the process of being written, full of potency, and crying out to be touched and nourished with new meanings. To me, the eroticism is the spatial void that is the by-product of choreographic structures, charged with chemistry and caught up in negotiation between ideologies of body and culture and gender and corporeality. It lies dormant in the 'third space'. The eroticism I speak of is not necessarily of a sexual nature alone (as embodied by the 'post men' framework) but one that comes attached to the ability to move with an autonomous corporeality, released from the postcolonial conditionings surrounding spatial configurations of the Indian classical dancer in general and construction of masculinity, male sexuality and male identity in particular. If and when the space eventually does close in and the bodies actually do touch, and such release of the erotic is allowed to surface in the physicality, perhaps a more dynamic male dancer will emerge from Khan's practice. This male dancer could potentially embrace the sensation of touch and move it beyond a technical and clinical point of contact to an emotional and visceral experience for both the dancer and his audience.

zero degrees, Khan and Larbi Cherkaoui's explosive collaboration, explores the volatility of several significant nuances of diasporic life in twenty-first-century Britain. A creative process and a performance that sits comfortably in this liminal 'third space' of flux, zero degrees marks the beginning of a long-term project of Khan's repertoire that investigates the phenomenon of how the body is marked by the processes of in-betweenness and how it negotiates space—social, geographic, political, artistic, cerebral and corporeal—to find an empowered existence within today's globalized reality, characterized by transience and instability. Khan's work is relevant to our times and self-referential. In this, he embodies the philosophy of performance-making as laid down in the Natyashastra which 'requires performance to be grounded in the lives of performers and their audiences' and is opposed 'to any mode of performance laying claim to authenticity or permanent value' (Brown 2001: 50). Removing any sense of permanence from his repertoire, the vulnerability of having to learn anew with each project, the discomfort in revealing one's imperfections and the conscious prevention of banal configurations, while characteristic of European dance-theatre, are completely unfamiliar in his classical background where repetitive mastery and presentation of virtuoso technique stand for one's art. Thus, by not entering the mode of repetition and reproduction, by rejecting categorization of his practice within existent terminology and by accepting the open-endedness of each creative project as new and challenging and vulnerable, Khan's embodiment of diaspora is in the process of being written, forever shifting, always in transmission. It remains to be seen if the precise ways in which Khan's artistic and aesthetic vision will perhaps come to represent 'the explicit body' (Schneider in Lepecki 1999: 130) on the British dance stage. By already occupying a significant and influential position in mainstream British dance, Khan's *otherness* is being rewritten in full view of the public as he renegotiates his corporeality as an ongoing endeavour. That his presence in British contemporary dance has significantly challenged pre-existent frameworks and subsequently demanded the acknowledgement of a new identity for the genre is now an undeniable reality.

*Notes*

1   Kathak is a north Indian classical dance and is distinct in its aesthetic and cultural heritage from its southern counterparts. The name 'Kathak' is derived from the Sanskrit word *katha*, which means story. A hybrid dance form in itself, Kathak combines the storytelling tradition of the *kathakars* of fifteenth and sixteenth-century northern India with the key features of Persian dance (which accompanied the foreign invasions from approximately the twelfth century AD), characterized by its mathematically complex and precise rhythms, geometrical shapes and linear alignments of the body. Thus not only is Kathak a culturally hybrid art form but also it embraces a religious duality in its identity: on the one hand, one can identify its Hindu storytelling tradition, and on the other, its Islamic corporeal artistry. It is said to have been nurtured through patronage in the Mughal courts in northern India.

2   A critique of this attempted homogenization of essentially heterogeneous ethnicities, performance traditions and cultural heritage falls outside the scope of this essay. However, an excellent appraisal of this logocentric categorization and the politicization of the history and practice of British Asian dance is undertaken by Alessandra Lopez y Royo in her article 'Dance in the British South Asian Diaspora: Redefining Classicism' (2004).

3   In a recent paper presentation at Research Day conference entitled 'Asian Theatres: Traditional, Contemporary, Diasporic, Intercultural', organized by Royal Holloway College, University of London, in June 2007, Ann David astutely observed the resurgence of Hindu identity and its intricate relationship with

community arts in the Indian diaspora in Britain. David's paper explored the reinstatement of Indian classical dance (particularly Bharatanatyam) within Hindu temple contexts in Britain, despite its highly contested history, reiterating the significance of Hinduization of the classical dance forms in the community life of the Indian diaspora.

4   I must stress here that while I argue that a secular identity encourages disengagement with any religious associations, I distinguish this clearly from the spiritual associations inherently present within the art forms.

5   This in itself is an interesting fact about his hybrid condition. Khan is a second-generation British Bangladeshi Muslim, practising Kathak, a north Indian classical dance form that is renowned as a hybrid dance form in its amalgamation of both Hindu storytelling traditions and Persian Islamic arts in fifteenth- and sixteenth-century India.

6   Akram Khan continues to perform traditional solo Kathak pieces (*Polaroid Feet* in 2001, *Ronin* in 2003 and *third catalogue*) in parallel to his contemporary experimentations (*Loose in Flight, Fix* and *Rush* in 2000, *Related Rocks* in 2001, *Kaash* in 2002, *ma* in 2004, *Variations for Vibes, Strings and Pianos* in 2005, *zero degrees* in 2006 and *Sacred Monsters* in 2007).

7   In 2006, Khan was awarded the Critics' Circle National Dance Awards prize for Outstanding Male or Female Artist (modern) and *zero degrees* was nominated for Laurence Olivier Awards (Best New Dance Production). In 2005, Khan became an Associate Artist at Sadler's Wells Theatre and was also awarded an MBE for his services to the UK dance community. In 2004, he received an Honorary Doctorate of Arts from De Montfort University for his contribution to the UK arts community. In April 2003, Khan became Associate Artist at the South Bank Centre. In 2002, he was announced Winner of Time Out Live Award for 'Best Newcomer' and was also made Choreographer in Residence at the South Bank Centre. I provide these details of his public recognition to demonstrate his steady and remarkably fast-paced journey in British dance.

8   A land that was once one and the same as Bengal and was part of the eastern land mass of India, until the Partition of Bengal segregated a race of people bound by a common culture and language on the premise of religion.

9   At the recent Congress on Research in Dance (CORD) and Society of Dance History Scholars (SDHS) conference (June 2007) in Paris, entitled 'Rethinking Practice & Theory/Repenser Pratique et Theorie', I had the privilege of

receiving feedback from Ramsay Burt after my paper presentation on the topic of representations of masculinity in Khan's practice. Burt clarified to me his intentions of never using the term 'post men' as anything more than an irony as a chapter title. He specified that he was not theorizing the raw, volatile and erotic masculinity as represented in recent European dance-theatre and physical theatre practice through the term 'post men'. While I accept that it was not his intention to do so when he introduced the chapter title as 'post men', I find his ironic construction of the phrase very useful in discussing the masculinity of the men in DV8, Ultima Vez, Pina Bausch, Liam Steel, and others. Therefore, my take on Burt's chapter title of 'post men' extends this phrase further into becoming a theoretical model with which to approach the masculinity of postmodern men as evoked and represented in recent European dance-theatre works.

*References*

ANTHIAS, Floya. 2001. 'New Hybridities, Old Concepts: The Limits of "Culture"'. *Ethnic and Racial Studies* 24(4): 619–41.

BHABHA, Homi K. 1994. *The Location of Culture*. London: Routledge.

BOSE, Mandakranta. 1998. 'Gender and Performance: Classical Indian Dancing', in Lizbeth Goodman and Jane de Gay (eds), *The Routledge Reader in Gender and Performance*. London: Routledge, pp. 251–4.

_____. 2001. *Speaking of Dance: The Indian Critique*. New Delhi: DK Printworld.

BROWN, John Russell. 2001. 'Voices of Reform in South Asian Theatre'. *New Theatre Quarterly* 17(1): 45–53.

BURT, Ramsay. 1995. *The Male Dancer: Bodies Spectacles, Sexualities*. London: Routledge.

_____. 2004. '*Kaash*: Dance, Sculpture and the Visual'. *Visual Culture in Britain* 5(2): 93–108.

COUNSEL, Colin and Laurie Wolf (eds). 2001. *Performance Analysis: An Introductory Coursebook*. London: Routledge.

DAVID, Ann. 2007. 'Performances of British Hinduism? Sacralization of Space and the Place of Pilgrimage in the UK'. Conference paper presented at Asian Theatres: Traditional, Contemporary, Diasporic, Intercultural, Drama and Theatre Department, Royal Holloway College, June 2007.

DAYAL, Samir. 1996. 'Diaspora and Double Consciousness'. *The Journal of Midwest Modern Language Association* 29(1): 46–62.

FOSTER, Susan Leigh (ed.). 1996. *Corporealities: Dancing Knowledge, Culture and Power.* London: Routledge.

GRAU, Andree. 2003. 'Political Activism, Art, and the Many Histories of Indian Classical Dance'. Available at: www.soas.ac.uk/ahrbmusicanddance/newsletter/-musicanddance2.pdf (accessed 10 March 2005).

GREHAN, Helen. 2003. 'Rakini Devi: Diasporic Subject and Agent Provocateur'. *Theatre Research International* 28(3): 229–44.

KAUR, Parm. N.D. 'Dancing Home'. Available at: bak.spc.org/poet/pdfs/dancing_-home.pdf (accessed 12 October 2007).

KHAN, Akram. 2005a. 'Personal Profile'. Available at: www.akramkhancompany.net/html/akram_home.html (accessed 18 February 2005).

———. 2005b. *zero degrees.* DVD. Akram Khan Company.

KOTHARI, Sunil (ed.). 2003. *New Directions in Indian Dance.* Mumbai: Marg Publications.

LEPECKI, Andre. 1999. 'Skin, Body, and Presence in Contemporary European Choreography'. *TDR* 43(4) (T164): 129–40.

LOPEZ Y ROYO, Alessandra. 2003. 'Classicism, Post-Classicism and Ranjabati Sircar's Work: Redefining the Terms of Indian Contemporary Dance Discourses'. *South Asia Research* 23(2): 153–69.

———. 2004. 'Dance in the British South Asian Diaspora: Redefining Classicism', in *Postcolonial Text.* Available at: pkp.ubc.ca/pocol/view-article.php?id=138 (accessed 10 March 2005).

MEREDITH, Paul. 1998. 'Hybridity in the Third Space: Rethinking Bi-cultural Politics in Aotearoa/New Zealand'. Available at: lianz.waikato.ac.nz/PAPERS/-paul/hybridity.pdf (accessed 8 October 2007).

MITRA, Royona. 2005. 'Cerebrality: Rewriting Corporeality of a Transcultural Dancer', in Johannes Birringer and Josephine Fenger (eds), *Tanz im Kopf* [Dance and Cognition]. Munster: Lit Verlag, pp. 167–83.

MOCK, Roberta. 2000. *Performing Processes.* Bristol: Intellectual Books.

PHELAN, Peggy. 1993. *Unmarked: The Politics of Performance.* London: Routledge.

RAM, Kalpana. 2005. 'Phantom Limbs: South Indian Dance and Immigrant Reifications of the Female Body'. *Journal of Intercultural Studies* 26(1–2): 121–37.

ROJEK, Chris. 2003. *Stuart Hall (Key Contemporary Thinkers)*. Cambridge: Polity Press.

SANDERS, Lorna. 2007. '"I just can't wait to get to the hotel": *zero degrees* (2005)'. Available at: akramkhancompany.net/docs/zerodegrees.doc (accessed 3 September 2007).

JENN JOY

Eyes breathe. Like open wounds (Waldrop 1998).

Standing in front of the photograph, my reflection disturbs the surface, casting a shadow that imposes a particular way of seeing that obscures the image in the very moment I attend to it. Confronted by the seeming obviousness of the nude figure posed on the studio floor, I am seduced by its clean surfaces yet haunted by its silence. This exposure of flesh reveals little intimacy or erotic force as it turns away from and into itself in a contraction of muscle and sinew. Sculpted curves along the edge of the buttocks appear where the head should be; minor indentations along the waist direct the eye into the articulated pulse of the spine. Sustaining a virtuosic pose captured in time as a still, *Cyc-7* (2007)[1] by artist Bill Durgin becomes uncomfortable in its resistance to my gaze and to recognition (Figure 1). Twisting away from the camera, the figure also proposes a twist away from the edges of representation, revealing the skeletal pull of gesture working at its limit to obscure markers of body and of expression. Inverting the verticality of the body simultaneously turns corporeal hierarchy on its head, literally balancing it on its shoulders. Without limbs, ambulation appears impossible, forcing a

FIGURE 1. Bill Durgin, *Cyc-7*. C-print. 2007.

different consideration of movement as something interior. Staging the relationship of figure to ground as an inversion of flesh and concrete, the contracted figures foreground the tension of gesture as a precondition for movement, suggesting perhaps that their immobility is merely a momentary pause in a tremulous choreography of isolation. If the history of photography has been narrated as sequential revelations of invisible movements—Muybridge's horse hovering above the ground—then Durgin's photographs secret these movements away, proposing a choreographic stall as body turned figure contracts in stilled distortion. This precarious tremor shifts the grounds of the photographic to speak as choreographic image, an image that unsettles as we move closer and farther away from it. Here Durgin presents us with an object of *ekphrasis*, torquing the language of the photographic to speak as choreographic proposal.

This tendency to play the boundaries of medium is also to play the boundaries of spectatorship and points toward what Jacques Rancière describes as an 'emancipated spectator [. . . sited at] the strategic intersection between art and politics' (2007: 217). For Rancière, this new spectator breaks with the speculative passivity denounced by Plato, the cruel immersive theatrics of Antonin Artaud and the distancing effects of Bertolt Brecht to announce a new mode of watching as a participatory act. To imagine the photograph in terms of the participatory and thus of always moving relationships foregrounds the choreographic surround of its process, its presence and its reception. The stain of my own shadow on the photograph's surface forces me to shift my weight in order to see it more distinctly. Trespassing into the lonely space of the contracted figure, I engage the blurry edges of critical spectatorship as a site of moving mutual interrogation.

Oscillating along the threshold—of figure and ground, of photography and dance, of stillness and mobility, of recognition and incommunicability—also imagines a political potency for the choreographic as a movement of body and of language that imagines the 'beyond' of something else: what I call the spasm. The choreographic spasm produces a conceptual distortion between forces disfiguring or reconfiguring elements in interaction. Spasms call attention to the kinetic potentials of individual bodies—pushed into movement, caught in stillness, reverberating in between—questioning philosophical and psychological notions of subjectivity. Not only a physical move-

ment, the spasm is simultaneously a theoretical labour marked by the difficult and at times uncomfortable proximity of ideas that contort and convulse
when brought into dialogue. As a movement of thought, the spasm interrogates the visual through the kinetic, the body through language, expression
through emotion, performer through witness, pain through pleasure. It is
not stagnant even when appearing as latency; in these moments, it quivers
and trembles.

The spasm is a convulsion: a gesture beginning in stillness, it crescendos
to extreme intensity and then dissipates. It reiterates its presence unexpectedly yet is not exactly repeatable; sometimes its effects linger along the surface and at other moments it disappears immediately. It resembles the
conception of the image as described by Jean-Luc Nancy. The image, he
writes,

> is therefore not a representation: it is an imprint of the intimacy of
> its passion (of its motion, its agitation, its tension, its passivity). It
> is not an imprint in the sense of a type or schema that would be set
> down and fixed. It is rather the movement of the imprint, the stroke
> that marks the surface, the hollowing out and pressing up of this
> surface, of its substance (canvas, paper, copper, paste, clay, pigment,
> film, skin), its impregnation or infusion, the embedding or the dis-
> charge effected in it by the pressure applied to it (2005: 7).[2]

This image, which Nancy also refers to as 'the distinct', must be defined
through a complicated tuning of language to render what it is and is not, to
point to its transitive potential without trapping it in proximities of medium
or surface. Like the spasm, the image-distinct maintains a distance from representation through its inclusion of the absence within itself of the very thing
it resembles (ibid.: 22). A sacred space, the image-distinct quivers with energy
that both empties and fills it and touches the surface it acts upon, affectively
reaching out beyond its figure or frame to touch the witness as well.

To consider another photograph *Cyc-9* (2007), under the influence of the
spasm, I witness a slightly fleshier figure bending into the wall at an oblique
angle, her head disappeared into the seam of the elbow. The pale figure appears still. Yet this stillness is undercut by the shadow bleeding along the
wall and under the body; it creates a hazy outline, capturing minute vibrations of effort as if the figure is bowing to meet itself. The vanishing point of

the lens lingers along this edge of skin and shadow, delineating an uncomfortable visibility. This is not a glamorous or virtuosic body but a fleshy vulnerability, a more intimate and idiosyncratic rendering of body reduced to sculpture or object. The remainder of the body hides in shadow, alluded to by the play of light passing through the distortion. The shadow also revels in the lie, the moment of possible escape and impending or latent motion. Against the controlled figure—body taut, knees locked, arms clenched, shoulders integrated along the spine—the shadow quivers just a little along the edges, an effect of tension and lighting. The space of the studio seems to weigh her down, taking over presence, forcing her into herself and registering an uncanny tension not quite beautiful, not quite abject. Possessed by an exquisite emotional and representational limit, the figure appears trapped but not immobile, captured but not quite contained (Figure 2).

The seeping presence of the shadow imagines a movement of flesh in a single frame that questions figurative representation and relies instead on a more affective or perhaps sensational relationship to figuration not bound by contour. The shadow is of the body, but not it; it marks an escape from the body and an escape from the rigidity of figuration assumed by representation. It is as if the body steps out of itself through the shadow, witnessed in Francis Bacon's *Studies of the Human Body* (1970) when the figure lifts a leg and staggers or bends over bleeding into the ground. As in the photographs, the seemingly distinct figure becomes unrooted, falling into the inverted ground even as it attempts to walk across it. Bacon's triptych renders a serial instability that offers a glimpse of contracted movement at that very moment of its concealment. The quiver of the photographic shadow appears in the painting as a thickened brush stroke, a blur of disfiguring oil. Bacon's working method notoriously moves between photograph and painting: he claimed that he could only work from intimate photographs because live models were too disturbed by the violence he commits to their image.

> What I want to do is to distort the thing far beyond the appearance, but in the distortion to bring it back to a recording of the appearance. [...The models] inhibit me because, if I like them, I don't want to practice before them the injury that I do to them in my work. I would rather practice the injury in private by which I think I can record the fact of them more clearly (Bacon, in Sylvester 1975: 40–1).

FIGURE 2. Bill Durgin, *Cyc-9*. C-print. 2007.

The damage Bacon does to the image, the figure and the subject (what could perhaps also be described as the forces of the spasm) also inspires Gilles Deleuze's meditation on Bacon's painting. Here, Deleuze proposes an unusual break from art-historical conceptions of figuration as he writes against periods, movements, biography and social art history and focuses instead on aesthetics in terms of movement—what I would describe as the choreographic impulses at work in visual art. Deleuze speaks directly of the shadow as a break from representation—the imperative to which figurative painting previously aspires.

In Bacon's paintings, Deleuze sees the rendering of the shadow-spasm as a limit not only of movement but also of a notion of subjectivity; the spasm performs the body at the edges of representation and of recognition, at the limits of sense as it moves into sensation. He describes the shadow itself as a moment of spasm:

> in which the body attempts to escape from itself *through* one of its organs in order to rejoin the field or material structure [. . .] the shadow has as much presence as the body; but the shadow acquires this presence only because it escapes from the body, the shadow is the body that has escaped from itself through some localized point in the contour (2003: 16).

Particularly in the 'stilled' work of painting and of photography, the shadow reveals the choreographic impulse acting out a kind of 'athleticism' (ibid.: 13)—a latent spasm effect.

In Durgin's photographs, the athleticism of the body is contained within the tension of the gesture, limbs hidden from view; the figures are not digitally manipulated, so the bodies in the studio must sustain awkward, uncomfortable poses for the duration of the shot. Their nudity revels in the accidents of flesh, the lines and weight of age, the hyper-articulation of the spine. Naked, the bodies appear constrained or reduced to almost pod-like objects, yet it is the shadow echoing on the white floor and wall that hints at the excess of figure that cannot quite be contained. Durgin's rendering of the figure–shadow relationship offers one perspective on the choreographic potential of the spasm, described by Deleuze: the shadow-spasm reveals 'not the relationship of form and matter, but of materials and forces; to make these forces visible through their effects on flesh [. . .] To make spasm visible' (ibid.: xxix).

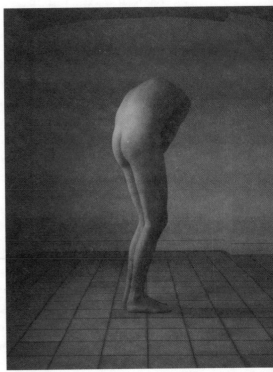

FIGURE 3. Bill Durgin, *Rue Vieille du Temple*. C-print. 2006.

As twinned figures twist away from each other in Durgin's diptych *Rue Vieille du Temple* (2006), we see this flickering spasm on the surface of the flesh as the ribs push against skin, muscles flex and cellulite curdles (Figure 3). The explicit nudity of the figures not only forces us to see what is happening on the surface of the body, but also hints at what is happening within. The difficult anatomical effort required to hold these gestures simultaneously informs their expressive vulnerability and tense isolation. As Deleuze again reminds us, 'Now it is inside the body that something is happening, the body is the source of movement. This is no longer the problem of place, but rather of the event. [. . .] It is not I who attempts to escape from my body, it is the body that attempts to escape from itself by means of [. . .] a spasm' (ibid.: 15).

The spasm happens from within as the body attempts to escape from itself. These spasms are sensational-perceptual events, distinct from a notion of spasm as clinical seizure or involuntary vibration. Deleuze's use of the word *spasm* as a sensate aesthetic effect retains traces of this involuntary action, yet, important in the context of his work and mine, spasm is not only aligned with a negative medical definition of madness or disease. The sensational-perceptual spasm spreads out from the interior of the body and is experienced as the kicks and pressures of a perpetual motion machine: I imagine it like the becoming baby that rolls and shifts unexpectedly, calling my attention to my own previously ignored interiority, tendons, muscles that remained invisible and numb before this other presence makes itself known. His subtle movements perform a series of spasms that arrive without warning, are out of my control, yet still extend out of the body as force. Importantly, this spasm as event is not a notion of interiority tied to a depth model of psychology, but a more phenomenological experience. It is not a layering, but a series of shifting chiasmatic sensations moving in both directions simultaneously, disorienting exterior and interior notions of figuration and a static relationship between the painted (or photographed) subject and the subject approaching the painting. The spasm moves along the material surface of the canvas through the tremulous effects of shadows to touch the viewer, and back from the sensations of the viewer to the work of art as a mutually destabilizing interrogation.

The shadow-spasm is a dance: light intercepted by the figure is thrown against the ground as darkness illuminating the potentials and residuals of movement. Thinking through this sensational dance requires a constant negotiation of presences—those within and attending to the photographic image and those who dance along signification's edge—as the language of movement constantly turns to a movement of language and back again. Thus the shadow-spasm is perhaps a paradoxical site, a moving still or stilled movement that leads us across disciplinary lines and further into the question of what the choreographic might mean. As described by Adrian Heathfield:

> Choreography is the impossible attempt to remove the paradox of the stillness inside movement. Choreography is a transaction of flesh, an opening of one body to others, a vibration of limits. Choreography is given to the erotic: it tests out, seduces, and proposes without ever saying anything. Choreography is a corporeal passage in which the body is both a question and an inaccessible answer (2007).

Heathfield's mediation on choreography's ontology traces its sensual qualities and oscillating physicality; choreography acts in relation and yet resists the very meanings it opens up. Choreography becomes, like Nancy's image-distinct, an unstable site that 'dispute[s . . .] representation' and signification (Nancy 2005: 33). While the image-distinct is described as a kind of seizure (ibid.: 9), it still hovers along philosophical peripheries, perhaps longing to trespass into a body and onto the stage.

Naked, two dancers lie face down on the darkened stage. They tremble; a mild convulsion passes through their bodies, which transforms into a creeping mobility as they slowly peel their bodies from the floor, edging away from the light. No longer completely recognizable, the slow progression of almost larval forms emerging from and disappearing into the darkness approaches abstraction as they ambulate using only their shoulders, chin and hips. Thick muscular flesh slaps against the floor, amplifying their difficult horizontal mobility.

In these moments of *Glory*[3] choreographed by Jeremy Wade and performed by Wade with Marysia Stoklosa, we encounter an extreme choreographic articulation of the spasm. *Glory* exhibits the generative excess of the spasm as the bodies attempt to expel themselves from their limits through what Wade describes as 'a three-dimensional kinesthetic blur. Add levels of speed, levels of rhythm, add fluids, flesh, chemical, emotional, behavioral bodies, add detail, memory, position, history, character, add light, sound'

(2007a). In the rehearsal process, he works with authentic movement scores[4] and improvisation to locate gestures internally as dancers move under the influence of specific words—empathy, anger, repulsion, shame, ecstasy, intoxication, anxiety, attraction. Subjecting the resulting gestures to the de-representational play of improvisation, the extreme states of shaking, convulsing, trembling, falling are continually refined to interrogate language. For Wade, improvisation is not simply a random series of actions, but rather a structure—determined initially by the particular associations of words—that is destabilized, subjected to precarious failures and ambivalent gestural oscillations as shame becomes ecstasy becomes anxiety in the process of experiential relational movement. This play between physicality and language enacted in the rehearsal studio and on the stage challenges techniques of representation and signification, creating new choreographic possibilities, or what Giorgio Agamben might refer to as communicabilities for excessive, spasming subjectivities to move. Here, Agamben's theory of communicability as a force of exposure—of ideas, of community, of 'revelation'—is explicitly tied to reimagining the work of gesture as a profoundly political act. When he writes, 'Exposition is the location of politics' (2000: 93), the visual and the gestural become intertwined, proposing a theory of politics as an always shifting encounter between image and movement. This is perhaps the creative power of the choreographic, as a generator of mutant identities and political potentialities.

'A work of art,' as Félix Guattari proposes, 'is an activity of unframing, of rupturing sense, of baroque proliferation [. . .] which leads to a recreation and reinvention of the subject itself' (1995: 131). For Guattari, the work of art is itself a moving encounter that reimagines aesthetics as a producer of alteric modes of subjectivity. His choice of 'baroque' becomes important because it alludes to a kind of spiritual or ecstatic excess, a seductive and at times repulsive display of expression and sensuality rendered through the dark shades of chiaroscuro, waves of light and shadow.[5] *Glory* performs the baroque in multiple ways as the dancers crawl into and out of darkness and, even more specifically—or perhaps art historically—as the iconic image of *The Ecstasy of St Teresa* tattooed on Wade's back shivers as he moves. Folds of flesh melt into the drawn folds of fabric draped across Teresa's body as she lies, mouth open, head turned from the attending angel.[6] Her fingers seem almost to quiver and her toes hang taut, her body trapped in the intermediary space of ecstasy, as Wade's body continues its stuttering ambulation across the floor.

Obscured in shadow, the bodies appear at one moment prostrated on the floor, at another as a messy pile of limbs becoming less visible and less distinct as if absorbed by the surrounding space.[7] A low light illuminates part of a torso, then flickers along the thighs or buttocks; yet, as these figures make their way along the ground they remain only partially in view, haunted by the sound score—an industrial roar marked by moments of silence or the moaning tendons of the cello. In shadow, the sound acts as animal accomplice lamenting the painful, hysterical process of becoming—a process haunted by violent excess.

This duet of shadow and sound played across the body continues until the dancers pause at the edge of the stage. Stoklosa grabs Wade's mouth with her own, she appears to be chewing or consuming him as they roll over, onto, into each other. As they intertwine she whispers, building to a scream, 'the road is long and I am tired and small.' In this moment of the extended kiss, the mouth becomes, as Wade describes it, a 'devouring machine' (2007a). Until this moment the states of spasm occur as individual gestures in parallel, as a duet or a mirror, yet in this phrase distance dissolves under the intensity of attraction disfiguring and refiguring their relationship. Sweat moves across and between bodies, limbs become more confused. This is communicability, as all consuming, submerged in an erotic and volatile physicality. It is a body almost possessed, desperate, messy, intimate, disorientated and disfigured in a moment of relational–sensational plexus.

Witnessing the climax of the spastic duet convulsing into a singular spasm while recoiling from this intimacy reveals the spasm as a beautifully grotesque gesture, relational yet resilient. The choreographic spasm poses as extreme anatomy of attachment and desire, even of disfiguration. Yet, in Wade's work the spasm resists a complete dissolving of subjectivity. Rather, the spasm functions as an interrogator of subjectivity and communicability. This becomes clear as the versions of *Glory* evolve. In the first version of *Glory* (2003), the dancers begin naked on stage, waiting for the audience to arrive. The process of becoming is always already underway; the bodies have transformed into surreal objects and their sculptural flesh anticipates the event of movement. Yet in the second and third versions (2007), it is the audience who waits, contemplating the empty space as Wade and Stoklosa walk onto the stage. Standing side by side, they pause. This dramaturgical shift directs attention to the quotidian presence of the bodies, to their easy orientation and calm physicality as if offering a foil for the drama to come. Clothed, the gestures seem less confused and vertiginous, forcing us to pay attention to the face, which alone remains open and naked to our gaze.

The dancers begin to smile, or almost, as a halting series of facial tics morphs from smile to frown to yawn to gag. Her eyes roll back into her head. His tongue reaches grotesquely out of his mouth. Performing an atrophic virtuosity, the dancers' faces appear to be choking on the very air that surrounds them. As their expressions accumulate and retrograde—eyebrows distort, tongues thrust, noses torque, mouths become gaping voids, hysterical laughter—they transform from micro-spasms of the face to contorted staggering movements of the entire body across the floor. At the precarious edge of collapse, the dancers' bodies appear disarticulated and out of control, severing choreography's anticipated relationship to mobility and stasis, graceful expertise and beautiful uncertainty. Pausing, they remove their clothes, arranging them in abject piles at their feet, and then carry them off-stage.

Subverting a virtuosic notion of dance through an existential examination of extreme facial gesture, the dancers direct our attention away from the figure to the expressive potentialities of the face, a move not unlike Samuel Beckett's *Not I* (1972). Also trapped in darkness, only a Mouth with glistening teeth is visible as she narrates her own coming into being, coming into language. She speaks of the impossibility of speech even when her own voice cries out, screaming, spasming against its limits, describing her own sound score as a 'buzzing' not in the ears, but in the skull (Beckett 2006: 411).[8] A kind of embedded, inscribed, inescapable soundtrack. Yet in place of Beckett's flood of hysterical language spoken by the disembodied Mouth, Wade choreographs the momentary (seemingly) disembodiment of the face as a site of impossible speech interrogating possibilities of representation and language through expressions of ecstasy, of despair, of shame, of pleasure, of pain. The bleed between these seductive and repulsive, recognizable and illegible expressions performs an excessive polyvocality not contained by the significatory logic of representation. Instead, the face becomes a site of alteric and affective communicability. *Glory*'s faces use the choreographic function of the spasm to differentiate between language as a function of representation and communicability as a transitive poetic address. Describing the face

FIGURE 4. Marysia Stoklosa (*foreground*) and Jeremy Wade. Jeremy Wade, *Glory*, 2007. Photograph by Mathias Trostdorf.

FIGURE 5. Marysia Stoklosa (*left*) and Jeremy Wade. Jeremy Wade, *Glory*, 2007. Photograph by Mathias Trostdorf.

as the site of 'communicability', the place where politics must be exposed, Agamben writes, 'Be only your face. Go to the threshold. Do not remain the subjects of your properties or faculties, do not stay beneath them: rather, go with them, in them, beyond them' (2000: 92, 100). Agamben's choreographic imperative argues for a rethinking of political language as passionate gestural expression spreading out from the face that resonates with the disorientating decompositions and recompositions of the face in *Glory*. Here, the spasm as choreographic address proposes an almost impossible body, one that rejects coherence and unity, striving instead to articulate a more vertiginous flux of subjectivity.

Naked, the body becomes an extension of the face. As facial tics saturate the dancers' bodies, we witness flickering sensations of weight, of balance, of fragility, of effort across their muscular flesh. This intensely intimate, sensual and perhaps violent dependency participates in the extreme gesture of the spasm as it 'devours' a coherent conception of bodies and subjectivities, forcing an, at times, illegible and distressing vision of the inability of language and movement to account for Wade's and our experience. This is the site and possibility of the threshold that Agamben imagines in the face—a zone of communicability that calls us to action, breaking with passive spectatorship to open up to the disturbing affective modes of sensual address.

Sensual address as communicative mode is a rare and subtle phenomenon, often obscured by legislative acts of consumption, erasure and violence. Crossing the photographic with the choreographic and back again, spasms image an alteric legibility that participates in an almost violent thrust, yet these extreme gestures are tempered in their directionality and force. Against the hyper-legibility of violent acts as perhaps the defining gesture of this particular historical moment,[9] the spasm undoes legibility through its supplementary excess—both stilled and danced—to propose a notion of subjectivity that challenges the regimes of the operative or quotidian. Against these dominant patterns, the anatomies of spasms disrupt. They quiver, they tremble, they repeat. They trip over folds of flesh: a figure escapes the bounds of representation through corporeal disorganization. Confrontational yet intimately inward, spasms as performed in the work of Durgin and Wade communicate an atrophic virtuosity that undoes gesture as it works on itself and on the spectator.

Lingering at the edges of the frame or stage, I no longer stand passively as my reflection obscures the image in the moment of its appearing. I am now called to continually bend toward or away from the obscuring shadows, to look into the shadows to encounter the tension passing across the terrains of paper and of skin. Perhaps this is the moment Roland Barthes describes as 'the painful burn of proximity' as he searches for some almost inexplicable identity in *Camera Lucida*. He writes: 'If my efforts are painful, if I am anguished, it is because sometimes I get closer, I am burning: in a certain photograph I believe I perceive the likeness of truth [. . .] Yet on thinking it over, I must ask myself: Who is like what? Resemblance is conformity, but to what? to an identity' (1981: 100). His tenuous encounter with a truth of the image performs communicability in its poetic destabilizing of my reflection along the grounds of the image. The choreographic impulse of the spasm is here revealed as subtly stilled, yet always moving, flashes of recognition through gesture that resists conforming. As the naked body becomes face, becomes the site of communicability, gestural spasms invite me to witness in fragments what is never quite recognizable, never quite identifiable identity, but instead a lingering suspension and stuttering hesitation. Yet this end is never final, suggesting only a place of exhaustion from which to begin again.

*Notes*

1   The photographs discussed here are part of the *Figurations* series (2005–08) by Bill Durgin. The *Cyc* in the title refers to the *Cyc* wall of the photo studio—a wall, curved along the bottom and usually painted white, used for shooting objects devoid of context—in which Durgin composed and shot his images.

2   Interestingly, this text first appeared in a catalogue for a show entitled *Heaven: An Exhibition That Will Break Your Heart* at Kunsthalle, Düsseldorf/Tate Gallery, Liverpool, 1999–2000. Jean-Luc Nancy argues for a notion of the image as a sacred space, a thing 'set apart, at a distance' (2005: 1). Yet the exhibition itself collapses religion and art to celebrate 'desire, consumerism, idolisation, glamour, identity and authenticity'—qualities seemingly at odds with his text (Tate Liverpool 1999).

3   The first version of *Glory* premiered in 2003 at the Kitchen in New York City as part of Dance Works in Progress when Jeremy Wade was based in New York

City. This version was performed with Lyndsey Karr. In February 2007, he per-
formed a second version at Dance Theater Workshop with Jessica Hill, with
music by Loren Dempster and Michael Mahalchick, lighting by Jonathan
Belcher, dramaturgy by Leigh Garret and Yvonne Meier. After moving to
Berlin, Wade created a third version (described here)—performed with
Marysia Stoklosa, music by Loren Dempster and Michael Mahalchick, lighting
by Fabian Bleisch, dramaturgy by Jenn Joy—which continues to be performed.
As Wade writes, 'We will continue to explore, tweak, question, and perform
"glory." It is alive and malleable' (2007b). See www.jeremywade.de for upcom-
ing performances.

4   In the practice of authentic movement, one mover begins by lying on the floor
with her eyes closed and follows the inner sensations of her body, transforming these sensations into images or impulses for movements, sounds or words.
Another individual witnesses the process of moving and later re-performs
these movements for the original mover. Scores can be created from these relational improvisations as an extended rehearsal strategy or transposed into
the performance.

5   For a more detailed examination of the baroque as 'operative function' crossing disciplinary genres through an endless proliferation of folds, see Gilles
Deleuze (1993).

6   Here, pain mingles with pleasure as she describes her experience: 'The pain
was so great that I screamed aloud; but at the same time I felt such infinite
sweetness that I wished the pain would last forever. It was not physical pain
but psychic pain, although it affected the body to some degree' (in Janson
1991: 57).

7   When I asked Wade what role images play in his choreographic process, he
responded with many possibilities, visions, memories, but two seem particularly vivid in relation to this section: 'images of the Jones Town massacre bodies sprawled out like dominos falling in an elegant pattern [. . .,] a picture of
a Pentecostal revival in which the congregation was in prostration face down
with only their hands reaching upwards' (2008).

8   Like the two dancers in *Glory*, the Mouth in *Not I* is not alone on stage. Her
hysterical linguistic spasm is always attended by the choreographic presence
of another. Completely cloaked in a black djellaba, the Auditor stands at an
oblique angle to the audience on an 'invisible podium' facing the Mouth (Beck-

ett 2006: 405). Four times during her monologue the Mouth stops and the Auditor's arms rise and fall slowly from the sides of the body in 'a gesture of
helpless compassion' (ibid.: 405).

9   In the final stages of this writing, I read Carrie Noland's evocative 'Introduc-
    tion' to *Migrations of Gesture* (2008) that begins with Theodor W. Adorno's
    lamentation on the fate of the subtle gesture, written in 1951: 'Technology is
    making gestures precise and brutal, and with them men. It expels from move-
    ments all hesitation, deliberation, civility. It subjects them to the implacable,
    as it were ahistorical demands of objects' (Adorno 2005: 40). Now in 2008, it is
    not only technology that pressures gesture to conform to regimented or op-
    erative brutality, but the nexus of forces of capitalist flow and mediated sat-
    uration of images that legislates gesture.

*References*

ADORNO, Theodor W. 2005 [1951]. *Minima Moralia: Reflections on a Damaged Life*
    (E. F. N. Jephcott trans.). London: Verso.

AGAMBEN, Giorgio. 2000 [1996]. *Means Without End: Notes on Politics* (Vincenzo Binetti
    and Cesare Casarino trans.). Minneapolis: University of Minnesota Press.

BARTHES, Roland. 1981 [1980]. *Camera Lucida: Reflections on Photography* (Richard
    Howard trans.). New York: Hill and Wang.

BECKETT, Samuel. 2006. *The Grove Centenary Editions, Volume III: The Dramatic Works
    of Samuel Beckett* (Paul Auster ed.). New York: Grove Press.

DELEUZE, Gilles. 1993 [1988]. *The Fold: Leibniz and the Baroque* (Tom Conley trans.).
    Minneapolis: University of Minnesota Press.

———. 2003 [1981]. *Francis Bacon: The Logic of Sensation* (Daniel W. Smith
    trans.). Minneapolis: University of Minnesota Press.

GUATTARI, Félix. 1995 [1992]. *Chaosmosis: an Ethico-Aesthetic Paradigm* (Paul Bains
    and Julian Pefanis trans.). Bloomington: Indiana University Press.

HEATHFIELD, Adrian. 2007. 'Thema/Theme #7: Was Ist Choreografie/What Is Cho-
    reography?' Available at: www.corpusweb.net/index.php?option=com_con-
    tent&task=view&id=660&Itemid=35 (accessed 12 April 2008).

JANSON, Horst Woldemar. 1991 [1962]. *History of Art*. New York: Harry N. Abrams.

NANCY, Jean-Luc. 2005 [2003]. *The Ground of the Image: Perspectives in Continental Philosophy* (Jeff Fort trans.). New York: Fordham University Press.

NOLAND, Carrie. 2008. 'Introduction', in Carrie Noland and Sally Ann Ness (eds), *Migrations of Gesture*. Minneapolis: University of Minnesota Press, pp. ix–xxviii.

RANCIÈRE, Jacques. 2007. 'The Emancipated Spectator'. *Artforum* 45(7) (March).

SYLVESTER, David. 1975. *The Brutality of Fact: Interviews with Francis Bacon*. New York: Thames and Hudson.

TATE LIVERPOOL. 1999. Press release for *Heaven: An Exhibition That Will Break Your Heart*. Available at: www/tate.org.uk/liverpool/exhibitions/heaven/default.shtm (accessed 29 April 2008).

WADE, Jeremy. 2007a. Email correspondence with author, 22 June.

_____. 2007b. 'Programme notes for *Feed & Glory*'. *Performance Space* 122 (February).

_____. 2008. Email correspondence with author, 25 March.

WALDROP, Rosmarie. 1998. *Blindsight*. New York: New Directions Books.

# PART II
ASSEMBLING RELATIONS

# PARADOXICAL BODY[1]

JOSÉ GIL

We know that the dancer evolves in a particular space, different from objective space. The dancer does not move *in* space; rather, the dancer secretes, creates space with his movement.

This is not too different from what happens in theatre, or on other stages and in other scenes. The actor also transforms the scenic space; the gymnast prolongs the space that surrounds his skin—he weaves with bars, mats or simply with the ground he steps on, relations of complicity as intimate as the ones he has with his own body. In a similar way, the Zen archer and his target are one and the same. In all of these cases, a new space emerges. We will call it *the space of the body*.

It is a paradoxical space on many levels; while different from objective space, it is not separated from it. On the contrary, it is imbricated in objective space totally, to the point of being impossible to distinguish one from the other. The transfigured scene where the actor performs—is it not already objective space? Nonetheless, it is a scene invested with affects and new forces—the objects that occupy it gain different emotional values according to the actors' bodies; and although invisible, the space, the air, acquires a diversity of textures—they become dense or rarified, invigorating or suffocating. It is as if they were enveloping things with a surface similar to the skin. The *space of the body* is the skin extending itself into space; it is skin becoming space—thus, the extreme proximity between things and the body.

We can perform the following experiment: let's immerse ourselves completely naked in a deep bathtub, leaving only our heads sticking out of the water; let's drop onto the surface of the water, near our submerged feet, a spider. We will feel the animal's contact on the entirety of our skin. What happened? The water created a space of the body defined by the skin membrane of the bathtub's water. From this example we can extract two consequences pertaining to the properties of the space of the body: it prolongs the body's limits beyond its visible contours; it is an intensified space, when compared with the habitual tactility of the skin.

The space of the body is not only produced by gymnasts or by artists who use their bodies. It is a general reality, present everywhere, born the moment there is an affective investment by the body. It is akin to the notion of 'territory' in ethology. As a matter of fact, it is the first natural prosthesis of the body: the body gives itself new extensions in space, and in such ways it forms a new body—a virtual one, but ready to become actual and ready to allow gestures to become actualized in it. Let's consider the simple fact of driving an automobile: if we can pass between two walls without touching them, or turn left without running over the sidewalk, it is because our body partakes of the space and the contours of the car. Thus we calculate distances as if they referred to our own body (at the front of the car, it is my body that risks running over the sidewalk). In a general manner, any tool and its precise manipulation presupposes the space of the body.[2]

The dancer presents that particular characteristic of apparently not needing any kind of object, or any kind of body, in order to form his/her own proper space. All dancers, choreographers and thinkers who refer to the space of the body have always described it as emanating from a single body that is surrounded and made autonomous *by* the space of the body.

Rudolf von Laban conceived the space of the body in the shape of an icosahedron; that is, in the shape of an invisible polyhedron with 20 faces whose points of intersection mark the possible directions of the movements of a dancer (who remains at its centre). The energetic points in space are defined by the intersections of three faces of the icosahedron. Spatial directions are figured by planes and energetic nuclei by points. Dance produces a space of the body that implies forces and that feeds itself through tensions. Laban's icosahedron surrounds the dancer in a form that he transports from one point in space to another, while at the same time movement erupts in the icosahedron, thus transforming it and preserving it through its mutations.

Others have conceived the space of the body as an egg or as a sphere. But all describe it as a lived experience of the dancer, who feels himself moving within a kind of container that *supports* movement.

We can attribute at least two functions to the space of the body: (a) it augments the movement's fluency by creating a proper milieu, with the least amount of viscosity possible; (b) it makes possible the positioning of virtual bodies, who multiply the dancer's point of view.

Indeed, the space of the body results from a kind of secretion or reversal (whose process we will have to clarify) of the inner space of the body toward the exterior. This reversibility transforms objective space, giving it a texture close to the one of internal space. The dancer's body no longer needs to move as an object in an exterior space—from now on, the dancer's body unfolds movements as if traversing a body (its natural milieu).[3]

An image will help us apprehend this kind of corporification of space from which the space of the body emerges. We can see the body as a receptacle for movement. In possession dances (in the tarantella, in the 'Saint Vitus dances' and in many others), it is the body itself that becomes a scene or a space of the dance, as if someone—another body—was dancing inside the possessed subject. The dancer's body unfolds in the dancing body-agent and in the body-space where it dances, or rather, the body-space that movement traverses and occupies. So that dance—and no longer possession—can begin, it is necessary that there is no longer interior space available for movement. It is necessary that interior space partake so intimately of exterior space that movement *seen* from the outside coincides with movement lived or seen from the inside. Indeed, this is what happens in danced trance, where no space is left free outside of the consciousness of the body.

In other words, movement in possession *aims* at dancing. But it faces a resistance or inner viscosity that manifests itself in disorganized movements, as if only the *full* transfer of gestures and of an interior disorder toward the surface of the body could channel the energy for an unblocked fluency. But only an outside space without viscosity allows such a transfer, a space like the space of the body—where interior and exterior are one and the same.

All of this shows that dancing movements are learned: it is necessary to adapt the body to the rhythms and to the imperatives of the dance. Muscles, tendons, organs must become the means for the unimpeded flow of energy. In terms of space, this means to tightly imbricate interior space and external space, the inside of the body invested with energy, and the outside where gestures of the dance unfold. Interior space is coextensive with exterior space.

The learning of classical ballet technique shows this clearly. Before the mirror, the student learns how a certain position of limbs corresponds to a certain kinesthetic tension, thus constructing a kind of interior map of those movements that will allow him to move in a precise manner but without having to take recourse to an exterior image of the body. But what is an energetic map of movements if not a device that turns exterior space interior and vice versa?

The body must open itself to space, must become, in a certain way, space. And interior space must acquire a texture similar to the one of the body so that gestures may flow as easily as movement propagating through muscles. The space of the body—as exterior space—satisfies this demand. The body moves in it without facing the obstacles of foreign, objective space—with all its objects, its density, its prefixed orientations, its own points of reference. In the space of the body, it is the body that creates its own referents to which all exterior directions must submit themselves (thus, Laban's icosahedron also comprises vectors).

Another function seems to be tied to the space of the body: it ensures the narcissistic position of the dancer by multiplying the virtual images of his body. Why is it that one always considers the dancer's body as essentially narcissistic? Let's compare it to the actor's body: both intensify the common narcissism that always accompanies the exposure of any body in space. As Maurice Merleau-Ponty described so well,[4] a seeing body enters into a field of vision that sends back its own image, as in a mirror: to see is to be seen. The body carries with it this reversibility of the seer and of the seen, regardless of whether there is or there isn't another body in the visual field. This is why Merleau-Ponty talked about a 'narcissism of vision'.[5]

Because the scene constitutes itself as an appropriate object for the gaze, bodies augment their narcissistic potency in it. They find themselves in it just to exhibit themselves. But while the narcissism of the actor is divided among other elements beyond the body (the play of voice and word), with the dancer it is fully concentrated in corporeal presence. Whether or not the dancer wants it, he carries with him a powerful narcissistic capacity.

Now, the dancer's narcissism does not only summon the gaze. It is true that one 'sees' dancing, but it is also true that one 'listens', and, even more profoundly, one 'senses' dancing (because one 'touches' or 'experiences' the movement: the reflexivity of the body is total). There is no single visual or kinesthetic image of the dancing body, but a multiplicity of virtual images produced by movement that mark so many *points of contemplation* from which the body perceives itself.

The dancer senses his dancing. The dancer does not see himself as an object in motion across space, but accompanies his body's movement (seen from the outside by the spectators) with virtual images formed according to the map he has created from the choreography. It is something different from a mirroring, because the virtual image is never built in itself (while the visible gestures are—they are the virtual image's actualization). The dancer sees his dancing 'as in a dream'—thus opposing his body image to the one presented by reality. On one hand, the danced movement pulls the body back upon itself; on the other, it projects its multiple images toward points of narcissistic contemplation, points that are necessarily outside of the body proper, and that are found in space. But in which space, since it can be neither objective space nor interior space? It is the space of the body that provides the exterior–interior points of contemplation. Indeed, the narcissistic relationship of the dancer with his body implies a complicity that objective space, neutral and homogeneous, cannot provide. And it supposes a distance—of contemplation—that interior space refuses to provide. Only the space of the body, with its intense exterior, can satisfy both demands.

The dancer contemplates the virtual images of his body from the multiple points of view of the space of the body. Paradoxically, the narcissistic position of the dancer does not demand an 'I'. Rather, it demands (at least) one other body that can detach itself from the visible body and dance with it. Thanks to the space of the body, the dancer, while dancing, creates virtual doubles or multiples of his/her body who guarantee a stable point of view over movement (to Mary Wigman, to dance is to produce a double with whom the dancer dialogues).

Complicity and distance of the actual body in relation to all virtual bodies are thus accompanied by a contemplation of the movement that simultaneously partakes of that movement and distances itself from it, in order to acquire a consistent perspective at the interior of movement itself.

To dance is to produce dancing doubles. This is what explains the existence of duos (or, in a general manner, of a series of 'n' dancers making identical or complementary movements). The actual partner realizes the virtual double of the dancer. It is quite natural that the partner occupies such a place: he sees himself in the other, he adjusts gestures and rhythms according to the other, augments the same impulse, contemplates himself from the place of the other.

It is necessary above all not to identify the production of doubles by dancing movement with a phenomenon of mimesis. The partners in a duo do not enter into any mirroring mimetic relation; they do not 'copy' forms or gestures from each other. Instead, both enter into the same rhythm, while marking within it their own differences. This rhythm surpasses both partners, given that the difference perceived in one of the partners bounces back and resonates on the movement of the other reciprocally. Thus, a plane of movement[6] is formed that overflows the individual movements of each dancer and acts as a nucleus of stimulation for both. The two partners will actualize other virtual bodies and so on. A duo is an arrangement for building multiplicities of dancing bodies.

A partner's movement tries to enter the rhythm or the form of the other's energy—as a matter of fact, one partner becomes the other, becomes the other's dancing energy. From this we can derive the constitution of series—as if the same energy would spread from one body to another, traversing during the entire process of such a becoming all the bodies that comprise the series. Dance has the vocation to form groups or series.

In this sense, a duo or an indefinite series of bodies makes dance more than the serial production of virtual bodies—all of them doubles, since the original virtual body initiated a becoming-double, that are then added to the multiplicity inherent to doubles. (This is what Anne Teresa De Keersmaecker understood very well in *Rosas danst Rosas* [1983], for instance.)

Dance is also an art of constructing series. (It would be of interest to choreographic analysis to adopt this methodological point of view more

often.) Danced movement creates most naturally the space of doubles, of multiplicities of bodies and of bodily movements. An isolated body that starts to
dance progressively populates space with a multiplicity of bodies. Narcissus
is a crowd.

Many other paradoxical aspects of the space of the body are clearly manifested in the dancer's movements: the absence of internal limits when, seen
from the outside, it is a finite space; the fact that its first dimension is depth,
a topological depth, non-perspectival in such a manner that when it blends
with objective space it is able to dilate, shrink, twist, disperse, unfold, or collect itself in a single point.

From the start, the first aspect creates a deep impression on the spectator looking at the dancer on the stage (the spectator will endure simultaneously a process of becoming-dancer): all of the body's movement, or all
movement coming out of the body, smoothly transports the spectator across
space. No material obstacle, object or wall, impedes the spectator's trajectory,
which does not end in any real place. No movement ends in a precise location
within the objective scene—just as the limits of the dancer's body never
prohibit his gestures from extending beyond his skin. There is an infinity
appropriate to danced gestures that only the space of the body is able to
engender.

Let us remember that the space of the body does not come about except
by the projection-secretion of interior space on exterior space. The body, as
we saw, also becomes space. The movements of the space of the body do not
stop at the frontier of the body itself, but they implicate the body in its entirety: if the space of the body dilates, this dilation will impact on the body
and its interior.

Depth as a dimension radically distinguishes the space of the body from
objective space, because it is not a matter of a measurable depth—as with a
length moving 90 degrees to measure the distance separating an observer
from the horizon. What is characteristic of this depth[7] is its capacity to tie
itself to a place, so we may call it topological: it is a certain link between body
and place that carves in it its own depth. The space of the body is that spatial
milieu that creates the depth of places. If a certain scenic place all of a sudden
becomes unlimited, if the height toward which Vaslav Nijinsky projects himself acquires an infinite dimension, it is because a depth was born there.

Depth is the primordial dimension of the dancer's space. It allows the dancer to mould space, to expand it or to restrict it, to make it acquire the most paradoxical forms. It is even from depth that one may create depthless choreographies with marionette bodies. In short: because the space of the dancer's body is riddled with virtual vacuoles, he can make it into an eminently plastic matter.

Thus, units of space–time that characterize the dancer's movement are formed. And because the dancer does not move in common space, his time transforms the objective time of clocks.

This has nothing to do with the appearance of a represented event whose own time irradiates through the behaviour of the actors, as in theatre. In dance, the event, regardless of whether we are referring to a narrative or to an abstract dance, refers to transformations of the regime of energy flow. This is due to the fact that such transformations of energy mark the passage to another level of meaning. The event is real, corporeal, modifying the very duration of the dancer's gesture. A leap, a figure, may not constitute an event if they are coming from the same regime of energy. On the other hand, a gesture as simple as a turn of the head, or the lifting of an elbow, may testify to the irruption of decisive events on the choreographic path. Dance is composed of a succession of micro-events that ceaselessly transform the movement's meaning.

To every transformation of the energetic regime there is a corresponding modification of the space of the body. Such modification always consists in certain forms of contraction or of folding, in certain forms of spatial dilation or of distention, which are all made possible by depth. These are, so to speak, dilations and foldings *in the same place*, and not in objective extension. For instance, only the unfolding of space brought about by depth allows the dancer to acquire an 'eternal slowness' when executing the movement: if a (same) distance has become too wide, the dancer need not traverse it in a hurry, under pressure from an external force. We know that Nijinsky over-articulated movements, thus de-multiplying distances by means of microscopic decompositions of movement. He thereby dilated the space of the body: he gave the impression of having all the time in the world, dislocating in space with the superb ease of someone creating (unfolding) space as he moved.

The same happens with any great dancer, regardless of technique. In truth, there is no fixed and autonomous space of the body. The space of the body varies according to the velocities of its unfolding, in such a way that it is dependent upon the time movement takes in opening the space of the body. This time depends on the texture—more or less dense, more or less viscous—of the space of the body, which is born from the energy involved. Energy creates space–time unities. The dancer does not traverse the space of the body as he would traverse an objective distance in a given chronological time. While dancing, the dancer produces singular and indissoluble space–time unities that confer a force of truth to metaphors such as 'a dilated slowness' or 'a sudden enlargement of space' used to describe the dancer's gestures.

So that we can understand how dance transforms the body, we need to have a more precise idea of this body, which we talk about all the time as if it was an unquestionable evidence. Yet, at the very moment we question the body, it becomes almost ungraspable. From the start we find ourselves before a multiplicity of points of view, all different, often unarticulated, but nevertheless all pertinent.

We have the body of Western anatomy and physiology, consisting of organ systems and of more or less independent functions—a body image about to change thanks to recent contributions from microbiology, neurosciences and all the advanced scanning and scoping technologies. We have the Eastern or Asian body, a multiple body—the yoga body and the Chinese medicine one, defined by other organ cartographies, and predicated upon a physiology of energy flows. Both systems of knowledge refer mostly to the body's interior.

Among the several types of body found in the 'psych' therapies, and in many body therapies, the interiority of the body and its organs are either reduced to representations that gain symbolic values and significations according to sign structures (as with psychoanalysis); or they are understood within complex systems that combine relational and behavioural positions with signifying values.

There are some rare attempts in Western medicine to articulate the point of view of symbolic analysis—we can cite the case of psychosomatics whose intelligibility remains quite precarious.

The merit of phenomenology lies in its consideration of the body in the world. It is not a therapeutic perspective (even though it spawned a whole psychiatric school), but a study of the role of the body-proper in the constitution of meaning. The notion of 'body-proper'[8] encompasses the perceiving body and the living body, that is, the sensing body, and the notions of 'Flesh' in Edmund Husserl, Merleau-Ponty and Erwin Strauss. With this notion, the description of the body in a situation takes precedence over all other considerations of meaning or function. We can measure the significance such an image of the body had for choreographers and for dance theory (particularly in the United States after the Second World War) in the work of authors such as Susanne Langer.

However, the phenomenological body (particularly the one found in Husserl, and not so much the one in Langer) did not understand two essential elements of living particular to dancers: what they call the body's 'energy', and the body's space–time.[9]

Here, we would like to consider the body no longer as a 'phenomenon', no longer as a visible and concrete perception moving in the objective Cartesian space, but rather, we would like to consider the body as a meta-phenomenon, simultaneously visible and virtual, a cluster of forces, a transformer of space and time, both emitter of signs and trans-semiotic, endowed by an organic interior ready to be dissolved as soon as it reaches the surface. A body inhabited by—and inhabiting—other bodies and other minds, a body existing at the same time at the opening toward the world provided by language and sensorial contact, and in the seclusion of its singularity through silence and non-inscription. A body that opens and shuts, that endlessly connects with other bodies and elements, a body that can be deserted, emptied, stolen from its soul, as well as traversed by the most exuberant fluxes of life. A human body because it can become animal, become mineral, plant, become atmosphere, hole, ocean, become pure movement. That is: a paradoxical body.

This body is composed of special matter, which gives it the property of being *in* space and of *becoming* space. That is to say, this body has the property of combining so intimately with exterior space that it draws from it a variety of textures. Thus, the body can become an interior–exterior space producing multiple space forms, porous spaces, spongeous, smooth, striated, Escher's or the Penroses' paradoxical spaces, or quite simply a space of asymmetric symmetry, like left and right in the same body-space.

It is a fallacy to say that we 'carry our body' like a weight we always drag around. The body's weight constitutes another paradox: if it requires an effort so we can make it move, it also carries us without effort across space.

As shown to us by Picasso's *Women Running on the Beach* (1922)—their legs and arms spreading like the very space that their running, the horizon, the sea and the wind generate—the body's texture is spatial; and, reciprocally, the texture of space is corporeal.

This paradoxical body is constantly opening and shutting itself to space and to other bodies—a capacity that has less to do with the existence of orifices marking the body visually than with the nature of skin. Because it is mostly through the entire surface of the body, rather than through the anus or the vagina, that the body opens itself up to the outside. These orifices are at the service of organic functions of exchange between interior and exterior—but rarely do they control the total opening of interior space (except in sexual pleasure and in speech).

The 'opening' of the body is not a metonymy nor a metaphor. It is really the interior space that reveals itself once it returns to the exterior, transforming the latter into the space of the body.

But why should one want to open the body and project it toward the outside? We know: in order to build the space of the body and, at the limit, to form the plane of dance's immanence as the last transformation of that space. And why should we want immanence? In order to reach the highest intensities, the ones (Merce) Cunningham called 'of fusion'. But, finally, why should we want to dance?

The moment we try to answer this question we are immediately redirected toward desire, toward the very nature of desire—which is tied to a simple verb: to assemble. This verb coming from Gilles Deleuze and Félix Guattari seems to us to be the most adequate one to express that which in desire is most implicated in the desire to dance.

Desire creates assemblages. But the movement *to assemble* always opens itself up toward new assemblages. This is because desire does not exhaust itself in pleasure but augments itself by assembling. To create new connections between heterogeneous materials, new bonds, other passageways for energy; to connect, to put in contact, to symbiose, to make something pass, to create machines, mechanisms, articulations—this is what it means to assemble. To ceaselessly demand new assemblages.

In this way desire is infinite—and it will continue to produce new assemblages unless exterior forces no longer come to tear, break and cut its flux.

Desire wants above all to desire, that is, to assemble, which is the same thing. The assemblage of desire opens up desire and prolongs it.

If assemblage opens and prolongs desire, it is only because it has become *desire's matter*; not its object, but its proper texture, participating in desire's force, in its intensity, in its *'élan vital'* to use Henri Bergson's expression.[10] In other words, desire is not only desire for assemblage, it is already assemblage—it transforms what it 'produces' or 'builds' into itself. If the desire of a painter consists in the assemblage of certain colours in a certain way, the resultant painting's force is desire. The assembled colours and spaces desire.

Regardless of the type of assemblage, desire always seeks to flow through it. In thought's movements as well as in the makings of the artist, or in the elaborations of speech, to desire is to assemble in order to flow—to assemble so that the power to desire increases. This is why desire leads back to itself; it transforms, metabolizes all elements that it touches, traverses or devours. For desire, everything must become desire.

What is a danced gesture if not a particular assemblage of the body? All gesture is, in itself, an assemblage. But in general, gesture assembles the body with an object or with other bodies. To say 'see you later' while oscillating the arm from left to right is to reconnect a body with another at an imminent rupture of contact. The danced gesture articulates the anterior posture of the body with a new position (often) without the help of an object or another body. The result is a passageway for energy and for movement that, rather than arresting them, increases their flow and intensity.

What do danced gestures assemble? We can say: they assemble gestures with other gestures; or an actual body with all the actualized virtual bodies; or still, a movement with other movements. In all cases, danced gesturality experiments with movement (with its circuits, its quality, its strength) in order to obtain the best conditions to execute a choreography. In this sense, to dance is to experiment, to work all possible assemblages of the body. This work is precisely what assembling consists of. To dance is therefore to assemble the body's assemblages.

As an articulated and fluidic machine, the body is made to connect with objects and other bodies. Dance operates as a kind of pure experimentation with the body's capacity to assemble, thus creating a laboratory where all possible assemblages are tested. Dance not only puts the body in motion by assembling its limbs (which usually only articulate according to functions), but dance enchains this motioning over the pure vital movement the body shelters. Dance unearths it, makes it gush out and awaken other potencies of movement. Dance assembles 'trivial' movement with that vital movement, thus discovering new assembling possibilities for corporeal gestures. In order to look for a new form, its matter—movement—first searches for an assemblage. It works in order not to assemble limbs, body parts, organs, but precisely to assemble that which assembles them—like a certain assemblage of legs and arms assembles itself with a certain assemblage of head or torso. And so on and so forth. How does this assemblage of assemblages enter into a combination with a certain falling movement; and how does this assemblage of assemblages of assemblages . . . ? Dance is an abstract machine of assemblages exposing and hiding them endlessly. Dance always wants to assemble assemblages and not organs with other organs.

This is how the map created by the dancer aims at energy and not at concrete movements: the most abstract and subtle modulation of energy is enough to actualize the most concrete bodily movements. Energy is what assembles assemblages; the energy map is what composes the most abstract tracing of movements.

It is in this sense that we can talk about the body as a totality. Not as an organism where we could find a global function operating in each part, but as a body-total that constitutes in and of itself a map of the assemblage of all possible assemblages. This totality naturally produces a body without organs, a plane of immanence.

This is why dance realizes in the purest way the assembling vocation of desire. Which explains, without a doubt, its very powerful—yet so often de-eroticized—presence in most courtly and royal dances. The desexualization of bodies accompanies the deployment of the movement of assemblage; that is to say, of danced movement as the movement of desire. If dance de-eroticizes bodies, it is because danced movement has become desire (desire to dance, desire to desire, desire to assemble). When eroticism breaks through and possesses bodies (namely in popular dances), it is because the movement of assemblage of assemblages was itself taken up by a concrete erotic assemblage. Then, everything is inverted: it is the movement of concrete gestures that sustains the *continuum* of abstract assemblage, while a whole choreography becomes impregnated with eroticism, like a wave or an atmosphere.

These three realities—(a) desire desires to assemble; (b) desire desires immanence; (c) desire desires to flow—all demand a space, a territory where desire may desire. To desire is already to start building such a space or plane where desire can flow and unfold its power (*potência*). This is a space from which all obstructions, all flux-breaking, flux-cutting and flux-vampirizing machines have been brushed off by the very intensity of the flux.

This plane, as we already know, is the plane of immanence or the 'body-without-organs'. Why this expression of a body that has no organs? Why does such a body compose a plane of immanence?[11] Let us say simply that the habitual body (the body-organism) is formed by organs that impede the free circulation of energy: in it, energy is invested and fixated on the organism's system of organs—this is how one builds those 'interiorized sensori-motor systems' that Cunningham talks about, and that for him always represent an obstacle to innovation. To untangle from these systems, to constitute another body where intensities may be taken to their highest degrees, such is the task of the artist and, in particular, of the dancer.

How do we make this body-without-organs, this plane of immanence of desire? In this case, the plane of movement immanent to the dancer?[12] Let's take as an example a therapeutic ritual as described by ethnologist Andràs Zempléni in his fieldwork with the Wolof from Senegal (Zempléni 1984: 325–52). In many cultures, therapeutic dances aim at curing by means of trance. Among the Wolof, trance is also entered through dancing and other procedures; and it arrives only through the destructuring of the body-organism.

This is how the Wolof proceed: they remove the entrails of a sacrificed animal and cover the body of a female patient with them. After bathing the patient with the blood of the sacrificed animal (an ox or a goat), the animal's intestines are emptied out and then,

> cut, and after that *tied*, bit by bit, to the body of the patient: to her left wrist and to her right ankle (or vice-versa); to her waist, like a belt; to her chest and back, as if it was a crossed brassiere tied under her breasts. Finally, a part of the animal's stomach, emptied out and *turned inside out*, is attached to the patient's hair like a small coif. Under a blanket of coagulated blood, the patient will wear these visceral adornments and this coif made out of stomach until the ritual bath she will take the next day in the lustrous waters of her new altars (Zempléni 1984: 332; italics in the original).

It should be underlined that all of this extremely complex process is unfolding while the patient is in a trance undergoing the strongest intensities she can endure (frequently, the patient will faint).

This ritual operation consisting in the extraction of organs from the organism and in the emptying out of interior space has several objectives: by extracting the organs and by splaying them out one destroys the organization of the organism. In this way, *one frees the affects invested in and fixated on the organs* that had been organized according to precise and stable structures and strata.[13] (All of this supposes, quite obviously, an 'identification' with the animal—or, more accurately, a 'becoming-animal'. This is quite explicit and well defined among the Wolof by means of chanting and ritual gestures.)

Secondly, one creates an interior 'paradoxical' space, which both is and is not in space. Being empty, and being of the order of the *non-incorporated corporeal*, interior space is composed of 'interstitial matter', that is, of the matter proper of becoming par excellence. This matter will allow: (a) the whole body to become surface (skin), given that the interior no longer separates in terms of thickness (viscera) the different oppositional planes of the body (back and front, anterior and posterior); (b) the exterior to attract upon itself the entirety of the interior's movement, most particularly the motion of affects. Interstitial matter has no thickness: it has become pure matter transformable into surface energy. It is matter for becoming; it is the matter of becoming.

As Deleuze insists, everything in the BwO is a question of matter (see Deleuze and Guattari 1980: 189–90). Building the BwO consists in determining which matter is adequate to the body one wants to build: a body of pictorial sensations, a body of pain for the masochist, a body of loving affects as in courtly love, a body of thought for the philosopher, a body of health for the sick, a body of movement for the dancer. In each case, desire chooses the adequate matter.

We perceive the interstitial nature of interior space by noting that it is not a lived aspect of consciousness. It is empty (void, a floating body), but it has the power to attract toward itself all sorts of 'matters' and to transform them into particular intensities (intensities of thought, of colours, etc.). Why is it that interior space attracts toward itself all sorts of matter? Why is it that it becomes the object of operations (for instance, as we saw in the Wolof ritual, operations of 'reversal' toward the outside, or of 'turning inside out', as a glove) in order to become a 'body of thought', or a BwO of sensations, or a plane of movement? Because interior space composes an interface with the skin. No longer a content, having become empty, it has a tendency to confuse itself with the container (the skin). It establishes an intimate connection with the skin, becoming a sort of inner atmospheric wall of the skin. In this interior space–skin machine, atmosphere constitutes the very texture of the matter of the BwO.

Let us remember that the skin is not a superficial membrane, but has a thickness; that it indefinitely extends itself into the body's interior: this is why tactile sensations are localized a few millimetres within the skin and not at its surface. This is what allows the formation of the machine interior space—(or atmospheric matter) skin: an interfacial machine situated between an organic interior that tends toward disappearing and an exterior that tends toward occupying it entirely.

Now, this space allows the liberated affects to run freely, as well as any other matter it will attract toward itself—thought, emotion, wood, mineral, supernatural being, ancestor (who enters the Wolof patient): they all tend to flow within it just as energy flows in the dancer's body. We can thus talk about a body of emotions or a body of intensities.

To flow like energy in the dancer's body: this indicates first of all a privileging of the dancer's 'body (or plane) of movement'—as if the machine interior space–skin of the dancer composed a surface where all movements could be transformed into danced movements; as if the dancer's movement could attract toward itself all other body movements just as the body empties itself out and loses its organs. Finally, this would mean that there would be no such thing as articulation; rather, a fluid circulation of intensities over a given matter, a skidding of energy fluxes one over the other, 'multiplicities of fusion', as Deleuze and Guattari write in *Mille Plateaux: Capitalisme et Schizophrénie 2* [A Thousand Plateaus: Capitalism and Schizophrenia, VOL. 2] (1980).

Two conditions are required for forming a body where intensities flow: (a) interior space, emptied out, must fall back toward the skin, thus constituting the matter of the BwO; (b) the skin, impregnated with interior space, has to become the body-matter of the full body (including the space of the body).

It should be noted that these two conditions imply immanence. There is no longer—or no more—the separation body/mind or mind/matter; no transcendence comes to disturb the movements of intensities. In the case of the

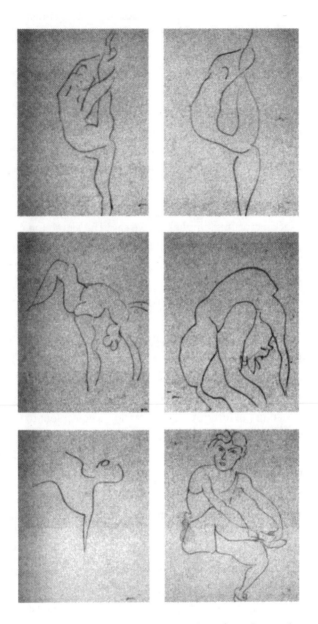

FIGURE 1. Henri Matisse, *Danseuse Acrobate* (Female Acrobatic Dancer), Plates 1–6. © 2008 Succession H. Matisse/Artists Rights Society (ARS), New York.

patient of the therapeutic ritual, it is trance that ensures immanence: thought, visions of ancestors, are acted by the dancing body—they all dance in that body they now inhabit.

Let us consider more closely the formation process of the BwO. The body is emptied out of its organs. Their removal leaves a floating cloud of affects, a mist of sensations in an atmospheric space. This milieu is, above all, affective. It is traversed by chaotic dynamisms with no anchoring point. The falling back of the milieu over the skin implies the transformation of the latter: because, on one hand, affect attracts to itself matters that become confused with the skin and, on the other hand, because the skin becomes the matter of becoming.

Falling back, returning, implies, as we saw, the attraction exercised by the skin over those affects populating the emptied-out interior space. Skin attracts them and impregnates them. It attracts them from within, because skin itself has ceased to be the map of the dissolved organism. Skin itself is in mutation, it changes nature, it wrinkles, it dilates—it searches for ways to become a new map for new intensities. It allows exterior and interior to penetrate it (this is clear in the Wolof ritual). It becomes an extremely porous interface, diaphanous, allowing all sorts of exchanges, confusing inside and outside. Skin no longer delimits the body-proper, but it extends beyond it across exterior space: it is the space of the body.

The reversibility of interior on the exterior is equivalent to the progressive disappearing of the interior. Everything will happen now horizontally: the becoming of matter–body–skin will transform it into a BwO where intensive affect will circulate.

How does the dancer achieve such a reversibility? By creating, thanks to danced movement, a very particular device: his body becomes a kind of Möebius strip—a Möebius strip (an interior space–skin machine) that forms itself as it absorbs interior affect-forces and makes them circulate at the surface. The reversion that the BwO of the dancer builds, its plane of immanence, is realized by this device that transforms the dancer's body into a moving Möebius strip, ceaselessly making and unmaking itself, absorbing and dissolving the interior without stopping, making it climb to the single-sided surface (única), the surface without obverse.

That the dancer, through movement, transforms his body into a Möebius surface results from the very constitution of the body: covered by a single skin, it simulates on its back a quasi-obverse of the front—an opposition that rotation immediately annihilates, thus forging a single 'frontal' surface, so to speak.

The obverse of the skin would be constituted precisely by this invisible interior wall: the 'inside' of the outside, whose existence the major orifices (particularly the anus and the vagina) constantly testify to. Danced movement precisely shuts its orifices: the energy flowing over the unified body demands a *continuum* no organ can cut.

In short, the BwO is constructed by danced movement because this movement: (1) empties the body of its organs, destructuring the organism, liberating the affects and *directing movement toward the periphery of the body*, toward the skin;[14] (2) creates a continuous space–skin surface, one that prevents orifices from inducing movements toward the interior of the body. Quite on the contrary, breathing becomes almost dermic, sounds make the skin vibrate, vision happens totally at the surface. If the female ballet dancer erased all trace of her genital organs, contemporary nudity in dance paradoxically does nothing else than emphasize the continuity of the unified surface of the skin, by also not allowing interior organs to become manifest or visible; (3) builds, thanks to movement, a Möebius strip-like body: pure depthless surface, without thickness, without obverse, body-without-organs freeing the strongest kinesthetic intensities.

It was this Möebius body (as paradoxical as the strip) that Matisse saw in the dancer. In his drawings and in his panels on 'The Dance', individual bodies as well as grouped bodies retrace Möebius strips. In his series of drawings *Danseuse Acrobate* (Female Acrobatic Dancer, 1931–32) here reproduced (Figure 1), the second drawing traces a Möebius ring: when the dancer lifts her leg vertically, the front becomes back and vice versa—and the whole body emerges from the tracing of a continuous line.

*Translated by André Lepecki*

*Notes*

1   'Paradoxical Body' was originally published as 'Corpo Paradoxal' in *Movimento Total: O Corpo e a Dança* (Lisboa: Relógio d'Água, 2001).

2   Irony of technology's destiny: the technological universe not only finds within itself that paradoxical or 'magic' capacity that the body has of secreting a proper space, but it also finds in that capacity its own limits—precisely because of what the space of the body allows, i.e. the *immediate* knowledge of space without any need for calculation. This immediate knowledge represents perhaps one of the absolute limits set before artificial intelligence (see Dreyfus 1999).

3   The 'reversal' proposed by José Gil departs from but also expands Maurice Merleau-Ponty's proposition (outlined in *Phenomenology of Perception*) that the body is not 'in' space, but it is 'of' space. In Gil's case, we would have to say that both body and space are 'of' the 'space of the body' (see Merleau-Ponty 2000).—Trans.

4   Particularly in *Le Visible et l'Invisible, suivi de Notes de Travail* [*The Visible and the Invisible, Followed by Working Notes*] (1964).

5   The full quote can be found in Merleau-Ponty's essay 'The Intertwining—The Chiasm': 'Thus since the seer is caught up in what he sees, it is still himself he sees: there is a fundamental narcissism of all vision' (1968: 139).—Trans.

6   Gil's notion of 'a plane of movement' directly refers to Gilles Deleuze and Félix Guattari's notions of 'plane' developed in *Mille Plateaux* (plane of immanence, plane of consistency, plane of composition, plane of desire, etc.). Deleuze and Guattari explore the semantic ambiguity of the word 'plan' in French, which refers not only to a geometric figure but also to 'map' and to 'making a plan'. See particularly the subsection 'Memories of a Plan(e) Maker' in their chapter '1730: Becoming-Intense, Becoming Animal, Becoming-Imperceptible . . . ' (in Deleuze and Guattari 1980).—Trans.

7   What Deleuze calls *spatium*, in *Différence et Répétition* (1968). Deleuze introduces the notion of *spatium* to distinguish his own understanding of spatiality from that of Merleau-Ponty, which Deleuze saw as still reminiscent of the Cartesian notion of space as extension.—Trans.

8   The 'body-proper' (*corps propre*) is a key concept in Merleau-Ponty's *Phenomenology of Perception*, the matrix from which all phenomenological accounts could arise: from within the body of the subject. Merleau-Ponty would revise this notion of body-proper later in his posthumous *Le Visible et l'Invisible, suivi de Notes de Travail* (1964). Here, the body-proper becomes no longer the matrix but an 'exemplar' for Merleau-Ponty's notion of flesh in its constitutive reversibility. More recently, neuroscientist António R. Damásio has used the term to oppose it to what he terms 'the brain'. For Damásio, 'the brain'

encompasses all parts of the nervous system, including all neurologically induced chemical discharges in the blood system. What is not 'the brain' is the
'body-proper' (see Damásio 1994).—Trans.

9   Such critiques also apply to the semiotic approach. An exception could be
found, perhaps, in the refined analyses of an author who claims such an approach, Susan Foster (see Foster 1986).

10  The reference is to Henri Bergson's use of the term in *Creative Evolution*
(1911).—Trans.

11  It is known that Deleuze borrowed this expression 'body-without-organs' (or
'b-w-o' or 'BwO') from Antonin Artaud's poem 'To be Done with the Judgment
of God' (1947). The expression appears in Deleuze for the first time in *Logique
du Sens* [The Logic of Sense] (1969), but without the full signification it would
acquire later on in *L'Anti-Oedipe: Capitalisme et Schizophrénie* [Anti-Oedipus: Capitalism and Schizophrenia] (1972), and, most significantly in *Mille Plateaux* [A
Thousand Plateaus] (1980), where it designates the plane of immanence.

12  In *Mille Plateaux*, there is a whole chapter dedicated to the subject: 'How to
Make Yourself a BwO?' However, after reading these very dense pages, the
mystery remains regarding 'what should one do' to avoid the strata and build
a full body (Deleuze and Guattari 1980: 199). We still cannot quite see what
transformations the body must endure so that it can become a plane of immanence. What we would like to show, in this essay, even if in a general way,
is how the dancer proceeds with this task.

13  It is important to remember at this point that Deleuze and Guattari followed
Artaud by saying that the enemy of the body is not the organs but the *organization* of the organs imposed by social-theological forces (see Deleuze and
Guattari 1980: 158). This means that all anatomy is already desire-organized
according to hegemonic laws that 'properly' assign functions to the organs.
'The organism is not at all the body, the BwO; rather, it is a stratum on the
BwO, in other words, a phenomenon of accumulation, coagulation, and sedi-
mentation that, in order to extract useful labor from the BwO, imposes upon
it forms, functions, bonds, dominant and hierarchized organizations, organized transcendences' (ibid.: 159). If we think about the legal organization of
body orifices and their 'properly assigned' functions—for instance, in sodomy
laws in the USA—we can see how legal-juridical systems linked with the
judgement of God constantly attempt to organize organs into a system of
(re)production. The full BwO is not a body free of organs, then, but free of the

judgement over how organs should behave, of how they should access and produce their own plane of immanence; that is: their own plane of consistency of desire.—Trans.

14 This is what makes dance fascinating: as the dancer experiences his whole body being transported to the periphery thanks to centrifugal movement, he feels increasingly more 'centred' and reunited with himself.

*References*

BERGSON, Henri. 1911 [1907]. *Creative Evolution* [L'Evolution créatrice] (Arthur Mitchell trans.). New York: Henry Holt & Co.

DAMÁSIO, António R. 1994. *Descartes' Error: Emotion, Reason, and the Human Brain.* New York: G. P. Putnam's Sons.

DELEUZE, Gilles. 1968. *Différence et Répétition* [Difference and Repetition]. Paris: Presses Universitaires de France.

_____.1969. *Logique du Sens* [The Logic of Sense]. Paris: Les Editions de Minuit.

DELEUZE, Gilles and Félix Guattari. 1972. *L'Anti-Oedipe: Capitalisme et Schizophrénie* [Anti-Oedipus: Capitalism and Schizophrenia]. Paris: Les Editions de Minuit.

_____. 1980. *Mille Plateaux: Capitalisme et Schizophrénie 2* [A Thousand Plateaus: Capitalism and Schizophrenia, VOL. 2]. Paris: Les Editions de Minuit.

DREYFUS, Hubert. 1999 [1972]. *What Computers Still Can't Do: A Critique of Artificial Reason.* Cambridge, MA: MIT Press.

FOSTER, Susan Leigh. 1986. *Reading Dancing: Bodies and Subjects in Contemporary American Dance.* Berkeley: University of California Press.

MERLEAU-PONTY, Maurice. 1964. *Le Visible et l'Invisible, suivi de Notes de Travail* [The Visible and the Invisible, Followed by Working Notes]. Paris: Gallimard.

_____. 1968. *The Visible and the Invisible, Followed by Working Notes* (Alphonso Lingis trans.). Evanston: Northwestern University Press.

_____. 2000. *Phenomenology of Perception.* London: Routledge, pp. 67–148, 203–98.

ZEMPLÉNI, V. Andràs 1984. 'Possession et Sacrifice' [Possession and Sacrifice], in *Le Temps de la Réfléxion* [The Time of Reflection], VOL. 5. Paris: Gallimard, pp. 325–52.

# THE ELASTICITY OF THE ALMOST

ERIN MANNING

> Movement is not explained by sensation, but by the elasticity of sensation, its vis elastica . . . (Deleuze 1981).

*Relational Movement*

Walking is the constraint. When you walk, you keep one foot on the ground, always. Two feet off the ground and you're jumping. With one foot on the ground, you can move in three directions: forward, backward, sideways. If you move sideways in the 'wrong' direction, you move across. This is one of the ways you can move around. Take a sidewalk: you are walking quickly, trying to get through the crowd to catch the bus. You have two blocks to navigate and your speed makes it difficult. You weave through the people, taking bigger and smaller steps, looking for the holes and then filling them, inhabiting them momentarily before they close. Hopefully no one is following you: sidewalk holes are rarely big enough for two people.

Relational movement[1] asks the holes to fit two people. But these people are not walking side by side, or one behind the other. They are walking face to face, body to body. Walking together means: when you walk into the hole I cannot walk alongside, I must walk-with. This walking-with is more than taking a step with you; it is creating a movement with you.

Creating a movement is initiating a dance. This dance demands grace, a grace that is not a succumbing to an outside, but a feeling of the inside, inside out. 'Grace is like the paradigm of intensity that escapes all quantitative reduction of movement' (Bergson 1970: 12–13). Grace is never felt in a step. Grace is the becoming-dance of the step, when walking flows in the between of directions, when the holes become emergent openings rather than missed opportunities.

Relational movement means moving the relation. Moving the person will never result in grace. Intensity of movement can only be felt when the in-between—the interval—created by the movement-with takes hold. This interval is ephemeral, impossible to grasp as such, essential to the passage from a step to a graceful movement.

I begin by taking her in my arms. We embrace, her left hand around my neck and over my left shoulder, right hand in my left hand, her cheek barely grazing mine. Our upper bodies are connected with a sense of horizontal intensity, not a pressure, not a weight, but palpable engagement. This first embrace signals to both of us that we are open to invention, that we will move the constraint.

We walk. I am leading. But that doesn't mean I am deciding. Leading is more like initiating an opening, entering the gap, and then waiting to follow her response. How she follows, with what intensity she creates the space, will influence how our bodies move together. I am not moving her, nor is she simply responding to me: we are beginning to move relationally, creating an interval that we move together. The more we connect to this becoming-movement, the more palpable the interval becomes. We begin to feel the relation.

Having both danced for many years, our bodies incorporate dance, a pastness of movement that allows dance-already-danced to move through us. This is not a learning by heart. It is not a choreography. It is improvising with the already-felt. It is a deep feeling of becoming-ground that we nurture as we continue to learn how to walk. Walking together feels like moving spacetime. Our walk is not the walk of the toddler, where each step fulfils itself in a fall, the fall almost part of the experience of getting ahead. Ours is a walk where the in-between of the steps takes on a consistency. The falling-to-walk of the frustrated toddler is transformed into a sustained reaching-toward. This reaching-toward is a walking that feels like a horizontal force rather than a taking of steps. A change of direction signals not an immanent fall but the potential to invent.

In an intimate embrace, we walk together counterclockwise around the dance floor, our bodies beginning to take on the rhythm of the interval we are creating. This interval—fed by the lead, or the pre-acceleration that is the feeling of the movement-to-come—is the virtual node through which each step becomes a movement. In the interval, the direction we've chosen gains a texture that encourages the step to become a fold. When our bodies begin to fold around the interval, we know we are creating a dance.

Relational movement is always improvisational. For sustained improvisation, constraint is essential. Without the rules of walking, we could invent infinitely, but this infinity wouldn't necessarily produce an interval. The constraint of the walk makes pre-acceleration essential. This keeps our movement poised at its incipience, rather than focusing on the displacement as such. Without this constraint—without the feeling of your movement before it comes—the very real possibility emerges that we will walk on each other's feet and lose the connection. To displace another body rather than moving the relation is to move-beside rather than with. Besides, the creation of a virtual centre is less essential. The essence of relational movement is the creation of this virtual node, the in-between that propels the dance, that forms the grace that is not of the body but of the movement itself.

As I walk with her, the constraint of the walk holds me to a certain pattern. I create out of this pattern, asking of the interval that it fold the movement. This folding is the transduction of a step into the reaching-toward of a directionality out of which a relational movement will be produced. She feels the pre-acceleration of my movement even before I move, responding by taking a step back around me, across the front of my body. I have not yet taken a step, but intensively, my movement is alive. As she steps across me, backward yet still facing me with her upper body, I inject the movement with a velocity that invites our two bodies to participate in a centrifugal force. With her body in my arms, across mine yet still in front, I take a small step forward which creates a spiral. This spiral is intensive—it does not move away, it moves-with. Moving-with, our bodies spiral together, turning on a shared axis that emerges out of the movement itself. Grace in the making.

The language of tango—out of which relational movement finds its consistency[2]—identifies this centrifugal spiralling as a *colgada*, a hanging: a hanging spiral, where the interval is wider at the top while our feet stay together, our centres still facing one another. Intervals are not stable. Relational movement insists on morphogenesis. I may lead you into a *colgada*, a hanging-out, which creates a triangular interval, closed where our feet touch, opening upward and out, or, as we hang together in a *colgada*, I may reverse it into a leaning-in, a triangular form that opens downward into an intensive ground—a *volcada*, centripetal.

Either way, what occurs is a qualitative reshaping of a triangular force. Formed by the pre-acceleration of the movement, and sustained by the movement itself, the triangulated interval folds into an intensive expansion, or an expansive intensity, languidly 'holding' the movement. This holding is not structural; it is elastic. It is almost the next movement, almost the next axis, almost the next equilibrium, but not quite yet. This elasticity of the almost is the intensive extension of the movement, a moment when anything can happen, when our bodies are poised in a togetherness that begins to take shape. The next movement has not yet come. The past movement is passing. No step is taken and yet in this elastic the microperception of every possible step can almost be felt.

*Folding*

It is a question of the curve. For Gottfried Wilhelm Leibniz, the curvature of the universe expresses itself in three fundamental notions: the fluidity of matter, the elasticity of bodies and elasticity as mechanism (in Deleuze 1988: 7). Matter springs into curvature. Matter would not in and of itself curve, writes Leibniz (ibid.). It curves because force acts upon it. We would not curve to fill the hole if there were no one in our way. 'But the universe is compressed by an active force that gives matter a curvilinear or vortical movement, following a curve without tangent' (in ibid.). Beyond the tangent that expresses a straight line, there is a folding curve, a curve replete with micro-tornadoes that produce microperceptual intervals. A curve within a curve within a curve. The movement we dance is infinitely curved.

As we move together this folding can be felt, but only when we move the relation and not the body. When we begin by moving her body, what we feel is resistance. The movement becomes a series of steps that we fall into, always a little early or a little late, our balance in disequilibrium, pulling and pushing. Relational movement pushes and pulls in a different way, in a togetherness of the infinite curve that moves through a single intensive equilibrium that is always more than stable: meta-stable. This doesn't mean that we never lose our balance. It means that balance can no longer be lost or gained because what is at stake is not a tangent but a curve. There is no stable axis around which we move. We curve together, creating a folding interval out of which our moving bodies take form.

Folding undoes form. Form does emerge, but always after the fact, in the moment of passing that is the actual movement emerging. The form emergent is a transience, a becoming-spiral, a becoming-turn, a becoming-triangle. But these forms have no resonance in and of themselves—they form because they curve movement. Emergent forms are more than steps. They are porous steps; porous because unidentifiable as such ('What was that?!' she will ask as the movement completes itself), yet felt. You will know that something happened, that your body became something, but the 'what' of the step will rarely reveal itself as such.

It is not simply the speed of the movement that keeps it from holding to a step. It is its wave, of which the elastic is the emergent force that holds it to itself. As the wave forms, we feel the interval creating itself. As it holds, we feel the elasticity, the becoming-form. This is almost a microperception, active only in transition, almost virtual. As the elasticity compresses, the impetus will be infinite. But if we lose it, if we want to hold on to it for too long, or if we compress it too quickly, the intensity of the movement will evaporate and only the step will be felt.

The labyrinth of folds virtually active in the interval are becoming-bodies of movement. They are not steps, nor can they be translated as such. They are potential directions, potential elasticities, potential pre-accelerations. Separating them out is impossible. Their indivisibility is what gives the interval its intensity. Intensive movement is always populated by such microperceptions. When we move the relation, we are creating these microperceptions and they are expressing themselves (virtually) in that very movement. It is not that they pre-exist the movement or that they can be called forth as such. They are the potential that is felt in the incipiency of the action, the potential that transduces matter into form. Mattering-form becomes movement not as an identifiable figuration, but as an intensive figure.

An intensive figure does not represent. It durationally evokes. It provokes and propels. A figure is active transience from one form to another, a molecular mattering-form that transduces. For Cézanne, the figure is what produces sensation. As Deleuze writes, 'The figure is the sensible form that relays to sensation; it acts immediately on the nervous system, which is of the flesh' (1981: 39). Sensation is what is produced, but not a sensation of, a sensing-with and toward. Moving relationally we sense not the step per se (though we do step it, otherwise we would not move)—we sense the intensity of the opening, the gathering up of forces into which we move. As we step into these openings, what we sense is the force acting upon our movement. And as the movement begins to fold into another movement, the elasticity takes form, opening the movement to its inevitable deformation.

The sensation of moving the relation is a rhythmic sensation, a topological transformation that is a fold to infinity. The sensation is multiple but not multiplied. It works on many levels at once—macro and microperceptual—operating on planes rather than in divided sequences. These planes of sensation are amorphous—they never produce a recognized feeling that can be repeated in the same way—and are therefore felt not in their form but in their effects. Sensation is accumulated, coagulated, always operative between levels. As an element of capture, sensation engages all kinds of movement, from pre-acceleration to displacement to the elasticity of the almost, folding itself into all of their microperceptual becomings. Sensation is in and of movement.

Infolding folds. The folds take form elastically. It is not that they did not exist before. It is that they were not yet materialized. Virtual, they are felt only in their effects. Elastic, their form becomes palpable. In the amodal tactility of elasticity, force is stored and then released. Elasticity acts on the movement. The release liberates the becoming-step, not a step that was there all along, but one that is virtually creating itself in the interval even while the interval becomes elastic. Almost-virtual.

'How to conceive of the elastic if we do not suppose that the body is composed, that the body can therefore contract itself by chasing from its pores those particles of subtle matter that penetrate it, and that in turn this more subtle matter must expulse from its pores another even more subtle matter, to infinity?' (Deleuze 1988: 10)

The folds of potential movement ingress into the dance. It is a folding–unfolding as much as an involution–evolution that propulses the movement. This movement is alive in the associated milieu that is the interval, productive, brimming with sensation. Rhythm, the aliveness of the associated milieu, is the transducer of sensation, the élan vital that provokes projections of sense into the becoming-movement. Without rhythm, becoming-movement tends to divide and become diffuse. For relational movement, intensive rhythmic movement is key—diffusion guarantees confusion. This does not mean that we move *to* a rhythm. It means we move rhythm—the very becoming of the movement is rhythmic. But this rhythm can change into measure, into a movement-to, and it has a tendency to do so when the intensity of the movement is unexpectedly diffused into a displacement. It happens when the direction pushes me back into my step rather than pre-accelerating me toward an intensive movement. This diffusion of rhythm into measure is experienced when you move not into the space I physically open, but into the space I hesitated toward before leading the direction I expected you to follow. You move where the movement was moving us—where I thought about going—rather than where I went. Although I never actually moved in that direction, you felt a kind of doubled pre-acceleration and what you responded to was its first tendency: the direction I thought but I didn't actually lead. You moved into my hesitation. Of course, this is part of moving together. I will follow your lead, moving into the spacetime I didn't think I had opened up. But this kind of moving is a falling-into. What is qualitatively missing from our displacement is elasticity. To move the relation once more, the virtual centre of our relational movement will have to be reintensified, the elasticity reinvigorated. Because at the onset of this redirectionality, what we have first and foremost is a step.

Relational movement's becoming-step is elastic, its elasticity felt more than seen. It is an intensive curve, a following-curve that was never led as such, because it was created relationally. The law of curvature is the law of folds, and folds have a tendency to refold, to pleat, to crease, to wrinkle. As the fold compresses, what results is not necessarily a smaller movement, but a more intensively compact one. This compactness produces a force that will open the movement to its form. The curve does not result from the movement. It is the movement, a movement that contracts its expansion into an elasticity that becomes a body-elastic. The body-elastic is the body of the between, the body of the almost, where the movement is on the verge, actual but almost virtual, hanging, pulsing, spiralling.

*Inflection*

The elasticity of the almost is part of the curve. It is the curve's point of inflexion. 'Inflexion is the veritable atom, the elastic point' (Deleuze 1988: 20). Inflexion is the genetic element of the active line. It is not a hard point, nor is it a point directed from outside the movement. The elastic point (inflexion) is of the movement: it is that which pulls out of the movement its becoming-form. This singularity carries the curve, is the event of the curve. This singularity is what expresses the virtual fullness of the interval, its plenitude. This plenitude is the worldness of the movement, the sense that the movement is composed of a world, that 'it is the world itself, or better its beginning' (ibid.: 21). That interval is world does not mean that it contains the world, but that it potentially expresses the infradimensional which is the worlding of the sensing body in movement. This worlding is the expression of movement's elastic gathering of spacetime into the becoming-body of dancers dancing, a movement that is co-constitutive of this very same experiential spacetime.

Inflexion gives expression to this worlding, and, in the elasticity of its activity, it makes palpable the tangibility of sensation. As the movement perishes, pre-accelerating into the next movement, the interval fills up with the potential still languishing in the pastness of the last movement. It is not that the new movement contains the specificity of the past movement—its steps. What the new movement contains are all of the micromovements, the pre-elasticities of the past movement. Movemented tendencies. Virtual events.

Inflexion is inseparable from infinite variation. There is no elastic point that resides on the curve in the same way each time. The curve creates the elastic point as much as the elastic point becomes the curve. The elastic point is a travelling node along a fluctuating line that has no beginning nor end, 'enveloping a world infinitely spongy and cavernous, constituting more than a line and less than a surface' (ibid.: 23). This is not a measurable point—its elasticity makes it infinitely malleable. It is a folding point, a curvilinear detour that moves not from point to point, but in an infinite circumvolution that is the movement itself. The interval created by relational movement is the plane of consistency of this circumvolution, elasticity the plane of composition.

The elastic point inflects the curve with an almost. This almost is the slight delay, almost imperceptible, that occurs at the interstice of the actual rebecoming virtual. The vortical force of the elasticity forms the movement such that it becomes fully actual at the same time as it recomposes itself through microperceptual intensities virtually active in the interval. The elasticity of the almost is a rare instance of an almost-actualization of the microperceptual within the actual. In the elastic moment, the movement becomes more-than, enveloping in its folds all of the potential of its pastness and its futurity. This elastic becoming-actual is thus also a becoming-virtual, an inflexion on the curvature of pure experience that demands that its effects be felt. In the elasticity of the almost, what is felt is the rhythmic sensation of the fullness of movement, movement beyond its actualization.

The elastic point is preemptive. It is the durational element in the becoming-curve of movement. It anticipates curvature. In the becoming-curve of movement, elasticity is always operative, but not always felt as such. Often, this elasticity is curtailed—for example, when a change of direction is fallen into rather than moved into. But when it is felt, it is always felt as though after its occurrence, an 'after' that is co-present with its actualization but feels differed because elastics take time.

Elasticity always produces spirals. Whether these spirals are extensive movements or whether they remain intensive, force is recombined with movement. The interval becomes intensively relayed with the force of the spiral, creating a turbulence that moves the relation. This turbulence feeds the spiral: movement is always turbulent. This can be a quiet, even serene turbulence, a graceful intensity, or it can be a wild, excessive turbulence; either way, it envelops the contours of the steps, creating a spur, a trace of the line of flight that characterizes the displacement of the moving relation.

The elasticity of the almost shifts the associated milieu of the interval toward a field of curvature. The movement curves and the two bodies moving feel the approach as a joining of the forces of movement. The effect opens the dance to an actualization that is not a displacement per se but a virtual intensity becoming actual. We become spiral. Intensive connection. To re-main in the elasticity for as long as possible is the goal—but remaining on the edge of virtuality is a challenging task. Sometimes we linger.

*Lingering Events*

The elastic point is eventful. It delivers the lingering of actuality as it begins to fold back into the virtual, pre-accelerating into the next movement. This lingering is part of the walk, part of the constraint: back, front, side. The in-finite potential in three directions makes itself felt in the elasticity of the al-most, but is as present in all of movement's stages. To improvise is to be able to pull the movement out of the steps, to create the elastic out of the curve (that itself becomes elastic), to capture the force and move with it: to create an event out of a series of improvised steps.

Events can also be related to what Alfred North Whitehead calls actual occasions.[3] An actual occasion is what I have been calling a movement. For an event to occur, the experience has to be pulled out of the indeterminate, activated from the virtuality of the not-yet. For Whitehead, this 'pulling out' is called prehension, and refers to a mode of activity provoked by the occasion in question. Yet, this provocation is not outside the occasion: it is the event. When we move together, I may prehend an opening to the front. This pre-hension is not simply a cue: it is a detail of activity that produces a relational movement. This relational movement is a becoming-world of our movement. Event-fully, we move the relation. As she steps into the opening (and I step to the side to maintain this opening), the forward–side movement transforms the directionality of our relation, creating a new interval. This new interval is the virtual node of that actual occasion, which is also the beginning of the becoming-form of the movement. As the elasticity of the curvature makes it-self felt—in Whiteheadian vocabulary, what I feel is the completion of the subjective form of the event—this actualization of the subjective form marks the almost-perishing of that actual occasion because it satisfies the event. Now the event has fulfilled itself and is ready to be backgrounded into the nexus of perished actual occasions. The affective tone of the almost-perishing of elasticity is the grace of moving the relation intensively.

The event is as much a vibration as an action. It can never be completely actualizable, since the actual is always replete with the virtual. The fullness of virtuality within the movement is its complexity. Without this, it would simply be a displacement, a falling-into steps. The extension of the event that creates spacetime is therefore a quasi-virtual experience, actual because all steps actually take place, virtual because all the microperceptions of pastness and futurity are enveloped in the movement. This fullness of past experience is located on what Whitehead calls the nexus of perished actual occasions. In relational movement, the nexus is the folds to infinity inherent in each movement.

The elasticity of the almost is textured, and its texture is that of unbounded creativity. It is the point that produces conjunction: not conjunction in a one-to-one relation, but the conjunction of the one–many, of the infinity of potential series coming together. This coming-together is a concrescence. Whitehead defines concrescence from the Latin meaning 'growing together', suggesting that it means a coming together in experience. This coming together, activated through the elastic point, is not a coming together of two subjectivities or two movements, but the creativity of pure experience expressing itself. 'No things are "together" except in experience; and no things *are*, in any sense of "are", except as components in experience or as immediacies of process which are occasions in self-creation' (Whitehead 1967: 236).

The elasticity of the almost brings together formed experience and pure experience, creating a doubled event that is always either on the verge of actualization or revirtualization, at once actual and virtual. ' "Pure experience" is the name which I gave to the immediate flux of life which furnishes the material to our later reflection with its conceptual categories' (James 1996: 93). The elastic point is pure experience in relational movement. It is an actualized event in the dance as well as a virtual opening to a virtual suspension. As we stretch the movement, we know that its perishing is near and we flirt with this nearness. If we find the inflexion, we can linger; if not, we will fall. Lingering is the pure experience of experiment with the almost.

*Perishing*

Perishing is inevitable. Events are only events because they perish. It is their perishing that completes the subjective forms of their potential. The perishing is not the end: it is the pre-acceleration of a new occasion of experience. Once the subjective form composes itself, the experience has been constituted and the event is nearing its completion. The perishing event has done its work. To feel the elasticity is always to know we are on the edge. When the elastic contracts, we feel at once the perishing of the event and the propulsion of the next pre-acceleration. This is because the elastic force is as present in its stretching as in its contraction, causing the intensive spiral of a new becoming-movement.

Perished actual occasions populate the nexus out of which experience is made. There is no movement that isn't nested within another movement with which it is in continuity. As events become and perish, they create openings for new events. Every opening in relational movement marks the potential for an infinity of approaches. 'When they perish, occasions pass from the immediacy of being into the non-being of immediacy' (Whitehead 1967: 237). Events do not perish into nothingness. But, like memories, they are reactivations. Reactivated, they become sensible. To reactivate an event is not to recreate the same movement, but to invent a new movement that carries an infinity of micromovements in its virtual centre. This new movement will always be virtually populated with the pastness that constitutes the experience of moving, and even of creating particular forms. In relational movement, once I know that it is possible for my body to move a certain way, it is much more likely I will experiment with that way of moving. To feel relational movement is to have known how to move. Whitehead calls these 'non-beings of immediacy' that populate that feeling of knowing in relational movement *stubborn facts* (see Whitehead 1979). They are stubborn because we are never completely free of them. They tense up our shoulders, lock our knees. But they also activate entries into otherwise impossibly small holes, inviting us to move-with in ways in which even yesterday we wouldn't have imagined possible.

*Affective Experience*

The different planes that compose movement are like modes. The movement composes itself through each of these modes in its own singular way. When the mode fulfils its process, another mode takes over. In relational movement, one way of thinking these modes is to analyse the movement as a shifting from pre-acceleration to the creation of an interval, to the moving of the interval (moving the relation) to the creation of the curve through the elastic point to the experience of the almost leading back into pre-acceleration. Although there is a certain linearity in these modes, it would be a mistake to think of them divisively. Each of these modes produces the opening for the next mode and together they constitute an event. This event produces an affective tone which gives rise to the consistency of that particular movement-experience, its sensation. This affective tone is also the concern—in Whiteheadian terms—for the event itself, its in-holding that places the moving bodies within the experience of movement. Subject and object—leader and follower—are no longer individuals expressing their roles through steps, but are constituted by the very experience they are relationally creating. Concern is not concern for, but concern with.

The event created by relational movement is not only concerned with those moving the relation. An occasion of experience always carries the many in the one. The modes of functioning that make the experience palpable—which constitute its eventncss—jointly constitute its process of becoming. These modes can never be separated out from the worlding of the event: each event contains the world within it. This means that each movement-event is invested with all of the currents of worldness that have made it possible and all of the futurity which will in turn create the nexus (the intensive background) out of which the next movements will emerge. The relationality of relational movement moves the world as much as the world moves through it.

Relations are inseparable from affective tone or concern. And affective tone is inseparable from the modes through which relations move and which relations create. The becoming-body of dance is the composition of its relation. How this becoming-body does what it can do is its concern. The body in this case is not the individual as leader or follower but the mattering-form that emerges from inflexion. In its 'taking form' this becoming-body is always relational, produced in the between of the mobile relation. It is a body without organs, an intensive body that is almost virtual.

Modes are always affective. In the mode of the interval, for instance, as she and I move together, we may feel the rhythm change, propulsed by a syncopation of the music that takes hold of the in-gathering of the movement and expresses it otherwise, taking us out of the interval and into a new pre-accelerated movement, the elasticity not quite experienced. What we feel more than a shift in our steps is an altered affective tone. Someone might nudge us from behind, infringing on our metastability and creating a displacement toward a direction we would like to resist, bringing on frustration and inner tension. Or, as I create an opening toward an extensive movement that will result in her leg rising behind her, I may find that she is about to step into the chair on the edge of the dance floor which I didn't feel was so close, and I may quickly change direction, thereby shifting the movement toward an intensive spiral, bringing the elasticity into the curve earlier than I thought I could, thus making both of us laugh as our bodies are transported in a direction we didn't quite anticipate. Improvisation makes room for all of these contingencies. Relation cannot be foretold; it must be experienced. And its experience is affective. Its modes will always change, perishing when no longer relevant, opening the way for new modes and thus different affective tones.

The relation is always already elastic. It expresses this elasticity in relational movement through inflexion. But that doesn't mean there are no other opportunities to feel its elasticity. Even a simple walk can feel elastic when the movement carries us, when the goal is not the first thing on our mind. The elasticity of the relation is perceptible in its affective margin, in the emergence of the unknowable where what is known stretches and contracts into a propulsion of experience. Every event is in some sense imbued with such virtual elasticity. What relational movement can do is to make this elasticity felt, to actualize it in an almost-form that takes shape in its deformation.

Relational movement depends on a fluid assemblage that operates always in the between of constraint and improvisation. Each mode acts both as constraint and as opening. 'We do not even know of what affections we are capable, nor to the extent of our power,' writes Spinoza. 'How could we know this in advance?' (in Deleuze 1990: 226). Affections here are our capacity to propel experience to its transmutational potential. Modes emerge and shift according to the requirements of the relation, altering the relation and opening it to new modes. Modes in this sense can be thought of as techniques of relation. These techniques of relation are operational in the sense that they open the way for relation to be experienced. But in themselves they do not constitute the relation. 'While a mode exists, its very essence is open to variation, according to the affections that belong to it at a given moment' (ibid.: 225–6).

Techniques of relation produce events. Every event is relational. Events create relation as much as relation creates events. We cannot know in advance what an event can do, any more than we can know what a body can do. Spinoza's question will remain unanswered, for to know of what a body is capable would be to divest a body of its elasticity. The essence of a technique of relation is not its content per se, but its capacity to become more-than and to create more-than. 'A conatus is indeed a mode's essence (or degree of power) once the mode has begun to exist. A mode comes to exist when its extensive parts are extrinsically determined to enter into the relation that characterizes the mode; then, and only then, is its essence itself determined as a conatus' (ibid.: 230). Conatus is an affirmative existence, a way of creating a more-than that is not added to the mode but is part of its technique. To create more-than is to always become in excess of what it seemed a body could do. This striving is not a reaching toward a goal, but the capacity to inhabit the almost-virtual of the more-than of experience. This more-than will always be the production of a new actual occasion, the creation of a pure experience out of which a world will emerge. Moving the relation is always a striving not toward an ultimate goal, but toward the ineffable experience of the elasticity of the almost.

*Notes*

1   I consider relational movement to be a way of moving that foregrounds the movement of the relation rather than simply the displacement or the actual bodies moving. Relational movement is both a dance and a way of walking, an ecology of practices that opens the way for a thinking of movement that begins in the interval and moves the people rather than the other way around. Gilles Deleuze's concept of a movement of thought is also a way of thinking relational movement. Relational movement as I work with it here is inspired by Argentine tango. For a more detailed exploration of Argentine tango and a politics of touch, see Erin Manning (2006); for a more comprehensive reading of relational movement as such, see Manning (2008).

2   Argentine tango as a social dance is improvised. This improvisation is based on the constraint of the walk, which means that infinite variations of movement are possible to the front, to the back and across, with one foot on the ground at all times. Relational movement begins here, focusing on how the arena of improvisation enabled by Argentine tango's complexly open vocab-

ulary provides an opening for thinking about how we move relationally. Whereas much work on tango—and much danced tango—relies on the vocabulary of 'leader' and 'follower', relational movement explores movement through the interval co-created by the dancer's movements. I consider the richness of relational movement to be the capacity to work jointly with incipient movement. In the tango lexicon, this requires that both 'leader' and 'follower' be capable of both 'roles'. In relational movement, although the movement is inflected primarily by one or the other dancer, the development of the movement is jointly experienced.

3   See Alfred North Whitehead (1967). A concept of the event is key to Whitehead's work, though some would argue that the durational specificity of the actual occasion can justify a thinking of it as an event of the event. The event is technically defined in Whitehead as the nexus of actual occasions with the single actual occasion as the limit concept of the event.

*References*

BERGSON, Henri. 1970 [1959]. 'Essai sur les données immédiates de la conscience' [An Essay on the Immediate Data of Consciousness], in A. Robinet (ed.), *Oeuvres*. Paris: PUF.

DELEUZE, Gilles. 1981. *Francis Bacon: Logique de la sensation* [Francis Bacon: The Logic of Sensation], VOLS 1–2. Paris: Editions de la différence.

————. 1988. *Le pli: Leibniz et le baroque* [The Fold: Leibniz and the Baroque]. Paris: Editions de minuit.

————. 1990 [1968]. *Expressionism in Philosophy: Spinoza* (Martin Joughin trans.). New York: Zone Books.

JAMES, William. 1996 [1912]. 'A World of Pure Experience', in *Essays in Radical Empiricism*. Lincoln: Nebraska Press, pp. 39–91.

MANNING, Erin. 2006. *Politics of Touch: Sense, Movement, Sovereignty*. Minneapolis: Minnesota University Press.

————. 2008. *Moving the Relation: Force Taking Form*. Cambridge, MA: MIT Press.

WHITEHEAD, Alfred North. 1967 [1933]. *Adventures of Ideas*. New York: Free Press.

————. 1979. *Process and Reality*. New York: Free Press.

# STROBOSCOPIC STUTTER:
## ON THE NOT-YET-CAPTURED ONTOLOGICAL CONDITION OF LIMIT-ATTRACTIONS

PAULA CASPÃO

## Opening

*Affect as critical point suggests that parasite affects and lateral barely percep-tible moves might be welcomed to undo any will to reach a too-managed critical judgement and remove any remaining mastery wishes from the process of crit-ically exploring.*

*A desire only:*

*might (also) writing and (also) reading cease to be practices of mediation to be-come inter-fused modulations?*

## Interfusion Pre-Story

*The interconnection of the senses was graphically illustrated by an experiment that ingeniously combined anesthetized skin and high-altitude flight. A scientist who was also an experienced pilot and had been trained to orient expertly during high-altitude manoeuvres anesthetized his own ass. Amazing but true: he could no longer see where he was. He could no longer orient. He had scientifically proven that we see with the seat of our pants. The interconnection of the senses is so complete that the removal of a strategic patch of tactile/proprioceptive feed makes the whole process dysfunctional* (Massumi 2002).

Inter-Logues (*jeux de piste*)

*Partitioning* senses or the politics of daily sensory experience.

*Some*-thing is fusty on the shelf of a much-reiterated *view* on dance and its performance as vanishing present bodies. That *view*—one anchored and inscribed in dance and performance's supposed ontological specificity—seems hard to re-move. Specifically, it still equates with a (pre-)*view* of both presence and movement as formal disappearances, displayed on the very grounding grounds of a measurable Euclidean space and with-*in* a perception of time as a flowing linear line. An assumption difficult to re-move not only from the sort of diffuse perception we have of our day-to-day moving bodies, at every step in our daily rounds, but also from more elaborate perceptions still moving through certain circles of dance and performance researchers,[1] as well as through a good portion of dance and performance practices.

The persistence of the assumption that dance and performance are best defined by the formal disappearance of present moving bodies calls for a re-framing of ongoing temporal and spatial perceptions, along with a reframing of subsequent perceptions of perception itself.

Before we move on, though, let us take some time to convey how intrinsically aesthetic and intrinsically political these matters are, and how intrinsically they collaborate. The common-sense notion that situates aesthetic perception in a flowing linear time and in a measurable Euclidean space is not contained in the realm of artistic practice alone, but concerns both aesthetic and so-called non-aesthetic experience. More exactly, it concerns what aesthetic and non-aesthetic experiences might have in common or lend to one another. This is the interface that inevitably acquires a political dimension, the point where we should ask to what extent that common-sense notion of perception limits both our conception of sensory experience and our modes of sensing, perceiving, moving and thinking. Furthermore, we should ask how far a notion that perpetuates a consensual order of the senses—assigning specific parts and positions to identified bodies, locating them within precise sociocultural frames according to their abilities or non-abilities—is or is not a political matter worth discussing.

At this point, I am following Jacques Rancière's most recent politico-aesthetic works (1998, 2000), particularly the concept of 'partition of the sensible' (see Rancière 2000), on the basis of which he argues that there is an intrinsic knot between aesthetic practices (including literature) and politics.[2]

According to Rancière, a 'partition of the sensible' can be understood as a first sense of aesthetics, which is to say, not as a set of artistic practices, not as a general theory that concerns these practices, and not as a theory of sensory experience in general; rather, aesthetics (as 'partition of the sensible') is 'the system of a priori forms determining what presents itself to experience' (ibid.: 13). As such, it can be understood in a Kantian sense (if revised by Michel Foucault's genealogy[3]). Hence, Rancière defines it as:

> the system of self-evident facts of sense perception that simultaneously discloses the existence of something in common and the delimitations that define the respective parts and positions within it. A partition of the sensible therefore establishes at one and the same time something common that is shared and has exclusive parts. This apportionment of parts and positions is based on a distribution of spaces, times, and forms of activity that determines the very manner in which something in common lends itself to participation and in what ways various individuals have a part in this partition (2000: 12).

Thus, the 'partition of the sensible' must appear as the dimension of experience that 'reveals who can have a share in what is common to the community based on what they do and on the time and space in which this activity is performed' (ibid.: 13).

This is to say, 'aesthetics' understood as a partition of the sensible falls into the dimension of sensory experience where appropriate parts and appropriate places and times are attributed to appropriate bodies, according to their presupposed abilities of thought, locution and action. Social positions are fixed according to these delimitations, and the partitioning of the sensible upon which the community is founded, and upon which politics becomes a possibility, ultimately determines which bodies, forms of sensing, making and speaking are recognizable as a part of a shared cartography, and which are excluded from its part-taking and part-giving.

Only on the basis of the partition of the sensible taken as 'primary aesthetics' (ibid.: 14) can we understand that aesthetic practices and politics are not two separate and permanently fixed realities. Putting aesthetics at the very basis of politics and politics at the very basis of aesthetics, Rancière considers that the arts only lend *what they can* to the 'enterprises of domination or emancipation' (ibid.: 25), which means the arts only lend to politics what they already have in common, what they inevitably share as partitions of the sensory dimension of experience. Consequently, what they share is nothing less and nothing more than 'bodies' positions and movements, speaking functions, [and] partitions between the visible and the invisible. And the autonomy they may benefit from, or the [political and aesthetic] subversion that can be attributed to them, have the same basis' (ibid.: 25).

Tautological as it might sound at first sight, such an assumption deserves further and closer consideration, as it neither compromises politics' nor aesthetics' autonomy. Nor does it engage them in submitting to one another—and this is not a negligible consideration. In fact, politics' and aesthetics' relation to one another only engages both and each of them in creating new bridges and gaps between different and even opposed levels of reality, in shifting the borders of what is considered artistic and of what is considered non-artistic, and also in shifting the borders of specific artistic or non-artistic genres and modes of being, speaking and making. In short, for Rancière both art and politics share the aim of modifying the 'sensory perception of what is common to the community' (ibid.: 63).

More radically, this equates with situating the relation between aesthetics and politics on a level that makes both politics and aesthetics one and the same with our most daily sensory experience (where artistic activities as such give up their usual *aesthetic* exclusivity).[4] It is a relation that works on the basis of the implication of both politics and aesthetics in the deconstruction and in the critical reconstruction of partitions of daily and less ordinary perceptions; precisely those perceptions that come to be felt as personal, despite the fact that they are shared according to common *partitioning*(s). Simultaneously personal and commonly sensed, these perceptions involuntarily pertain to particular forms of installing and moving in times and spaces, more or less visibly, more or less critically and creatively.

In this context, it becomes evident that both politics and aesthetics only become effectively political and effectively aesthetic when they are capable of interrupting a given order of the forms of sensing and of the forms of making sense; when they are capable of giving way to the eruption of singular sense combinations that don't necessarily fit in the consensually established ones. Their task is then not only to reconfigure the limits of each of our senses and their relations to one another, but also to constantly push those limits to tensional thresholds of *dis-sensus*, to produce a crisis in *consensus*. More precisely, their task is to force singular heterogeneous reorganizations of the sensible into everyday experience, namely suspending appropriate places, de-positioning bodies out of their appropriate positions, and listening to the polyrhythmic humming of erupting senses without formal recognition. For, as Rancière states, arts' and politics' aim is not to produce appropriately placed collective bodies: 'Instead, they introduce lines of fracture and disincorporation into imaginary collective bodies', thus calling into 'question any distribution of roles, territories and languages' (2000: 63, 64).

In a word, both politics and artistic practices should constantly and variably try to unfold the question: How can the imperceptible become perceptible within a given partition of the sensible that apparently has no place for it?

*Sewing Seams*

Concrete is as concrete doesn't (Massumi 2002).

Now taking into account that time and space, although they are indeed distinct dimensions of experience, aren't formally discernible as such, let us put it this way: what is missed by our most current perceptions of bodily presence and movement, occurring with-*in* a linear timeline and *in* a Euclidean space, is that the most embodied of our bodily experience always occurs in a relational spatiotemporal smudge whose end differentially loops back to its beginning.[5] It seems we keep '*looking forward to our own past and looking past into the future*, in a seeing so intense that it falls out of sight' (Massumi 2002: 194). It seems, we are all *Angelus Novus*.[6] It seems that the very daily empirical experience of an historically, culturally and sociopolitically embodied body half-involuntarily calls for the emergence of an abstract-virtual spatiotemporal surface of perception—radically *synesthetic* and *kinesthetic*, more than aesthetic and kinetic—that can only be conceived topologically in a non-linear temporality.[7] If the way we live is always entirely embodied, then 'you' can never be 'just about you', precisely situated in place ('where'?) and time ('when'?), '"you", just as you are' (entirely personal affair . . .), as we love to define ourselves. It means both that you are never isolated and that there is more to it: 'you' is always connected to other situations and dimensions, embedded in something brighter than 'you' in your places, times and timings.

It's not that we don't live in a measurable space and in a linear time as well, as we indeed do. They are not just optical illusions. Bodies don't just explode the laws of physics. Unavoidable then, it is also true that we live in

Euclidean spaces and in linear times: we build, we eat and we sit in Euclidean space and linear time. Fair enough. It's just that all this, as reassuring as it may sound, wouldn't make it to the surface where distinct materialities cross-reference concreteness and abstractness, where supposedly already perceived forms may re-emerge as just emerging perceptions, and potentially recolour our modes of thinking and perceiving. Without that inter-crossing dimension of dimensions, 'you' wouldn't be reading this, and 'I' wouldn't be writing it. In fact, we have to have Euclidean and topological geometries (many more? We don't really know how many, do we?) collaborating and co-attracting, their differentiation and mutual integration operating together within our perception.[8] Consequence: in-between, in interference and over-lapping, is where we always have to be, to really constantly re-become kines-thetically inter-fusing thinking bodies,[9] even when we are visibly positioned somewhere here, sitting and writing at home, in Paris, in France, in Europe, on Earth, on a St Valentine's Tuesday—or else visibly moving from some-where visibly here, to somewhere visibly there. 'A "surface" then,' Rancière very appropriately notes, 'is not simply a geometric composition of lines' (2000: 19). Rather, it is always intrinsically a (political) form of sharing/*partitioning* the sensory dimension of experience.

Get closer. Step aside. Intermingle: In-between is where we may inten-sively read, move, sing, think, walk, love, fall or write, and varyingly remain. In-affection. Still. Still varying.

*Chopping List*

I therefore suggest that new insights on time, space and perception might be found by introducing *relationality*[10] into the present essay. This can be tried both by rethinking AFFECT—affects as '*virtual synesthetic perspectives*' (Mas-sumi 2002: 35)[11]—and by letting go of the formal opposition between the con-crete and the abstract (as if abstraction had nothing to do with an excess due to very concrete moves of 'perception's passing'—perception as *aesthetics*, or a wonderfully pain-full *force* effect, posing for intensity).[12] Except that putting the above-mentioned opposition aside will *force*-fully affect the whole oppo-sites' family, namely co-relatives such as matter and mind, objective and sub-jective, quiescence and movement, visible and invisible, embodied presence and disembodied absence, present and past-future, space and time (as if we couldn't *see time in space*, in continuous future-past interplay . . . ).

Problem: to realize this list could extend almost infinitely to other well-known binary beings. Example (*au pied de la lettre*):

01. Nature and culture.

Comment: as if culture wasn't nature . . .

01. Real and symbolic.

No comment.

01. Event and representation.

Comment: as if representation wasn't a dimension of event-reality, re-entering the relational continuum, always re-becoming eventful sensorial perception . . .

01. Raw perception and rehearsed perception.

Comment: as if every so-called 'first-time' perception wasn't already half way . . . a memory.

Comment: as if none of the so-called 'higher' forms of perception had ways and means of re-plunging into direct contact with sensorial matter . . .

Comment: as if there wasn't only a possible way of rethinking raw and rehearsed perceptions: each across and all along the other, inter-modulating. And no question of culturally 'higher' cognition mediating naturally 'rawer' perception, which is the usual way 'to begin with' . . . [13]

01. Real experience and pure imagination.

Comment: as if experience itself wasn't a very imaginative multidimensional reality . . .

01. Anaesthetic and aesthetic.

No comment.

01. Mono-sense and cross-sense perception (synesthesia).[14]

No comment. Think about it.

Remember to add tri-oppositions like:

01. Forgotten, misremembered and remembered.

01. Cognition, perception and hallucination.

Comment: as if thought didn't hallucinate that it coincides with itself . . . [15]

Enough.

Press 'Pause.'

Move it! (Don't STOP)

Hesitate. For one time, oppose.

Stillness: for some reason I would like to try to understand why the trope of dance and its performance as vanishing present bodies still has currency and is still pursuing the same old routes and routines along collective and individual imaginaries. Almost everywhere I go (and read), I can still hear its echo. That's why I feel like saying it still resonates more or less subliminally in human practices where you wouldn't expect it to. You will find it still enchants a whole lot of literature, philosophy, visual arts, media and cultural studies, cinema and publicity. And you will find it still at work in many dance and performance practices, as well as throughout dance and performance studies.

The problem is that no matter how elaborate its new versions, this trope always leaves a residue of its old fellow traveller, the most enduring opposition colonized by Western thought: writing (and discourse in general) as a means to capture movement and sensation, and dance as a flowing vanishing art[16] (meanwhile turned into the art of vanishing? Remind me to get back to this . . . ).

Moreover, this approximately two-centuries-old opposition has it (even if only residually, very *au fond de soi-même*) that dance would have the unique privilege of accessing the body as pure movement and pure sensation—supposedly, the closest to the body a body can be, the (most on the) threshold to the body's most truly truth. A wonder. Or only just what reverberates in neoliberal official discourse on sensation and movement. Assuming: fluidity inspires and fascinates our next best (me included, I suspect). And there it goes, echoing and far reaching: 'Move it!'; 'Be flexible!'; 'Overcome yourself!'; 'Overcome your second best!'; 'Project yourself (be a projectile!)!'; 'Get a brand new "you"!'; 'Re-new!'; 'Do "it" yourself!'; (Whatever 'you' does:) 'Don't stop "it"!'; 'Don't stop!'; 'Move "it"!'

From here we will always risk returning (even if only very *au fond*) to a dance mystified as a pre-something, a pre-language, a pre-everything you can imagine, with no effective (affective) potential beyond its local appearing, only existing (desisting?) in a fascinating vanishing, unique body *here* and *now*, never again. And again: gone forever. Repeat it after me. Echo 'it'. After 'I' *has* disappeared into the realms of pastness. Document 'it', for 'I' wouldn't mind. By the way, 'who' said documenting was less (a-)live than live-arts? (Remind me to get back to this.)

*Cauliflower Effects: Affect as Critical Point*

Recapitulate: My point by now is that what has to 'vanish' from theoretical discussions on dance and performance is not only the very notion of specific ontological conditions proper to specific artistic practices, but also general notions of separately operating levels of reality, relating to each other almost exclusively under the mode of mutual exclusion. Separately operating levels of reality would then never intersect but only meet under the mode of distancing formal equivalence, and thus officially allowed, substitution of one another—describing or prescribing, documenting or regulating each other. Inevitably, such distinctions limit the field of operating possibilities when it comes to dance and performance theory. They only help perpetuate the same old set of action–reaction circuits, instead of helping to explore the interference and superposition circuits at work between distinct materialities, which in fact are mutually included in the same continuum of self-differentiating reality. That is why I argue that some key notions here could be 'resonating levels' of emergence, 'bifurcation' paths, or simply affect as 'critical point' (Massumi 2002: 33). These notions refer to affect's relational operative modes, and as such intermingle at the core of what we may call the turning points of any sensory experience (ibid.: 32). They intervene as openings for a more-to-come. It becomes clear that this is exactly the point where resonation levels are most active, giving way to the sensing of contradictory levels of reality belonging to multiple logics and spatiotemporal organizations. They present, as recapitulations of many versions of one and the same physical system, a continual doubling of the actual by its dimension of intensity (intensity equating with potential). Such a turning point in perception equals its becoming critical. It can only take place when affect appears as the point of emergence of all resonating levels remaining in many ways present (though not necessarily actual).

Now many present resonating levels cannot avoid bifurcating at many points, opening up a supplementary level of complexity in the intersecting of sensing, thinking, saying or making. Bifurcation paths are ways of simultaneously covering and uncovering rifts in the field of thought and sensory perception, making apparently distinct terms relate without making them coincide (for example: politics and aesthetics, or matter and mind).

As operative modes of affect, resonation and bifurcation are the conditions for the becoming critical of perception at large. This means affect brings about a multitude of openings for more senses, more thought, more action, more *whatever*, that leads perception to its becoming critical of what is right now, of what was or has just been, or of what will possibly be. In a register closer to Rancière, this also means it is through these operations that affect can render perceptible new networks of sensing. Affect functions as a 'critical point' in so far as it can dismantle legitimate orders of discourse as well as definite relations between words, bodies, minds, actions and objects. This is the way affect goes against modes of communication that legitimate the 'appropriate', those in which every body, every sense and every thing is attributed a place or a non-place. Blurring positions and functions, affect appears as a tool for opening up constant redistributions of the places attributed to every body and to every thing.

Is it just me, or is affect now resonating with Rancière's idea of democracy? It seems as if there is at least one level of affect that could bifurcate the political dimension of aesthetics and the aesthetic dimension of politics: the level that inevitably reveals a certain kind of indetermination, if not disincorporation, that survives even in the best identified identities. Let us read what Rancière writes about what the operative mode of arts shares with politics: 'artistic phenomena are [. . .] inhabited by a heterogeneous power, the power of a form of thought that has become foreign to itself: a product identical with something not produced, knowledge transformed into non-knowledge, *logos* identical with pathos, the intentional of the unintentional, etc.' (2000: 31). Let us also read what Brian Massumi writes about affect: 'an invitation to recapitulate, to repeat and complexify, at ground level, the real conditions of emergence, not of the categorical, but of the unclassifiable, the unassimilable, the never-yet felt, the felt for less than half a second, again for the first time—the new' (2002: 33). And then return to Rancière again to underline that the paths for political and aesthetic subjectivation are surely not those of identification but those of artistic (also literary) disincorporation (2000: 64).

FIGURE 1. (*From left*): Marek Lamprecht, Martin Nachbar and Jochen Roller. Martin Nachbar and Jochen Roller, *mnemonic non-stop: Ein Kartographisches Duet*, Steirischer Herbst, Graz/Austria, 2005. Photograph by Katrin Schoof.

In the meanwhile, note that affect cannot be reduced to subjectively captured and qualified emotion. Nor should it somehow be romanticized as only personal depth of each one's subjective experience. On the contrary, there is undoubtedly much to think over about the relations between affect–mobilized affect and the new non-ideological decentralized forms of power operating within late capitalism.[17] But first of all, before being captured, affect captures (and again: it captures even after it has been captured). It is given to the world as an impersonal gift: affect is merely 'the virtual co-presence of potentials' (Massumi 2003). And it is much more about (felt) transitional intensity than just about personal emotions or feelings, although it is surely also what allows personal feelings to intensify and enlarge their potential of actualizing differently. Affect then, is 'not just subjective, which is not to say there is nothing subjective in it' (ibid.). The same doesn't go for emotion:

> [A]n emotion is a subjective content, the sociolinguistic fixing of the quality of an experience which is from that point onward defined as personal. Emotion is qualified intensity, the conventional, consensual point of insertion of intensity into semantically and semiotically formed progression, into narrativizable action–reaction circuits, into function and meaning. It is intensity owned and recognized (Massumi 2002: 28).

That is the reason why an emotion is always just a very partial expression of affect. Affect on the contrary is 'all about the openness of situations and how we can live that openness. [...] With intensified affect comes a stronger sense of embeddedness in a larger field of life—a heightened sense of belonging, with other people and to other places' (Massumi 2003).

Call affect the reason why a body moves through life as a swarm of swirling potentials. Call it also the reason why the complex dynamics of the body's in-mixing of spatiotemporalities is neither conceivable nor conceptualizable if we don't take to exploring non-Euclidean ontologies and non-linear causalities. And finally, call affect the inhabitant of a cauliflower complex, the best way to suggest fractal modes of sensing.

Consequently, if we want to analyse the complexity of our perception, we will need to take all fractal, non-Euclidean and non-linear dimensions into account, as Massumi refers: 'The organization of multiple levels that have different logics and temporal organizations, but are locked in resonance with each other and recapitulate the same event in divergent ways, recalls the *fractal ontology* and *nonlinear causality* underlying theories of complexity' (2002: 33; emphasis added).

One thing is almost certain: affects are indeed analysable, namely as effects.[18] So why not try to diversify our methods of approach? Getting closer (from a varying distance)? (Question.)

Answer: 'The virtual is a lived paradox where what are normally opposites coexist, coalesce, and connect' (ibid.: 30).

On the not-yet-captured ontological status of becoming 'something other than' ... *disappearance*. Get back. Invert senses.

Talk about processes of disappearing ... ask where *it all* goes. Afterwards. Ask also if the place where a performance finds itself after public (re)presentation—should it be memory—is really exclusively invisible and distinguishable from the performance itself, differing both in *nature* (in *matter*) and in (choreographic) *genre*.

Some years ago, performance theorist Peggy Phelan wrote: 'Without a copy, live performance plunges into visibility—in a maniacally charged present—and disappears into memory, in the realm of invisibility where it eludes regulation and control' (1993: 148).

Today still, when I read this, questions run over each other through my mind. (Far from disappearing as fast as performances. If.) As a historically situated strategic move intended to challenge the politics of visibility and visibility as politically partitioned, this theoretical assertion may sound effective for a while. Only: can we really escape the trap of visibility (as politically partitioned) from its outside, especially when its 'outside' is here taken strictly as invisible 'inside'—namely, memory as the realm of invisibility— elusively protected from all visibility? Memory as capable of eluding 'regulation and control'? I wonder if Phelan's statements are not evoking a sort of freedom performed by personal memory unattainable by extrinsic constraints, and thus unattainable by politically partitioned visibilities?

Try to leave it open so far. Asking.

Isn't the only way to resist visibility to fight from within visibility? And by the way: is memory really the realm of invisibility? Is memory a strictly interior 'affair', and is interiority strictly invisible? The most intimate and personal memory, doesn't it forcefully have something to do with visibilities (though at different levels)? Does any memory, as intimate and personal as it may feel, really escape constraints, visible or invisible? Is memory really a boxed-in 'affair'? Never (also) collectively cued?

Change paths: 'Consider that there is no "raw" perception. That all perception is rehearsed. Even, especially, our most intense, most abject and inspiring, self-perceptions' (Massumi 2002: 66). Consider then, that memory is just a reactivating perception. Not some utopian escape from outwardly performed visibilities. Not that we are not following ourselves within our memories and other most intimate realms of experience. We really are (also), but following ourselves is already (also) following paths that politically partitioned perception has put in us: from the inside, from within our very openness to the outside, not from a separate, imposed-upon outside. So we never really do free ourselves from extrinsic constraints, we only sometimes find the leaks in them and more or less creatively convert them. This doesn't necessarily shrink our degree of freedom to some merely repetitive reconversion of something exterior to us. There is nothing to fear at this point: 'Wherever you are, there is still potential, there are openings, and the openings are in the grey areas, in the blur where you are susceptible to affective contagion, or capable of spreading it. [Only:] It's never totally within your personal power to decide' (Massumi 2003).

From here we may suppose that memory is not a realm immune to visibility. Moreover, there *have to be visibilities* within memory, many of them working together, for memory is as synesthetic as perception itself and 'synesthetic perception is always an event or performance' (Massumi 2002: 190) merging outward and inward dimensions along a one-sided surface. *See?* Memory is not only a realm that is in no way exclusively interior and invisible, it is also a realm that is crossed by and interferes with so-called exteriorly performed visibilities.

How can resistance against entropy then be performed not only 'against' entropy but from 'within' its utmost outside (visible and invisible)? Seemingly, misunderstandings persist, about where and how resistance can be performed: when we believe resistance must be performed from the outside (disappearing from visibility), we paradoxically replace it with an invisible inside (memory as invisible); when we believe resistance is only displayable from within, we just go straight back to the same spot (are we resisting resistance?), and afresh we tend to take this 'within' for an invisible interiority, opposing, escaping and finally getting rid of outside constraints.

*Loop the Loop*

Re-ask where *it all* goes. Ask also where *it all* comes from. Ask also where *it all* just becomes. Better, ask also if what comes *before* (as production-creation), what comes *during* (as public presentation) and what comes *after* (as documentation of) a performance is really completely distinguishable and different in *nature* (in *matter*) and in (*choreographic*) *genre*. Perhaps all these levels do differ from one another, but only otherwise. That is, not as ontologically different, and not as methodologically separate levels of emergence. Rather, they may, and generally do, resonate intertextually and interchoreographically in one another. For: 'The virtual self-standing of [any] vision actually takes place in a crowded bubble' (ibid.: 157).

Phelan defined performance ontologically as an experience that only becomes itself through disappearance. The refrain is by now well known: 'Performance in a strict ontological sense is nonreproductive' (1993: 148). And well re-enacted: 'Presence and theatre are instances of enactments predicated on their own disappearance' (Phelan 1997: 2).

In a legitimate theoretical move (though almost falling into moralizing, as I read it) pronouncing against documentation as 'photology',[19] Phelan strongly advises us to resist any desire to preserve, further represent, document or in any way illustrate performances as such: 'The desire to preserve the performance is a desire we should resist. For what one otherwise preserves is an illustrated corpse, a pop-up anatomical drawing that stands in for the thing that one most wants to save, the embodied performance' (ibid.: 3). 'Always failing to keep the real in view, representation papers it over and reproduces other representations' (Phelan 1993: 19). Sounds fair. Our archives are full of corpses and we should better acknowledge that what we have experienced once in a lifetime is not any more and will never again be exactly the same way. That, in a way, is life, and performance performing life. Only, it is not that simple. Corpses or any other stiff bodies are seldom that dead. Nonetheless, the refrain comes back, and insists: 'Performance's life is only in the present. Performance cannot be saved, recorded, documented, or otherwise participate in the circulation of representations of representations: once it does so it becomes something other than performance' (ibid.: 146).

FIGURE 2. Martin Nachbar (*left*) and Jochen Roller. Martin Nachbar and Jochen Roller, *mnemonic non-stop: Ein Kartographisches Duet*, Steirischer Herbst, Graz/Austria, 2005. Photograph by Katrin Schoof.

If I get it right, a degree of complexity is missing, a whole set of interference patterns between fields (has it just disappeared along with performance's current status as 'disappearance'?). Hereby, Phelan automaticaly strikes a note familiar to 'on-the-spot' notions of witnessing that insinuate the pressure to be right there at the right moment, to not miss it. Note how both the urge to document and its opposite, the need to 'resist' the 'desire to preserve' the performance, strangely join in a similar urge toward direct witnessing. For Phelan only mentions documentation as a direct consequence of direct witnessing, as something leading to infinite circuits of representations of representations, from which the 'real' live-performance is, on the grounds of its very ontological status, absolutely absent as such. No relation, no interference. I would now like to ask how close is on-the-spot witnessing (be it in order to document or in order to *not* document) to the process itself. It looks as if we have long ago left behind the age where we used to speak of 'the thing itself', but we still abide with the pressure to witness processes in 'real time', as the only valid circumstance allowing us to feel close to it.

Is there really an essential value difference between primary and secondary sources?[20]

Another consequence of Phelan's last-quoted assertion is that a neat line between performance and other genres is drawn. If I get it right, there is a certain genre stratification resonating here, between what I would call choreographic and non-choreographic practice, with no regard for what I would call affective/critical *contagion*. Could we for a while stop pulling the curtain around the 'unique present moment' displayed by performance, and around performance as a unique genre? Could we stop talking of 'disappearance' as 'becoming something other than performance', and start talking about 'changing' and 'becoming something other' within performance as well? For isn't 'becoming something other' something that works on performances from within? Aren't all the 'others' already performing within performance, exploding genre barriers all around? Are dance, performance and any sort of documentation really separate moves and genres?

I am thinking of choreographer and performer Olga de Soto,[21] who created the performance *histoire(s)* out of a documenting process. The choreographer not only transformed a documentation process into a performance, she also transformed the very act of performing into one of documentation, displacing both notions of documentation and of dance performance (see de Soto 2004).

Following an invitation from Culturgest (Lisbon, 2002) to pay tribute to the ballet *Le Jeune Homme et la Mort* (1946),[22] de Soto began with the question 'What does it mean to pay tribute?' (ibid.) and arrived at the conclusion that in the absence of direct witnessing, the best thing to do was to approach the memories of the individuals who had been to the premiere. This is to say, to get in touch with their mental, affective and physical spaces, and with their modes of telling and relating to their memories. So, instead of analysing the ballet itself or trying to reconstruct it in some way, de Soto followed the trace of the witnesses' perception of their own memories. Interestingly, the result doesn't help us identify the ballet in question; what we get is a choreographic recomposition of heterogeneous times, spaces, memories and perceptions, constructed around the projection of a *documentary* film. Projected on four screens of different dimensions, the film shows the witnesses de Soto contacted (this was not easy and the research took her quite a long time) quietly installed at their homes, in their intimate spaces, talking about their memories of the ballet. They were all filmed from the same distance; only the screens are placed and displaced by the dancers onstage, so visible physical distances constantly change, as they visibly constantly change in the mental and affective space of each pair of eyes we see on the screens.

Eventually, what we see in the performance of *histoire(s)* is an image of a deliberately biased archaeology of memory and perception that emphasizes the affective dimension of perception, of remembering, and of any project of documentation. We only see the performers onstage in their intervening role, actively but discretely catalyzing (manipulating, reorganizing) the diverse dimensions of experience at play in a choreographic pattern. And at the end we get the impression that the words and voices of the witnesses, their hesitations charged with affective force suddenly appearing as movement, as well as the questions they lead us to, could have been functioning as a choreographic score all the way through the performance.

Another effective realization of the precarious boundary between documentation and performance is *mnemonic nonstop: Ein Kartographisches Duett* (2005), a choreographic performance by Martin Nachbar and Jochen Roller[23] that also disrupts the apportionment of genres, spaces and times of aesthetic experience. In this performance, choreography, documentation and cartography patterns inevitably blur and inevitably change. Applying a method close to the technique of the *dérive* developed by the French Situationists,[24] Nachbar and Roller choreographed a performance out of the exploration of the affective anatomy of five European cities (Tel Aviv, Brussels, Berlin, Zagreb and Graz), collecting and noting impressions, photographing details, and drawing unconventional cartographies of those cities. Their method consisted of intermingling, for example, street events with mental detours, places observed with past encounters, present encounters with past impressions or emerging desires, or the other way around. In a way, this is nothing other than making heterogeneous levels of perception and memory intersect with heterogeneous physical spaces, by opening up the leaking holes between them and official mappings. About this practice, Nachbar states:

> When embarking on a walk through one of the cities, our attempt is to find holes and cracks in the official maps, so that we can crawl through them and map the city in a different way than the one we might find in our tour guides. We don't literally trespass onto forbidden territory, but we leave the commonly agreed upon passageways of a city. The result of our practice is a heightened perception and an ability to play with the situations we encounter. With this, we create passages that enable us to leave known territories (of land, but more so of perception); we de-territorialize and ideally, our passages become lines of flight. The space gets perforated, so that our passions can leak into the city and vice versa (2005).

Looking for modes of generating choreographic scores out of research on the ways we walk (live) through urban space, Nachbar and Roller produced a cartographic/choreographic mode of documenting the paths of our daily lives that questions and extends the borders of the three implicated methods: the choreographic, the documentary and the cartographic.

Onstage, the score for *mnemonic non-stop* is the projection of transparencies either containing the mappings that are the result of the artists' singular documentation process, or official ones; these mappings are progressively superposed, and each time the last one added proposes a new approach to the former. As Roller writes:

> When one copies the map of the city one is in onto a transparent foil, this foil can be put onto another map and hidden structures ap-

pear on them just like secret ink appears when exposed to its developer agent. When, for example, laying a transparent map of Brussels on to the map of Congolese capital Kinshasa, the superposed cities seem to plainly deconstruct the Belgian colonial past (2005).

Indeed, by traversing these altered cartographic and documentary proceedings, choreography itself can be approached otherwise. As Roller states: 'the patterns that evolve by superposing foils in a "mnemonic nonstop" simulate urban experiences: the choreography reorganizes space and becomes itself a map that describes this very re-writing' (ibid.).

Inevitably, 'proper' and officially mapped places are displaced; they become unrecognizable or recognizable otherwise. Besides, this deterritorializing (and reterritorializing) cartographing choreography can also work as a vivid document of a particular gesture: an invitation to rethink our modes of conceiving and delimitating physical and mental spaces, sense and sensorial terms, choreographic, documentary and cartographic modes of moving.

Look through: performances are often treacherous grounds from the point of view of attempting to stratify genres. Look around: contemporary and actual performances are frequently the most heterogeneous composites, effectively made out of the most diverse supports and out of the most diversely interconnected spatiotemporal dimensions—performance as an intermodal *kinesthetic* practice among others, as just one of many other intertextual and interchoreographic genres. This is where documentation's materiality as a (why not inter-choreo-*graphic*?) practice, and despite its being more or less illustrative, more or less affectionate toward representation, would start to move, enlarging its current ontological status of non-disappearing, unchanged and unchanging illustrative, representation mode. This is where documentation modes can also become treacherous grounds from the point of view of attempting to stratify genres. Reason enough to argue that performances' remains (documentation or others) do not necessarily just remain as post-mortems wandering along the representational corpses they give way to. Nor do they necessarily remain in boxed-in personal memories.

In short: potential for change is potentially everywhere. Just not always, and not always the same, in the same way.

*On 'odd fruits of experience that [sometimes] go "raw" '*

> There is an objective degree of freedom even in the most determin-
> istic system. Something in the coming together of movements, even
> according to the strictest of laws, flips the constraints over into con-
> ditions of freedom. It's a relational effect, a complexity effect. Affect
> is like our relational field and what we call our freedom are its rela-
> tional flips. Freedom is not about breaking or escaping constraints.
> It is about flipping them over into degrees of freedom (Massumi
> 2003).[25]

These considerations about 'relational flips' that allow degrees of freedom
into the most deterministic systems shall lead us directly to the relation between movement, perception and language. This is to say, directly back to affect. Rancière posits that literature, as a mode of locution belonging to a
specific partition of the sensible, 'lives only by evading the incarnation that
it incessantly puts into play' (1998: 14). So literature lives only to escape the
becoming-flesh of words, or their becoming recognizable as a specific body
that dictates meaning by incorporating words. In other terms, the conflict
that inhabits both literature and language is much like the one that inhabits
both politics and aesthetics: they only live on the basis of partitions of the
sensible, and they only live by disrupting those partitions and modes of communication that function to legitimate the 'appropriate', so that they can create new partitions and new modes of communication and thus give a part to
those who have no part; give a part to the 'inappropriate' or not necessarily
'appropriate', a surplus that can only be sensed and rendered effective
through connectedness—through affect. So, again, it should be noted that
Rancière's 'partition of the sensible' is a concept that has the advantage of
highlighting the fact that the sensorial delimitations it refers to are neither
merely physical nor merely discursive, but apply to the borders where conceptual sense meets the senses; exactly where affects best unfold and produce
turning points.

The issue is that in spite of its being direct—or better said, directly in
transition—and non-mediated (though not quite in the sense of being more
natural than other cultural deeds), affect does touch, re-include and move
highly elaborated functions like language. Still, we cannot deny that language
is first of all (at least for most of us) the most coded or conventional expression of affect. But there is more to it—something to get back to . . .

In the meanwhile, we will admit that we use words to capture, seize, tune into and express affects, usually as emotions. This is namely the more or less calculable part of affect, the one power recycles so well, provided we are not thinking of power as repression but as it effectively circulates nowadays: as a highly subversive inclusion and conversion, of the most subversive charge of affect. The good news is that affect doesn't just abandon already formed forms (whichever their relation to power circuits of regularization) to the delirium of seemingly stiff bodies. Affect moves through and reopens everything: 'There's an affect associated with every functioning of the body, from moving your foot to moving your lips to make words' (Massumi 2003).

So, affect doesn't just disappear from effectively actualizing or already actualized discourses, even the most dominating, mimetic or stereotypical ones. It just somehow remains off to the side, erratically, as a 'perpetual bodily remainder', as a not-yet-exhausted excess, a third and a fourth body, a more-to-come. In any case, more than just gone forever, sentenced to disappear by any of its past or present actualizations. For affect is not only an aspect of emerging unique events like live performances. For one thing, pronounced or written words, or any more or less arrested forms, affect us, for better or for worse, or neither of the two.[26]

The thing is that language is always about playing between constraint and the remaining room to *manoeuvre*. And it is always difficult to pin down the constantly refreshing emerging affects; and it becomes stale, when you think of it in the traditional way, namely as a tool for constraining or regulating, a means to describe or even command movement and affect, rather than just a boat to navigate through them, wherever this might lead. Just try using words not only to pin down but also to intercept and absorb irregular blobs of passing rhythms, to scratch your tongue, to stagger, or to do anything you can imagine. Just don't let words coagulate in and out of your throat. Give them other uses. Burst out laughing, stutter. Use your imagination, and your own language as a foreign one.[27]

Language is definitely amphibian. Two-pronged (many pronged? I wonder), as Massumi declares: 'If you think of language in the traditional way, as a correspondence between a word with its established meaning on the one hand and a matching perception on the other, then it starts coagulating' and distancing itself from the excess of affect that the experiencing of every situation brings about. Though, he continues:

[T]here are uses of language that can bring inadequacies between language and experience to the fore, in a way that can convey the 'too much' of the situation—its charge—in a way that actually fosters new experiences. Humor is a prime example. So is poetic expression taken in its broadest sense. [. . .] Experiencing this potential for change, experiencing the eventfulness and uniqueness of every situation, even the most conventional ones, that's not necessarily about commanding movement, it's about navigating movement (2003).[28]

Now if we think of perception as a synesthetic experience and accept its 'strange one-sided topology' (Massumi 2002: 189) as 'the general plane of cross-reference not only for signs, sounds, touches, tastes, smells, and proprioceptions, but also for numbers, letters, words, [and] even units of grammar', then we have to acknowledge that 'the learned forms that are usually thought of as restricted to a "higher" cultural plane re-become perceptions' (ibid.). This means that no given forms of discursive pinning-down and documentation, however descriptive, conventional and stereotyped they may be, ever go definitely stale. Keep in mind, knee and nose that their staleness is just as provisory as eventful experience itself.[29] And if they usually look like just another set of stubbornly persistent forms of arresting movement and affect to be poured into our monumental archives, they also practise other not yet given forms of *remaining*: as 'odd fruits of experience that [sometimes] go "raw"' (ibid.: 198).

And by the way, do dance and performance always have to equate with fluidity? Keep in mind, body and brain that real effects of affects are just not part of the 'formal definition of the figure' (ibid.: 185).

Lasting problem: a non-sequential one to be dealt with accordingly, or non-accordingly. (Just look how sequential forms of dealing with problems may also become effective in dealing with non-sequential ones.) Try.

Try 1: Perhaps stiff bodies are not only to be found in documentation, representation and other textual or imaged supposedly arresting movements!

Try 2: Perhaps fluid bodies are not only to be found in dance and performance! (What if dance and performance's materialities didn't really always flow?)

Try 3: Stiff and fluid bodies can be just everywhere. (Interconnectedness of all material supports—including human bodies—at work no matter where, when and how.)

Sound it:

The idea of 'flowing bodies' in a 'flowing flux' tinkles a tone familiar to that same linear line that goes from one point to another, from the very beginning and across the middle, right to the end. A-problematically.

We have not found the solution. We have just come back to the heart(s) of 'a-problems'.

Fluidity *Rocked*

There is a certain ongoing praise of movement, sensation, fluidity and even any sort of fluency that comes along with the conviction that they are necessarily going to lead us 'further', in whatever sense. This prevailing fascination (if not mystification) of movement (and all concerned so-called fluidities) as the privileged doorway both to one's own most human creativity and to one's most politically effective body and soul has come a long way. As Rancière reminds us: 'In the *cité* hostile to theatre and to written law, Plato recommended citizens to constantly rock their infants' (2000: 24).[30] Reason enough not to forget 'the very ancient link between citizen's unanimism and the exaltation of the free movement of bodies' (ibid.). Reason enough to make us think of the trouble there is in distinguishing 'fair mobility' and 'guardians of good movement' from 'fake mobilization' and 'actors of mobilization', as Peter Sloterdijk formulates it, should this be the 'good' way to formulate it (2000: 46, 67). For they are neither really formally separable, nor otherwise absolutely distinguishable, both ambiguously bifurcating, superposing and interfusing on the topological surface of our perception. In fact, to think of perception as synesthesia and synesthesia as a one-sided topological surface may help us grasp the highly subversive political (*partitioning*) charge occluded by our amphi-biological condition. This is to say: for better, for worse, or none of them. This is why it is important, as Sloterdijk suggests, to pay attention to lateral mobility. Notice then how affective connectedness is not just, and not necessarily, 'the good' part of *it all*. Rather, affect as connectedness is an uncaptured gift given to everyone and everything, but what is not given is how we are going to *live along*, if we don't just want to make something *out of it*. As anything else in this world, the most promising movements, perceptions, thoughts or affects can quickly turn into self-captures. Keep thinking: 'Think about the contradictory destinies of the choreographic model. Recent works have reminded us of the misadventures of the movement notation elaborated by [Rudolf] Laban in a context of liberation of the body that has nevertheless become the model for the big Nazi demonstrations, before it could recover a new subversive virginity within the anti-establishment context of performance arts' (Rancière 2000: 23, 24). Think also how any functionalized and nationalized affective capture 'feeds directly into prison construction and neo-colonial adventure' (Massumi 2002: 42).

Think also how much space and time (fluent) fluidity images are capturing and occupying all around and in us. Think also how *this all* is getting slippery. Which is not a reason to fasten seat belts—on the contrary. Let ambiguity play, and interplay (with) it.

STOP. Everything.

Time to ask where all theoretical attempts to define something ontologically essential to dance and performance come from and where they get to. Do they really help in conceptualizing dance's and performance's specific modes of appearing, doing and disappearing; or do they rather erase something *essential* to our understanding of the effective modes of moving (affecting) displayed by each singularly embodied performance? Is it fair to suppose that such attempts derive from a limited but much expanded view of what live arts (like bodies) are supposed to be? For what live arts are supposed to be is usually borrowed from reified assumptions of how a body is supposed to feel and move *in* space and time; where and when it is supposed to start and end.

In a sense, these assumptions are just logical consequences of a general ontology that prioritizes human over non-human, position over movement, and discrete terms over relationality.

Unfasten your seat belt. Try the upside-down version of this. See if you get to a non-hierarchical relationality continuum, where concrete-abstract human bodies and concrete-abstract non-human bodies and terms not only move from position to position, but also interchange their modes of changing. Together (but not too loud): *changing-movement* rather than Euclideanized position, *connectedness* rather than separate bodies and terms. And back to the middle, by the sides (erase priorities): suppose there is no specific kind of presence specific to dance and performance that wouldn't be shared by other embodied practice in any other of the officially separate domains of experience. Suppose what you find at stake in dance and performance is just what you will find at stake in any situation where the issue is connectedness, resonance and change, in any possible and impossible directions and dimensions. Change changes: suppose any situation where the issue is connectedness, resonance and change is an open 'domain' where human bodily-beings are neither prior nor non-prior. Now if there isn't anything prior to anything, if there isn't anything like merely arrested presence (or Euclidean position), if there isn't anything like merely isolated bodies (or isolated 'whatevers'), then there is nothing to discuss. There is nothing to be asserted about dance's and performance's particular ontological condition. Dance and performance melt into the topological surface of melting affects—a connecting movement that doesn't even belong to the embodied human body alone.[31] Dance and performance emerge out of the same experiential continuum of variation, and into those most mixed-up—human and non-human, bodily and bodiless—spatiotemporal dimensions that dance and performance studies, and me along with my writings, seem to have some trouble conceptualizing.

Stillness. Try again: convey all possible and impossible heterogeneous ontologies, logics, geometries, choreographies, kinetics and aesthetics you can imagine; use them all to rethink human and non-human changing co-presences, interconnected sensations and merging writings, even before you get to dance and performance. Was this methodology ever to be named, then it would be called 'amphibiology', the only inhabitable sphere for *mattering* thought, open for all sorts of heterogeneous, not-yet-thought-through operative methodologies of exploring *mattering* thought. Openness. Close to the 'amphibian anthropology' Sloterdijk (2003) once mentioned as 'informal thinking', and according to which we are constantly making something of a dimensional pass into another. Even when we move the least we can, to not frighten 'becoming', as Deleuze (2003) once wrote.

Les devenirs. *De-place* Moving Places.

De-place moving places. Put co-attraction in the place of presence (as disappearing movement). Put changing change in the place of movement (as

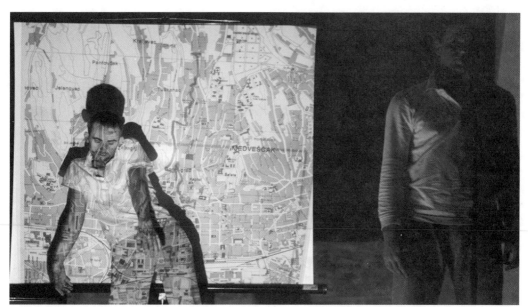

FIGURE 3. Martin Nachbar (*left*) and Jochen Roller. Martin Nachbar and Jochen Roller, *mnemonic non-stop: Ein Kartographisches Duet*, Steirischer Herbst, Graz/Austria, 2005. Photograph by Katrin Schoof.

disappearing presence). This will lead you to Baruch Spinoza (most quoted these days, but still very much uncaptured) and his writings on the body only in the pragmatic terms of its capacity for affecting or being affected, its capacity to step over thresholds. Instead of vanishing present bodies you get bodies as limit-attractions, simultaneously co-attracting and co-attracted, co-*absenting* and co-*presenting* along its varying virtual potentials. Try co-*incidence*: you get to affect. Keep writing: affected and affecting is an intensive body only co-*incident* (though not coinciding) with its charge of affect, provided affect is a never definitely fixed openness.

*OPENING*

*Notes*

1   André Lepecki (2004: 124–39) traces the genealogy and metamorphosis of this trope: from dance as 'ephemerality', a dance that should be accurately documented or else fall into complete forgetfulness (as it was diagnosed from about the late eighteenth century on—with and after Jean-Georges Noverre's 'mournful lament' about 'dance's flawed materiality'), until the current version of dance as 'disappearance', a dance that dismisses any documenting effort not only as unnecessary, but also as undesirable (dance's presence is still understood as perpetual self-erasure, but this time symmetric to a writing equally subject to the movement of perpetual *différance*—with and *after* Derrida's *trace*). May this essay move toward a reopening of the remaining ontological condition—*after*-Derrida—of dance and performance as 'disappearance' (in its latest versions appearing as historically, culturally and politically embodied 'disappearance').

2   '*Le partage du sensible*' in the original, alternatively translated as 'distribution of the sensible'. All quotations from Jacques Rancière's works are my translation of the French editions. Provided, as Rancière notes, we do not consider the aesthetic and literary core of politics 'as the perverse commandeering of politics by a will to art' (2000: 13), nor the political core of artistic creation as an intention of the artist to pursue a political programme. In fact, when he comes to rethink the relation between aesthetics and politics, Rancière dismisses the pertinence of distinctions between autonomy and submission, and radically questions what he calls the 'imaginary histories of artistic

"modernity"', lost in 'vain debates' that put 'art's autonomy' on one side, and its 'political submission' on the other (ibid.: 25). Taking us far back to Plato's *cité*, he claims there is an intrinsic *politicity* of the sensorial and an intrinsic *aestheticity* of politics specific to each particular time and to each particular place (not only during the 'mass age', where Walter Benjamin diagnosed an 'aesthetization of politics') (ibid.: 24). Without restricting politics and aesthetics to their mutual annulations, Rancière considers that figures of community are internal both to the possibilities of artistic creativity and to the possibilities of political stance. These figures are able to circulate as affects in non-art, in non-politics, and in every possible field of knowledge and practice. As a consequence, aesthetics and politics are, in Rancière's sense, always the place of conflict, of confrontation, or productive dissent. This is what Rancière calls a real condition for democracy: a non-authoritarian, non-'authorshiped' circulation of the senses, positions and parts played within a community.

3   At this point, we may recall Michel Foucault's genealogy of the human sciences conceived both as practices and as institutions (see *Les Mots et les Choses* [The Order of Things], 1966, where the author calls his genealogy an 'archaeology' of knowledge, a concept he developed later in *L'Archéologie du Savoir* [The Archaelogy of Knowledge], 1969). What is important to keep in mind in order to understand Rancière's reference to a possible analogy between his idea of aesthetics as partition of the sensible and Foucault's genealogical method (Rancière 2000: 13) is the fact that Foucault's project was neither to determine the transcendental a priori conditions of knowledge in a strictly Kantian sense, nor to describe the evolution of the human sciences toward a growing objectivity supposedly achieved by modern sciences. Rather, his goal was to study the human sciences' very conditions of possibility, understood as specific spatiotemporal configurations (we could as well call them 'partitions') in which specific conceptions of language, of representation modes, of beings and of things combine in hierarchies that give way to specific conceptions and practices of knowledge. Such conditions are not determined for all the times and places, but in a permanent process of configuration, deconfiguration and reconfiguration.

4   Rancière puts it as follows: 'No matter the specificity of the economic circuits along which they are displayed, artistic activities are not "an exception" over the other activities. They represent and reconfigure the partitioning displayed by other activities' (2000: 73).

5   This is, according to Brian Massumi, a recursive complex duration that is lost to our conscious awareness, but nevertheless constantly and recursively informs (and is constantly and recursively informed by) any elementary unit of thought. This has been experimentally confirmed:

> In famous studies in the 1970s, Benjamin Libet demonstrated that there is a half-second delay between the onset of brain activity and conscious awareness of the event. Cognitive scientists and theorists of consciousness have worried over this because, in brain terms, a half second is a very long time. [. . .] All kinds of things might be going on in autopilot as perception and reflection are taking off from chemical and electrical movements of matter. Thought lags behind itself. [. . .] All awareness emerges from a nonconscious thought-o-genic indistinguishable from movements of matter (2002: 195, 196).

This is where micro-perceptions emerge, which make thought think more than it thinks it does, I guess.

6   Massumi's (2002: 194) formulation reminds me of how Walter Benjamin referred to *his Angelus Novus*—Paul Klee's painting (1920), which became Benjamin's Angel of History.

7   Peter Sloterdijk refers to the human being as a 'topological enigma', a 'creature' that should ask us to constantly renew the question: 'Where is it in reality? On which latent scene does it operate as it does what it does?' (2003: 168).

8   See how Massumi describes interference and superposition between empirical and virtual dimensions: 'Without its passage into the empirical, the virtual world would be nothing lurking. Without the passing of the virtual into it, the empirical would functionally die. It would coincide so even-temperedly with its own unity and constancy that it would have no ontological room to manoeuvre: *entropic death by excess of success*' (2002: 159; emphasis added).

9   Drawing from Massumi again, on interference or resonation:

> It's not really discrete bodies and paths interacting. It is fields. Gravity is a field—a field of potential attraction, collision, orbit, of potential centripetal and centrifugal movements. All these potentials form such complex interference patterns when three fields overlap that a measure of indeterminacy creeps in. It's not that we just don't have a detailed enough knowledge to predict. Accurate prediction is impossible because *the indeterminacy* is objective (2003; emphasis added).

10 On 'relationality' as 'already in the world' and registering materially in our bodies, even before we become consciously aware of it, see William James (1996: 25, 42, 71–2).

11 What Massumi calls affect is the relationality inherent in every living thing:

> [a] two-sidedness *as seen from the side of the actual thing*, as couched in its perceptions and cognitions. Affect is *the virtual as point of view*, provided the visual metaphor is used guardedly. For affect is synesthetic, implying a participation of the senses in each other: the measure of a living thing's potential interactions is its ability to transform the effects of one sensory mode into those of another (2002: 35).

It should be underlined that Massumi's understanding of affect as intensity or potential connectedness owes quite a lot, as the author himself states (2003; 2002: 32), to the works of Henri Bergson, especially *Matter and Memory* (1988), Baruch Spinoza, *The Ethics* (1985), Gilles Deleuze and Félix Guattari, *Mille Plateaux. Capitalisme et Schizophrénie 2* [A Thousand Plateaus: Capitalism and Schizophrenia, VOL. 2] (1980), and to William James, *Essays in Radical Empiricism* (1996). Moreover, it is also indebted to their having been read together with recent theories of complexity and chaos.

12 If we keep following Massumi, we might accept that 'objects' could very well be just,

> anaesthetic specifications of the growth pain of perception's passing into and out of itself. The anaesthetic is the *perceived*, as distinguished from the perceiving: objects passing into empirical existence, sensation passing out of itself into that objectivity. [. . .] If the empirical is the anaesthetic, then the pain accompanying perception's passing forcefully into itself and continuing superempirically in flight from its objective quelling—what can this be but the *aesthetic*? (2002: 161).

13 A somewhat too long quotation may be helpful at this point, regarding the above-mentioned loop between 'primitive' and 'higher' forms of perception and cognition, so that we won't miss its far-reaching consequences for a reformulation of ongoing concepts of perception (that frequently draw a line/divide between natural and culturally mediated perceptions):

> The loop between 'primitive' perception and 'higher cognition' has been observed in [. . .] brain function. One of the most startling findings has been that a single neuron is capable of recognizing a face. /

> The feedback of 'higher' functions undermines the deconstructionist mistrust of 'naïve' or 'natural' perception. In deconstructivist architectural theory, this mistrust has often translated into an aversion to any talk of direct perception, shunned in favor of mediated readings. But, if social operations like recognizing a face or cultural operations of literate interpretation can dissolve back into direct perceptions, there is nothing to worry about. If there is never any possibility of raw experience to begin with, there is nothing to bracket or deconstruct. The most material of experience, the firing of a single neuron, is always already positively socio-cultural. Conversely, and perhaps more provocatively, *reading ceases to be a practice of mediation.* We are capable of operating socially and culturally directly on a level with matter. / It all becomes a question of modulation (Massumi 2002: 199).

14 About the interfusion of senses, see also philosopher and dance theorist Michel Bernard (2001: 101–21) who considers that our corporeality is mostly determined by the intersensorial modes in which our perception works. More precisely, the author posits a 'fictionary theory of sensation', exploring the idea that any sensorial experience, in its dynamics of subtle imbrications between sensation, expression and enunciation, is intrinsically fictionary.

15 As Massumi refers to it, the 'Libet Lag' (see note 5) determined that all 'awareness is "backdated"'. And though

> each thought experiences itself to have been at the precise moment the stimulus was applied, [. . . s]o the simplest perception of the simplest stimulus is already a fairly elaborate hoax, from the point of view of a theory of cognitive authenticity that sees truth in plain and present reflection. [. . .] The cognitive model would have to recognize that it, too, has been a matterful hallucination, on the half second installment plan (2002: 195).

16 Lepecki notes that 'such an ontology [the one attributed to dance] has a historical grounding' and that 'it exists only within the horizons of the mournful lament generated by the splitting of dancing and writing, a splitting propelled by the perception of movement and presence as markedly sentenced to disappearance' (2004: 137).

17 Massumi underlines that 'affect is now much more important for understanding power, even state power narrowly defined, than concepts like ideology.

Direct affect modulation takes the place of old-style ideology. [. . .] This post-ideological media power has been around at least since television matured as a medium [. . .]' (2003). Massumi further asserts that marketing itself, where words like 'connectibility' make careers nowadays, functions along affective lines. This is 'relational marketing', working on the grounds of affective contagion rather than by rational convincing: 'The ability of affect to produce an economic effect more swiftly and surely than economics itself means that affect is a real condition, an intrinsic variable of the late-capitalist system, as infrastructural as a factory' (2002: 45).

18 Concerning the possibility of analysing the effects of emerging affects, Massumi argues that 'affect is indeed unformed and unstructured, but that it is nevertheless highly organized and effectively analyzable (it is not entirely containable in knowledge but is analyzable in effect, as effect)' (2002: 206).

19 'Photology' is a term used here in reference to the project of documenting dance, as it emerged within early dance theory and within the frame of Western metaphysical tradition, namely in a sense analysed in detail by Lepecki: underlined is the fact that dance theory has largely developed out of a documenting effort where documentation turned into 'optical-descriptive obsession', echoing a 'mournful lament' (that same one that goes far back to the late eighteenth century) in the face of dance's ungraspable presence (2004: 124–39).

20 In a side note to a letter entitled 'Les Affects', included in a lecture text on collaboration, dance and performance theorist Myriam van Imshoot (2003: 342) imparts her desire to work on a co-conference project together with Jill Johnston (author and critic from New York who created a short series of performances, was deeply engaged in the arts and dance world of the 1960s, and was very close to the Judson Church 'family'). For the project, Imshoot would take Johnston's place, wearing the same jeans and imitating her silhouette as she appears on the cover photo of her anthology Marmalade Me (1971), and they would cross their visions on the dance of the 1960s. The project has yet to be realized, but Imshoot maintains that she is very enthusiastic about the idea of co-writing a text that would transcend the double rhetoric of the 'I've been to it, there you are, here's my experience' that can only take place with the 'Oh, if only I had been to it, and that's exactly what I regret.'

21 Conception, direction and choreography by Olga de Soto, in collaboration with Vincent Druguet. Co-production: ABAROA/Coto de Caza asbl, KunstenFESTI-

VAL des Arts, Centre National de la danse-Pantin. Commissioned by Culturgest, Lisbon 2002. Premiered at the *Centre National de la Danse* of Paris, on 6 December 2004.

22 Ballet *en deux tableaux*, choreographed by Roland Petit after Jean Cocteau's libretto, premiered at the Théâtre des Champs Elysées just after the Second World War, 25 June 1946. Dancers: Nathalie Philippart and Jean Babilée.

23 Co-production of Steirischer Herbst Graz, Klapstuk #12 Leuven. Premiered at Steirischer Herbst, Graz/Austria, 15 October 2005.

24 Developed in the 1950s, the technique of the *dérive* was conceived as a way of proposing an alternative mode of moving through a city, namely remapping urban spaces according to their psycho-geographic relevance. It should be noted that the use Martin Nachbar and Jochen Roller make of this technique largely transforms it into something other, far away from its well-known limits.

25 Keep thinking about this when, for example, reading Rancière:

> Think also about the long and contradictory history of rhetoric and the model of the 'good speaker' along the monarchic age, where 'excellence of word' was the imaginary attribute of supreme power, and nevertheless remained available to display a democratic function, lending its canonical forms and consecrated images to the subversive break through of non-authorised speakers onto the public scene (2000: 23).

26 About the interaction between discourse, relational psycho-affective dynamics, and the biological functioning of the speakers, see Boris Cyrulnik (1995).

27 Let me borrow some words from Gilles Deleuze and Félix Guattari:

> Proust used to say: 'masterpieces are written in a sort of foreign language.' It is like stuttering, but stuttering in language itself and not only in speaking. To be a foreigner in one's own language and not only as someone who speaks a foreign language. To be bilingual, but within one and the same language, in the absence of any dialect or patois (1980: 124, 125; translation by the author).

28 For an example of 'navigating' movement along writing, see the works of Hélène Cixous. Deleuze (2002: 320–2) refers to the writings of this author as 'stroboscopic', '*une écriture stroboscopique*' that merges fiction, theory, critique and colours in a way that produces unknown tones, using words to form vari-

able figures and to make us follow vertiginous speeds of connection in the process of reading.

29 Massumi points out that '[w]ords, numbers, and grammars recursively-dura-tionally smudge as messily as anything. They reenter the relational contin-uum. This means that no matter how conventional or even stereotyped they may be, they never really go stale' (2002: 198).

30 By the way, in Plato's partition of the citizens' activities into verbal and bodily practice (see Rancière 2000: 15, 16), the choreographic form comes as the 'good' one, countering theatre (a movement space where bodies double in scene simulacra) and writing (a non-moving surface of mute signs like paint-ing). Joining dance and singing in the rhythm of the chorus, the choreographic form corresponds, according to Plato, to the expression of authentic move-ment appropriate to communitarian bodies.

31 Quoting Massumi one last time: 'The concepts of nature and culture need se-rious reworking, in a way that expresses the irreducible alterity of the non-human in and through its active connection to the human and vice versa. Let matter be matter, brains be brains, jellyfish be jellyfish, and culture be nature, in irreducible alterity and infinite connection' (2002: 39).

*References*

BERGSON, Henri. 1988 [1896]. *Matter and Memory* (W. Scott Palmer and Nancy Mar-garet Paul trans.). New York: Zone Books.

BERNARD, Michel. 2001. *De la création chorégraphique* [Choreographic Creation]. Paris: Centre National de la Danse.

CYRULNIK, Boris. 1995 [1991]. *De la parole comme d'une molécule. Entretiens avec Emile Noël* [Word, Just as in Molecule: Interviews with Emil Noël]. Paris: Eschel.

DELEUZE, Gilles. 2002. *L'île déserte et autres textes. Textes et entretiens 1953–1974* [Desert Islands and Other Texts: 1953–1974]. Paris: Minuit.

———. 2003 [1990]. *Pourparlers* [Negotiations]. Paris: Minuit.

——— and Félix Guattari. 1980. *Mille Plateaux. Capitalisme et Schizophrénie 2* [A Thousand Plateaus: Capitalism and Schizophrenia, VOL. 2]. Paris: Les Editions de Minuit.

DE Soto, Olga. 2004. 'historie(s). journal de bord (extraits)' [history(s). a daily log (extracts)]. Performance notes. Bruxelles.

Foucault, Michel. 1966. Les Mots et les Choses [The Order of Things]. Paris: Éditions Gallimard.

———. 1969. L'Archéologie du Savoir [The Archaelogy of Knowledge]. Paris: Éditions Gallimard.

James, William. 1996 [1912]. Essays in Radical Empiricism. Lincoln: University of Nebraska Press.

Lepecki, André (ed.). 2004. 'Inscribing Dance', in Of the Presence of the Body: Essays on Dance and Performance Theory. Middletown, CT: Wesleyan University Press, pp. 124–39.

Libet, Benjamin. 1985. 'Unconscious Cerebral Initiative and the Role of Conscious Will in Voluntary Action'. Behavioural and Brain Sciences 8: 529–66.

Massumi, Brian. 2002. Parables for the Virtual: Movement, Affect, Sensation. Durham, NC: Duke University Press.

———. 2003. 'Navigating Movements: An Interview with Brian Massumi, by Mary Zournazi', 21MC Magazine. Available at: www. 21cmagazine.com/issue2/-massumi.html (accessed 27 October 2004).

Nachbar, Martin. 2005. 'How to Become a Trespasser or How to Produce a Crack in the Map'. Available at: www.e-tcetera.be (accessed 1 October 2006).

Phelan, Peggy. 1993. Unmarked: The Politics of Performance. London: Routledge.

———. 1997. Mourning Sex: Performing Public Memories. London: Routledge.

Rancière, Jacques. 1998. La chair des mots. Politiques de l'écriture [The Flesh of Words: Politics of Writing]. Paris: Galilée.

———. 2000. Le partage du sensible. Esthétique et Politique [The Distribution of the Sensible: The Politics of Aesthetics]. Paris: La Fabrique-éditions.

Roller, Jochen. 2005. 'Walking and Dancing-Locomotion in the Example of "mnemonic non-stop"'. Available at: www.jochenroller.de (accessed 1 October 2006).

Sloterdijk, Peter. 2000 [1989]. La mobilisation infinie. Vers une critique de la cinétique politique [The Infinite Mobilization: Toward a Critique of Political Kinetics] (Hans Hildenbrand trans.). Paris: Christian Bourgois Editeur.

———. 2003 [2001]. Ni le soleil ni la mort. Jeu de piste sous forme de dialogues avec Hans-Jürgen Heinrichs [Neither Sun nor Death. Scavenger Hunt in the Shape of

Dialogues with Hans-Jürgen Heinrichs] (Olivier Mannoni trans.). Paris: Pauvert.

SPINOZA, Baruch. 1985 [1677]. 'The Ethics'. *Collected Works*. 2 VOLS (Edwin Curley ed. and trans.). Princeton: Princeton University Press.

VAN IMSHOOT, Myriam. 2003. 'Lettres sur la collaboration'. *Etre ensemble. Figures de la communauté en danse depuis le XX siècle* ['Letters on Collaboration'. Being Together. Figures of Community in Dance after the 20th Century]. Paris: Centre National de la Danse, pp. 335–66.

RELATIONAL GESTURES:
*ALLITÉRATIONS* AND THE LIMITS OF THE CHOREOGRAPHIC

NOÉMIE SOLOMON

> The dance begins insensibly and the suspicion is for-med that it will remain impossible to decide where and when, in truth, it will have begun (Monnier and Nancy 2005).

The philosopher is on stage. When Jean-Luc Nancy, carefully reciting his text, inadvertently leans onto the odd table in front of him, the unstable surface gives way under his body. The shift of weight is sudden, barely perceptible, a slight stumble over a few thoughts on dance, yet it resonates vividly with the gestures of the other bodies located next to him—as Mathilde Monnier, Dimitri Chamblas and Erikm propose unexpected shapes and functions through a series of movements, sounds and still acts. In the midst of these co-gestures, the philosopher drifts away from a steady and coherent locus of enunciation. The performers' gestures emerge as driven relational edge-plays: the selves enacted here are pressed to a limit as the relational gestures impinge upon each other, working toward a suspension, dislocation and reinvention of subjectivity. These poetic functions occur within *Allitérations*, a creative collaboration between the choreographer Mathilde Monnier and the philosopher

Jean-Luc Nancy, realized through a performance and a related publication. In this essay, I propose to map the relational gestures at work in *Allitérations* as a series of encounters at the intersection of dance and philosophy that reimagine the space of the choreographic.

## Shaping Subjectivities

*Allitérations*, which toured extensively across Europe between 2002 and 2004,[1] stages four bodies, each performing in relation to a malleable latex table. As the performers enter the scene, they take a place behind one of the four tables located side by side at the front edge of the stage. Starting silent and immobile, the piece unfolds as the performers' gestures extend toward each other, deforming and reforming the tables as prostheses or foldings of the bodies. Thus, Chamblas shapes the surface of a table so it becomes a box, a supple and unsteady pocket enveloping his body, and the dancer repeatedly pushes his head in the direction of Nancy, stretching the surface to its limit of expansion, engaging it as a relational threshold. The movements and sounds seem to drag the performer toward an outside, toward an other, propelling the body ahead of itself and exposing a gesture as that which happens always already outside of a body. Enunciations of gesture are constantly interrupted, suspended: the stroboscopic music echoes Nancy's fragmented reading; Monnier's unfinished and lingering gestures as she hangs at the edge of a table resonate with and distort Nancy's densely imagistic text. As they slip away and extend themselves in relation to another (to a body, to a table, to a sound), the moving, talking and silent bodies are stretched, disfigured, refigured. The relational gestures compel the bodies toward limits, initiating and sustaining multiple kinetic connections. This relational force proposes a restless performing 'self', one that appears constantly 'out of itself'. Through its multiple performances of relationality, *Allitérations* thus works toward undoing coherences of meaning and experience; the performing bodies are grasped as moving singularities whose choreographic labour constantly reappropriates and expropriates a body never fully complete within itself.

The performance seeks to expose different bodies, techniques and elements of composition on the same plane of experience, next to each other. Relational gestures thus appear as the co-sharing of many perspectives and experiences around text, silence, movement, sound; as an exploration across the correspondences, divergences and tensions between dance, music, philosophy. The simultaneous occurrence of these phenomena is crucial here: as the diverse gestures unfold in the same time period, subjectivity is reimagined through synchronicity. The dancers never actually touch, yet their crossing are deeply affective, discursive and para-somatic, and thus impinge on each other's incorporeal surfaces. The components of the piece first appear as unrelated, different in themselves, remarkable—that is, singular. They do not rely on each other: there is no dependency or causal relation between a dancer, and a table, and a sound, and a spectator. Yet, the 'and' acts as a connective gesture, an in-between, a site of multiplicity, that which brings into relation. In this respect, the singularities at work in *Alliterations* can be defined after Gilles Deleuze as 'some elements that can be extended close to another, so as to obtain a connection' (1991: 94). Relational gestures coexist: they emerge on a plane of synchronicity. Paradoxically, that which unites these gestures—their simultaneous occurrence—also scatters them as it works toward saturating, reflecting and dispersing sense. As the synchronic gestures collide or echo each other, they encroach on one another, get mixed up and teased apart, bit by bit. This overlapping introduces gaps between Chamblas' production of movement and its perception, between Nancy's lecture and its signification. Instants arise where the text does not make sense any more: one can only listen to the words, to their vibrations, as they resonate with the sounds emanating from Erikm's gestures, and with Monnier's throbbing breaths from her hasty running in place, while negotiating her improbable balance on the wobbly support. While the juxtaposition of heterogeneous elements dislocates meaning and sensibility, it also produces a subtle intensive rhythm that composes new modalities of relating, new bodies. The singular modes of relationality of these synchronic gestures thus reinvent subjectivity by proposing multiple ways for the gestures to connect as they brush against each other.

The relational gestures at work throughout *Alliterations* propose subjectivity as a 'practical' issue, such as described by Gilles Deleuze and Félix Guattari (1987), who outline a body as it is shaped by its potentialities. Here, the binding of philosophical and performance practices explores the potential to dislocate, shift and create bodies; to invent relationalities, assemblages, becomings and processes of subjectification. The piece thus stages performing subjects as they drift away from stable loci of enunciation and experience a series of transformations. The bodies are here constantly made or formed through the experiment: the things it can perform, the linkages it can establish, the becomings it can undergo. 'It is not enough to think in order to be', argues Guattari: the performing 'subject' is not a disembodied cogito, but acquires its forms and cannot be dissociated from the imperatives of experimentation (1989: 23).[2] Inventing and doing are precisely what constitute oneself. And if, as a philosophical concept, 'the subject' can only be defined in terms of the functions it fulfils, Deleuze proposes 'to build the new functions and discover new fields that make it useless or inadequate', a task that calls for artistic experimentations and the creation of new sensory aggregates (1992: 285). In this respect, one might argue that the expressive functions at work in *Allitérations* call for modes of subjectification rather than for philosophical and dancing 'subjects'. These singular modes here function as dynamic concepts, consisting in 'the production of a way of existing that can't be equated with a subject' (Deleuze 1995: 98). In *A Thousand Plateaus: Capitalism and Schizophrenia*, Deleuze and Guattari have described these phenomena as 'haecceities'. Haecceities are distinct from a person, a substance or a subject, as they evoke a modality of being at work in a process of becoming, a process marked by facticity and 'thisness'. In *Allitérations*, these modes are singularly proposed by the work's relational gestures that trace a body as a 'set of non-subjectified affects' (Deleuze and Guattari 1987: 262). In this respect, the work could be located within a stream of contemporary dance practices such as those described by André Lepecki in *Exhausting Dance*, in which 're-thinking the subject in terms of the body is precisely the task of choreography [. . .] a task that is always already in dialogue with critical theory and philosophy' (2006: 5). One might thus grasp the choreographic bodies at work within *Allitérations* as they refigure philosophical and dancing 'subjects' as haecceities: these dynamic modes are always already assemblages and offer potential to establish connections with an outside; to create linkages with other bodies and to enter into composition with other intensities.

In the middle of the performance, Nancy recites:

The other, there, near in its distance, tensed, folded, unfolded, unlaunched, resonates in my joints. I do not perceive her/him properly by the eyes, the hearing, or the touch. I do not perceive; I resonate.

> Here I am curved of her/his curve, inclined of her/his angle,
> launched of her/his momentum. Her/his dance has started instead
> of me. He or she has displaced me, has almost replaced me (in Mon-
> nier and Nancy 2005: 139).

What do these words suggest? What can a 'curved', 'launching' or 'resonating'
philosopher do? In this passage, Nancy sounds nearly 'out of himself', affectively displaced by the gestures of the dancer. One might argue that we witness an instance of kinesthetic empathy: the performing body appears deeply
moved by the dancers, transported by their kinetic force. From this radical
relational stance, this singular affective encounter, language begins to dissolve: the words no longer assign stable meanings, nor impose an order for
things, nor act as a functional apparatus of representation. One might argue
that Nancy becomes 'a foreigner in [his] own language, tracing a sort of line
of flight for words' (Deleuze 1995: 41). It happens momentarily: the voice of
the philosopher becomes odd, distant, introducing delays and gaps between
the signs and their significations, the words and their apprehensions. One
can recognize the form of the spoken expression but cannot link this form
to a stable meaning. It happens not as an affection of the philosopher, but
rather as language itself becoming deeply affective and intensive. These singular gestures draw out processes of decodification and deterritorialization
for the linguistic body: they trace lines of flight for a discourse on dance, for
words, for movements. Such moves directly echo Baruch Spinoza's joyful
philosophical question as reformulated by Deleuze: 'What can a body do?'
(Deleuze 1990: 218). This line of practical philosophy proposes an active and
affirmative understanding of thought from which the potentialities of a body
can be drawn out not so much in its power to act, as agency, but rather in
terms of its power (*puissance*) to affect and be affected by other bodies: 'what
can a body do is the nature and the limits of its power to be affected' (ibid.:
226). One might argue that the relational gestures at work in *Allitérations* act
as an empirical exploration of bodies, by staging multiple ways in which the
haecceities interact and encounter: the performance exposes these bodies'
processes of composition, decomposition, compatibility and conflict. Nancy
and Monnier's enunciation of sounds, words, postures, silences or movements
alternately converge—becoming compossible—and diverge—echoing each
other. The co-gestures emerge sharing a vibratory existence, an ex-stasis.
*Allitérations* thus invents new expressive functions, new modes of composition

where art and philosophy echo what each other *does* and hence come into relation by the impinging of one onto another, 'as separate melodic lines in constant interplay with one another' (Deleuze 1992: 285). In this respect, relational gestures draw an autopoetics of subjectification as a process of many propositions for difference, variation and metamorphosis: they reimagine potentialities for encountering transversal corporealities.

*Across the Table*

For Monnier, *Allitérations* constitutes 'neither a danced conference, nor a performance, nor a lecture, and even less an improvisation' (Monnier and Nancy 2005: 16). In a subsequent published dialogue with Nancy, she claims: '[*Allitérations*] would rather be an essay where we cross our modes of expression on a common basis, which is the table' (in ibid.: 16). The work combines diverse forms of textual and gestural exchanges across a series of e-mails, conversations, letters and movements directed toward each other as these intersect on the slippery surface of the table. *Allitérations* is initiated by a text written by Nancy in 2000 entitled 'The Separation of Dance', which develops an idea of dance as birth, as the detachment of the body from the plane of the ground through its multiple unfoldings that open up toward the world. Yet the work *Allitérations* also encompasses Monnier's dancing response, as she sees in the writing 'an indirect correspondence with a choreography', and culminates with the publication of a book of the same title in 2005 (in ibid.: 14).[3] Throughout the creative and critical process, the table seems to play a vital role, functioning as a moving platform across which words, bodies, movements and sounds coexist. The table can here be grasped as a connective membrane, an edge between the different bodies, as it simultaneously folds them onto themselves and onto each other. The edge of a table: a connective plane that forms a moving boundary between the performing bodies. The performers' actions transform the tables into little stages, as if they were many intimate dancing territories, spaces which catalyse the singular encounters between skins, sounds, clothes, rubber and their respective motions of speed, slowness, rest. Erikm converts his table into a sonic tool hosting his body and electronic devices; Nancy gradually unfolds the rubber along the metallic structure until the table becomes a wobbly box; Monnier and Chamblas radically alter the aspect and function of their tables until they become unstable, vertical surfaces. The tables lose their proper functions to become

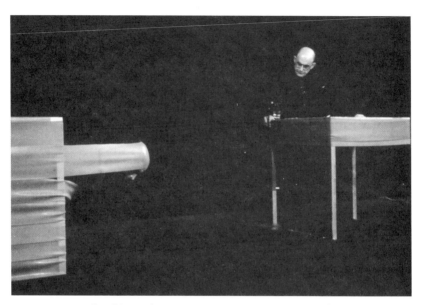

FIGURE 1. Dimitri Chamblas and Jean-Luc Nancy in *Allitérations*, 2002/2003. Photograph by Marc Coudrais; courtesy of the Centre chorégraphique national de Montpellier.

FIGURE 2. Mathilde Monnier and a technician in *Allitérations*, 2002/2003. Photograph by Marc Coudrais; courtesy of the Centre chorégraphique national de Montpellier.

improbable, uncanny or impossible things. The hard surface becomes flexible, folds itself to welcome a body, to host the hollow of a vibration, a movement, a silence. In this respect, the table constitutes a 'kind of matrix that is neither controllable nor comfortable'; it becomes an absurd table, one that offers nothing but an unsteady yet connective edge for body-thoughts (ibid.: 16).

One might see the table in *Allitérations* as a site that distributes the different relational gestures between the performing bodies, which answer or echo each other around the question of the dancing body's singular mode of enunciation of sense. Nancy refers to sense neither as the intelligible nor as the sensible, for meaning or perception, but as that which escapes or emerges from these distinctions. In reminding us that meaning is usually understood as a completion or a result, the philosopher proposes that the dancing body in *Allitérations* is precisely that which 'makes sense outside of sense', thus constantly reopening new directions for signification (Nancy in Monnier and Nancy 2005). The invocation of dance as a movement out of discourse and toward the sensate, an extra-rational movement altering the very way language and sense are apprehended, is actually one that has occurred throughout the project of Modernity. Various key philosophical texts, from Nietzsche to Nancy, including Valéry, Didi-Huberman and others, have cast dance as a potential for logical alteration: one could indeed follow philosophy's many gestures of exception, exclusion, fascination and oblivion in regard to choreographic creation, where the dancing gesture emerges always already at the very limits of philosophy, language and signification.[4] Yet Nancy's philosophical invocation of dance as a sense outside of sense is given here in proximity to the very force and practice that would dissolve philosophical enunciations. According to Nancy, the text he performs night after night is 'written in a certain tension toward dance' as it itself 'changes, fluctuates, stretches, folds or jumps on place' (ibid.: 17). In this respect, *Allitérations* stages the repetition and the exhaustion of sense, the sense outside of sense, as the dancing bodies offer possibilities to release what language has closed in an effort to secure meaning. What the choreographic gestures seem to do here is not to add to a systematic critique of language, but rather to propose new artistic functions for a (always already linguistic) body by shaping sensorial constellations in proximity to a philosophy in movement.

Moreover, the table in *Allitérations* seems to occupy a particular stance toward the question of the beginning: its surface enacts a singular tension between gestures of pure originality and those working toward the retaining of sense. During the performance, Nancy's text evokes dance as birth, as sheer invention in which the table seems to provide a fresh terrain each time, a sort of *tabula rasa*. Nancy writes to Monnier about his excitement at performing the piece: 'That is why I like to re-take (re-do) *Allitérations* with you and the performers: in the passage to the act and at each actualization, the beginning is a new beginning, without reserve' (ibid.: 79). At stake here is a recurrent obsession in the philosopher's discourse that sees dance as an ever-new beginning. Whereas Nancy admits he generally never reads his philosophical texts again, what fascinates him in the experience of performing is precisely this possibility of starting out anew. Furthermore, the title of the work also emphasizes an opening gesture. Indeed, 'alliteration' is a figure of speech that defines the repetition or redundancy of the first consonant, of the first sound. The piece reiterates and plays with different words and gestures in close connection with each other, while coming back to the surface of the table each time, repeating initial thoughts via a series of assonances and consonances. As the performance begins again and again, the repeated relational gestures cause the performance to stutter. Monnier also describes the dancing body as the place whereby sense escapes, yet she situates her practice in the movement of withholding sense, proposing a slightly different temporality for the dancing gesture:

> I have the impression that my work as a choreographer and a dancer is first to hold, to withhold (and to write as well) sense in this escaping [*échappée . . .*] Dance would be this art that labors to withhold the escaping of the movement in the body, and at the same time (simultaneously) to give sense to that which seems to escape (in Monnier and Nancy 2005: 18–19).

As dialogue, *Allitérations* explores a tension between Nancy's ever-new beginning and Monnier's holding onto sense, between the boundless enthusiasm of the philosopher as novice dancer and the 'fatalism' of the experienced practitioner of dance who sees its inevitable re-inclusion within sense. Between the two, the table offers a creative malleability, acting as affective membrane and nervous vector. This is a space in which the plane of the table as a ground of fresh inscription, the *tabula rasa* as virgin terrain, is disturbed. For here there can be no sense in which dance is separable from a scriptural discourse, but only a sense in which dance emerges in an unstable plane of conjunction between language and movement. Once again, the table functions as the limit of the many relational gestures, all at once accumulating, dispersing, retaining and inventing sense.

The table in *Allitérations* therefore appears as a vital ground for the choreographic, a critical and creative plane that composes new bodies. This gesture can be seen in the context of a stream of aesthetic practices: the table has indeed been a recurrent object in the European dance scene over the last decade, and one might suggest it has played an elemental role in the radical refiguring of the choreographic, within works by choreographers such as Xavier Le Roy, Meg Stuart and Boris Chartmatz, to name but a few.[5] The table constitutes a foundational platform in the history of thought and the disciplining of the bodies upon which scriptural economies and epistemologies have formed, a plane upon which their spatialization rests. The multiple uses of the table at work within contemporary creation seem to echo and subvert the modern project of Choreography—the writing of dance—which was itself inscribed upon a table.[6] Indeed, Choreography's table has functioned as a teleological apparatus upon which the *maître de ballet* writes the steps of the dances to be performed by absent bodies: by outlining the disciplinary boundaries of dance, Choreography establishes the authority of the dance text whose discourse overlaps, seeks out and reinforces movement itself. In *Allitérations*, the table is constantly remodelled via a series of artistic operations, and appears as a moving limit between words and bodies, virtual and actual, exposing an always-already textured surface. One might thus argue that *Allitérations* acknowledges the table as a constitutive plane of both philosophy and dance, and furthermore seeks to redefine the foundations and the limits of this ground. In this respect, the work not only stages the table as a common ground between dance and philosophy, between different bodies, but as an initial plane that must be destabilized, dematerialized and reshaped in order for the relational gestures to compose new, hybrid subjectivities. The table in *Allitérations* can thus be grasped as a prosthetic operation, a material and meaningful site for discursive and gestural play— a site of creative and critical contraband between dance and philosophy.

*Toward a Choreographic* Désœuvrement

*Allitérations* gestures at the edges of the choreographic, toward a virtual and utopian space shaped by its multiple experimentations, yet it does so while rendering the various failures and deceptions at work. Thus, the relational gestures implement a constant negotiation between agency and the potential for transformation, a tightening and loosening of the disciplinary constraints and thereby the orders of power that shape subjectivity. By unworking and reinventing sense and subjectivity, the multiple relational experiments at work in *Allitérations* as previously described enact a *désœuvrement*, an existential condition tied to the withdrawal of the work. The French word *désœuvrement* is articulated around the notion of 'œuvre'—work, body of work or artwork—and proposes a negative yet subtly active process that implies a range of meanings—idleness, inoperative, undoing, unfunctioning, worklessness, being at a loose end, a state of being without work, unoccupied—while suggesting the existential malaise associated with the very absence of work. It describes the material, corporeal, psychic, affective states of the one who has no work, as put forth by the writings of Maurice Blanchot and Georges Bataille. In referring to *désœuvrement* as a task that implies an active negation, those authors reveal an ambiguous and affirmative potential for inertia and corporeal inactivity. Unworking suggests a form of labour that would not be characterized by work itself, but rather its active absence:

> If action ('doing') is (as Hegel says) negativity, then there is still the problem of knowing whether the negativity of someone who 'doesn't have anything more to do' disappears or remains in a state of 'unemployed negativity.' As for me, I can only decide in one way, since I am exactly this 'unemployed negativity' [. . .] I think of my life—or better yet, its abortive condition, the open wound that my life is—as itself constituting a refutation of a closed System (Bataille in Baugh 2003: 123).

When the doing is done, when there is nothing left to do, being must exist in a state of *unemployed negativity*. Here, in his letter to Kojève, Bataille proposes a radical negation where that which no longer has anything to negate is affirmed. As the performing body is unable to invest itself in activity, it discloses a surplus of nothingness: the activity constitutes the very absence of the work as it produces itself throughout the work.

FIGURE 3. Dimitri Chamblas and Mathilde Monnier in *Al-litérations*, 2002/2003. Photograph by Marc Coudrais; courtesy of the Centre chorégraphique national de Montpellier.

If the multiple relational gestures at work in *Allitérations* emerge through the interweaving and the sharing of singularities—singularities that are always-already other, shared and exposed—one might argue that the repetition and the exhaustion of these gestures radically undoes or unworks not only the possibility of a stable and circumscribable subjectivity, but the stability of the performance as a single 'work'. 'The work, as soon as it becomes a work [. . .] must be abandoned at this limit,' says Nancy elsewhere (1991: 121). In *Allitérations*, the choreographic emerges as a common plane: it is posed in exteriority through the singular articulations between the performers and constitutes this being-together disclosed by moments of stillness, silence and nothingness. The common plane is at the limit; it *is* the limit. The choreographic is thus at the very limits of language, as it exceeds the horizon of signification. There is communication, but one that exceeds representation: there is sharing and co-gesture. This sharing happens precisely through the multiple interruptions that unwork choreographic labour, through *désœuvrement* as that which 'before or beyond the work, withdraws from the work, and which, no longer having to do either with production or with completion, encounters interruption, fragmentation, suspension' (ibid.: 31).

*Allitérations* epitomized a phenomenon of the European dance scene: it made manifest a correspondence which had long been felt within dance communities of the vital relation between contemporary practices of dance and contemporary philosophical speculation. In this respect, the conjunction of dance and philosophy within *Allitérations* seemed to answer a desire or demand for an epistemological claim long held within dance. The staging of a dialogue between dance and philosophy couldn't have been more literally rehearsed, embodied and enacted. As such, *Allitérations* carried a set of expectations for the release of potentialities for the creative and critical practice of dance itself. But what worked about *Allitérations* was perhaps its unworking. Once the possibilities for bodies to relate are exhausted, the performance enters the space that Blanchot describes: 'When there is nothing, it is this nothing itself which can no longer be negated. It affirms, keeps on affirming, and it states nothingness as being, as inertia [*désœuvrement*] of being' (1982: 110). Moments of boredom, of failure, of being stuck, of exhaustion, of repetition, of dance hoping for discourse, recognition, of philosophy hoping for an escape route, something beyond signification. These moments powerfully traverse the work, as the performing bodies increasingly renounce directed trajectories and focused aims, and stand, toward the end, barely immobile next to the tables. Inertia thus emerges as the accumulation of relational gestures and intersecting forces, as affective and existential stillness. In this space of unworking, *Allitérations* exposes a necessity for dance and philosophy not only to refigure the grounds of their correspondence, but to share the production of transversal subjectivities; to co-invent potentialities for bodies and new ways of existing through—and as—performance.

*Notes*

1   *Allitérations* was performed many times across Europe between 2002 and 2004 with slightly different configurations and numbers of performers. My analysis is based on a version seen live at the Centre Beaubourg, Paris, in 2003, and a contemporary video of the work. The set design is by Annie Tolleter and the light design by Eric Wurtz.

2   Translation from French of this text and *Allitérations* (2005) by the author.

3   The book includes four different sections: extensive email correspondence between Mathilde Monnier and Jean-Luc Nancy; a dialogue from 2001 around the question of the solo (originally published in Claire Rousier's *Le solo: Une figure singulière de la modernité en danse* [Solo: A Singular Figure of Modernity in Dance], 2002); a three-voice conversation between Monnier, Nancy and Claire Denis, who made documentaries on both Monnier's and Nancy's practices (*Vers Nancy* [2003] and *Vers Mathilde* [2004]); and finally a re-transcription of the sixth version of the text Nancy recites during the performance.

4   On this, see Paul Valéry's 'La philosophie de la danse' (The Philosophy of Dance, 1956); Georges Didi-Huberman's *Le Danseur des solitudes* (The Dancers of Solitudes, 2006) and Stéphane Mallarmé's *Ballets* (1945).

5   The work of Xavier Le Roy might be particularly explicit in this respect, as two of his pieces which one might consider as emblematic of the contemporary European dance scene (*Produits de Circonstances* [Product of Circumstances, 1999] and *Self-Unfinished* [1998]) stage the table as a key element of the choreography.

6   On this, see Chapter 2 of André Lepecki (2006).

*References*

BAUGH, Bruce. 2003. *French Hegel: From Surrealism to Postmodernism*. New York: Routledge.

BLANCHOT, Maurice. 1982 [1955]. *The Space of Literature* (Ann Smock trans.). Lincoln: University of Nebraska Press.

DELEUZE, Gilles. 1990 [1968]. *Expressionism in Philosophy: Spinoza* (Martin Joughin trans.). New York: Zone Books.

———. 1991 [1989]. 'A Philosophical Concept . . .', in Jean-Luc Nancy and Eduardo Cadava (eds), *Who Comes after the Subject?* New York: Routledge, pp. 94–5.

———. 1992 [1985]. 'Mediators', in Jonathan Crary and Sanford Kwinter (eds), *Incorporations*. New York: Zone Books, pp. 280–95.

———. 1995 [1990]. *Negotiations*. New York: Columbia University Press.

DELEUZE, Gilles and Félix Guattari. 1987 [1980]. *A Thousand Plateaus: Capitalism and Schizophrenia* (Brian Massumi trans.), VOL. 2. Minneapolis: University of Minnesota Press.

DIDI-HUBERMAN, Georges. 2006. *Le danseur des solitudes* [The Dancers of Solitudes]. Paris: Minuit.

GUATTARI, Félix. 1989. *Cartographies schizoanalitiques* [Schizoanalytical Cartographies]. Paris: Galilé.

LEPECKI, André. 2006. *Exhausting Dance: Performance and the Politics of Movement*. New York: Routledge.

MALLARMÉ, Stéphane. 1945 [1886]. 'Ballets and Autre étude de danse' [Ballets and Other Study of Dance], in *Œuvres* [Works]. Paris: Gallimard, pp. 303–09.

MONNIER, Mathilde and Jean-Luc Nancy. 2005. *Allitérations* [Alliterations]. Paris: Galilée.

NANCY, Jean-Luc. 1991 [1982]. *The Inoperative Community* (Peter Connor, Lisa Garbus, Michael Holland and Simona Sawhney trans.). Minneapolis: University of Minnesota Press.

ROUSIER, Claire (ed.). 2002. *Le solo: Une figure singulière de la modernité en danse* [Solo: A Singular Figure of Modernity in Dance]. Paris: Centre national de la danse.

VALÉRY, Paul. 1956 [1936]. 'La philosophie de la danse' [The Philosophy of Dance], in *Œuvres 1, Variétés* [Works I, Varieties]. Paris: Gallimard, pp. 1390–1403.

*SCÈNE* AND CONTEMPORANEITY

FRÉDÉRIC POUILLAUDE

Of the contemporary, there would be exposition. And perhaps even *scène*.

In this *scène*,[1] possibly choreographic, it is the spirit of the time, the figure of the epoch, which would obscurely give itself to be read. Human time would have an essential capacity to draw images of itself, to figure itself (*s'auto-figurer*), to stage itself; certain products traditionally named 'works of art' would be the privileged medium of this operation. So that having to talk of dance and of the contemporary, I would only have to try to decipher within the works produced and the milieu of their existence—precisely, the *scène*— something that could be read as an image of time, of *our* time.

This is precisely the path I will not follow.

For two reasons essentially. First—and here I am only suggesting a theory that goes further than my argument—what we hear *today* under the empty term of the 'contemporary' might consist of nothing else but the known impossibility of epochal figuration,[2] the inability of our time to represent itself. We do not believe any more in the *unity* of a time that is *ours*, in the possibility of a unifying and figurative presentation of *our* time. The names strategically given to this situation are multiple and ideologically heterogeneous: 'end of master narratives', 'end of utopias', 'death of art', 'postmodernity', 'end of

the avant-garde', 'end of History' . . . What is exposed through the monoto-
nous chant of loss and the heterogeneity of the elegiac discourse is perhaps
more determined than one believes: it is not History as such that would be
lost, but the capacity of time, of *our* time, to figure itself and to take hold of
itself as a One, a unity. In this apparatus (*dispositif*), the place of art, or rather
of a certain diagnosis made of its state, is, as one suspects, crucial. As the traditional authority of time's figuration and the epoch's presentation, art must
logically be at the centre of the crisis. Dead a first time, with Hegel, in the
grandiose completion of its ontotheological mission, this spectre would have
survived for some time until its secularization. Giving itself other tasks, it
would have found in the modernist discourse and the figure of the avant-
garde a form of theology, substitutive and atheist, able to guarantee its his-
torico-political inscription and its responsibility before time. But the
substitution would itself have lingered; indeed, today the spectre would be
dead, not because it would have achieved its mission, but because of the fading of all teleological structure able to assign to it a function. Art would have
entered a 'gaseous' regime (see Michaud 2003), untied from any responsibility,
floating among the infinite possibilities, and answering to no authority but
the play of institutional recognition, of empty novelty and subversion, immediately integrated and recycled by the Market or the State. Art would have
lost all power (*puissance*) of epochal figuration, and would content itself, in
the same way as any economic sector, to play the social game that is its own.
No more, no less. Thus 'the contemporary' would mean both the general incapacity of our time to take hold of and to figure itself as epoch, and the core
of such an incapacity, its cause, perhaps, a certain crisis of artistic production
or, at least, the entry of artistic production into a regime so foreign that, for
the moment, one could only think this regime from what was absented from
it. Therefore, it would be quite absurd to still want to apply to art, and in this
case to dance, the schema of epochal figuration—which is one that the very
expression 'the contemporary' seems to doubly deny. Such would be the first
reason for my refusal—even though one can say it is an exterior and insuffi-
cient one.

Indeed, it is not that easy to escape from the logic of epochality. Again,
it is in the form of an epoch, even though empty, that the incapacity of our
time to take hold of itself is presented, and it is again under the form of a
temporal figure, homogeneous and unified, though undoubtedly negative,

that our inability to constitute 'one' time that is 'ours' is apprehended. The distinctive feature, the 'proper' feature, of 'our time' would be neither to be one, nor *ours*. But this 'propriety', in so far as it is proper, would allow us despite everything to continue to talk about it as a One and to attribute it to us —even if this 'us' would indicate nothing else but our own impossibility. 'The contemporary', in its nominal and unifying form, would be precisely the emblem of such a contradiction. 'The contemporary' would be a name *remaining* —one which simultaneously dreams and annuls the unification in the zeitgeist, one which annuls the zeitgeist while conserving the empty place of its subject. Certainly, we do not believe any more in the idea of a unified and common time, in the idea of a substantial community in time, but the form of our incredulity is still a way to subscribe to it. In this, by the way, we are still pious.

But then this particular kind of representation called figuration must also, in some way, continue to operate. And, in fact, one cannot deny the perfect adequacy that links the new regime of art to the contemporary impossibility of self-figuration. 'The contemporary', by indicating simultaneously an epoch and its artistic productions, postulates nothing but this adequacy understood as a remaining and negative form of positive figuration: in art's contemporary incapacity to give shape to time, it is again the epoch, the spirit of time, that would give itself to be read negatively. Therefore my refusal would still be too naive. Despite the obsolescence of a positive reading of time's figures in art, a negative way would remain available, under two forms. On the one hand, one seeks to show, through interiority—the aesthetic description of these forms of art—that contemporary art ('postmodern', if one prefers) gave itself the essential task to figure the impossibility of figuration, to present the fact that there is an unpresentable, and one upholds that this is how it manages to represent the epoch. As Jean-François Lyotard himself recognizes, this negative figuration remains part of the modernist logic and is internal to the operation of art.[3] On the other hand, one is content to bring to light, through exteriority—the sociological description of these artistic behaviours—a straight renouncement of art, an abandonment or a fading of its historical task, and one makes this very renouncement the *symptomatic* figure, and very incidentally artistic, of our time: there would still be a figuration of time in art, but only according to the exteriority of the symptom, and not to the negative interiority of the symbol. Such would be the cultural and sociological way, where the general theme of the 'death of art', of the 'end of its myth', etc., is necessarily articulated alongside the crude (*brut*) exhibition of its factual and socioeconomic functioning. The works of Nathalie Heinich (1998) or Yves Michaud (1997) could, in a very diverse way, prepare the ground for this second way, 'in exteriority'.

I could try to apply this schema of negative figuration to the choreographic field. I could show that dance is also, particularly by its non-iconic use of the body, an experience of the unpresentable, a presentation of unpresentability. I could conversely seek to deflate empty theories, show that the choreographic 'field' is itself the place of artistic unbinding and irresponsibility, of insignificant eclecticism and singularity, and that all in all the social game of empty subversion and recognition is at stake here as well as elsewhere. I will not do it. And this for the second reason previously stated: while proceeding like this we would actually learn nothing more than what we already know, and, in any case, nothing specific to dance. Such an approach would remain exterior to its object, being satisfied to apply a network of concepts and problematics coming from quite different fields, generally those of the visual arts and literature. Doubtless such an approach would grasp something of dance, but only of that which generally takes part in this regime of art that is ours today. Hence the very specificity of dance's participation in this regime could not be seized (*prise en vue*). This is why I propose to start from elsewhere and to temporarily pretend we did not know anything at all of what has been said so far.

Putting aside the schema of epochal figuration, I will start from a specific and internal connection of dance to *contemporaneity*. 'Contemporaneity' does not indicate here an historical figure, an epoch, but a *structure of temporality*. In this case: a *neutral simultaneity*, a *contingent coexistence*. In its broader meaning and without indicating any epoch, 'contemporary' is *all that coexists*, all that belongs to a particular time. No need to base this coexistence on a sharing of features and identities, on some form of substantial community. The things, the people, the events coexist. There is no need for any further argument. As we said, the simultaneity is *neutral* and the coexistence *contingent*. But, at the same time, precisely because it authorizes the gathering of the different coexistences under a unique term (the 'epoch', the 'time', 'the contemporary'), contemporaneity seems to call for the surpassing of contingency. Thus, it is necessary that at some point the simultaneity gives an account of itself and establishes itself as a genuine community; it is necessary that an identity, a reason, a content, explains the *fact* of the coexistence, and reinsures it as being a matter of a truly *common* present. Therefore contemporaneity should be understood in the following way: a neutral simultaneity marking itself with an insufficiency and aspiring to the unity of a substantial community. I will acknowledge that dance, as a *scenic event*, is directly shaped by such a structure. Its own works have no other milieu of existence but the *scène*, and this one, as we hope to show, is nothing else but a structure of contemporaneity and therefore a structure of temporality. From there, I will come back to 'the contemporary' itself, and will expose a certain mutation that has happened in the choreographic field during the past 10 years. I will uphold that this mutation can only be understood in reference to the *contemporaneity* of the *scène*, which would be, as the reflective work of the performance, an awakening and radical establishing of the stakes.

Let us start with a simple axiom, though apparently exorbitant: *strictly speaking there is only contemporary dance.* Not, of course, that the genre of 'contemporary dance' must be considered as choreographic history's *terminus ad quem*, as a moment of assumption where the experience of movement would be revealed in its ultimate figure of truth. But, more simply, to say something obvious: dance has never given itself (to view) any differently than as a *presence* to *presence* in a space of simultaneity of itself (*à soi*) and to others, which is precisely what one names a *scène* and which has all the characteristics of a structure of contemporaneity. Doubtless one will object that the *scène* is not at all necessary to the experience of dance. One can indeed dance for oneself, without addressing oneself to anyone. And, if someone else is present, it should be recognized that this someone is also dancing, fully participative and never seated. Very well. It remains to be said that it is exclusively through the scenic structure that dance can constitute and offer itself as an *oeuvre* (a work).[4] As long as dance remains near itself, folded up in the intimate experience of its gesture, nothing emerges from it, nothing detaches from it that can assume the figure of an artistic object (at least, not without the intervention of an indelicate and voyeuristic look that turns into a spectacle what was not at all made to be seen). It is only by means of an intentional address and an explicit exchange between performers and onlookers (*regardants*) that a third object can be extracted from dance, opening the possibility for a work. And if it is a matter of speaking here about dance as an art, as a mode of production and presentation of objects by which those who are doing and those who are not come to meet each other, then we have to renew without scruples this reduction of dance to the *scène*.

By this reduction, the tying of dance to contemporaneity is reaffirmed, since the solipsistic experience of movement is by no means concerned with contemporaneity. Its time is certainly that of presence, but of a presence all folded up on itself, without any dialectic articulation, as a perfect sphere of pure self-affection. Unfurling in and for itself the continuation of its own kinesthesis, the only temporality of the dancing body is a present eternity from which any possible coexistence has absented itself. Several dancing bodies will probably not change anything in this regard. One dancing body will only slightly displace the general question: one will simply be solipsistic in a group, in an intensively fusional and non-dialectic form of experiencing what is common to all in the group.[5] In order for contemporaneity to genuinely experiment itself, coexistence must not be reabsorbed immediately in a fusion without an outside; a hiatus has to be reintroduced, and the cleavage of the *scène* has to appear.

Thus, let us reduce dance to the *scène* and make the latter the emblem of a possible articulation between dance and contemporaneity. Let us recall, however, that we still do not know what a *scène* is and how it functions. Let us try then to describe the thing, in a falsely phenomenological attempt.

People are there, gathered together in indifferent multiplicity, without any other reason for being there but to be there. A kind of local heap. They do nothing, or barely anything, or not really anything. They wait for some event. Others, in front, or behind, or on the side, or among them—it does not matter—make that something, that event, happen. That something is carried out, possibly in the form of nothing, but in any case in a way sufficiently clear to emerge, to extricate itself, from the heap. In return, those people whom we first mentioned, the heap precisely, constitute themselves as an *audience*. Perhaps we are too quick in putting forward the term 'audience'. Perhaps this term only masks its underlying phenomenon. All that we know for the moment is that on the one hand people are waiting and doing nothing, and that on the other hand people are acting, carrying out, moving (or not). Above all, we know that these two things have to happen *at the same time*, according to a form of coexistence that for now we have to qualify as *contingent*. Those who are doing and those who are not do not actually have any reason to be there, and even less to be there *together*. A certain event, the very one in the name of which the *scène* delimits itself, opens a space of coexistence—founds an 'us' of simultaneity. But this 'us' has for the moment no other content than that of the empty wait and of its fulfilment. Therefore nothing is actually done yet. This wait cannot be satisfied by the bare event, by that which, happening here and now, has *ecceity* as its only merit. Something more has to happen. Presence alone is not enough. For we are already fully immersed in it: that which gives itself to be seen, over there, on the *scène*, gives itself as an authentic firsthand, inducing in everyone the very lucid consciousness that nothing will ever repeat itself identically, wherever this may be, and, therefore, wraps itself up in an *aura*. But we know well that such a presence is factitious, that such an aura is mechanically induced by the heap's inoperativity (*désoeuvrement*)[6] and the vacuity of its time. It is necessary to go that way, it is an impassable condition, and one even finds a certain pleasure in it. However, it is still for something else that one waits. One waits for the coexistence of those who are doing, of those who are not, and of their ensemble, to escape at last from the pure absence of foundation by which this coexistence is originated, and to re-establish itself around some 'commonality'. One waits for something of Truth, of Presence (a supplement of presence, or rather a transsubstantiation of 'p' to 'P') to redeem the slightest bit of the initial contingency and give it back under the form of a recognized community, of a present truly shared. The applause, which at the end will finish off the matter, is the delayed indication of such a hope, its ultimate and disappointing substitute.

The *scène* is nothing other than a structure of contemporaneity, intensified and complexified. Here, coexistence is folded in two, complicated by the inoperativity (*désoeuvrement*) of some and the intentional address of others; the contingency is at once thematized for itself and no longer simply in itself.

Very well. But how does this *directly* concern dance? Isn't the scenic structure as relevant for theatre or for a concert? Indeed. Except that the choreographic work, contrary to the musical or theatrical work, does not have another place of subsistence but the *scène* itself, and for the choreographic work to access the *scène* it must by necessity participate by giving itself in *presence*. This is for two reasons. First, the choreographic work does not establish any particular element of the performance as a condition of identity. Whereas the identity of an opera or a theatre piece is only defined by one of its fields and can therefore be interpreted and staged in various ways, the dance performance conserves the heterogeneity of the spectacular elements without hierarchizing them. Everything then contributes to the definition of the work, including these seemingly secondary elements that are the settings, the costumes or the lights. Thus, to talk about Odile Duboc's *Trois boleros* (1996) is not only to refer to Duboc's choreography and to Ravel's music, but just as much to Dominique Fabrègue's costumes, Sélim Saïah's settings, Françoise Michel's lights. Such a work remains therefore radically veiled (*dérobé*) except for the eventhood of the scenic encounter of its constitutive fields.[7] The Ballets Russes would be a point of departure and a paradigm of this eventhood of the heterogeneous work, extremely well described by Vladimir Jankélévitch:

> There are no Ballet Russes 'works'; rather there is at the meeting point of several arts a pneumatic work that is paradoxically a work of the moment, one that appears and disappears in the course of the same evening, without leaving any deposit in the archives except a more or less illusory electromagnetic recording. This instantaneous 'work' is the miraculous conjunction of music, choreography, and a setting; and one can call it 'semelfactive', in the sense that, even repeated, it appears each time for the first time, each time for the last time, each time for the first-last time! (1979: 167)

By not reabsorbing the heterogeneity of the performance into a single element, the choreographic work cannot subsist without the *scène*, in the semelfactive temporality of the event and the contemporaneity of performers and onlookers.

Furthermore, supposing that the work can define itself solely from the identity of the choreographic *text*, it is still necessary to note the ambiguous and uncertain character of this very text, which is generally oral. Few dancers or choreographers know how to read or write a choreographic score. The notation, when it takes place (which is rare), functions more as a means (*dispositif*) of exterior consignation (an *archival* fixing) than as a principle of identification authorizing re-enactments foreign to personal transmissions (a *corpus*). Because notation was never really integrated into dance practices, the passage to the allograph that it announced (and through which the work could have been abstracted from its local conditions of production and transmission) went unheeded. The works have continued to be transmitted in a way that is largely oral, from body to body, from presence to presence. The very composition has remained submissive to this imperative: inconceivable in the abstract and solitary space of the page, composition can only happen through the singular body of chosen performers, working at once in the co-present space of the studio. Not having the procedures of absence authorized by the text, dance indexes itself to a horizon of generalized presence. Therefore its giving still remains doomed to contemporaneity (see Pouillaude 2004).

The 1980s in France were oblivious to this dependence. More exactly, it was put into brackets, without being questioned. For it was primarily as *indifferent reiterability* that the works were defined. The pieces, being part of a company's repertoire, were meant to be independent from their local conditions of actualization and they endured without complaint the heterogeneous calendar of evenings and tours. These 'all-terrain' works, to some extent, play a game of denial by abstracting themselves from the eventhood of their giving to view. An evening here, another there, in such-and-such a theatre, and yet, imperturbably, the *same* work.[8] This putting into brackets of the fact of the performance situation had as a consequence the absence of a challenge to its very form. The scenic structure and its parameters were approached in accordance with the obviousness of an unquestioned and therefore unavoidable medium. What one still called at that time 'dance performance' seemed obvious, and the essence of the *performance*—to do something in real time in front of people who are not doing anything—seemed not to raise many issues.

The mutation we are talking about (which could date back to the mid-1990s) must be understood as the exact opposite of this state. Variously named by the critics, who reduce it to the state of a local avant-garde—'New French scene' (*Nouvelle scène française*), 'Young dance' (*Jeune danse*), etc.[9]—this mutation constitutes, however one judges it, more than a fashion or a passing tendency; it announces a radical change of regime within the production of the works. And, actually, this change has already occurred. Today, for anyone who seeks to work in dance, there are impossibilities, there are some things that one simply cannot do any more, or at least not with the same naiveté: narration, expression, as well as composition or virtuosity.

What are the features of this mutation? For the clarity of the analysis, we will isolate five features, which can be subsumed in a single syntagma: 'the *reflective* work of performance'.

The first feature consists of the dissolution of fixed companies. The team of stable and salaried collaborators—what one formerly called a 'company'— is replaced by temporary and local coalitions, individuals handling their own artistic careers in an autonomous way gathering around a defined project. This model, both liberal and libertarian, referring the work to the temporary character of its mission and to the limited consent of its participants, is not only an answer to economic factors. The dissolution of the Mathilde Monnier Company in 1999 proves this. It came about as a result of no real financial necessity (the company benefited from its good reputation, and thus from the subsidies owed to every National Choreographic Centre (*Centre chorégraphique national*). The dissolution rather attempted to respond to the impasse created by salaried work within the company (what Monnier calls the 'familial neurosis'), and the realization that the reciprocal commitment of the dancer and the choreographer could not extend beyond the immediate needs of such-and-such a project. The precariousness of the workforce then becomes an internal artistic norm. The lack of a Contract of Indeterminate Duration (*Contrat à Durée Indéterminée*; or at least a commitment to a long-term contract) is no longer something to lament; on the contrary, it is something that has been rejected for reasons internal to the new modes of artistic production. Therefore, the regime of intermittence is not a compensation for an ideal salary-earning situation that everyone should strive to reach; rather, it simply accompanies, at a social level and in an absolutely essential way, a liberalism fully assumed by the actors. Here, it is necessary to quote French choreographer Boris Charmatz's exemplary formulation, where the intermittence is defined as '(social) precariousness assumed to the benefit of (artistic) exchanges' (Charmatz and Launay 2003: 139). The punch lies, of course, in the play of the parentheticals: once the 'artistic' parenthetical is eliminated, what is it that remains but a formulation of MEDEF's[10] economic programme?[11] This mutation of dance's labour is not without consequences for the very concept of the work (*oeuvre*). Two related elements are weakened through this mutation: the author and the repertoire. The work ceases to be only the choreographer's project and becomes the local and temporary result of a coalition that is also local and temporary: as in, 'Artists have consented to work together for a given time, and here is the result . . . '.[12] Therefore it is also the notion of repertoire that disappears, since it is difficult for the work to subsist beyond the coalition that authorizes it. Works are constituted in repertoire only if the author's signature is enough to identify them and only if a fixed company—one that is directly related to the choreographer's name —is there to actualize them. This general mutation of choreographic labour (which is also a mutation of the work), I interpret as the awakening of the necessarily local and temporary character of the *performance*, as the recognition of its inescapable contemporaneity which had remained obscured by the structure of the 'company' and of the 'repertoire'.

The second feature consists of the integration of the works into the economic context of production and of presenting/touring (*diffusion*). It is a question of treating the financial parameters of creation not as secondary and contingent elements over which it would be necessary to draw a modest veil, but as constitutive and proper features. Choreographers intend to adapt the work, each time in a different way, to the places and structures that host and finance it. Therefore, they abandon the universal figure of the 'all-terrain' work that, abstracting itself from its material conditions of production, was dominant in the 1980s. The mutation consists, economically speaking, in fusing together production and presenting/touring. Within the production company, the partners give money for a new work to be created. Booking agents are satisfied with buying a ready-made piece that will simply be actualized on the stage. Each performance on the tour (each actualization of the work) is today required to be simultaneously a premiere production and a re-creation. *Bords* (2001) by Emmanuelle Huynh is the perfect example of this fusion. This piece has metamorphosed in each of its actualizations and is sold only under the express condition that time for (re)creation is allowed for each presentation. There again, the performance has to be adequate to its own concept: its necessary *contemporaneity*.

The third feature lies in the mutation of the concept of 'writing' (which does not refer to graphic notation but to *composition*: as such, it indicates the ensemble of procedures enabling the identification and fixing of the choreographic object as a stable and reiterable entity). Today, choreographic writing no longer consists of fixing a determined gestural trace that the performer would have to mechanically actualize from one evening to the next, but rather of setting open aparati that would have to be re-encountered and re-experimented with in a different way in every instance. The opening of writing thus implies that an element of improvisation is lodged in each actualization, so that the scenic event precisely ceases to be mechanical actualization and becomes partial re-creation. The writing by *matter*, being contented to determine the general parameters of the gesture's identity without fixing its form, constitutes one of the possible modalities of this renewed writing.[13] Though prevalent today, one finds an exemplary case in the work of Monnier, and particularly *Multi-materials* (2002) and *Déroutes* (2002). By this mutation of writing, the work still only aligns itself with the necessary eventhood of its giving to view (see Pouillaude 2006).

The fourth feature consists of the loss of an obvious notion of the medium 'dance'. The 1980s saw a relative consensus concerning the identity of dance. Despite the diversity of styles, there was an obvious demarcation in regard to pedestrian and everyday movement, a demarcation that remained constitutive and unchallenged. This obviousness is dead. Everything can be dance today, including (and above all without a doubt) the more banal gesture or even the more absent and still one. This calling into question of the identity of the choreographic can be read as a determined return to the American postmodern dance of the 1960s and 1970s.[14] Except for one thing: whereas postmodern dance was understood as the analytic questioning of an essence (What is dance?), operating by eidetic variation and testing the limits (How far can one go without ceasing to produce dance?), our mutation seems rather to shift the questioning toward the essence of *performing* (To what extent is there an event when I do something—or not—in front of somebody who does not do anything?). It is only from this calling into question of performance itself that the medium 'dance' is, in its turn, requestioned. *Mùa* (1995) by Emmanuelle Huynh proves this. In this solo wholly made of stillness, silence and darkness, it is only by a general calling into question of spectacular parameters that dance comes to question itself.

Therefore our fifth feature—the reflective opacification of the medium 'show' (*spectacle*)—actually confirms the truth of the previous one. In the 1980s, dance worked through a clear naiveté regarding the spectacular form, treating it as a medium that was impassable, neutral and transparent. Through this medium, some choreographic 'worlds' were directly displayed, distant and autonomous, unaltered by relation and indifferent to the fact of giving themselves. The show was only a glimpse of these choreographic worlds and did not modify them at all. Within this apparatus, some memorable works were produced. For instance, *May B* (1981) by Maguy Marin evokes a Beckettian universe closed on itself, simply presenting itself to spectators without providing a thematized offering. This approach has now become impossible. Today, the performance would be necessarily reflexive. The show could only escape its essential duplicity by thematizing onstage its operation and in becoming its own object. Without the reflexivity of the spectacular medium, there can be no salvation! Jérôme Bel's pieces, whose titles —*Le dernier spectacle* (The Last Show, 1998) and *The Show Must Go On* (2001)— speak for themselves, are a striking example of such an imperative.

These five features can be subsumed in a single syntagma: 'the *reflective work* of performance'. The eventhood of the performance, as such, comes to take itself into sight, to the extent of becoming immanent to the concept of work (*oeuvre*) (points 1, 2 and 3). The spectacular giving becomes its own object and thus authorizes itself to become forms of internal calling into question (points 4 and 5). Our gesture is therefore to push the argument further, by referring this mutation to the dialectic *contemporaneity* of the *scène*, which would make it both an awakening and a radical establishing of the stakes.

One has the right to interrogate the historical status of such a mutation. We previously believed that we could put aside any question of epochality. Justly, this question has caught up with us. Nevertheless, here again, we will only answer negatively. We will uphold that this mutation escapes the terms ordinarily used in considering the historicity of the arts. The mutation is neither modern, nor postmodern. It does not consist of, as per modernism's claims, a moving forward of art toward what is appropriate: it is not 'dance' as such that is the object of reflection but rather the performance event, which is accidentally and not essentially related to dance (it would have been sufficient that notation became an everyday pratice for the dependence of dance on performance to be considerably weakened). Moreover, this mutation only repeats and adjusts a mutation that has already happened (that of the American postmodern dance), so that the repetition comes to break the figures of progress and of successive breaks with conventions of the modernist logic. But it does not mean that the mutation is postmodern. The repetition possesses a real internal consistency that prevents it from lapsing into the simple eclecticism of the 'return to' and from escaping the pure fading of historicity that postmodernity supposes. Furthermore, the American 'postmodern dance' that it repeats is actually everything but 'postmodern'. For the historic names that dance dresses itself in are out of sync with their artistic content. Indeed, at the risk of being paradoxical, we have to insist that 'modern' dance (Laban, Wigman, Graham . . . ) is *classical*: it is entirely organized according to the expressivity of a creator subject. And, in parallel, that the American 'postmodern dance' is *modern*: it moves by transgressing the limit and exceeding that which it is supposed to be, toward the elucidation of its own feature.[15] As for our mutation, it would be neither modern nor postmodern. It would be *contemporary*, in an extra-or parahistorical sense. It would attempt to take into consideration the necessary *contemporaneity* of the performance (which is not an intrinsic feature but an accident); it would try to reflect in its very work what it is to expose the contingent coexistence of those who are doing and those who are not. Two motifs are then tied together: the *presence* (the necessary eventhood of that which can only give itself in an act), and the contingency (the dialectic insufficiency of the neutral simultaneity), motifs that our mutation attempts to raise to self-consciousness. The work is no longer abstracted from the eventhood of its giving, and the contingency comes to be thematized for itself, through forms of reabsorbtion essentially deceptive or absent (it will be a question of producing null events, invisible dances, still gestures, and thus to go against satisfying any expectations). Therefore, it is an immanent definition of performance that comes to us: a thing that is possible only in presence and conditional to its *failure*.

*Translated by Noémie Solomon*

## Notes

1   '*Scène*' in French means both an abstract place for an event or a representation ('*la scène de l'histoire*', '*la scène du crime*', etc.) and more precisely and concretely the stage.

2   Our time, our epoch, would be unable to draw figures of itself. By 'figuration' I mean a certain kind of representation that simultaneously unifies and pres-

ents something, in a sensible form. The traditional Greek term for that is *skhèma*, the Latin is *figura*.

3    Jean-François Lyotard states: 'A work can only become modern if it is first postmodern. Postmodernism thus understood isn't modernism at its end, but in its birthing state and this state is constant. [. . .] The postmodern would be that which in the modern shows the unpresentable in the presentation itself' (1988: 22–3).

4    *Oeuvre* (work of art) in French refers generally to a singular object and not to the whole production of an artist through his life.

5    Here, one should be extremely careful since the contemporary creation is mostly oriented around a search for a non-fusional form of community. On this, see *Les lieux de là* by Mathilde Monnier (1999; Théâtre de la ville, Paris) which launches such a search.

6    'Inoperativity' (*désoeuvrement*) is used here as a marginal term, describing the position of the audience sitting, passively waiting for the performance. In my other work (*Le désoeuvrement chorégraphique: Etude sur la notion d'oeuvre en danse* [The Choreographic Inoperativity: A Study of the Notion of the Work of Art in Dance], 2009), this concept becomes absolutely central. It tries to describe, through historical developments, the very complex relationship between dance and work. This concept is then reinscribed in its genealogy: Georges Bataille (see 'Lettre à Alexandre Kojève, 6 décembre 1937', when Bataille describes himself as an 'unemployed negativity' [1961]), Michel Foucault (the 'absence of work', at the end of *Histoire de la folie à l'âge classique*, 1972) and Maurice Blanchot (*L'entretien infini*, 1969). For me, the political issues of inoperativity, first developed by Jean-Luc Nancy in *La communauté désœuvrée* (The Inoperative Community, 1982), are yet to be understood.

7    While the same could be said of theatre, opera and about certain performances and recordings of music, in theatre, opera or musical performance, there's an abstract and identified work behind the event of the performance. In dance, not really or less clearly. This point receives fuller attention in my book *Le désoeuvrement chorégraphique* (2009).

8    For example, Dominique Bagouet's company (*Déserts d'amour*, 1984; *Le saut de l'ange*, 1987) or Maguy Marin's company (*May B*, 1981).

9    Without being exhaustive, let us mention a few names: Alain Buffard, Jérôme Bel, Boris Charmatz, Emmanuelle Huynh, Xavier Le Roy, Alain Michard, Laurent Pichaud and Loïc Touzé.

10 MEDEF, Mouvement des Enterprises de France (Movement of French Enterprises) is the largest association of employers in France.—Eds.

11 On the liberal mutation of the arts of spectacle (*arts du spectacle*), thought about in its relation to the general precariousness of labour within the 'ordinary' economy, see the remarkable analyses of Pierre-Michel Menger (2002).

12 The project of Alain Buffard for Montpellier-Danse 2003, *Mauvais genre*, cancelled because of the artists' strike and conflict over intermittence, is exemplary of such a mechanism. This piece was planned to gather about 30 choreographer-dancers, each of whom had a solid reputation from their own works, including Régine Chopinot, Xavier Le Roy, Mathilde Monnier, Rachid Ouramdane, Mark Tompkins and others.

13 Following the French use, 'choreographic writing' here means 'composition'.

14 On the relation between the 'new French scene' (*nouvelle scène française*) and the American postmodern dance, see Denise Luccioni (2002).

15 Here we follow the analysis of Sally Banes:

> [H]istorical modern dance was never really *modernist*. Often it has been precisely in the arena of post-modern dance that issues of modernism in the other arts have arisen: the acknowledgment of the medium's materials, the revealing of dance's essential qualities as an art form, the separation of formal elements, the abstraction of forms, and the elimination of external references as subjects. Thus in many respects it is post-modern dance that functions as *modernist art*. [. . .] But since 'modern' in dance did not mean modernist, to be anti-modern dance was not at all to be anti-modernist. In fact, quite the opposite (1987: xv).

*References*

BANES, Sally. 1987 [1980]. *Terpsichore in Sneakers. Post-modern Dance*. Middletown: Wesleyan University Press.

BATAILLE, Georges. 1961 [1937]. 'Lettre à Alexandre Kojève, 6 décembre 1937' [Letter to Alexandre Kojève, 6 December 1937], in *Le coupable*. Paris: Gallimard.

BLANCHOT, Maurice. 1969. *L'entretien infini* [The Infinite Conversation]. Paris: Gallimard.

CHARMATZ, Boris and Isabelle Launay. 2003. *Entretenir* [Conversing]. Pantin: Centre national de la danse.

FOUCAULT, Michel. 1972. *Histoire de la folie à l'âge classique* [Madness and Civilization: A History of Insanity in the Age of Reason]. Paris: Gallimard.

HEINICH, Nathalie. 1998. *Le triple jeu de l'art contemporain* [The Triple Game of Contemporary Art]. Paris: Les Éditions de Minuit.

JANKÉLÉVITCH, Vladimir. 1979. *Liszt et la rhapsodie* [Liszt and the Rhapsody]. Paris: Plon.

LUCCIONI, Denise. 2002. 'Un miroir tendu à la danse française' [A Mirror Held to French Dance], in Sally Banes, *Terpsichore en Baskets* (Denise Luccioni trans.). Pantin: Centre national de la danse, pp. 7–11.

LYOTARD, Jean-François. 1988. *Le postmoderne expliqué aux enfants* [The Postmodern Explained to Children]. Paris: Galilée.

MENGER, Pierre-Michel. 2002. *Portrait de l'artiste en travailleur: Métamorphoses du capitalisme* [Portrait of the Artist as Worker: Metamorphoses of Capitalism]. Paris: Seuil.

MICHAUD, Yves. 1997. *La crise de l'art contemporain* [The Crisis of Contemporary Art]. Paris: Presses universitaires de France.

———. 2003. *L'art à l'état gazeux: Essai sur le triomphe de l'esthétisme* [Art in the Gaseous State: The Triumph of Aestheticism]. Paris: Stock.

NANCY, Jean-Luc. 1982. *La communauté désœuvrée* [The Inoperative Community]. Paris: Bourgois.

POUILLAUDE, Frédéric. 2004. 'D'une graphie qui ne dit rien: les ambiguïtés de la notation chorégraphique' [Of a Speechless Graphy: The Ambiguities of Choreographic Notation]. *Poétique* 137: 99–123.

———. 2006. 'Vouloir l'involontaire et répéter l'irrépétable' [Wanting the Involuntary and Repeating the Unrepeatable], in Anne Boissière and Catherine Kintzler (eds), *Penser la danse contemporaine* [Thinking Contemporary Dance]. Villeneuve d'Ascq: Presses universitaires du septentrion, pp. 145–63.

———. 2009. *Le désoeuvrement chorégraphique: Étude sur la notion d'œuvre en danse* [Choreographic Inoperativity: Study of the Concept of *Oeuvre* in Dance]. Paris: Vrin.

# CREATIVE ENDURANCE AND THE FACE MACHINE:
## ROSEANNE SPRADLIN'S *SURVIVE CYCLE*

VICTORIA ANDERSON DAVIES

I guess we're looking at exposure in a different way—we're looking at people's faces, we're listening to their words . . . but the words are not all that important . . . the words mostly function as another way to look at the faces. So it's mostly about the faces (Spradlin 2006).

You don't so much as have a face as slide into one (Deleuze and Guattari 1987).

*What does it mean to endure?* I am seated comfortably in the audience of the Dance Theater Workshop in New York City reading 'Anatomy of Melancholy', an editorial published in the Fall 2006 issue of *Movement Research Journal.* In this provocative and confessional critique, veteran dance critic Elizabeth Zimmer laments the diminishing standards of both criticism and dance in NYC. Freshly laid off as the dance editor for *Village Voice* after 14 years, Zimmer claims that dance criticism has reached a new level of crisis. Her woes are as follows: *Village Voice*, which once devoted 2,400 words to dance per week, is now topping off at a meagre 675 words and covering only one dance event per issue; dance concerts in small venues often don't run long enough to justify reviewing them to commercially driven editors; the increased use of the Internet as an inexpensive marketing and networking tool is only serving to further limit the audiences of dance to other performers and their immediate families; and even worse than all this—more 'depressing', as she describes it —is that Zimmer herself is suffering from burnout. After the vivisection of logical reasons for the crisis she is enduring, she finally discloses her most personal struggle:

> After close to 35 years of covering dance on both coasts of two continents, I've basically lost my appetite for it, I can now usually tell, just by looking at a press release, whether the event in question is going to be worth my time. I've become bolder about leaving a dance at intermission; since I am rarely writing I am not sacrificing anyone's bid for media immortality (2006: 6).

It would be easy to dismiss the entire editorial at this point as the result of sheer exhaustion and bitterness. Her boredom as a critic and complaints about word count pale in comparison to the efforts of artists who are breaking their backs to get those venues for one or two weekends, and who are coming up with creative solutions to their own struggles with funding and real estate. But dismissing her plea entirely may be too easy; anatomizing one's melancholia in public has its benefits. By working her way through her complaints piecemeal, she provides the dance community with a clear portrait of a critic losing her ability to cope, a woman a little on the edge. And isn't there some thrill, some catharsis in the fact that she allows us into the sight of her undoing? We feel the weight of years as the mask of the critic crumbles under time's force and we are left to gaze at the vulnerable human being behind the pieces. The drama lies in wondering just how, or if, she will endure. So, maybe the value of Zimmer's 'Anatomy of Melancholy' is less in arguing the thinness of its obvious points—she condescendingly advises, 'One thing that the downtown community [. . .] needs to face is the fact that it's in the entertainment business' (ibid.: 7)—and more in considering how the tactics of endurance, survival and creativity play out under the splintering forces that threaten us from within, and from without. After all, there is no conversation about making work of any kind that does not include an anatomy of how hard it is to make ends meet and how that affects the artistic process. As Bessie Award-winning dancer Walter Dunderville once put it to me, the act of creation nowadays is 'all about the psychodynamics of poverty' (2006a).

So, there are forces that gnaw at us slowly and relentlessly over time, and ones that knock us to our knees all at once. Given the fickle nature of such storms, brute stamina may not suffice. We need more innovative strategies and tactics. We need to revise the question too—*What does it mean to endure creatively?* Just as I finish reading Zimmer, as if on cue, the lights dim for Rose- Anne Spradlin's *Survive Cycle* (2006). The work opens with Dunderville's face projected onto a massive screen at the back of the Dance Theater Workshop stage. In the background, a low vibratory moan emanates from the keyboard of composer Chris Peck, who is visible half on/half off of the dance space at stage right. The screen is so immense that our eye is invited to close in on the subtle micro-movements of pupil, nostril and brow. Dunderville gazes out at us with obdurate calm. After what feels like forever, his face quickly fades and is followed by extended close-ups of the three other performers: Paige Martin, Cédric Andrieux and Tasha Taylor. This is not the wry, meditative, black-and-white humour of Andy Warhol's *Screen Tests* in the mid-1960s, nor are we privy to the distanced, fleeting contemplation of Thomas Struth's minute-long *Video Portraits* (which hovered over Times Square on the Astrovision screen in 2003). Within the intimacy of the Dance Theater Workshop, we have the chance to visually ski the slopes of the physiognomy of face in full colour, to earnestly trace the rhythms of thought as they proceed across the temples and cheeks. This proximity also allows us to chart the myriad pieces of the lives lived by the face: the blows, caresses, cuts and gutters of its experiences; the high vistas and loved ones held in the gaze; the forces of time and circumstance; the winds and early morning feedings; the privileges and struggles. It is straightforward but loaded. We face Dunderville; he faces us back.

The experience of projecting such narratives and figures on to the folds and shadows of faces feels utterly hypnotic and disturbingly familiar. Where else but in the cinema is this seduction more obvious? In his haunting essay 'The Face of Garbo', Roland Barthes submerges us in the polar forces that comprise the face of Greta Garbo, whose snowy visage reached such a point of perfection she was also known as 'The Divine'. Her mask-like countenance is that of the face as an awe-inspiring archetypal mask, while in other ways she veers away from the Platonic ideal of a perfect surface and toward the harmonic signature that details more mortal faces. Barthes, never one to be trapped by dichotomies, conceptualizes Garbo as the moment of transition between the two: 'Garbo's face represents this fragile moment when the cinema is about to draw an existential from an essential beauty, when the archetype leans towards the fascination of mortal faces, when clarity of the flesh as essence yields its place to a lyricism of Woman' (1993: 57). One cannot help but linger forever when contemplating such surfaces, and it is especially worthwhile in order to trace such subtle transitions. But these variations seem to be the fleeting surfaces of a deep armature, a hidden system. What exactly is the glue that holds us again and again to gaze at, and be gazed upon, by those looming facades? And what sparked the impulse to begin this choreography of survival with the face?

In their chapter 'Year Zero: Faciality' from A Thousand Plateaus, Gilles Deleuze and Félix Guattari shine light onto the mechanisms that make the hypnotic magic of the facade possible. They unearth a semiotic facial machine that is lodged at the intersection of language and consciousness, and is firmly entrenched in the history of the West. The face they evoke is not a particular, singularly recognizable face, nor is it an archetypal mask or method of signification organizing an unformed, prelinguistic surface that precedes it. It is a 'special mechanism' (Deleuze and Guattari 1987: 167) that functions as a result of an 'abstract machine of faciality' (ibid.: 169). This abstract machine, existing at the threshold of the white wall of 'significance' and the black hole of consciousness, is linked to the signs and hierarchies of language but is so much more. For, a 'language is always embedded in the faces that announce its statements [. . . ;] choices are guided by faces, elements are organized around faces: a common grammar is never separable from a facial education. The face is a veritable megaphone' (ibid.: 179). And the four faces of the performers of Survive Cycle that inhabit the screen one by one harbour silent, hidden projecting mechanisms even when they do not speak. Their mobile, shifting planes indeed 'slide' (ibid.: 177) into and between the unspoken and often unacknowledged narrative tropes that are conjured through them. In silence they speak to us with visible micro-movements and half-restrained tics, and yet they retreat somewhere unknown. We slide along with them, hallucinating fever dreams that resurrect half-forgotten narratives. The semiotic mechanism of the face machine is at work. You cannot touch it or see it, but we are magnetized by the results of its labours. Maybe Spradlin began this way because she sensed the power of this hidden mechanism at work in the performers, and what it could evoke in the audience. Blue-eyed

Dunderville is all symmetry and light and strength and distance—after a long engagement with the lens of the camera his eyes shift down and to the side, his eyelids drop. His serene countenance coupled with his penetrating gaze is almost sage-like and mystical. Amongst the many narratives emanating from within the folds of his particular face are the discernable echoes of Christ's looming presence as rendered on canvas since the Middle Ages. According to Deleuze and Guattari, it is not the faces that produce the machine of faciality but the machine itself, the armature of the white wall/black hole system (which has its own liquid variations) that creates the possibility for multiplications and digressions. But there is a subtle contradiction at work in the interpretation of the ubiquitous face of Christ:

> Painting has taken the abstract white wall/black hole machine of faciality in all directions, using the face of Christ to produce every kind of facial unit and every degree of deviance. In this respect there is exultation in the painting of the Middle Ages to the Renaissance, like an unbridled freedom [. . .]. It was under the sign of the cross that people learned to steer the face and processes of facialization in all directions (ibid.: 178–9).

The hidden armature of the face machine makes the facade possible; people then steer faciality in new directions and variations.

Deleuze and Guattari direct our attention to Giotto's *The Life of St Francis* —*Scene XII* (1305–06), which depicts Saint Francis' body in the process of becoming the image of the hovering Christ. Christ's stigmata function as rays of connectivity and also kite strings; Saint Francis is being acted upon and, in turn, is directing the winged 'Christ-turned-kite-machine' (ibid.: 178). The image is startling and strange, emerging as it does from the white wall/black hole system of the craggy white landscape and the mysterious darkening sky.

But for the purpose of explicating the direct, frontal gazes of the looming faces of *Survive Cycle*, it may be better to look at Matthias Grünewald's *Resurrection* (1515) from the Isenheim altarpiece. It does not just depict the face machine as it works upon another, but through a face-to-face encounter with the glowing Christ-face (becoming moon-face), the moment of Christ's resurrection enacts the face machine directly upon the viewer, striving to lock her in through the penetrating gaze of the rising body. The white wall/black hole system is evident in many variations and reversals here: Christ's golden halo tinged with green is set off by a velvety black night punctuated with tiny glowing stars; his eyes doubled by the upheld palms whose dark wounds look out at us, level with his eyes. The halo becomes the bulbous head of another face for which Christ's body provides the outline of slightly skewed facial features. The altarpiece itself, a three-dimensional interactive face machine, has two sets of wings, displaying three configurations. The outermost wings show a Crucifixion scene, flanked by images of Saint Anthony and Saint Sebastian. But how does the Christ-face come to rest upon Dunderville? It seems that faciality and the hidden mechanism that makes faciality possible are in a kind of subtle sequential dance, rippling across time and space, multiplying and regenerating. The echoes of all the Christ-faces that were ever painted seem to find a moment of accumulation within Dunderville's gaze, under which we cannot help but allow ourselves to be enveloped in some way. Indeed, the resonance of the face of Christ in all its variations may be a momentary haunting layer to all the faces that gaze down at us with knowing eyes from the screen.

But we should not allow ourselves to blanket the fantasy of the Christ-face with any sense of permanence. For, the moment we think we can name what pins us to our seats in the audience, we slide again, from a faciality we think we recognize to a sense of emerging and shifting abstract planes. We must constantly revise. And, according to Deleuze and Guattari, there is a powerful correlate that intersects with faciality that should be considered—the landscape: 'All faces envelope an unknown, unexplored landscape; all landscapes are populated by a loved or dreamed-of face [. . . ;] what face has not called upon the landscapes it amalgamated, sea and hill; what landscape has not evoked the face that would have completed it, providing an unexpected complement for its lines and traits?' (ibid.: 173). We tend to make faces in the clouds, turn eyes into limpid pools. Dunderville conjures forested snow-capped mountains and sky-blue vistas, while Paige Martin's features curve like delicate hills into a white sky. The two close-ups in succession create a sense of journey through dynamic landscapes.

This mysterious polarity between face and landscape has a specific history as well. Deleuze and Guattari cite how manuals by reformist educator J. B. de la Salle, in which pupils coloured in and arranged faces and landscapes, formed part of a Christian education in the seventeenth century (ibid.: 172). But what we observe on the screen is never so blatant; it only gets its

FIGURE 1. Paige Martin in *Survive Cycle*, 2006. Dance Theater Workshop, New York City, 7 November 2006. Photograph by Roger Gaess; courtesy of RoseAnne Spradlin.

FIGURE 2. Tasha Taylor in *Survive Cycle*, 2006. Dance Theater Workshop, New York City, 7 November 2006. Photograph by Roger Gaess; courtesy of RoseAnne Spradlin.

FIGURE 3. Walter Dunderville in *Survive Cycle*, 2006. Dance Theater Workshop, New York City, 7 November 2006. Photograph by Roger Gaess; courtesy of RoseAnne Spradlin.

momentum from the same abstract machine which is always on the move. Martin's cheekbones evoke hills, her neck a descending slope. And in the next instant she gives us something else to contemplate. Her brown eyes are impossibly energized orbs of permanent surprise that refuse to look directly into the camera. When she finally does we are pinned to our seats by wells of darkness; no longer comfortably in the dark but decidedly the target of her sharp stare into which we fall like Alice into the rabbit hole. What feels obvious here is the way faciality makes meaning in conjunction with the white wall and digs away at consciousness through the black hole.[1] With Martin, we surface into language and plunge into being with ferocious intensity.

But it is not only the visual arts that contain seminal versions of the face machine. Cédric Andrieux receives the pressure of the lens (the black hole par excellence) with apparent ease, no sign of tension here, but the easy yielding to gravity, a sleep, a trance state. He slides into that literary trope groaning at the dawn of the novel in Western literature,[2] the sleeping knight that Deleuze and Guattari claim is able to dismantle the face, even if for a fleeting moment, because he is 'continually drawing a line of absolute deterritorialization, but also losing his way, stopping and falling into black holes' (ibid.: 174). The perfect foil to Dunderville's and Martin's intensity, Andrieux is not unaware entirely but definitely *elsewhere*. Last to inhabit the screen is Tasha Taylor, offering her face without censure. Through the lines and folds we reckon with poetry and time; unspoken stories etched into fragile porcelain. Her unwavering gaze and the camera are in collusion to bring us into the uncharted waters of our own lives that lie just below the calm surface. In complicity with the video, we make a many-faced machine that creates an atmosphere in the theatre that is like hot glue, adhering us to the pressure of an eternal moment in which the face machine forces us to come face to face with ourselves.

If part of Spradlin's genius is to hold us to the task of allowing this four-faced machine to work upon us so that we experience it viscerally, then Deleuze and Guattari make explicit why faciality so overwhelms our senses. It is partly because we are participating in a long tradition of lingering within its variations, whether maternal, passional, political or filmic (ibid.: 175). We fall into faces and see them in landscapes and objects, receiving signals from and re-projecting faciality on to computer screens, cars and telephones. 'Facebook me', a student cheerfully says to her classmate. The face acts as a threshold through which communication takes place and as a register of status. We fear at times we may, like Zimmer, get fired and 'lose face'. Seen in this light her public melancholia can be read as courageous, for shaming makes us want to hide our faces. Watching the four close-ups in succession we want to, must, turn away. But are we ashamed? No, we are scared. Any face this close, for this long, becomes an estranged kind of beauty that is also a kind of nightmare: '*The face, what a horror*. It is naturally a lunar landscape with its pores, planes, matts, bright colors, whiteness and holes: there is no need for a close-up to make it human, it is naturally a close-up, and naturally inhuman, a monstrous hood' (ibid.: 190).

Another aspect of this nightmare is that this abstract machine of faciality has a racialized core, for it is not 'of the white man: it is White Man himself' (ibid.: 176). The abstract machine of the face 'rejects the faces that do not conform, or seem suspicious' (ibid.: 177) but does not ever acknowledge true alterity for, 'from the point of view of racism, there is no exterior, there are no people on the outside. There are only people who should be like us and whose crime it is not to be' (ibid.: 178). Faciality manifests itself in endless variations but is not benign; it is a locus of power that can be a trap, an inhuman limit that should be taken apart. But how? Deleuze and Guattari suggest that the only way to dismantle this repressive mechanism of reproduction is through the very abstract machine that is the source of the habit-of-face. '[K]now them, know your faces, it is the only way you will be able to dismantle them and draw your lines of flight' (ibid.: 188). In the end, we must resist the temptation to escape through the fantasy of a utopian prelinguistic state, or the fantasy that we will find new, fresh configurations in the construction of voyages to an exotic elsewhere for 'it will be only taking more photos and bouncing off the walls again' (ibid.). We must sit tight: 'subjectivity and the facial machine are impasses, the measure of our submissions and subjections and it is there we must stand battle' (ibid.: 189). In order to effect 'lines of flight', it seems that we must invent new ways to use these inherited tools of signification. This may not sound like a return, or exploitation, but such rhizomatic flights have the quality of a deeply beautiful transcendence—into madness if one is not careful, into gratefully becoming the landscape if one is, like the Knight, willing to risk losing oneself completely to the intersection of time and space.[3] So Spradlin does more than hold us to the task of acknowledging the power of these faces; she reckons with the question of faciality in just the way Deleuze and Guattari suggest, by sinking more deeply into its strata. But the results of her exploration have little to do with a gentle chivalric flight into becoming-landscape. By making the faces huge and by lingering on them each for such intense durations, her work begins to understand, in kinetic ways, the consequences of faciality itself. For what of those of us who, like Zimmer, are struggling with issues of creative endurance much closer to the ground? What are we to do with such nuanced philosophical flights and dismantlings?

It is the dancing—a quaking, throbbing, cacophony of limbs, eyes and organs—that reveals what it means to struggle creatively with seemingly overwhelming outside forces. After the four intimate video portraits, it is startling to watch the dancers take the space, to witness what appears to be a subtle schism between face and body. They arrange themselves in the space without ceremony. They are wearing the crisp designs of Jennifer Goggans: formal black-and-white outfits that signal a cocktail party. The men are in sleek pants and collared shirts, the women in whimsical party dresses. Taylor is sprightly, quick and light, contradicting the poetic gravitas of her gaze; Martin is more earthbound and sure-footed than we might expect. From the abstract power of faciality, we switch gears to the primordial movement of the back. Once they have entered, the dancers turn their backs toward the audience and begin to rock a hidden mechanism deep inside their torsos. We are awakened from the sound of a low vibration to the ear-shattering and percussive wrenching that will accompany us for the rest of the dancing. Between the increasingly searing score and the rocking motion, which gradually increases in scope and force, we are sent into a land of frenzy and turbulence. Taylor steps front and centre, her rumblings now an earthquake shattering the seams of her once composed dancing self. Her mouth is open as if she is singing. She shakes out a demon or two. She is shuddering, convulsing, her body a wet blanket whipping in the cold air; it goes everywhere at once and her arms, hands and head ride the convulsions to the end. These are not strangely 'facialized' bodies; they are something else. Any perceived schism between face and body has disappeared. *Survive Cycle* has allowed the faces to become absorbed and is taking off from deep inside the rib cages of the performers, making their whole bodies new, strange and somehow alien. The dancers don't lose their faces because of shame or some kind of return, but because they are operating on a different stratum altogether, exceeding through sheer kinetic vibration Deluze and Guattari's parting hallucination in which they bid a fond farewell to the face and embrace a new kind of futuristic inhumanity: '*Face, my love*, you have finally become a probe-head' (ibid.: 191). Spradlin veers away from the sleek, silent violence implied by such futuristic probe-heads. The shuddering performers are dancing the essential human animal, not through a return but through an acknowledgement of what is right there, on the pulsing surfaces.

And there are phrases too. Funky urgent quartets and duets of male-to-female pairings start out with formal goals, and then are disrupted by unstable quaking. A momentum-filled running-and-spinning lift series started by Dunderville and Taylor is punctuated by Martin bending backwards from a squat over the shoulders of Andrieux. There is lurching, staggering, and whipping arms and legs that settle resolutely into deep lunges. Everything is repeated while quaking. What was once the hurried and prescribed ritual of this makeshift family/cocktail gathering is now falling apart at the seams. Still, they struggle forwards in a million shimmering pieces. Martin's act of virtuosic acrobatics on the shoulders of Andrieux is repeated, taken to its quivering threshold as she reaches her trembling arms and tottering head into the dangerous void. They even enter and exit the space quaking: one spies Andrieux wobbling deep offstage before his entrance. While Taylor's spasms seem to let inner demons out of their cages, Dunderville's furious thrusting gestures rocket from the centre of his torso, channelling the pseudo-pugilistic arm movements of a rapper at the height of his poetic fury. In this way he recalls the searing punching gestures of LL Cool Jay in his now classic 'Momma Said Knock You Out' (1991). A brush with danger here: is Spradlin courting the kind of racialized deterritorialization that Deleuze and Guattari warn us of? She might be, but, even in this mimetic form the quaking is not a gestural stroke of imitation, it is part of the thick fabric of the movement. It crescendos through Dunderville like electric waves and, in so doing, it seems to require him to pick up on vibrations and stories and impressions embedded in the air. Are the dancers acting as mediums? Who finds them? They keep going no matter what or who surfaces. And the music keeps screeching, and the tremors continue. The hairs on my arms stand up a bit in the presence of some kind of apocalypse. We are not just uncomfortable now; we are twitching and jerking right along with them. While Deleuze and Guattari give us the idea of dismantling the face machine and imagine what might greet us on the other side, Spradlin shows us what these experiments with new thresholds might look and feel like, and how the body will endure the storm.

And there is even more to the dancing. All the excess is coupled with wilful restraint. It takes effort, but they lock themselves in place when they need to. There are moments of exhausted plastique repose, the dancers all held and silent once in a tight geometrical quartet, once spread at the edges of the wingless stage half-on/half-off along with the composer. Amidst the chaotic rocking, their hands often remain specific, folded into their collarbones like soft paws. Because *Survive Cycle* dances the forms and tactics through which we might cope with life's storms and invite new intensities, it also dances the idea that what we endure—the annihilations, tremors and unforeseen fragilities—doesn't necessarily destroy everything, but leaves us with new and ever more complex pieces to pick up. And whether we asked for it or not, we are often better for the dismantling. The cycles we manage to survive force us to create things we cannot begin to imagine. And there is something here that dance offers particularly, for it is through the dancing that the peaks and folds of the energy necessary for the cycles become sensate. The dancers exit and a brief but intense video by Glen Fogel pulses like a strobe light on the screen. The sound and sight of scissors cutting into clothing brings home the notion of excision as a terrifying but vital component to our creative endurance.

*Survive Cycle* lands with the performers enacting a methodical process of remantling. Dragging bags of clothing scraps onstage, they piece together a huge mosaic on the floor. Though their individual cobblings eventually intersect with one another, this is work done entirely alone. They each begin in a far corner of the stage and interconnect each other's careful designs with restrained ceremony. On the screen we are returned to the faces, and this time they speak to us. Nightmares, fears, break-ups and the fraught process of the creation of *Survive Cycle* weave personal narrative with the formal act of piecing together the new ground in a way entirely devoid of melodrama. And yet there is a refreshing theatricality in hearing intimate details. Tasha Taylor had a dream someone was shoving drugs down her throat, but was really kind. Martin dreamed her mother tried to kill her. It gets even edgier and funnier when Martin looks toward someone beyond the camera (possibly Spradlin) and asks, 'Is that good enough?' Dance doesn't often give us such intimacy with its performers, when dancers enter into their dancerly natures in a given performance; they usually come to represent community or humanity, a cohort of sorts that can melt into couplings and trios. But often the sacrifice to the mutably abstract world of dance is something of the particularity of the performer, their physical and verbal syntax erased. This is not always a bad thing, of course—through the abstraction and the negation of the personal we leap to a universal plane—but Spradlin manages to straddle both realms here, thereby challenging both realms. This ability to be resolutely in the universal, and to challenge its edges through the familiar, or personal, has always been there in her group work, especially *Empathy* (1999) and *Under/World* (2002). These two trios meshed and intertwined and layered the dancers' bodies until the three became one. And yet one had clear images of each individual as well. But this capability was also present in her solo *Take 2* (*The Oklahoma Piece*) (2000) in which Spradlin found a way to reckon complex personal emotions surrounding the death of her father with the omniscient power of an oncoming tornado, filmed from the inside of a car. With Spradlin we are at once on beautifully particular and beautifully universal terms with the dancers and the dancing.

The final moments of *Survive Cycle* have us glancing from the screen to the growing mosaic on the ground, returning the evening to a slowly encroaching, though stilled world of surface. In the process of showing us how bodies behave under the pressure of cutting and mending, disintegration and immobility, confession and transcendence, *Survive Cycle* turns the creative act of endurance inside out. 'Year Zero: Faciality' suggests we should use the resources of art to dismantle that which inhibits our creativity, but not to stop there, for 'art is never an end in itself, it is only a tool for blazing life lines' (ibid.: 187); *Survive Cycle* does not 'blaze' but rumbles until it oozes over its own edges, revealing the (sometimes fraught) inner seams of its own process to us, as well as the valuable lesson that while destruction is inevitable, remaking is required.

And where do these lessons in survival leave Zimmer? Turkish Nobel Prize winner Orhan Pamuk, who was put on trial in 2005 for speaking out about the Armenian genocide, puts endurance in the context of a writer's life:

> As I sit at my table, for days, months, years, slowly adding words to empty pages, I feel as if I were bringing into being that other person

inside me, in the same way that one might build a bridge or a dome, stone by stone [. . .]. The writer's secret is not inspiration—for it is never clear where that comes from—but stubbornness, endurance (2006/2007: 84–5).

Sometimes to endure creatively means to persist in the impossible, in the unforgiving processes of dismantling and remantling until a new being is created. This work is never done from a position of passivity or comfort. Spradlin and the performers in the work explore an embodiment that seems destined to reiterate familiar patterns and rituals with its symmetry and plastique forms but is shaken, literally and sometimes dangerously, to the core. They rattle the rusty chains of the face machine, shaking new possibilities out of thin air. The risk associated with this serious work seemed to be part of the atmosphere that weekend. Across town at St Mark's Church another choreographer, Luciana Achugar, presented *Exhausting Love at Danspace Project* (2006), a choreography that threatened the edges of her dancer's endurance through mind-numbing repetition and feats of athletic stamina. The performers ran, skipped, kicked and spun to a point of nausea. Then suddenly, at my feet, lay performer Hillary Clarke. Having destroyed some kind of internal barrier through the intense discomfort of her pounding heart and exhausted limbs, she slithered and slid at the feet of the audience, her body groping, reaching and surging toward a new stratum, weaving a web of endurance, survival and regeneration in time and space. I wanted to lay my hands on her, to gather all her sweaty roving parts and collect them safely into a cohesive whole but I dared not interrupt this mysterious dance for it was something bigger than my own desire to contain, and therefore be comforted by, that which I can recognize and name.

But does all our work have to be so serious? Contain such weighty gravitas? In another section the performers of *Exhausting Love at Danspace Project*, as if fed up with their own bodies, turn their energies on each other, wrestling one another to the ground with serious slapstick glee. And in a transitional moment in the middle of *Survive Cycle* there is a darkly absurd procession in which each performer totes a jet-black stuffed-animal crow (Dunderville wears his on his head; Taylor carries hers like a purse), satirizing the morbid determination with which we carry our psychic burdens. Lastly, in the same issue of *Movement Research Journal* in which Zimmer's piece appears, Dunderville offers an imaginative surprise in 'Notes on Nothing (in particular)'

(2006b). Upon the backdrop of simple graph paper and amidst a large ink-drawn portrait of a woman with a snowy serene face (not unlike Garbo's), he conducts a hilarious interview between his 'inner-self' and his 'icky-self' about the relevance of making a dance from nothing. Humour lightens the load, gives us the fuel to undo what we have done and the stamina to keep going. And so does the possibility of what is on the other side. Of the necessary cyclical process of creation and destruction, Martha Graham wrote:

> From all the things that life offers us we have spun a net, a necessary cause that chains and enslaves us. But we retain the possibility of undoing this Penelope's web for we ourselves have woven it; once we have freed ourselves from the servitude into which our actions lead us we find ourselves at the scene of our great task [. . .] (1973: 319).

And what do the faces have to do with this ongoing cyclical process of weaving and unweaving? The face, in that it is made up of so many shifting and collapsing parts, strives to be a whole. The endeavour of the face to put the tics, grimaces, sighs and gazes together, though never really successful, makes explicit with every subtle shift both the unravelling of the whole and the inevitable process of remaking—restless, surprising and fraught with significance. Zimmer is now working freelance, earning just 25 per cent of her former salary. But a kind of rebirth is at hand, for she has a deep desire to get back to the studio: 'When I shut up and listen to my body I want to be dancing' (2007). And on 5 April 2007 it was announced that RoseAnne Spradlin was awarded a Guggenheim Fellowship. When asked if she'd been celebrating she replied, 'I've been mostly in shock' (2007). Just on the other side of destruction is regeneration; the possibility of a new, mysterious task.

*Notes*

1   Gilles Deleuze and Félix Guattari remind us: 'Significance is never without a white wall upon which it inscribes its signs and redundancies. Subjectification is never without a black hole upon which it lodges its consciousness, passion, and redundancies'—but then they qualify this by emphasizing the many combinations of white wall/black hole expressivity (1987: 167).

2   In 'Year Zero: Faciality' we are referred to the novel *Lancelot the Knight of the Cart* by Chretien de Troyes (1176) within which the character of Lancelot embodies the 'catatonic Knight seated on his steed, leaning on his lance, waiting, seeing the face of his loved one in the landscape; you have to hit him to make him respond' (in ibid.: 174).

3   Deleuze and Guattari explore the possibility that to be truly mindless like Lancelot could be the first step in riding the forces that point toward an escape. D. H. Lawrence, who, the authors claim, has been linked to the figure of Lancelot, writes of just such an escape through the landscape of the shore: 'To be alone and memoryless beside the sea [. . .] far off far off as if he had landed on another planet, as a man might after death [. . .]' (in ibid.: 189).

*References*

BARTHES, Roland. 1993 [1957]. *Mythologies.* London: Vintage Press.

DELEUZE, Gilles and Félix Guattari. 1987 [1980]. *A Thousand Plateaus: Capitalism and Schizophrenia* (Brian Massumi trans.), VOL. 2. Minneapolis: University of Minnesota Press.

DUNDERVILLE, Walter. 2006a. 'Notes on Nothing (in particular)'. *Movement Research Performance Journal* 30 (Fall): 40.

———. 2006b. Personal correspondence.

GRAHAM, Martha. 1973. *The Notebooks of Martha Graham.* New York: Harcourt Brace Jovanovich.

PAMUK, Orhan. 2006/2007. 'My Father's Suitcase'. Nobel Prize Speech. *The New Yorker* (25 December–1 January): 82–96.

SPRADLIN, RoseAnne. 2006. 'Artist Dialogue: Carla Peterson in Conversation with RoseAnne Spradlin'. Programme for *Survive Cycle.* Dance Theater Workshop, New York City.

———. 2007. Personal correspondence. 13 April.

ZIMMER, Elizabeth. 2006. 'Anatomy of Melancholy'. *Movement Research Performance Journal* 30 (Fall): 6–7.

———. 2007. Phone interview. 13 April.

# HOW TO KNIT YOUR OWN PRIVATE POLITICAL BODY?
## ON DEUFERT + PLISCHKE'S *DIRECTORY* PROJECT

JEROEN PEETERS

Since they first met in March 2001, the German performance theoretician and performer Kattrin Deufert and the German choreographer Thomas Plischke have been sharing work and life. When you hardly know each other, how do you mould living together? You exchange memories and stories, share experiences and end up creating a common fund of material as a basis for work. 'A life in work'—or to speak through both their work and their lives—is the project deufert + plischke set about to shape. Their body of work can be regarded as an ongoing process, a work in progress that leaves traces in the many products and events their collaboration yields: performances, video works, visual installations, laboratories and workshops. Their endeavour to negotiate the borders between life and work is most clearly developed in the *Directory* trilogy (2003–06), which they announce as follows: 'How does the life of the artist write itself into an artistic work? How does the work change the life of the artist in return? How do we share the place with our inventions?' (2007).

Developed over a period of several years, the *Directory* project reflects distinct moments in deufert + plischke's collaboration. Initially conceived as a lecture demonstration to introduce their work, *Directory 1: Europe Endless* (2003) eventually took the form of a 'visual audio play', which interweaves the respective stories of deufert + plischke prior to their meeting. *Directory 2: Songs of Love and War* (2005) integrates their memories into a broader reflection on issues such as memory, mourning and narrativity. From that piece onward, they started to refer to themselves as the 'artist twins' deufert + plischke. This meant a deliberate shift of focus: along with this new self-description, they claimed a specific method and outlined a specific poetics which are the subject matter of *Directory 2.*

Similar in form, both parts are often presented together as one programme, called *Directory: In Be Twin*, which also makes the older *Directory 1* appear in retrospect as a work by the 'artist twins' deufert + plischke. How a memory-ridden process of writing (their method) translates into movement and into a critical notion of choreography as knitting (their poetics), is at stake in *Directory 3: Tattoo* (2006). A group choreography, *Directory 3* also points at the limits of the artist twins' fiction—prompting deufert + plischke to address the social aspects of theatre and of collaboration as a prerequisite for their self-narration.

To puncture the borders between practice and theory is another recurring concern in deufert + plischke's work, which results in its hyper-formulated and dense character, sometimes reaching the hermetic, given their work's whirlpool of theoretical references. And even though these references are freely appropriated by the artists and integrated into their fiction, it is tempting for the writer to follow some of the theoretical leads hidden in the work—not simply to bring them back to the realm of theory 'proper', but as a dramaturgical point of entry that can allow for the probing of some of the work's main notions and presuppositions. At the risk of losing myself in deufert + plischke's phraseology or of identifying myself too strongly with *Directory*'s imaginary other, I hope that in following these hidden leads some friction or distance will occur that would allow for both translation and reflection. But to arrive there and construct my own theoretical fiction, I will first rummage through a selection of materials, tropes and references, borrowing deufert + plischke's motto as a guide: '*How to knit your own private political body?*'

1

Accompanied by visual elements on a large screen mounted on the theatre stage, such as highlighted keywords or quotes, photographs, videos and film by deufert + plischke, the 'visual audio play' *Directory 2: Songs of Love and War* unfolds mainly through loudspeakers. Memories are unleashed through myths, as we listen to narrator Gillian Carson's warm voice, relating with a Scottish accent genealogies and intrigues of Greek gods. We hear how the bold Chronos cuts off his father Ouranos' genitals with a sickle, how Hermes falls in love with Aphrodite, and how their son Hermaphrodite is merged into one body with the nymph Salmacis. Cutting and merging hint at the erasure of sexual difference, gestures that are also at work in deufert + plischke's fiction of the identical twins, a fiction that seeks to wipe out difference altogether. Throughout *Directory 2* deufert + plischke explore the fiction of themselves being 'identical twins' and put it to a test, probing the notion of difference *ex negativo*.

On the screen, we see from time to time digital images of 'identical twins': mirrored images of a body dressed in white knitted tights, seen from the back. It is either Deufert or Plischke who is being shown, the image converted into twins by the cutting process of digital editing—a futile erasure of difference, as it is severed from time and space. A critical approach to the use of digital media is evident from the images' juxtaposition with analogue photography, which has an indexical relation with reality. deufert + plischke identify with American photographer Diane Arbus' 1967 photograph of identical twins—two girls dressed in identical clothes. '*The clothes give us a feeling of how it is to be identical, but then in the expression of their faces a difference appears.* [. . .] *Diane, you make appear the difference of the smallest detail and thus you show us how afraid we are that it might disappear, that it might vanish in the identical.*'[1] These images of identical twins furthermore contrast with the *Directory* project's narrative endeavour: '*It has already been some time now that we share a life in work to become twins in our fiction. Instead of sharing the same DNA our plan was and still is to share the same protocol, to share a work in life. We wanted to bring all our memories and knit one fictional twin body to work and live in, simultaneously*' (D2).

Twins appear on at least four levels in *Directory 2*: in digital and analogue photography, and in the piece's narrative, which all seek to flesh out deufert + plischke's self-description as 'artist twins' and the impossible desire to coincide with the other. deufert + plischke started to talk about their work as the artist twins deufert + plischke to slightly twist the dominant social fiction of the heterosexual couple. The fiction of the artist twins gives another label to a project of sharing life and work: a practice of mutual witnessing that transforms all their shared activity into work. All these fictional approximations run into difference as their limit and ground, and hence yield reflections on identity politics and the possibility to narrate oneself.

In *Directory 1: Europe Endless*, it is also a myth that mobilizes the process of remembering and mourning, of telling and sharing stories. We listen to the myth of Europe, interwoven with Deufert's story, which is voiced by narrator Martin Hargreaves. While playing by the seaside in a bridal dress, Europe was seduced, abducted and raped by the beautiful bull Zeus. Do we still remember the drama of a violated and displaced woman that gave her name to a continent and a community? Commuting between Brussels and Berlin in the year 2000, Deufert is inquiring into Europe's myth and, at the same time, pondering her own identity crisis and lack of place. To her, Europe's is a myth about territory, about taking and naming the land, about the homelessness of women.

Landscapes and imagery related to travelling are recurring motifs throughout the *Directory* trilogy. Sometimes we see Deufert or Plischke stretched out in nature, posing in a pair of tights. '*We have lain on your grounds many times, making pictures of ourselves, over and over again. We hoped to meet you, catch you at the edges of our pictures. [. . .] We will never find Europe again. Maybe we are able to reknit her bridal dress*' (D2). Deufert's account and her identification with Europe complicate the artist twins' genealogy and their desire to coincide with the other: displaced and charged with history, one doesn't coincide with oneself in the first place. People are marked by their own difference and their partial opacity to themselves.

Europe's is also a myth about rupture, about moments in which life's narrative thread snaps: '*Cutting oneself off the net means to lose the thread into the net of the time. The net is Europe and Europe was the first spinner who had to tear the thread. Entanglement of the time . . . I will always be for myself but I won't run anymore. Running into nowhere doesn't make sense anymore*' (D1). To cut the thread is to lose oneself: how to relate to the net of time and earn oneself a place? Interestingly, the issue of narrativity as that which grants us a 'place', a 'life', a 'world' is introduced in *Directory 1* immediately through textile metaphors: thread, net and entanglement, tearing and spinning.[2] During the whole performance, deufert + plischke are present on stage as the masters of ceremony, announcing each chapter in the piece with small actions, but mostly they are immersed in the act of knitting a piece of cloth. A first explanation of this omnipresent metaphor: knitting is an activity that aims to restore a torn narrative fabric. But where and how to begin—by cutting oneself loose, by darning the holes or by knitting a new tissue altogether?

*'The image of knitting starts with something simple, a thread, and via movement it becomes something quite complicated. It loses its beginning and in the end it has no end. How to knit, how to speak?'* (D2). The omnipresent knitting metaphor in *Directory 2* is inspired by Portuguese poet Fernando Pessoa's reflections in *The Book of Disquiet* on the (im)possibility of writing one's biography: 'Living is knitting according to the intentions of others. But as we do it, our thoughts are free and all the enchanted princes can stroll through their parks between the instants when the hooked ivory needle sinks into the yarn. I crochet things . . . I digress . . . nothing' (1998: 6). Knitting is a movement that allows one to create something on the basis of a single thread, and as easily to undo the figure, return to the thread and start over again. But yarn is resistant; its material quality defines the figure's eventual form. And once undone, the yarn is somewhat crumpled, as a witness of the process, of the repetitive movements that have transformed it into something else. Is it possible or desirable to knit oneself a life narrative, as a mere work of fiction, drained of life itself? To knit a body oblivious of the movements and transformations that shape it?

In *Giving an Account of Oneself*, Judith Butler discusses the subject's possibility to respond to the question 'Who are you?'. Butler lists the limits of self-narration as follows:

> There is (1) a non-narrativizable exposure that establishes my singularity, and there are (2) *primary relations*, irrecoverable, that form lasting and recurrent impressions in the history of my life, and so (3) a history that establishes my *partial opacity* to myself. Lastly, there are (4) *norms* that facilitate my telling about myself but that I do not author and that render me substitutable at the very moment that I seek to establish the history of my singularity. This last dispossession

in language is intensified by the fact that I give an account of myself to someone, so that the narrative structure of my account is superseded by (5) the *structure of address* in which it takes place (2005: 39).

The multiple temporalities of this structure point backward in time, as if self-narration has a choreographic memory: 'To be a body is, in some sense, to be deprived of having a full recollection of one's life' (ibid.: 38). And they point forwards in time, as self-narration requires a 'scene of address' that ties exposure to possibility: 'The other represents the prospect that the story might be given back in new form, that fragments might be linked in some way, that some part of opacity might be brought to light' (ibid.: 80). The link with the *Directory* project is at hand: as a project of mutual witnessing and self-narration, the concept 'artist twins' provides a scene of address for deufert + plischke, which entails an investigation of the right distance to the other and to oneself. At some point, we'll have to return to another scene of address: to the question of the spectator and the theatre, since this is after all the place where deufert + plischke perform their accounts. But let us remain in their fiction for a bit longer.

2

> *Could I knit better, I'd knit myself my own place! How identical can we allow ourselves to be with the places and characters of our past? I tell you memories and I receive yours. And how these memories have been placed in sequence will be made clear in remembering them, together. [...] Is it possible to share places of memory? Is it possible to share places of fiction? Is it possible to share places of distant terror and thrill? Place, where do you take place?* (D2)

*Directory 1* relates moments of Deufert's and Plischke's childhood and family life, stories of coming of age with art. The performance doesn't retell the life of two artists from A to Z, though. Most of the narrated memories are heavy and circle around similar themes, such as identity, gender trouble, loss, mourning—they point at both remembered and desired traumas. In a fashion reminiscent of Michel Foucault's genealogy, the performance addresses the singularity and contingency of events that have marked deufert + plischke and that have made them who they are—as people and as artists. It is an associative and fragmentary account that focuses on coincidences and details:

a history of two lives that doesn't trace origins so much as the disparity of events inscribed onto the body's surface. To reveal the many regimes that mould the body and to go against the grain of traditions that define the reassuring stability of life and nature is what Foucault calls genealogy. He reminds us that knowledge of history is made for 'cutting': 'History becomes "effective" to the degree that it introduces discontinuity into our very being—as it divides our emotions, dramatizes our instincts, multiplies our body and sets it against itself' (1977: 154).

In a Foucaultian vein, Gabriele Brandstetter analyses the role of the anecdote in contemporary performance to develop a different understanding of narrativity in the theatre (2005: 119–21). For Brandstetter, the anecdote functions as a break or a cut; its eventful contingency interrupts the narration, thus revealing and unsettling the ties between facts and the imposed order of writing history. In *Directory 1*, anecdotes are indeed a tool to unnerve dominant narratives of family life and gender, but also of art and work. To gain a better understanding of the 'cut' in *Directory 1*, let us listen to two fragments of Plischke's story, as voiced by narrator Kaethe Fine.

Family life and gender trouble are introduced by the anecdote of the grandmother's Christmas present for the seven-year-old Thomas Plischke. Dreaming of a Playmobil fire brigade, he is more confused than disappointed to discover that the parcel contains a pair of white long johns. '*My mother and grandmother saw my confusion and explained to me that now that I was a "real" boy, it was time to stop wearing tights and start wearing long johns*' (D1). As we learn, the main difference between these two garments is that long johns don't cover the feet. '*I had to suppose that gender identity was manifested as something "real" at the age of seven at the feet, and that this manifestation concerned boys only.*' Sexual difference is clear enough at the age of seven, but the difference between a boy and a 'real' boy? The young Thomas Plischke starts to mistrust his intimate social surroundings and decides upon an act of resistance: '*I took a pair of scissors and cut the long johns in many places so I would get a pair of tights again.*' His mother fails to read his protest, though, and simply buys him a new pair of long johns—after which comment the soundtrack strands in a loop for about five minutes: '*But my mother bought new white long johns. I cut them again.*'

The anecdote's incisiveness contrasts with the young Plischke's recalcitrant but vain action of endlessly cutting his long johns. Still, the ripped cloth is a witness to the belief that insistence and repetition will eventually induce difference or change. By 2001, tights have become a central motif in Plischke's work, inspired by the title of visual artist Rosemarie Trockel's ironic collage *Leben heisst Strumpfhosen stricken* (To live means to knit tights, 1998). Plischke films himself in tights for the video work *AESS* (November 2000–September 2001), aiming to establish the piece of cloth as a container of memories. Again, his desire to create a different narrative fabric to constitute his understanding of the body, of gender and anatomy, is haunted by repetition. Plischke's myth is that of Sisyphus—AESS stands for 'autoeroticselfsisyphus'—who endlessly rolls the same stone up the same hill. Sisyphus is a male figure with a clear space but without history, with a life but with an unfinished death. '*Place, where do you take place?*' (D2). How to write your own biography? How to write your own life? How to begin?

In spring 2001, Plischke finds himself with two colleagues in a *favela* in Rio de Janeiro for a workshop and the creation of (*não*) *se pode falar* [speaking not allowed] with a group of local teenagers. A report of the living conditions, contacts with the local drug mafia, and the creation make clear the setting is anything but idyllic; poverty, drugs and violence mark the horizon. On the projection we see various pictures of Plischke posing in tights, alternated with secretly shot footage of a 14-year-old demonstrating the use of a Kalashnikov. Out of meditative music for string quartet, *Directory 1*'s soundtrack grows thick with noise, barking dogs and people yelling. Then the images and narration are briefly interrupted to share the event of '*Rua do Andarai. Balcony of our House. 26th of May 2001.* [...] *Suddenly just outside the house, machine-gunfire. I freeze in fear of death*' (D1). On the screen, we see Plischke posing in tights, while the machine-gunfire hits the eardrums. After a minute, the narration is resumed without further comment. Yet, this time the staged disruption reaches far beyond the anecdote's impact on life's narrative fabric: charged with the possibility of death, the ultimate limits of meaning come into view.

3

Sometimes deufert + plischke are reproached for doing therapy on stage, for using art to deal with their personal traumas. Their endeavour has always been a broader one, though, as they explain in an interview:

How can we create a place for mourning? In Germany there are a lot of monuments and memorials, but they are mainly a social gesture which releases people from the activity of remembrance, so that in the end nothing changes. Germans have for example a highly aestheticized image of the Second World War, formed by television and visual culture, which leaves no space for a process of rendering. We don't want to experience the aesthetics of recollection from a fixed place. There are so many unresolved memories, not only regarding the war, but also concerning sexuality and gender. Sharing memories and stories makes me think of pain. The experience of pain can totally occupy you, but you can't share it. Does that also hold for stories? For history? (2005a)

'Could I knit better, I'd knit my own death. Is this a suicide?' (D2). Our thoughts travel back to *Directory 1*, to Deufert's accounts of early artistic collaborations in baroque opera and theoretical research on John Cage, to the dramatic story of her mother's suicide attempt. '*My relationship toward family has changed radically as well as my relationship toward art. Everything got very close, private life and work, I could not see any difference anymore. I didn't want to see a difference anymore. There were only a few things that I could stay interested in: the loss of subjectivity through the use of chance operations in Cage's works and the possible perception of transcendence in the stepping out of the single voice in Monteverdi's* Orfeo' (D1). She calls the latter a '*highly artistic portrait of human failure*', which charges all opera with the task of singing forever about something lost.

In his unceasing exploration of the relation between language and death, the French author Maurice Blanchot developed an important analysis of Orpheus' myth. While descending into the underworld to bring his beloved Eurydice back to daylight, the poet-musician will eventually break the law, look behind him and lose her a second time, now forever. Orpheus' impatient, insouciant gesture in which everything is lost contains for Blanchot the gist of literature: 'All the glory of his work, all the power of his art, and even the desire for a happy life in the lovely, clear light of day are sacrificed to this sole aim: to look in the night at what night hides, the *other* night, the dissimulation that appears' (1989: 172). Already in the underworld, seduced by the night and eager to transcend the law of an absolute separation of life and death, Orpheus wants the impossible: not Eurydice, but Eurydice as lost, as engulfed by the night. When he turns around to look, with eyes that inevitably belong to the regime of the day, this experience is immediately lost, hidden by the appearance of the 'other night'. What Orpheus really wants to witness is that movement of withdrawal; he wants to fathom his blind spot.

The experience of loss and the desire to cope with death point to something else: since language will always precede human experience and action, it entrusts literature with the 'incessant', 'interminable' endeavour to address the impossibility to begin. To write or to exist is always to begin again. Blanchot's 'other night' speaks about the impossibility of grasping the first signifier, about the insecure and inaccessible place of the subject's inscription in the symbolic order which grounds our ability to speak and write, and underpins narrativity as life's fabric. At that point, the reality of loss and trauma is not only intimately connected with impossibility, but also with the imaginary and a sense of possibility.

4

In an early version, *Directory 1* bore the subtitle 'How to risk work with work.' As a motto, it is inspired by Blanchot's poetics: 'The work of art is linked to a risk; it is the affirmation of an extreme experience' (ibid.: 236). Indebted to Orpheus' look, Blanchot connects two radical approaches to work: its exposure to death and the uncertainty of eternal starting over. It provides a perspective for deufert + plischke's preoccupation with death, violence and trauma throughout *Directory 1*, sketched above. But what about the second term, the destruction of the work? Stated in relation to deufert + plischke's meeting in Brussels, the piece's last words are: '*We stopped working with the methods we already knew. All we know about method is that when we are not working we sometimes think we know something. But when we are working, it is quite clear that we know nothing*' (D1).

Rather than rehearse the intricacies of Blanchot's philosophy of writing, it is worthwhile to dwell on the way deufert + plischke developed it into a method of their own. Blanchot remarks that '[t]he writer never knows whether the work is done. What he has finished in one book, he starts over or destroys in another' (ibid.: 21). It sets us on the way to understand deufert + plischke's drive to continually rework their pieces. Two performances of the same piece are seldom alike, although deufert + plischke's work is hyper-formulated and doesn't embrace an informal aesthetics of improvisation.

Pieces are thoroughly reworked overnight or from city to city, but work in progress is not a matter of improvement—sometimes quite the contrary—nor of a desire to create the ultimate piece. It is an issue of principle, in line with Orpheus and Blanchot: to rework means to destroy, out of a compulsion to face death and begin at the beginning. Hence the adage 'How to risk work with work?'

This principle permeates the work on all levels, mobilized by a method of 'formulating and reformulating', which is practised by deufert + plischke between themselves, but also in workshops and in the creation of group pieces. All the participants who take part in this process receive a notebook to write down personal memories. Afterwards, they pass their writing on to their neighbour, who makes alterations to it and passes it on to the next person. Step by step, memories lose a clear source, transform into fiction and gain a more precise form through the many accurate reformulations. deufert + plischke comment on their method:

> For us it is important to practise a lot of formulating and reformulating in our work in order to keep it constantly (re)thought and thus alive for the repetition of the performance. We tell each other our memories and then we try to write them down (for the other), create a story, a context, a place. Then we read it again and experience both how it changed and that it is impossible to archive or store memories. They change but via telling them at least they don't disappear (2005b).

The relation between memory and change is crucial to understanding the method's potentiality for narrativity. deufert + plischke comment, hinting at the myth of Europe:

> Deterritorialization is not what our method is concerned with, rather the desire to return to a moment even before territorialization took place. Through the reformulation of your memories by others, you start to doubt a place in your own memory that you thought was familiar to you. Eventually you touch upon a moment before the territory of your memory is set. It's about an active approach to your own memory (2005a).

Again, a deeply melancholic drive propels the work: it belongs to what always precedes it and aims to grasp its impossible origin. And charges it with the compulsion to risk work with work: 'During the reformulation of perform-ance texts we go even as far as to destroy all the intermediate versions. There is no genealogy of a text and its development. It keeps you alert and attentive, and moreover it entails a calm: you lose the anxiety to lose things' (ibid.).

5

'*How to knit myself a difference?*' While we watch footage of a fitness programme on television, the narration of *Directory 2* focuses on the body. A critique of the anatomically correct body is an ongoing concern in the work of deufert + plischke, who deconstruct an essentialist view of the dancer's medium in order to imagine different bodies. This aim to unsettle the pretence of unifi-cation and identity resonates again with Foucault's genealogy:

> The body is the inscribed surface of events (traced by language and dissolved by ideas), the locus of a dissociated Self (adopting the illusion of a substantial unity), and a volume in perpetual disinte-gration. Genealogy, as an analysis of descent, is thus situated within the articulation of the body and history. Its task is to expose a body totally imprinted by history and the process of history's destruction of the body (1977: 148).

This approach to the body as a contradictory terrain of experiences, lan-guages and cultural practices prepares us for an alternative understanding of anatomy.

On the screen of *Directory 2*, we follow a camera that wanders through a museum, to stand still in front of a showcase with a human skeleton on dis-play. Then the camera wavers and glides along another showcase with knitwear—bonnets, gloves, socks. '*Dear body, you are in movement, like the story lines cross, mix, appear and disappear. Anatomy is a story we invented, a story of fixed body parts, a picture of a body. We like to tell it as a transporter of morals, truth, form, content. The picture of anatomy replaces a life lived in movement. Nobody con-sists of the same stories and this is why nobody walks the same way although we share the same fiction of anatomy*' (D2). Anatomy is not unequivocal, the body not a mere image, but a container of stories, the witness of a life lived in movement. For deufert + plischke, anatomy is what most strongly conveys dominant cul-tural ideals of the visible body in dance, and thus what requires a critical ap-proach to practice and training. Once opened up, anatomy's potentiality for choreography becomes clearer: the ties between movement, memory and narrativity propel the imaginary in deufert + plischke's work.

The melancholic drive of the imaginary does not only circle around the horizon of an ideal image; it is also pulled about by a string of absences. Throughout the memories and stories in *Directory 1* and *2*, exactly that becomes intuitively clear: the outline of a poetics of holes. Ouranos' severed genitals and the young Plischke's ripped long johns indicate deliberate acts of cutting. Life's narrative fabric is torn and punctured, the body bears marks and inscriptions: the thread tore when Europe was seduced, abducted and raped; the penetrating sound of gunfire unleashes myriad memories of death, loss, trauma; anecdotes remind us of anatomy, gender and the violence of culture imposed on the body. The subject's inscription in the symbolic order remains an insecure one: the futility of digital editing testifies to the impossibility of coinciding with the other and wiping out difference; the first signifier recedes, Orpheus' endeavour to trace the origin is trapped in the interminable character of the work.

Then, what is choreography as knitting? To let the needle sink into the yarn and connect holes with holes. That is to incorporate loss, trauma and remote memories in a tissue of myths and shared stories, to create a place for mourning. That is also to continuously formulate and reformulate one's work in order to stay alert, resist prescribed patterns of anatomy and gender, and put identity at risk. That is to acknowledge one's inscriptions and finite access to the world in order to embrace the social—in collaboration and in the theatre—as a space where meaning can circulate and difference exist. The underlying question is: '*How can I knit myself my own private political body?*' (D2).

6

In his book *Abwesenheit* (2006), the German dance theoretician Gerald Siegmund proposes a theory of absence and a model for the analysis of dance that adopts a Lacanian vocabulary. Siegmund connects the symbolic with culture as it is represented in the conventions of the stage and in dance technique, the imaginary with body images as projected by both dancers and spectators, and the real with injury, pain and the body's materiality.[3] Both the subject's insecure place in the symbolic order and the impossibility of signifying the real open up an imaginary realm. The interaction between the three levels is what constitutes a 'negative space', which 'opens for the subject an individual *Freiraum* [a free zone for self-development] of thinking, feeling and perceiving' (Siegmund 2006: 172). It is the mental space of the desiring subject on stage, thick with memories and projections, but 'de facto physically absent' (ibid.). In Siegmund's aesthetics, potentiality and agency, as they are shaped in the imaginary of dance performances, appear always in relation to their cultural embeddedness and against the horizon of death.

In deufert + plischke's phraseology, this imaginary negative space opened up in performance is a product of knitting, epitomized by a pair of tights. As a metaphor for the imaginary, knitting relates to both a layered process (self-narration, genealogy, reformulating, choreography) and a product (a fabric of memories, a different anatomy). *'Could I knit better I'd knit myself my own biographical clothes!'* (D2). Driven by a desire for difference and change, deufert + plischke are trying to knit themselves their own place, their own death, their own body, and suggest that 'cloth' and 'clothes' contain all these imaginary elements. Yet the costumes in the *Directory* trilogy are nothing more than generic grey dance trousers and a tank top: not exactly clothes that evoke certain references. While the narration of *Directory 2* talks about clothes as a place to get started, deufert + plischke project images of themselves dressed in tights: first on a piece of cloth, then travelling through the theatre space and eventually upon their own bodies. The action introduces an explicit connection between the actual bodies of Deufert and Plischke and the narration: *'Thinking of my own biography I grasp it like a bunch of clothes. Nobody without memories escapes into migration. Nobody without clothes escapes into migration. Nobody without stories escapes into migration. No-body'* (D2). As a dancer, to begin to travel into the imaginary one needs clothes, an awareness of life's perforated narrative fabric as much as of one's dress.

Following Siegmund's remark that the imaginary negative space doesn't find a physical equivalent on stage, we could say that deufert + plischke are dressed in narrativity and even in sound, wrapped in an acoustic imaginary. In *Directory 2*, the rhythm and many repetitions of the text call attention to Gillian Carson's voice, which is combined with a meditative soundtrack that underscores the narration, creates cross-references and triggers memory. But, if choreography as knitting takes place on an imaginary level carried by narrative and sound, then what about the visual component: what does the 'actual' dance look like?—because Deufert and Plischke are dancing, indeed, their sparsely lit bodies engaged in what appears at first sight only as noodling and doodling. Their movements have an easy and curiously nonde-script quality, they resist reading, they skirt the illegible, as if led by a non-visual logic—in sharp contrast to the pictorial video imagery of nature and travelling. The presence of Deufert and Plischke is inward, pensive, silent. They are dancing with closed eyes, as if guided by an internal voice, awakened by listening. Most striking is the detachment of the narration and the dance: Carson's voice doesn't have a body; the bodies of Deufert and Plischke are mute. In that gap between the auditory and the visual resides Siegmund's negative space, exuding the heterogeneous imaginary realm of different, strange and possible bodies.[4]

The principle of separation between the visual and the acoustic inspires the French philosopher Jean-Luc Nancy in his reflections on the painted por-trait. A portrait is deprived of the person's voice, but makes the sonority of silence heard that reminds us of the irreducible 'not-totality' of the arts. The latter opens up an endless resonance between different media. Similarly, the medium of dance includes alterity—or even: the movement that induces res-onance in the order of the body and unceasingly slices it in 'eidogenous zones' is the very core of dance. Nancy calls the resonance of forms the 'ground' of things and connects it with his notion of 'methexis' or participation, as a fun-damental part of any mimesis. Unlike imitation, mimesis craves the inim-itable; methexis is what unsettles the alleged unity of visual regimes (Nancy 2004: 172–9). Crucially, Nancy's argument revolves around the sensorial mode of listening as a form of participation. We are in the sound (and not opposite of it), and we hear ourselves sound and resound to a certain extent (while it is impossible to see ourselves see). It is while listening that we are touched and moved, that our cogito is in the resonance: 'not any longer as *punctum caecum*, but as *corpus sensitivus*' (ibid.: 179).

Nancy doesn't seek to reconstitute a fulfilled, unified and transparent subject, though, as the subject is perpetually immersed in the multiple tem-poralities of desire. Peter Sloterdijk points out that the ear orientates us in the world, that subjectivation is in the first place related to listening. He speaks about the 'sonorous cogito', the self-hearing of our inner voice of thought. Subjectivity is not fundamental but medial in nature, as a sounding board: unsteady and susceptible for arriving acoustic presences, immersed in a sphere already brought to resonance by others (Sloterdijk 2007: 66–8,

72). That we *hear* our bodies as a multitude of intensities, images and practices: such is also deufert + plischke's approach to anatomy, gender and desire, and ultimately to choreography. In *Directory 2*, listening to memories guides this self-reflexive moment and prepares both performers and spectators to imagine alternative bodies and subjectivities. The inaudible makes itself heard in the silence of the dancing bodies, a resonant gap that reminds us of alterity and entrusts us with a sense of possibility.

## 7

'If I tell the story to a "you", that other is implied not only as an internal feature of the narrative but also as an irreducibly exterior condition and trajectory of the mode of address', writes Judith Butler (2005: 38). Beyond the artist twins' mutual witnessing and reformulation that shapes their self-narration, beyond their reflections on difference and the subject's opacity to itself, how does deufert + plischke's work actually communicate? What about the 'you' in the theatre, which is also a group of individual spectators responding to an address?

As the sound dramaturgy of *Directory: In Be Twin* is so dominant, audience members find themselves literally in the sound, and are as a consequence almost lured into deufert + plischke's imaginary realm. This contrasts with deufert + plischke's visual presence on stage, which is inward, distant and withdrawn from the audience. *Directory 2* has an open ending, a persistent silence that is not resolved by deufert + plischke, who remain seated at the side of the stage, but don't return to greet the audience. The only moment of direct address through eye contact happens at the end of *Directory 1*, where deufert + plischke walk over to the audience and hand out small presents, such as pieces of knitwear: as traces or documents they affirm the spectators' complicity as witnesses to the alternative places they've been knitting out of narrative. Addressed as a witness or via an imaginary you, the audience travels into a heterogeneous, foreign world. But at the same time deufert + plischke cherish an inclination to withdraw themselves into their hermetic, personal mythology—a flirt with solipsism that seems to contradict their poetics. Does *Directory*'s hyper-formulated construction allow for deufert + plischke to surpass the fiction of the 'artist twins'?

After several years of work as 'artist twins', exploring bubble life and the impossibility of coinciding with the other, deufert + plischke created the group choreography *Directory 3: Tattoo*. It takes up the issues from the first two parts of the trilogy as a point of departure, but unfolds them in an altogether different way. deufert + plischke's interest in choreography has never been in developing an aesthetics or movement language, rather in questioning how one relates to movement. This reflects on the way one trains, thinks and speaks about movement as a way to risk the dominant order of the body. Yet, how do they combine the poetics explored in the *Directory* project with the actual writing of movement? Together with three other dancers (Maria Baroncea, Eduard Gabia and Willy Prager), deufert + plischke tried for the first time to apply their method of formulation and reformulation to the development of movement material, guided by the question: is it possible to share physical memories? But now it also concerns a collaboration that extends to a group of people, foregrounding the social aspects of both method and subject matter. The passing of notebooks between the dancers creates a specific scene of address in the studio, which combines the solitary effort of writing with the physical presence of other people. How does this 'proto-social' scene transform, once it is moved from the closed studio environment to the stage?

The title *Directory 3: Tattoo* reminds us of Sloterdijk's comment on Blanchot regarding the impossibility of beginning at the beginning. For Sloterdijk, writing (and art in general) is indebted to what always precedes it, and this is not only language, but also the 'preliterary text of life' (1988: 15). Life is marked, the soul is tattooed with sense connections and learning processes: it is in learning to speak that one gains distance and freedom from the signs and inscriptions that one is, that a world and a realm of potentiality open up. Unlike Blanchot's writerly solitude, Sloterdijk's space of literature is the space of philosophy and the space of theatre. It is devoted to natality (rather than mortality) as a sign of human finitude, and it requires the public sphere as a stage for symbolical actions of world initiation. Going public is coming into the world, distancing oneself from one's tattoos, sharing them with others and running the risk of acquiring new tattoos. Sloterdijk's poetics and anthropology are reminiscent of Foucault's genealogy of descent, which ties itself to the body. But Sloterdijk pushes the use of the bodily metaphor even further: 'The inscriptions are often situated in withdrawn places, where no proper looking or sensing can reach—at the soul's blind spot, at the inaccessible borders, at the downsides and back surfaces of the dark body, which I

am' (ibid.: 26). This thought also contains the core of Sloterdijk's Orpheus interpretation: Orpheus' turning around speaks about his impossibility to look
himself between the shoulder blades, where his inscriptions reside. We need
the gaze of others to come to terms with our own invisibility to ourselves
(see Sloterdijk 1988; 15–19, 25–9 specifically). In *Directory 3: Tattoo* the social
is linked with a specific scene of address: how to symbolize our proper difference in the public space of the theatre?[5]

8

The stage is dimly lit by a few fluorescent lamps. A low electronic soundtrack
zooms in the background. The space is empty, apart from a table, two chairs,
and at the right side a diagonally placed black wall, like a blackboard: a
writer's resort or a school class rather than a dance studio. The only view
upon the world outside is a small window, actually a video projection of a
camera travelling through a landscape. At the bottom of the wall, a projected
text rolls by, sentence after sentence, throughout the entire performance—
is this the actual choreography, as text? Bits and pieces are reminiscent of a
process of formulation and reformulation: '*Restart. This is the place for a new
beginning.*' Or: '*The space is a place full of biography, alive and out of breath. Lots of
memories which are breathtakingly alive. Move along the corners and the borders of
the clothes and furniture of your biography*' (D3). In between, the text unveils
personal memories, which are also translated into descriptions of movement,
as a score waiting to be performed: '*Drop to the floor and lie down on your back.
Place your hands next to your ears with the palms on the floor. Roll over on your left
side. This is my space. Show us your space with your hands. I am not alone*' (D3). The
piece is a series of exercises in socialization—or, better, in world initiation.
'*Today is the first day of the rest of my life*' (D3). How to begin?

The choreography of *Directory 3: Tattoo* unfolds slowly, as the dancers perform solos, one by one dispersed in the space. The movement material is
highly idiosyncratic but articulate—and in that respect very different from
the quasi-formless movements in *Directory 2*. The choreography's imaginary
is unleashed by physical memories, readable in meaningful details: from hints
at early body memories such as sucking and crawling to joyful jumping and
games like hopscotch. These elements pop up in longer phrases that embrace
a certain level of abstraction, which betrays a choreographic process of

articulation and reformulation. Throughout the performance, repetition functions both as a structuring element for the choreography and as a way to touch upon reformulation and change. Processes of knitting temporal difference, as introduced in the first two parts of *Directory*, here find a choreographic equivalent. Halfway into the piece a blackout occurs, the performers 'erase' the video projection with chalk. Then, a caption states: '*Again (from the beginning)*.' Now, Hubert Machnik's electronic sound score dominates the space, an auditory movement scanning into the past and involving performers and audience in a ghostly listening experience.[6]

Although the five dancers are mostly immersed in their own worlds, they also establish relations by observing each other. They engage in quasi-unison dances and exchange parts as if guided by the question of whether it is possible to share physical memories. At this point, many differences between the dancers become apparent: their bodies have different physicalities and training, and they are shaped by different lives and stories. Mutual difference is addressed in gestures of comparison and juxtaposition, a choreography that is both simple and infinitely intricate. It is tempting to read the piece on a political level, involving change (difference over time) and living together (mutual difference), but isn't that a quick analysis? If *Directory 3* talks about coming into the world and socialization, then difference needs to be discussed also on a third level: subjectivation requires the social, as it ultimately revolves around the inaccessibility of one's proper difference.

How to symbolize one's invisibility to oneself in the theatre? Haunted by the paradox that this invisibility cannot simply be made visible, the impossible access to one's origin must be addressed through a 'symbolic' relation that is a formal recognition. In this respect, the theme of repetition in the choreography can be regarded as a symbolic activity reminiscent of Blanchot's incessant writing. But a symbolic approach is also at issue on the level of the movement material itself. The performers bring the space behind their backs repeatedly into focus: by performing with their backs toward the audience, by bending and exposing their backs, by lying on the floor and shielding their backs, by a swinging arm probing that blind space. And sometimes the drama of these 'inaccessible borders, at the downsides and back surfaces of the dark body, which I am' (Sloterdijk 1988: 26) crystallizes in a single gesture: a hand placed on one's own back, with an open palm. It is a symbol that marks one's vulnerability, retraces the tattoo of one's inscriptions, and gestures toward the others.

But then, what to think of the insistent falling back on memories as a field of reference, even reaching toward early childhood? Can narrativity and memory be regarded as an indirect address, or as a circumvention of one's inaccessible origin? If the latter eludes visual regimes, can it perhaps be heard, as Nancy suggests? In *Directory 3*, the bodies are stunningly silent, as if deprived of their voices, yet they do 'speak' in all the gestures and movements that evoke memories, stories and symbols. In contrast to the music, the bodies' silence reminds one of Nancy's ground of things, as a resonant gap unsettling the order of the body. Not so much the 'irreducible not-totality' of the arts is at stake here, but the reverberation of a more fundamental silence, which Sloterdijk calls the '*sprachlose Kinderanfangsnacht* [speechless children's night of beginning]' (ibid.: 51).

The interest in early memories circles around a gap: the absence of consciousness and memory of one's own coming into the world. Though deufert + plischke's method of formulation and reformulation aims to return to a point before the territorialization of one's memory, it meets the same hole as a limit. One can't start with oneself as a speechless being, prior to language. 'That is why he [man] covers up the gap of origin with stories, and starts to be entangled in narratives, because he is a being that can't own his beginning' (ibid.: 39). A radical sense of self-narration does not just spring from 'life's preliterary text', but addresses its precarious character: that we have speechless children's nights behind our backs also means that we don't begin, but that we *are* begun. Tradition takes our place and relieves us, though not without imprint: at some point it calls for self-realization, for resistance and deliberate cutting, for formulation and reformulation (ibid.: 42–51). '*This is the empty space of my life. But when the breathing continues maybe this noise outside will stop. I open my eyes*' (D3).

## 9

Let us return a last time to deufert + plischke's motto: 'How to knit your own private political body?' *Directory 3* seems to embrace a tension between the appropriation of a private body and the theatre as an arena to act it out politically. Though we are in a theatre, the set design suggests that the dancers are still in the closed studio space: a kind of experimental space, removed from the outside world, rather than an actual social environment. The 'outside' is symbolized by video projections of a landscape (the 'world') and text ('language'), and also seems to percolate through the dancers' bodies. Yet, the dancers are mostly immersed in their own world, locking out the spectator (the 'other'), even withdrawing themselves from the theatre. *Directory 3* is not concluded by the performers greeting the audience, but by an open ending. For about 20 minutes the five performers stand still, nodding their heads as if in a trance. Their eyes are closed: a symbol for our constitutive blindness, a suspended choreography of memory, a gesture of listening to inner voices, silences and arriving acoustic presences. All the while it is silent and the text states: '*Again (from the beginning)*' (D3).

Does *Directory 3* propose a solipsist universe then, nothing more than reluctant exercises in socialization that time and again are enmeshed in repetition and closure?[7] Over against Butler, Nancy and Sloterdijk, who all link narrativity as life's fabric with possibility and a movement toward the social, deufert + plischke also insist on Blanchot's incompatible position, which is perhaps inscribed in their method of reformulation: a sense of *impossibility* tied to the solitary moment of writing. This conflict courses through the *Directory* trilogy, stays deliberately unresolved and fuels the utter strangeness of *Directory 3*. How to knit your own private political body? Though the choreography is hospitable to difference, to other perceptions, opinions and possibilities, these are not merely celebrated as tropes of emancipation—which would risk embrace of the comfortable expressivism of the enlightened subject. *Directory 3* finds its urgency and political potential also elsewhere: in paradoxical choreographic gestures that symbolize a sense of impossibility —rather than express solipsism. Subjectivation happens through this symbolical activity that allows for a certain distancing from one's tattoos, by giving them a place without totally overcoming them.

That deufert + plischke keep commuting in *Directory 3* between the extremes of worldly and solitary perspectives thus appears to be a strategy to address difference in relation to one's proper difference. As a spectator, one cannot simply lean back—it is not just happening 'over there'. The performance's lack of resolution provokes a strong discomfort in the spectators, who are left in the end with the dark mirror of a persistent silence, knitting everyone's blind spots into the performance's fabric. The result is an uncanny boomerang effect, *as if* everyone present is sent back into a solitary space of reflection: audible in the unending silence that concludes *Directory 3* is the profound muteness lingering in one's own drama of coming into the world. Yet, in their efforts to make sense of it, both dancers and spectators are exposed and involved in a shared symbolical activity—we are in a theatre, after all.[8]

*Notes*

1  Performance text *Directory 2*, unpublished. All the quotes taken from the performance texts of *Directory 1, 2* and *3* will be put in italics and additionally referred to in the text as D1, D2 or D3 if required.

2  Remark that Kattrin Deufert's reflections on the myth of Europe stem from her unpublished essay 'Mythos Europa', written in German, which hints also at a relation between knitting (*stricken*) and entanglement (*Verstrickung*).

3  For a detailed introduction to Gerald Siegmund's model, see Siegmund (2006: 171–231).

4  Siegmund devotes interesting pages to the 'acoustic imaginary' in the work of choreographers Boris Charmatz and Meg Stuart, in which the separation of the visual and the auditory plays a central role (see Siegmund 2006: 172, 199, 223–36, 427, 441–2).

5  My thoughts below on the relation between one's proper difference, the public space and symbolical visibility are indebted to the Belgian philosopher Rudi Visker (2007: 11–67, 103–39).

6  Hubert Machnik's sound score is based on his composition *Empty Rooms* (2000). As basic material, Machnik recorded signals for the blind at street crossings. Then he sliced the original recording into bits and pieces of only a few seconds each and looped them, moving backward through the material. The result is a soundtrack scanning itself, moving from the future toward the past, which creates an uncanny experience that addresses memory. See also www.hmach.com.

7  For an inspiring analysis of the historical ties between choreography, subjectivation and solipsism, see André Lepecki (2006: 17–44).

8   In September 2007, deufert + plischke premiered the new group piece *reportable portraits*, and for the first time returned to the stage to receive the applause and greet the audience. This explicit acknowledgement of the audience steered their work into an altogether different direction, while still negotiating the tension between the social and the solitary. For an extensive discussion (which can be read as a sequel to this essay), see Jeroen Peeters (2008).

*References*

BLANCHOT, Maurice. 1989 [1955]. *The Space of Literature* (Ann Smock trans.). Lincoln: University of Nebraska Press.

BRANDSTETTER, Gabriele. 2005. *Bild-Sprung. TanzTheaterBewegung im Wechsel der Medien* [Image-Leap: DanceTheaterMovement in Changing Media]. Berlin: Theater der Zeit.

BUTLER, Judith. 2005. *Giving an Account of Oneself*. New York: Fordham University Press.

DEUFERT, Kattrin and Thomas Plischke. 2005a. Interview with author, Leipzig, June.

——. 2005b. Interview with author and Myriam Van Imschoot, Leipzig, September.

——. 2007. 'Statement by Deufert and Plischke Introducing the Directory Project'. Available at: www.artistwin.de (accessed June 2007).

FOUCAULT, Michel. 1977 [1971]. 'Nietzsche, Genealogy, History', in Donald F. Bouchard (ed.), *Language, Counter-Memory, Practice. Selected Essays and Interviews*. Ithaca, NY: Cornell University Press, pp. 139–64.

LEPECKI, André. 2006. *Exhausting Dance: Performance and the Politics of Movement*. London: Routledge.

NANCY, Jean-Luc. 2004. 'Das Bild: Mimesis & Methexis' [The Image: Mimesis & Methexis], in Jörg Huber (ed.), *Ästhetik Erfahrung* [Aesthetic Experience]. Zürich: Edition Voldemeer, pp. 171–89.

PEETERS, Jeroen. 2008. 'Restless Portraits. On deufert + plischke's *Reportable Portraits*'. *Dance Theatre Journal* 23(1) (October): 24–9.

PESSOA, Fernando. 1998. *The Book of Disquiet. Composed by Bernardo Soares, assistant bookkeeper in the city of Lisbon* (Alfred Mac Adam trans.). Boston: Exact Change.

SIEGMUND, Gerald. 2006. *Abwesenheit. Eine performative Ästhetik des Tanzes* [Absence: A Performative Aesthetics of Dance]. *William Forsythe, Jérôme Bel, Xavier Le Roy, Meg Stuart.* Bielefeld: Trancript.

SLOTERDIJK, Peter. 1988. *Zur Welt kommen—Zur Sprache kommen* [To Come into the World: To Come into Language]. *Frankfurter Vorlesungen.* Frankfurt am Main: Suhrkamp.

———. 2007. *Der ästhetische Imperativ. Schriften zur Kunst* [The Aesthetic Imperative: Writings on Art] (Peter Weibel ed.). Hamburg: Philo & Philo Fine Arts/EVA.

VISKER, Rudi. 2007. *Lof der zichtbaarheid. Een uitleiding in de hedendaagse wijsbegeerte* [Praise of Visibility. An Outroduction in Contemporary Philosophy]. Amsterdam: SUN.

# PART III

EXPANDING CHOREOGRAPHY

DRAWING WITH FEET, WALKING ON HANDS:
ROBIN RHODE'S *FREQUENCY*

ANDRÉ LEPECKI

*Frequency*

> 1. The state or condition of being crowded; also concr. a numerous as-
> sembly, concourse, crowd.[1]

A dance at Haus der Künst, München, September 2007.

In one of the museum's galleries, a large, rectangular, raised platform covered
with a light grey surface occupies most of the space. On the platform, delim-
iting one of its narrower sides, by the gallery's entrance, we find a perfectly
lined-up row of white and black shoes. The white shoes are made out of chalk,
the black, of charcoal. Across the platform, next to one of the corners, a bicycle completely painted in light green lies on the floor; next to it, a tin bucket
filled with water. Detail: the bicycle is made out of soap, and thus the bucket
of water is immediately recast as an imminent threat to the formal integrity
of the object lying next to it. Around three of the platform's sides, sitting on
the floor or standing against the walls, the audience squeezes into the narrow
spaces. On the remaining side, also on the gallery's floor, next to the line of
chalk and charcoal shoes, we find a drum set, a prepared grand piano and a

percussion set. The piece is short, about 20 minutes—but this is long considering the timing of most of the live actions created by South African artist Robin Rhode—which sometimes last no longer than a couple of minutes. Another distinguishing factor: the performer is not Rhode but one of his closest collaborators, the dancer and acrobat Jean-Baptiste André.[2]

The whole piece is structured around a conceptually simple, but physically challenging set of tasks. The dancer must try to reach the other side of the platform alternating between wearing either a pair of chalk or a pair of charcoal shoes. This is not as easy as it sounds, for as soon as André, head and neck completely covered with a black hood, begins to walk on the grey platform, his shoes start to crumble, slowly collapsing under his weight. André drags his feet in order to leave chalk or charcoal marks on the floor, and the attrition also contributes to the shoes fast falling apart. Under the effect of these physical forces, André's walking becomes a slowed-down stumbling, a hesitant stop-and-go dance of precarious equilibrium. As he progresses, he leaves behind a trail of crooked black and white lines, broken bits of chalk and crumbled chunks of charcoal. Once each pair of shoes is completely destroyed (which does not take that long, sometimes only a few seconds), the hooded dancer halts, balancing on the tiniest crumble of matter under his foot or feet. Without the possibility of continuing tracing, of marking his crooked path, the dancer's task becomes a new one: to return to the perfectly lined up shoes at the edge of the platform without ever touching the grey surface with his feet. To do so, he must reverse his path and step exactly on the bits of matter left and on the lines he has just drawn. As André carefully retraces his steps, it becomes clear that his previous task of marking the floor had also been one of creating choreographies for future returns: the white and black lines on the grey floor function as temporal bridges, marking potential paths, waiting to be stepped over again. The problem is that those choreographic lines are spotty, broken, smudged, imperfect, discontinuous. To follow them back, to re-step exactly on the broken bits of chalk and charcoal without touching the floor or without falling, becomes almost an impossible task. Eventually, and repeatedly, André will completely lose his balance, and start to fall. For these moments, Rhode arranged a precise choreographic solution, repeated throughout the piece: as soon as André hits a dead end on his path, or as soon as he is about to fall, he must swiftly revert to a handstand, and walk on his hands to return as directly as possible to his point of departure. Once there, he can regain a normal stance, slip into a new pair of shoes/tracers, and start tracing forward, on the platform, once again.

It is striking to see how André's difficult walk, his dragging of feet, his precarious balancing act, becomes a dexterous skittering thanks to a simple body reorientation. There is much to be said about this easiness, this dexterity in the inverted stance, particularly in a racialized context, which is the context of a work created by a brown-skinned South African artist for a white-skinned French dancer-acrobat. The inversion of the body's stance through a headstand or a handstand is a particularly important choreographic gesture in hip-hop dance, to which the visual art works of Rhode directly refer to. Inversion is also an act that radically re-territorializes both ground and body. Louis Kaplan reads in the performance of bodily inversions within a racialized field a deconstructive practice that is also a politics (2007: 19). This practice unites the theoretical with the kinetic, and both with the political. Kaplan reminds us how Jacques Derrida in his aptly titled book *Positions* casts 'inversion' as a *theoretical operation of spacing* that nevertheless allows for the material irruption of the new within an existing regime of power. This irruption of the new surpasses, for Derrida, the purely theoretical to include also the innovative act, gesture or mode of living life: 'Thus, we must also mark the interval between inversion, which brings low what was high, and the irruptive emergence of a new "concept", a concept that can no longer be, or never could be, included in the previous regime' (1981: 42). Inversion deconstructs. But given its capacity for cutting, for spacing space, once inversion is practised by a moving body it becomes also a fundamental act of deterritorializing the body itself and, by extension, its political and social grounds.

Writing on how the Afro-Brazilian dance and martial art *capoeira* 'developed as a way of dealing with very immediate material, historical and political pressures' linked to the history of slavery in Brazil (a way where a particularly virtuosic acrobatic athleticism of inversion is central), Barbara Browning finds in *capoeira*'s emphasis on body 'inversions' a kinetic-political project of active resistance under racist and colonialist oppressions, where 'the important thing was being able to see the *world* upside down' (1995: 109, 116). In thinking about the centrality of the handstand in Rhode's *Frequency*, the eruption of this particular mode of inversion becomes an insistent or persistent political-kinetic gesture that erupts whenever one finds oneself precariously moving on a violently racialized field; whenever one progresses on a mislead-ingly smooth ground crisscrossed by black and white lines.

Upside down, André's hands do the walk, efficiently and with no hesita-tion, away from the lines he has just drawn with his feet. Upside down, he moves directly, quickly, inventing a new possibility for standing. Let's remem-ber that his face has been erased, hyperbolically, by a black cloth—so that he becomes a moving figure with a faceless black head. Here, we are reminded not only of the ways Browning describes the crucial role of de-facing in capoeira's handstand—a powerful counter-move to escape the scopic regime in which the black body is inscribed by the colonial project ('the upside-down face, like those magical cartoons from your childhood where the hair became a beard and the creased forehead a smirking, lipless mouth, grins at your at-tempts to fix it. And still those eyes are on you' [ibid.: 89]); we are also re-minded of how the faceless head is the figure Gilles Deleuze uses to describe (in *The Logic of Sense* [1990]) the mesh of bone and meat that expresses a whole history of violence of which the body is both protagonist and ground.

As André, upside down, returns to the line of shoes, he reverts to a nor-mal stance, immediately slips into a new pair (in the back and forth which becomes the rhythm of the piece, André always alternates between black and white shoes, between chalk and charcoal), and promptly resumes his difficult walk, always exploring new directions, new velocities, new pressures; always trying to go as far as possible toward the opposite end, always tracing graf-fiti-like black and white lines as if the grey empty platform was a fallen wall. The more he fails and returns, the more marks he leaves—tenuous tracks that are as many timelines between his recurrent origin and his final goal. Each line a tortuous labyrinth, just as all the accumulating lines, in all their con-vergences and divergences, weavings and overlaps, map out so many possi-bilities for choreographies yet to be danced—choreographies for the past as well as for the future. Some non-choreographic elements contribute to the piece's overall atmosphere. The three musicians, playing a score by Austrian composer and pianist Thomas Larcher, use their instruments to create high-pitched sounds, interspersed with crashing bangs reminding us of those 'per-cussive affects' that 'constitute blocs inseparable from the material' Deleuze and Guattari write about in *What is Philosophy?* (1994: 195). The clattering and high-pitched sounds create an overall noisy rather than melodic or harmonic effect, a sonic counterpart to the broken lines and the difficult progression of the dancer. Finally, or firstly, this dance piece for a black masked, white-skinned dancer-acrobat is titled *Frequency*.

## Zigzag

The question is how to put in relation disparate singularities (Gilles Deleuze, 'Zig-Zag', in Boutang 2004).

Since the early 1990s, Robin Rhode has been engaged in a systematic smudging away of many of the constitutive, proper and proprietary marks of differentiation that well-established artistic genres try to keep in place as unmistakable traits of their identity. When working in photography, Rhode's prints are profoundly sculptural; when working in video, his films are profoundly sonic (even if silent); while working in performance, his acts are profoundly painterly; while working in dance, his choreographic scores are conduits for the creation of drawings or sculptures (most often sculpture-drawings); and while drawing, he is often performing in front of an audience, and using surfaces other than paper (sometimes tri-dimensional ones) as support. It is as if Rhode's main task as an artist were to constantly ensure the creation of adequate conditions for a permanent and uncontrollable mobility between forms, traditions, materials and tools. There is a fundamental athleticism in this mode of approaching work—a dynamic, incessant, experimental and thoughtful zigzagging that for all effects could be termed, non-metaphorically, dancing.

Zigzagging between genres, between media, between still photos, slowed-down videos, live performances, sonic creations, animated short films, drawings and the creation of dances for film (*The Storyteller* is the title of a short film made by Rhode in 2006 mixing animation, installation, and again André dancing, quite often upside down) as well as for live performances, Rhode moves as that intriguing element that Deleuze called, in *The Logic of Sense*, 'the articulator': a non-locatable, incessantly moving absent-presence that constantly weaves surfaces and meanings with depths and bodies. For Deleuze, the necessarily unstoppable zigzagging of the articulator is precisely the condition of its constitutive placelessness, of its belonging only to movement. That is: to a physically concrete, endlessly belabouring *imperceptibility* that nevertheless creates and sustains and propels all forms of expression. In *The Logic of Sense*, first published in 1969, Deleuze gives as an example of an articulator the famous 'purloined letter' that titles Edgar Allan Poe's 1845 short story.[3] Given its fictional and literary source, this example could be seen as a metaphor. But, in the same book, Deleuze gives two other examples of articulators: the actor and the dancer. For Deleuze, the dancer/the actor is an articulator precisely because he/she is the agent that puts in relation all the disparate singularities of surface and depth, meaning and body, expression and content. This connective zigzagging, this putting in relation of what should 'properly' remain foreign, or estranged, this *athletic articulation*, is the dancer's privileged belabouring. That is why Deleuze writes, 'the present of the actor, dancer or mime—the pure perverse "moment" [. . .] is the present of the pure operation' (1990: 192). For Deleuze, the articulating operation performed by the dancer is certainly not a metaphor, even if it is always also traversed by metaphors.

In *The Logic of Sense*, Deleuze depicted the operation performed by the zigzagging articulator as a dynamics springing from structurally opposite elements—depth, which Deleuze sided with the body, and surface, which he sided with meaning/sense. About a decade later, the paintings of Francis Bacon lead Deleuze to rethink and complicate the play of opposition between depth and surface he had described earlier. In *Francis Bacon: The Logic of Sensation*, first published in 1981, Deleuze explores how depth and surface intermingle in the mutual co-creation of a geometry of sensation. Here, the body is that which excavates unsuspected depths in the thin (yet endless) layers of meaning; while meaning is that which ravages the body, revealing in the body's depths inescapable planarities. Revising his theory of sense via the uncovering of a logic of sensation, Deleuze maps how bodies and meaning both are composed by a multiplicity of exfoliating planes and all sorts of depths. Still, even in this new formulation, the particular dynamism and the blurring kinetics characteristic of the articulator remain. Its zigzagging is described by Deleuze in relation to the material conditions of art-making, and it gains a new name: the 'diagram'. For Deleuze, the diagram is not only, or not mainly, or not necessarily, a visible sketch, but the actual practice of the 'affective athleticism' through which painter and painting continuously and very concretely fold back onto and into each other in virtual and actual exchanges, in mutual co-creation (2003: 81). Deleuze emphasizes many times that the diagram is an 'act' and, as such, it has a specific autonomy, a specific 'manual' intelligence, and a specific agency that supersedes and reverses all the stifling over-determinations of the preconceived. In this sense, we could say that the diagram conjures and activates all the powers of the improvisational—if we substantially reduce the function of the spontaneous from this notion (without totally getting rid of it). Indeed, the diagram has all the force of an open experimentation with chaos, a mastery of both chance and the yet-to-come, both chance and the pre-planned, opening up all sorts of lines of flight before all sorts of repressive over-determinations: meaning, property, genre, habitus, telos and cliché.

In *Frequency*, Rhode performs and displays the creation of a kind of slow diagram, where precarious, broken-down, smudged zigzagging tracings and the athletic inversions of what hands and feet are supposed to 'properly' do in art-making, displace the slightly epic, or heroic, tone underlining Deleuze's description of the diagram's function in painting. Instead of the struggle between hand, canvas and chance, Rhode emphasizes the struggle between feet, floor and gravity. Thus a pedestrian diagram emerges: a diagram of nothing but itself, a diagramming of how all tracing always tracks past, present and future; a diagram that displays the political imperative of blurring away from the space of inscription the mode of marking that marks predominant or hegemonic regimes of expression and oppression. Indeed, if Deleuze saw 'blurring' as the operation that defigures the intrusion of the normative in the tracing of a figure in Bacon's painting, we can say that the verb-effect-event that best describes Rhode's athleticism as he creates his art by zigzagging in between a multitude of genres, media, supports, is: to smudge. In Rhode's work, smudging is not just the name of a response to an impetus toward interdisciplinarity (between drawing and dancing, or between sculpture and music, or between acrobacy and installation), but the outcome of an inevitably experimental dynamics where what matters is to cross back and forth between all sorts of boundaries in order to keep creating.[4] There is a risk to this crossing—the least of which is not to be taken seriously as an artist. And, indeed, in several of his live pieces, Rhode attaches to the virtuosic fast-paced athleticism that defines the task of the articulator a very strong sense of impending danger. He shows up at a time when the gallery or museum is filled with an audience, awaiting the arrival of the artist; he pushes his way into the crowd, sometimes even rudely, with the directness of a fighter, or maybe of a burglar, creates an action usually around the making of a drawing or a painting on an empty wall, and then leaves, as fast as possible. Get in, do the job, get out. Fast, in a narrow moment—since no one ever knows what the future may bring.

It is crucial to note that there is a formal and direct relationship between the particular qualities of Rhode's way of mobilizing the body in performance (whether his or André's) and the qualities of his very personal way of drawing a line. Rhode articulated the correspondence between his drawings and his performances by stating that his work at large 'essentially exists as drawing' and that 'ultimately, the performance exists as a kind of drawing study' (in Bellini 2005: 92). What feeds the correspondence between these apparently distinct art forms, what intensifies both their maximum amplitude, like a composite sound, is Rhode's emphasis on performing before an audience the work of creating a line—and then, on performing the necessary complementary act of smudging that line right away, of blurring its place, as if to show that even the straightest of lines does not function to mark or define a boundary but rather to indicate an infinitely fast zigzagging act.

Now, this athletic dynamics in Rhode's work, the performative identification of this boundless place for moving is, I would say, also a politics—one addressing the current effects created by the recent history of racism, of colonialism, of postcolonialism and of apartheid, which have defined the place we now call (perhaps too optimistically) 'the global'. Thus, a history and a politics not only confined to the particularities of South Africa's recent past and current present—but one also tied to (new) cosmopolitanisms that characterize today's mode of living and building the urban in a planetary order we now call (certainly too hastily) 'postcolonial'.

It is here, in our planetary postcolonial condition, in our new world order of rehashed colonial relations under thinly disguised neo-imperial bureaucracies, in our strangely quotidian spaces and motions built by old-new racisms, in the brand-new city-ruins of old colonies, that certain bodies are framed and perceived in such ways as to be condemned to live and move under conditions of permanent exceptionality, to use Giorgio Agamben's famous expression. Paul Gilroy expands Agamben's notion of 'state of exception' by stating that 'histories of conquest and famine alike reveal that colonial government contributed to the manifestation of bare life in historically unprecedented quantities and circumstances', and shows how permanent exceptionality is not at all a trait of the colony, nor even of the post-colony, but it is the political and affective constitutive condition created by and for the 'hyperdeveloped' West so that it may stay hyper-active in its hyper-development (2005: 48). This condition is totalitarian, we could say: it conditions all racialized bodies to engage with movement and to express movement in ways that remain both unexpected and dangerous.

In Rhode's *Frequency*, improvisation is what allows for the creation of the unexpected, of the non-charted, the boundless; agile inversions and ineffi-cient bipedalism are the modes of moving that take for themselves the task of making and unmaking new lines of flight. Thus the political need for ath-leticism. Thus the necessity of creating agile inversions and reversions; thus the perseverance of the dancer to keep going even while treading on treach-erous terrain; thus the stubborn action of always trying to leave a mark for future feet to walk (back) on—even if marking is the most excruciatingly frus-trating task one can do with one's feet. All these elements, performed by a faceless figure with a black head, animate Rhode's very particular critique of movement, a *kinetic* critique of how movement may invent new ways of moving on the old-new grounds of our immense planetary post-colony—a deceptively smooth ground, streaked by white and black colour lines, of which *Frequency* bespeaks, performs, enacts and makes visible, as a stumbling dancer draws broken lines with his crumbling shoes and then skitters quickly upside down, walking with his hands as in a controlled fall, surrounded by clatter and high pitches, white skin, black mask.

### The Crypt/the Fall

> The opening to the new city and the new world is this: the crypt where his falsetto (interruptive-connective bridge of lost and found desire, lost and found matter) and her dying fall (the sounding, mu-sical descent where action is made possible) glance and brush. Dance (Moten 2003).

In the crypts of the new cities of the globalized postcolonial, a *he* emits a high frequency that animates air and flesh and bone—a frequency that cuts across the urban, stitching away a line of flight, launching an arrowed-soul. While out there, in the harrowingly open openness of the new world, a *she* endlessly falls in a dying that also has no end, a dying whose (re)sound(ing) tracks the path delineated by a history of lost and found matter, lost and found ground, lost and found voices, meaning and lives. The exchange between these two lines of flight (one traced by high frequency, the other by the accelerating acoustic descent of matter), between glancing and brushing as two modes of being in the world is, Fred Moten tells us, precisely, a dance. Period. No metaphor.

Or not only not metaphor—at least not as long as the question of the glance, of the brush, of falling, and of high-frequency emissions and of acoustic descents remains attached to the question of racial and sexual difference, to a history of colonial violence, and to the forces animating the dance that cuts across and scrambles these questions, histories and forces, as so many entangled, crooked, zigzagging black and white lines.

Here, it would be crucial to remain for a moment with our three main elements, which are both present in Moten's writings as well as in Rhode's *Frequency*: a high-pitched vibration, a falling or descent, and a brushing effect. What looms, above and below, inside and outside, manifesting the possibility of these three elements to articulate themselves in a dance, is the eternally zooming, eternally moving ground, the ground of history, and the ground of the body-affect, where the crypt is dug, and toward which one endlessly keeps falling-dying, even if falling upwards, following the high pitch's arch, as in a headstand—'upside down, the sky is the ground beneath your feet, and the only heaven is the earth to which you are bound' (Browning 1995: 112).

In Rhode's *Frequency*, these elements merge in powerful assemblage: the high-pitched sounds of the live music, where measured rhythm never takes hold; the erasure of the face of the dancer, and the emphasis on a black head without eyes, or mouth or nose, creating a black stub, like a burnt piece of meat and bone; the athletic and effortless inversion of the body in recurrent headstands, as indexical gesture to a falling that is without end whenever one is not able to leave a choreographic mark on one's ground. And mostly, the unexpected agility of the body in this upside down stance, its amazing lightness and quickness as it moves around the platform, embracing and mastering the fall—so distinct from when it painstakingly and slowly and precariously walks–traces–dances while wearing the crumbling shoes of chalk and charcoal.

*Frequency*

> 3. a. The constant use or repetition of (something); frequent practice.
> Obs.

Moten invokes brushing and the glance as the mode through which this encountering of falling down and falling up may happen in the new cities of the new world. Given Rhode's explicit engagement with painting and drawing and their relationship to movement, we should remember that the recent history of painting could be summarized as revolving precisely around a crisis in the ongoing (non-metaphorical) dance between glancing and brushing under the spell of the gravitational pull. The advent of that set of practices that Amelia Jones correctly termed 'the Pollockian performative' (Jones 1998) marks the moment when brushing is exactly what can no longer be taken for granted in painting. In this mode of the performative, we are before a deterritorialization of the painter's hand that is constitutively bound to a re-territorialization of the painter's feet with regard to the canvas, which becomes the ground upon which the painter stands, moves about, walks or (non-metaphorically) dances. In this departure of technique, which is also a departure from a certain understanding of representation, and certainly from an understanding of how to represent the act of presenting representation, the quick tempo that characterizes the brush's and the glance's strikes on the canvas's surface is replaced by an extremely agile, zigzaggingly swift, but certainly weightier vision, by a gaze and a hand and a use of paint profoundly entangled with the bodily kinetic, with feet sliding on smudged surfaces, with the brush becoming a stick or a stump, and the painter's whole body becoming a conduit for paint to yield to gravity. There is a pulling down of both glance and brush, a new proximity between heart and ground, a necessary embracing of a falling that would be nothing more than the direction of a new regime for painting, and a remapping of the limits of the realm where the painter's sovereignty is reaffirmed as authorial.

In *Frequency*, we witness the postcolonial aftermath of this strange history of re-territorialized painting, glancing and brushing. The key factors are the choice of chalk and charcoal as markers, and the defacement of the dancer-draftsman, his hybridity displayed by the conjunction of the faceless black head with white hands that serve no longer to mark, but to walk. Crumbling powder replaces the liquid flows of paint, the grey horizontal becomes an enormous canvas, and the history of action painting as the assemblage of colour and dance appears contained in the stilled, gaping mouth of the unused bucket at the end of the dancer's path. Remember that to this open mouth, or hole or crypt, the dancer-draftsman must walk, but his crumbling shoes turn his walking into a sad spectacle of precarious equilibrium, and what starts to appear on the horizontal surface are not splatters, drips and stains but thick broken lines, crushed blocks of chalk, crumbled charcoal and smudges. Lines are drawn up to a point, but end abruptly in little piles of white or black, tracing a history of effort and of failing. In the history of Western choreography, the line has always been the smooth index of an ideally unbroken, teleologically driven movement, one drawn by feet fantastically reduced to a singular mathematical point isomorphic to the stylus's point—as, for instance, we can find in the eighteenth-century dance notations following Feuillet's method.[5] However, in *Frequency*, Rhode proposes a different history of/for inscription. If there is a goal, the path that leads to it is tortuous, filled with falls and fissures, detritus, mistakes, cuts, blocks and blockages. As with action painting, here the canvas remains the ground—but with the difference that the marks it bears reveal the specificity of a particular mode of inscription: the pressing and skimming and brushing that are proper to *drawing*.

Perhaps this is why Rhode has carried his line's qualities, which are the qualities it captures from movement, to all sorts of urban supports—with a clear privileging of tarmac and asphalt, cement and brick walls. Whether drawing on the outer walls of the House of Parliament in Cape Town (*Park Bench*, 2000), on the pavement of some Cape Town street (*Street Gym*; *He Got Game*, 2000) or on the inner walls of a ruined building in Mexico City (*Untitled/Landing*, 2005); whether drawing on empty white walls at the Walker Art Center (*Drawing Car*; *Washing Car*, 2003) or at Houston's CAM (*Exit/Entry*, 2004), or at the Perry Rubenstein Gallery in New York City (*Night Caller*, 2005), Rhode's concern is not only about deciding how to draw his lines (which is a question of style) but also about deciding *where* to place his lines and his art (which is a question of ethics and of politics). Thus Rhode transforms his drawings and performances into studious enactments of a politics of place— which is the work of the graffiti artist, perhaps the major genre in which certain artistic expressions are still overtly criminalized. As Rosalind E. Krauss writes on the graffitist: 'entering the scene as a criminal, he understands that the mark he makes can only take the form of a clue' (1993: 260).

Indeed, it should never be forgotten how the question of place (and of belonging to that place, of having full access to place) has informed, from the start, Rhode's work. 'Initially, I took a more political position, performing in the public realm in South Africa so as to reach out to an audience who had little or no contact with contemporary art. I am still motivated in realizing art as a need' (in Bellini 2005: 91). From this moment on, the urban landscape becomes an immediate partner, or 'a form of thought process', as Rhode puts it, a process which, in his case, appears as a fine mapping of those forces shaping the plundered terrain he chooses to create his art on: a terrain that, as native soil, was tainted by a long history of colonial violence and racist violations, a history of systematic exclusion and criminalization of black and brown bodies whose direct impact Rhode's paler brown skin colour could not have spared him from experiencing first hand. Not by chance, in many of his performances (*Night Caller*, 2004; FSRR, 2003) Rhode appears wearing a blue sports jacket with the initials W. P. S. S. S. U. (Western Province Senior Schools Sport Union), an organization prominent for its history of anti-apartheid initiatives and actions.

*Tracking Tracing Marking Lining*

> For the formal character of the graffito is that of a violation, the trespass onto a space that is not the graffitist's own, the desecration of a field originally consecrated to another purpose, the effacement of that purpose through the act of dirtying, smearing, scarring, jabbing (Krauss 1993).

In *The Optical Unconscious*, Krauss narrates the many (masculine) appropriations and interpretations of Jackson Pollock's drip paintings by a generation of artists such as Andy Warhol, Cy Twombly and Robert Morris. In her reading of Twombly's interpretation of Pollock's gestures, Krauss suggests that Twombly's replacement of the brush by the pencil is indicative of the specific kind of violence constitutive of any act of marking (any act of inscription). 'By 1955,' she writes, 'Twombly had stopped making paintings with the expressionist's loaded brush and had started using the sharp points of pencils to scar and maul and ravage the creamy stuccoed surface of his canvases instead. He had begun, that is, down the attack route which is that of the graffitist, the marauder, the maimer of the blank wall' (ibid.: 259).

Krauss' readings on the relation between violence, danger and the replacement of dripped paint by the inscribed line made by pencil (or by charcoal or by chalk . . .) allow us to understand yet another element that transpires from Rhode's drawings (as in his drawings of cars, but also, for instance, in his drawings for the films *Microphone* [2005] or *The Shower* [2004]), from his particular mode of 'jabbing' the canvas/wall which I have called smudging, and from his performances: a subtle yet very particular, very well defined, very pervasive temporality. This temporality (which arises mainly from his gestures' exactness, quickness and sharpness of focus) could be qualified as one of urgency, even of danger—as if Rhode's speed keeps reminding us that something not necessarily pleasant could be about to happen, may perhaps be already happening. This sense of impending danger in his actions and performances generates a sort of temporal paradox that traverses the experience of Rhode's work at large. This paradox can be described as a rare mix of the (apparently) quasi-impulsive way he approaches walls to quickly compose his drawings—or the way he dashes in and exits from galleries and museums—with the contemplative, almost endless time that erupts from his drawings, endless time enduring as the instant's content. The result is the odd mix of high physical energy and an almost melancholy affect that traverses his work (particularly in his more recent pieces: the touching *Color Chart*, the danced *The Storyteller*, and the amazingly filmic *Candle*, all from 2006). But if one considers for a moment life in colonized contexts, life under the rule of institutionalized racist laws, it becomes clear that there is almost a survival imperative dominating the paradoxical time required to keep on living in such violent places—places where historically the exercise of contemplation by the subaltern was perceived by colonialist powers as proof of native endemic idleness, and where the subaltern's active, agile and imaginative engagement with the world was cast as the manifestation of a dangerous, rebellious (if not plainly criminal) character. This is why Rhode, in the interview with Bellini, has to clarify: 'In order to survive in the world you have to develop a particular strategy and psychology' (in Bellini 2005: 92). In Rhode's case, this strategy produces a temporality that simultaneously places his work in the past (thus the crucial task of smudging his own drawings which he performs many times in front of an audience), makes it interpellate the present (thus the intensity of his live presence in performance), while producing a plurality of futures (thus the mix of contemplation and anticipation happening at the infinite speed of thought). The point is to displace time, or, as Robin says, the point is of 'locating the work beyond past, present and future' (in Gule 2005: 28). The point is to displace the present as stable referent. This is why even when Rhode steps into museums and galleries to quickly engage in a clear action (drawing, painting, erasing, smudging), it's as if his demeanour and sense of urgency purposefully displace the eventfulness of the event away from any material objecthood, away from his corporeal presence, even away from his drawings and smudges, in order to redirect the whole eventfulness of the event directly toward the sensation that something indefinable 'is about to happen'. The creation of a pervasive yet indefinable awareness that 'something is about to happen' would be the real event of Rhode's events. It's almost as if Rhode prepares the gallery space for a crime that is about to take place. If the gallery is a scene where Rhode performs, this scene is not totally dissimilar to a crime scene.

*Crime Scene*

> If we ask a modern subject 'where were you at the time of the crime?'
> the answer is: 'I was where the crime took place' (Sloterdijk 2000).

It was Peter Sloterdijk—in a short essay on the relationship between the temporality of the artwork and the globalization of the 'monstrosity' (*das Ungeheure*) he identifies as constitutive of our late modernity—who reminded us that to live in late modernity is to live in a permanent, and all-encompassing, 'crime scene' (ibid.: 9). For the German philosopher, the methodical transformation of the planet into a globalized crime scene—a transformation Sloterdijk sees as a direct effect of 'the Eurocentric era of 1492–1945'—is a result of the concerted acts of 'human agents, entrepreneurs, technicians, artists and consumers' (ibid.: 20, 9). The creation of the same (crime) scene as a place of choice for our living discloses modern subjectivity as 'the renouncing of the possibility of having an alibi' (ibid.: 10).

If Sloterdijk is correct in his assessment, we could nevertheless add that in the globalized 'crime scene' (a scene whose settings coincide with the setting into motion of the European colonialist project), even if no one is supposed to have an alibi, even if there is no possibility of finding a *place* that is not also a crime *scene*, there still remains the possibility for anyone to claim agency, to resist the setting up of life and living as a voyeuristically macabre forensic spectacle. There always remains the possibility of resisting the traps set up by representation in the persistent renewal of the conditions under which monstrous crimes are staged once and again, without relief, before our eyes, in our streets, with rigorously predefined and anticipated steps: the steps of habit and indifference. To accuse and to reveal the global as a crime-scene set up by the impetus of the colonial project—the reason why Rhode must refer so frequently in his performances to burglaries and small crimes (for instance, the amazing performance at the Walker Art Center in May of 2003, when Rhode performed a two-minute long piece to the blasting sound of a car-alarm, where he tried to climb a white gallery wall, only to leave all sorts of smudged tracks on it, and then leave as fast as possible), to a generalized state of emergency and of danger. For in these performances, he places us all, without exception, and emphatically so, within modernity's crime scene. This is why Rhode so frequently invokes modernity's emblem, the automobile, as a recurrent theme that must be reclaimed, erased, burglarized, destroyed (*Car Theft* [2005], *Untitled* [2003]).[6] Against this fantasy of a self-propelled subject, following the colonial imperative of hyper-mobility and hyper-development, the inverted body walks on hands, putting the world upside-down.

*Percursive Skins/Revealed Flesh*

[. . .] the descent, and the inverted head that reveals the flesh (Deleuze 2003).

The black hood, the mask, conceals the face, or rather turns the head into a black stump. The upside-down agility of the dancer indexes a being-for-falling as a condition of life. The high frequency of the music irrupts–interrupts–disrupts any sense of temporal and spatial linearity or coherence. The smudging of the choreographic lines on the floor indicates how to draw the present while aiming for future returns. All these elements of *Frequency* indicate that there are localized particularities in the dying falls and their soundings that Moten writes about: particularities that reverberate across all those 'new cities' in all those 'new worlds' opened up, ravaged, cut through, mapped, organized, brutalized, invented, quickly built and even more quickly ruined by the kinetic forces gathered and unleashed by the hypertrophied colonial impetus that animates the condition of globalization.

In the fantasy of our current postcolonial demise of these acts as something of the past, in our collective fantasy that describes current living as one taking place in a non-colonialist new era called 'globalization', it is important to keep listening to the concrete singularities of those particular sounds and falls Moten writes about: not only to learn how sounds and bodies resonate and clatter against each other on the violent grounding of the world, but to identify the conditions of their mutual co-creation and co-destruction. It is crucial to identify how the material conditions of sound production and movement production are predicated upon specific (political-desiring) arrangements of bodies. These arrangements reveal chiasmatic superimpositions of the sonic and the kinetic that produce a reverberating, resonating body that may very well be the biopolitical ground for countering the (re)current national-racist projects in the West. And it is not only that Deleuze may have indicated a possible way for thinking about this political-desiring resonance in *The Logic of Sense*, when he found in the skin the organ for a biopolitical calling where 'we stretch our skin like a drum, in order that the "great politics" begin' (1990: 84). This percussive–political–kinetic proposition for the body would have gained much if race had been explicitly invoked by Deleuze.

Talking drums, percussive skins, faceless heads, stumbling feet, falling bodies, screaming bodies, resonating each other in a high-frequency dance. It is precisely in the ongoing cryptic and cosmopolitan (re)arrangement of these corporeal-material realities and affects, these moving movements, which are always racialized realities and affects, that the performance of certain kinds of gestures, athleticisms, inversions and frequencies may initiate so many political and choreographic counter-movements, to reveal more desirable modes of living and moving in this crime scene we all stand on, move on, make move, and call, not so innocently 'the global'.

Notes

1  All the entry definitions of the word 'frequency' throughout this essay were excerpted from the *Oxford English Dictionary*.

2  I am keeping here to Jean-Baptiste André's own self-description as a performer, as found in a 2007 essay on his work by Nancy Wozny: 'Straddling two

worlds André remains close to his circus roots. "A lot of people consider my work as dance performance, and I want to draw their attention to this point. I am basically a circus artist and I defend it." '

3  For a discussion of Lacan's seminar on Poe's *The Purloined Letter* and for an acute critique of it by Jacques Derrida, see John P. Muller and William J. Richardson (1988).

4  I have written specifically about smudging in Rhode's work in *Robin Rhode*: *Walk Off* (2007).

5  For a discussion of Feuillet's method of writing as choreographic inscription, see André Lepecki (2004).

6  On the automobile as modernity's emblem, see Peter Sloterdijk (2000).

*References*

Bellini, Andrea. 2005. 'Robin Rhode. The Dimension of Desire'. *Flash Art* (October): 90–2.

Boutang, Pierre-André. 2004. *L'Abécédaire de Gilles Deleuze*. DVD. France: Editions Montparnasse.

Browning, Barbara. 1995. *Samba: Resistance in Motion*. Bloomington: Indiana University Press.

Deleuze, Gilles. 1990 [1969]. *The Logic of Sense* (Mark Lester trans.). New York: Columbia University Press.

——. 2003 [1981]. *Francis Bacon: The Logic of Sensation* (Daniel W. Smith trans.). Minneapolis: University of Minnesota Press.

Deleuze, Gilles and Félix Guattari. 1994 [1991]. *What Is Philosophy?* (Hugh Tomlinson and Graham Burchell trans.). New York: Columbia University Press.

Derrida, Jacques. 1981 [1972]. *Positions* (Alan Bass trans. and annot.). Chicago: University of Chicago Press.

Gilroy, Paul. 2005. *Postcolonial Melancholia*. New York: Columbia University Press.

Gule, Khwezi. 2005. 'At the Centre's Edge'. *Art/South Africa* 4(1) (Spring): 28.

Jones, Amelia. 1998. *Body Art/Performing the Subject*. Minneapolis: University of Minnesota Press.

Kaplan, Louis. 2007. 'Yahweh Rastafari! Matisyahu and the Aporias of Hasidic Reggae Superstardom'. *CR: The New Centennial Review* 7(1) (Spring): 15–44.

KRAUSS, Rosalind E. 1993. *The Optical Unconscious*. Cambridge, MA: MIT Press.

LEPECKI, André. 2004. 'Introduction: Presence and Body in Dance and Performance Theory', in André Lepecki (ed.), *Of the Presence of the Body: Essays on Dance and Performance Theory*. Middletown, CT: Wesleyan University Press, pp. 1–9.

———. 2007. 'Smudge', in *Robin Rhode: Walk Off*. Ostfildern: Hatje Cantz Verlag.

MOTEN, Fred. 2003. *In the Break: The Aesthetics of the Black Radical Tradition*. Minneapolis: University of Minnesota Press.

MULLER, John P. and William J. Richardson. 1988. *The Purloined Poe: Lacan, Derrida, and Psychoanalytic Reading*. Baltimore: Johns Hopkins University Press.

SLOTERDIJK, Peter. 2000. *L'Heure du Crime et le Temps de l'Ouevre d'Art*. [The Hour of the Crime in the Time of the Work of Art]. Paris: Calmann-Lévy.

WOZNY, Nancy. 2007. 'One Clown, One Room, Jean-Baptiste André Returns to Houston.' Available at: dancehunter.blogspot.com/2007/11/one-clown-one-room-jean-baptiste.html (accessed 26 May 2008).

FOUR YEARS LATER

RALPH LEMON

*Modern memory may indeed be archival, relying entirely on the materiality of the trace.*

—Pierre Nora

Well, there is what I plan, prepare; a particular knowing and there is what I know cannot, will not happen. The in-between tension is the reality of both knowing and not knowing. My prepared plan provides a semblance of courage. The illusion of courage is necessary in giving the shape/form to the amorphous and imprecise nature of what will actually happen: a daily event appropriate to uncontrolled circumstances and my precise daily discipline of being structurally available to this unknown.

To what unknown uncontrolled circumstance.

Walter Carter represents a kind of human nature weather. I can know wind, rain, cold, blue sky, the difference between atmospheric conditions, but I cannot forecast with any accuracy what any day will be like. I can only reasonably forecast the seasons, and my favoritism and/or annoyance with what a particular season will bring to my remembrance.

Walter also speaks to what James Young terms "the rhetoric of ruins." He is a very old man, a "debris" of the past, and a fragmentary element of an imagined history, a particular (peculiar) mark in that history. But it would be a mistake to mistake his mark in history for history itself, however often the distinction collapses.

A memorial marker. I can ask Walter to dance, because he and I both know he recently remembers his old dances; the one-step, two-step, and the slow drag, if he has not already forgotten. His dance and the trace that it recalls, its living history, speaks for itself. I'm not sure what else his body invokes.

> *Memory is blind to all but the group it binds. History on the other hand, belongs to everyone and no one, whence its claim to universal authority.*
>
> —Pierre Nora

I called his home three times. No answer. Away for the holidays, perhaps. I couldn't imagine where he would be. He hates to travel, I remember him complaining.

> *Instead of a fixed figure for memory (a monument), the debate itself perpetually unresolved amid ever-changing conditions would be enshrined.*
>
> —James Young

*3 January*

I called again at 10.30 a.m. the next day and a man answered, deep-voiced, "No sir, they're not home." It was Tavorus, a nephew, someone I'd not met. "They went to Yazoo City, they'll be back around 1.30," Tavorus said. Tavorus, that's an interesting name, I commented. "Yes, sir," he said.

I was relieved. Walter may be unhappy traveling but he was alive, in Yazoo City. And there he is "monumental," a fixed presence, representative of a past, not because he's in Yazoo City but because he is alive. Monumental, until we meet and again he becomes human temporality, an ordinary human presence, extraordinary and modern, collapsing time.

And then I thought, Walter may not be unhappy traveling; in fact, he may enjoy traveling a lot. It's his old body, worn out organs, and bodily functions that reject the experience of travel. Maybe that's the complaint I remembered.

*4 January*

Counter-mythology. Getting there, on a commuter flight from Cincinnati, Ohio, to Jackson, Mississippi, I was surprised at how remote I felt from the wonderment of going South, further South. As though I knew it, already, from before, as though I had had enough years of excitement and surprises down there a few years ago, in my beginning naive research, and now it was different, prosaic in fact, and no longer research. As if my family down South is prosaic, was always down South and prosaic, and not ever research.

The fear factor was different, a kind of cultural boredom. I was mostly interested in the weather, temperature. And this time I looked mostly at black people. Reading them for any potential infraction, what they might be capable of, on planes, in airports, at motels, and sucking pork rib bones in a nearby Shoney's. A baleful reading, that black folk seem to be in such critical suffering there, such as they seem in a lot of places. Before then I mostly looked at white people, attending the same spaces, also sucking pork rib bones, Mississippi white people, as if they were mythological monsters. Now I don't seem to care. This does not mean I am now fearless.

Our non-smoking motel room in Jackson smelled like cigarettes. Yes, this fact was terrifying and sad. I don't really know the South. I also didn't have much of a plan for being there this time other than some strange concocted experiment with Walter that I had designed and know and he doesn't know, and who knows what this encounter will ultimately bring and why it should bring anything. It will bring something. It is this charged ordinariness that is disconcerting and urgent. A new kind of research after all.

*5 January*

Counter-research. A dark thin man helped us put air in our front tires. "Twenty pounds too low," he critiqued. "Oops, it stopped. You'll have to put another 75 cents in the machine, if you want me to finish, and I gotta finish cause I'm on the clock," he said, with odd authority.

"I forgot that people talk funny here," Chelsea comments under her breath, without thinking.

"There, now this car will ride better, you'll feel it immediately."

I gave him 5 bucks and it startled him.

"Oh my. Yep, you can ride all the way to New Jersey on those tires."

We went scouting at a Family Dollar Store for some of the items on our list. Earlier I had described to Chelsea the tasks I imagined Walter decoding (or ignoring). She was obviously confounded.

"You're not going to make him wear a rabbit suit. How demeaning!"

I had bought the rabbit suit in San Francisco, at a costume shop on lower Haight Street. The other items we had to try and find there:

1. Box for the rabbit costume

2. Car grease

3. Screwdriver

4. Large ceramic vase

5. Ceramic rabbit (almost any size)

6. Ten-foot rope

7. Four or five old vinyl albums with jackets from the 1960s or 1970s

8. Baseball bat

9. Watering can

I immediately sensed the beginnings of the drastic culturally specific translation of our event. Family Dollar had its own confounding item list, stock and clientele. There were no ceramic rabbits but there were six-inch round ceramic basketball banks. No rope but there was white, purple, and blue plastic shiny cord and 10-foot black speaker wire. No baseball bats, not even the plastic kind. Surprisingly, there were large ceramic vases, Egyptian blue. I assumed Walter already had a chair, a metal washbasin, an empty soup can, and maybe an old baseball bat, discarded somewhere. We also shopped for phone cards. I bought one but later discovered that the checkout woman neglected to activate it.

Hello, may I speak to Edna? "Hold on," a young girl yelled, almost too fast to perceive, and then it sounded like she dropped the phone. Edna is Walter's second wife, his caretaker, although she always says he's getting around a lot better than she is, him being 20 years or so her senior.

FIGURE 1. Installation view of Ralph Lemon's (*The Efflorescence of*) *Walter*. Photograph by Eileen Costa.

"I got to go to the beauty parlor tomorrow, early, as early as I can. Don't know when I can be back, you know hairdressers, you gotta wait to make an appointment and then you gotta wait to git yo hair fixed and then you gotta wait to see what they did. And all the talkin' in-between, hard to say when I'll be back. Just can't say."

What time you think you'll leave your house? I tried to calculate, imagine how many hours she was unfolding.

And then she said, "Oh, maybe 9–9.30. It takes me a while to get dressed and out the house. Walter gets around better than I do these days."

Well, call us once you're finished with the hairdresser and maybe we can meet you on your way back home, on the hill, the gas station in Little Yazoo. We'll wait by the phone.

"If you say so. Sounds crazy to me but if you say so. I'll call y'all once I'm done with the hairdresser."

Walter lives somewhere in-between Bentonia and Yazoo City, near Little Yazoo, down and around quite a few small indistinct dirt roads. It was impossible to visit Walter without Edna, driving halfway to meet us on Highway 49, on the hill, at the gas station in Little Yazoo. So I made a plan to wait by the phone the next day, for as long as it took.

*6 January*

> If the place of memory is "created by a play of memory and history," as Pierre Nora believes, then "time may be the crucible for this interaction."
> —James Young

It was 10 a.m. and I looked at my haunting score. It seemed outrageously cryptic. I wondered what actually could be done, that is, if Edna called. If Edna did call, I assumed much of the day would be spent hashing out (in person) what could actually be done with Walter. And there I saw a courage issue: how available was I for pushing and easing up on what I wanted to have happen, to what would obviously be a more give-and-take conversation with Walter. What would be appropriate and not exploitative? And was not exploiting possible? I wouldn't know until we met and began.

The endeavor began to feel a lot like the mysterious neverland of 90-something Hicks Walker and the inscrutable Buzzard Lope transmission, on Sapelo Island, Georgia, many years back. An imagined ring-shout dance was all in my head . . . and there it stayed, it seemed. Hicks Walker controlled the entire endeavor. There was no exploitation, other than the exploitation of my own venture and aspiration. I didn't learn the undocumented Buzzard Lope from Hicks Walker. I did learn a lesson about how memory is mostly made up of air. We made up our own version of the Buzzard Lope, with the help of his daughter's loving second-hand, third-hand data. It would surely be a moot issue with Walter, as well. I doubted he'd be pushed around.

Waiting, looking out the window of my motel room. There's a great open field nestled behind the Best Western. Long sweeping brown grass and a few dark spots of large sink holes. A dozen tiny new pine trees popping at different spots around the sinkholes, at different heights, even in the bright cold. And young occasional deer, appearing and then disappearing.

The Gujarati Indian proprietors have a sizeable garden directly behind the building: greens, herbs, peppers, asleep and winterized. It goes well with the adjoining open field, all of which is sinking.

Okay Edna, call . . . call, I waited.

At 1.00 p.m. I called again. Another new voice, a young woman, disarmingly polite, Lawonda. "They're in Yazoo City. My grandmother's getting her hair done. Not sure when they'll be back. It takes a while, usually 2 hours."

They? Walter went to the hairdresser with her?

"Yes."

What time did they leave the house?

"Oh, about 12.45. They should be back by 3.30."

Damn, I thought to myself, sunset's about 5. I hate driving through the dark pitch woods of Mississippi at night. My eyes, it's my bad eyes that hallucinate.

Our motel room also started to sink. Stuck there, waiting.

Chelsea reminded me that this was the part I really loved.

Love? Glorify, maybe, but "love" waiting, frustrated? I couldn't imagine that kind of love . . .

" . . . [T]*ime may be the crucible for this interaction.*"

Edna called at 2.30. "Ralph, we're back home, finally back home. And I'm sure tired."

Could we still come by today? And then I didn't give her any time to answer. Ah, well, we're ready to go, we can meet you at the gas station in 15 minutes.

There was a long pause.

"Boy, you drive fast," she giggled. "I'm gon' need a little time, 20 minutes, half hour . . ."

We pulled up alongside Edna's dark blue '81 Chrysler. Walter was in the front passenger's seat seemingly asleep, until he saw us, and then, bright-eyed, opened the car door and almost ran to where we were parked. Not really a run, no, not even almost, more like a broken wobbly hop, mastered. I hugged Walter and felt his frailness, the jacketed bones, that of a young boy, teenager. I asked Edna if it was okay for Walter to ride with us. Walter was already in the front passenger seat of our car.

Following Edna's '81 dark blue Chrysler, I asked Chelsea to videotape our journey, making sure we had a repeatable and precise road map for returning to the motel, especially in the dark. And just in case: Mr Carter, where do you actually live? What's it called, Yazoo City, Little Yazoo, Bentonia, Oil City?

"Ain't got no name, I live in the country," he said.

As it turned out we had plenty of time and daylight and road.

Driving with Walter through these roads felt very familiar. I checked to see that his seat belt was secured.

So Walter, I have these things I'd like you to do, for a video play I'm directing. Simple tasks, things we all do every day that seem ordinary but that are in fact sacred, but we don't know that they are sacred but maybe some of us do . . . As important to our lives as prayer, whatever we pray to, and we all pray but maybe don't recognize we're praying, until we find something, and have to think about what it is we found. Something like that, like your running around the house every night before going to bed, so that you can sleep, because you have too much pulsing, vanishing energy.

Anyway, it's about you and me. I'll do them first, the tasks, and then you'll do them, however you remember them. I'll do them my way and you'll do them your way. And you can make as much noise as you want. And then we'll

FIGURE 2. Installation view of Ralph Lemon's (*The Efflorescence of*) *Walter*. Photograph by Eileen Costa.

FIGURE 3. Ralph Lemon, *Walter Carter in his bedroom in spacesuit*, 2006. Photograph © Ralph Lemon.

rethink what it was we just did and call them "events," because "events" sounds more determined than "tasks."

That's not what I really said. This is what I actually said to Walter on the way to his house: "Walter, It's so good to see you. I'm going to be here a few days and would like to visit you, come by every day and talk, do a little documentary videotape and take some photographs. I can't believe you're still alive."

Walter, excited, hearing what little he hears, yelled, "Yeah, sure, anytime . . ."

"Go on in, go on in," he yelled, once we were out of the car, rushing us into his small brick house, 1856 Cessna Road, the address on his mailbox.

We sat in his dark front room catching up, admiring Edna's becoming roaring twenties hairdo and Walter's unbounded childlike energy and faux lizard skin cowboy boots. I apologized for not following up from my last visit, the research of trying to get him to New York, two and a half years ago, to be part of the theater I was conjuring. To them it could have been yesterday, and so there's neither disappointment nor resentment, it seemed. I shared nothing of *Come Home Charley Patton*. Its ultimate descriptive process and experiences seemed completely irrelevant here.

There was a long conversation about their grandkids, lots of exotic names and different states, Walter's from another marriage and Edna's from another marriage, how many they might have and if they should count the dead ones. Lawonda and Tavorus were brought into the conversation and after a while everyone concluded that Edna alone has about 15, "But probably more like 16 or 17." With Walter they got as far as, "Ol' boy, let me see . . ." and the counting ended there. There were two great-grandkids present, Lawonda's kids; Tré Darious, who I thought was a little girl, who must have been the little boy with a high-pitched voice who yelled too fast and dropped the phone a few calls back, and Shakyla, a beautiful dark four-year-old, with six tiny gold front crowns. "I've never seen that on baby teeth before," Chelsea remarked, deeply curious.

There was a shorter conversation about the Sago mine disaster. "People expect too much from God. He gave you eyes, and a mouth, and ears, what else you want?" Walter mused, almost angry.

And I learned a few corrections to my earlier field trip notes; that "Gary" was actually "Jerry" and that "Gator Limb," the tree where they hung Gary, I mean Jerry, is actually "Jerry's Limb." I learned that the uncle who blew his brains out after seeing "the big black buzzard-like bird, a prophesy bird" actually saw a "big blue cock bird," which may also be a "prophesy bird," and then had his brains "blown out" by someone else. It was not a suicide. "It was late at night, in the dark. He had just finished workin' in the field, on his way home. He was a rough'un anyway, so who knows," Walter reminisced.

I also learned, with some karmic appreciation, that Captain Taylor, the sheriff behind Jerry's lynching, a long time ago, killed himself, committed suicide.

Walter was on a roll: "Colored folk don't kill themselves, they too interested in living, most of them. But white folks will kill themselves, commit suicide all the time. I could name six, seven folks used to live right round here. White folks don't care if they die, that's why they dangerous."

"White folks, black folks, that's a tall fight with a short stick," Edna added, finishing Walter's thinking.

We took a walk, scouted his yard, and discovered these possible event item translations:

A broken dangling basketball hoop in a tree

An old sardine can

A hose to replace the watering can

You got a washbasin Walter?

"A what?" he said.

Like that, I said, pointing to three metal tubs hanging from a shed.

"Oh, them is tin tubs, got three," he said.

A large empty soldering gas tank

A big pile of colorful wires

A wheel barrel sans wheel

A chewed-off deer leg . . . "White boys, hunters, and then the dogs got to it," Walter comments.

A shovel. And he said he could dig a hole, "Guess so, guess so."

An empty sheet metal dog house, with "Dog House" written on it in red letters.

An odd-shaped capped glass jar.

FIGURE 4. Ralph Lemon, *Walter Carter in his bedroom in spacesuit*, 2006. Photograph © Ralph Lemon.

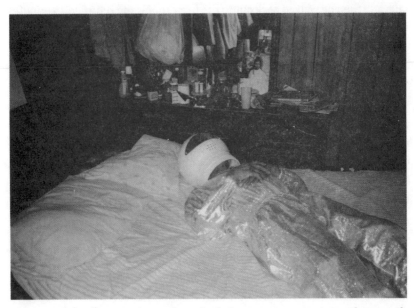

FIGURE 5. Ralph Lemon, *Walter Carter in his bedroom in spacesuit*, 2006. Photograph © Ralph Lemon.

At some point in the walk Walter tripped and fell, completely flat onto his stomach. He quickly stumbled up to his feet, in a body language I'd never encountered, like he was reminded down there that down there was waiting, calling. He stood, shaking a little and brushed himself off, embarrassed. "I ain't fallen like that in a long time!" He repeated, twice.

Early Sunday. Chelsea and I drove back from Jackson with a porcelain rabbit in hand, four 78 records, and three or four fading bright-labeled 45s, from a flea market. But no baseball bat. Other than the baseball bat and car grease, it seemed we had everything we needed for the rest of the week.

We met up with Walter at his house, after he returned from church. Edna let us in. We found Walter in his bedroom, lying across his bed fully clothed and asleep. He heard us at his door and woke up immediately as though sleep were always present but never deep enough to keep him away from the mindfulness of being alive . . . or something numinous like that. While Walter put on his shoes, tied his shoes, which took a while, Edna offered us some lunch; turnip greens, pork, black-eyed peas, and okra—food prepared by a friend from church because Edna "barely cooks anymore." Walter came into the kitchen surprised that we were eating: "I thought we was ready to go," he said, and then he walked back out to the front room, and returned 15 minutes later, exactly the moment Chelsea and I had finished eating. We said goodbye to Edna, who continued to sit and eat. Want to come along? I asked. "I'll probably be sleep when y'all get back," she smiled.

The plan was to drive Walter to the spot of the "old plum tree" where Jerry was hung 90 years ago and then to the Blue Front Cafe juke joint in Bentonia, to visit Jimmy "Duck" Holmes. But unbeknownst to us, Walter had other plans. As soon we were all in the car Walter told us we needed to do some other things first. What about Jerry's Limb? I asked, a little shocked. "Later, later," he mumbled.

Walter sat in the front passenger's seat and in a remarkable vocal calling, matching our car's velocity, rattled off which race lived where, owned which set of grass, hills, trees, and skyline, on either side of the many roads we ventured. "That's colored, that's white, that's white, white, that one's colored, colored . . . that used to be white, now it's colored . . . white on both sides . . . white on both sides . . ." This went on for 10 miles or so, obsessive, speeding up and slowing down with the pace of the car. We turned a corner and then it started again. A profound vocal marker of nondescript landscape. And rarely, almost never, was there a distinct house, yard, car, truck, person in sight.

First stop, he told us, was to be his grandson's trailer pub, where Walter was surreptitiously given a pint of Seagram's 7. He also asked for any old baseball bat that might be lying around the property. His grandson looked around his property and in his truck but found nothing. "Yeah, we need a bat and they gon' have me digging a hole with my shovel," Walter gamely announced, curiously.

Then we were off to his oldest daughter's house, whom he hadn't seen since the new year, who's a beauty at 70, and who maternally demanded that Walter get rid of a small shed trailer sitting in her yard. She told him if he didn't take it she'd burn it. "Don't burn it, I'll take it. But I'll need some time and help," he responded.

At all our stops Walter introduced Chelsea and I as the folks who were supposed to bring him to New York for a theater performance. And everyone greeted us and smiled with a tad of polite suspicion. I realized that Walter was more than disappointed that the New York trip didn't happen. He was also showing us off to his family, proud of something I couldn't translate.

At the end of the day he finally directed us to the place where "Jerry" was hung, what I had been expecting, planned, since morning, since 2002, when I heard the story for the first time, a visit to the "old plum tree," "Gator Limb," "Jerry's Limb."

Pull off the road over here, over here, he directed, as though he had given this exact tour before. He got out of the car and fell again, backwards, sliding against the car door, but didn't seem to notice this time, not even the dirt on his shirt. Got up, didn't brush himself off and hurried to a nondescript place off a side road, in the country, near Bentonia.

One would have to imagine it, the historical place and scene, 90 years ago. There was a trace of something there, in the landscape, in the ground and sky of its history, depending on who's looking. I could imagine a "tree hanging over the road," a different road, a different sky. I imagined it, because there was not much there except a dirt road and off the road a little gully, surrounded by wild grass.

And as we videoed Walter there, telling the story once again, the sun was be-hind us, creating shadows, which threatened whatever it was we were hoping to capture and preserve.

Walter also diverted any memorial event emotionality, by reminding us that it happened, "a long time ago," when he was a little boy. And how he and his friends were never going to play in that tree again and what a shame that was. And now the tree is completely gone and so are all his friends. Walter was actually more interested in talking about the field across the road, where he had first ploughed a field, as a teenager, First World War time, back then.

We ended the day, sunset, at the Blue Front. It was good to see Jimmy "Duck" Holmes, who all of a sudden is an in-demand Bentonia Blues recording star, playing the blues of Skip James and Jack Owens, who at the moment was ter-rified of a possible date he had in Italy. "How long does it take to fly to Italy? They say it takes nine hours, over the water the whole time. That's too long!" he pleads. I told him he had to go, that there were drugs he could take and that he wouldn't feel a thing. And that maybe from Mississippi it wouldn't take as long.

Among the regulars, Duck's older brother, Franklin, was there; he told me, "It's a shame Walter couldn't go to New York," and that if he had been in-volved he would have got him there, that he knows the right people. He also told me that Walter saved the life of his uncle, Wash Ellis, who killed a white man in 1936, right in front of where the Blue Front now sits. A white man slapped Wash's wife and Wash later killed the white man with a knife. Walter helped get Wash out of town, and away from a pursuing mob. Walter walked the man, his friend, through the woods, four miles out of town, in the middle of the night, got him to a train that took him to St. Louis and then Detroit.

Ah, Walter, the hero, who was out of sight. I found him at a small table in the corner of the Blue Front, sitting asleep, and woke him. He was a little drunk. We looked at each other and he told me he'd had a good day. I got my camera and took a photograph. He was not at all afraid and stared straight into the lens. I asked Walter later, while driving him home, why he hadn't mentioned the Wash Ellis story before, along with all the other remarkable things he's shared with me. "Oh, I forgot all about that," he replied. "Yeah, if it weren't for me he'd be dead."

Monday. The day began cloudy, overcast. Chelsea assured me that that was a good thing, for the light. We began the first event.

We knocked on Walter's bedroom door. He was sitting in a worn tan velveteen lounge chair next to his bed and window, watching television. I told Walter that today we'd videotape some more, but no lynching site this time and no authentic Blue Front juke joint, no traveling, just him in his backyard, moving stuff around. And instead of a baseball bat we'd use a brick, any ol' brick, and instead of car grease we'd use Crisco shortening.

*Event #1*

*The Music of Breaking Rabbits or How to Dig the Wrong Hole*

Walter, the warrior, holding a shovel, stood under a broken dangling basketball hoop, barely hanging from a tree, in his front yard.

Walter, carrying the shovel, walked into the scene of the event, a space in his backyard, behind two leaning sheds, with interesting yard debris cluttered all around: a large empty soldering gas tank, a big pile of colorful wires, a wheel barrel sans wheel, a large empty Kwanzaa detergent can, a chewed-off deer leg . . .

Walter then walked down a slight hill from the two leaning sheds and began to dig a hole. And found three buried 78 records, unjacketed:

(a) *How Many Times*/Orrin Tucker and his Orchestra

(b) *Singing The Blues*/Guy Mitchell with Ray Coniff and his Orchestra

(c) *Down By The O-HI-O*/Ben Bernie and his Orchestra

He retrieved the records, brushed them off; dropped them one at a time, back up the slight hill, marking his path, to a sitting tin tub.

He paused.

He reached into the tin tub and retrieved a set-in-place screwdriver and sardine can, filled with Crisco. He took the screwdriver and can filled with Crisco to a blue Egyptian vase standing on a worktable with a brick resting in its mouth.

He smeared the Crisco onto the vase with the screwdriver, greasing it up and down with a vertical action.

FIGURE 6. Ralph Lemon, *Walter Carter in his bedroom in spacesuit*, 2006. Photograph © Ralph Lemon.

FIGURE 7. Ralph Lemon, *Walter Carter in his bedroom in spacesuit*, 2006. Photograph © Ralph Lemon.

He repeated this action for four or five minutes.

Once finished, he placed the sardine can filled with Crisco and the screw-driver down onto the table and took up a nearby green glass water pitcher filled with water, carried it to the tin tub, poured the water into the tin tub.

He paused.

Still holding onto the empty green pitcher, he walked over to the vase with the brick, and took the brick from the mouth of the vase.

Carrying the brick and the pitcher, he walked to the tin tub and pulled it a few feet closer to a porcelain rabbit sitting nearby. (A long thin rusted cable connected the brick and tin tub.)

He moved to a stance directly next to the rabbit, agilely knelt and with the brick smashed the porcelain rabbit.

He stood and paused, holding the empty pitcher, dangling the cabled brick in the other hand.

He dropped the brick.

He picked up the broken porcelain rabbit pieces scattered on the ground and placed them in the empty pitcher.

He carried the pitcher full of broken porcelain rabbit pieces down the slight hill to the freshly dug hole.

And buried the broken pieces.

The event ended with Walter standing over the grave of the broken rabbit, holding the shovel, using it as a natural rest prop, for a very long time.

The event did not go as planned. We started with another score, one that made more sequential sense to me, but Walter forgot certain things and en-acted as many of the instructions as he could remember, doing the event his way. And I fought for what I thought it should be, and lost, was battered. The hardest part throughout was getting Walter to not ask us if he should begin a sequence: "Now? Dig now? Want me to give it to 'em now? Smash it now? Go over there . . . now?"

When we finished, three hours later, Walter sat down in a white plastic chair, panting a little, humming.

So, Walter, how was it?

"I don't know. I broke a rabbit and dug a hole. Hmm, I still don't know," he hummed. He did seem to relish digging the hole and smashing the rabbit, a thorough and precise work. But his smearing Crisco on the vase took on a surprising otherworldly obsessive sacredness.

What did it mean to him? Nothing, nothing he cared to ask about or tell. It barely meant something comprehensive to me, but it is dangerously meaningful in that it's something I'm desperately trying to figure out, a complex repatterning of the ordinary, living mundane debris of life, made sublime and unknown. Now, with Walter's co-opting, I could start analyzing it anew, from scratch. This "event idea" became freer, because it's completely something else, a prize. And the work light of the day was perfect.

And for Walter there was always, at every moment, an exquisite position to action: digging, greasing, moving, breaking, forgetting . . . it is the work that is understood, biologically mastered, a long time ago, a direct work, not pampered, rehearsed, politicized, intellectualized nor aestheticized—how fucking stunning. Walter was paid a $100 a day for a few hours of his fearless unquestioning time.

For the next day's work we planned, talked about trying another event iteration. I also proposed that we should look at the video of the work done thus far, to get his approval or not. "I don't care," he responded, "Don't need to know. It's nice, it's nice. I'll sleep tonight." And then, "Money on Monday is good luck!"

On Tuesday it was supposed to rain.

And rain it did.

But before it rained, the morning sky's gray-blue light matched yesterday's cloudy shimmer. It had the look of another good but softly pale day. A tractor taking advantage of the momentary weather mowed the long grass in the field behind the Best Western. I thought we'd be lucky; I thought we could redo some of the shots that did not go as planned yesterday, not from Walter's unpredictable point of view but from Chelsea's and my camera angles and technical timing requirements. Of course, redoing meant creating the zone for some completely different action, and then what?

When we got to work, we tried a beginning sequence of an idea and then it would begin to rain and then stop and rain again and stop. We only accomplished a process of maybes. Walter had to change clothes twice. Finally, it just rained. And that was helpful. We went indoors, to the screened-in porch, and stayed.

*Event #2*
*Recording Rain*

We gathered all the recovered, unburied 78s from yesterday's work, now mostly broken in several pieces (from the shoveling and dropping), these "emblems of brokenness," and brought them inside to the screened-in porch and documented Walter putting all the parts back together, puzzle-like, with wide gray electrical tape and scissors, using the top of his white porch freezer as a work station. Those were the only instructions given. He chose his own setup this time. We also provided a dainty little clamp work light, with a 40-watt bulb, bought at another dollar store, this time a Fred's Dollar Store. He took an hour, took his time, deliberate, getting three records fairly reconfigured and the fourth, *How Many Times* by Orrin Tucker with Orchestra, interestingly disordered (thanks to the tape). "Destruction and the impossibility of recovery" in the abstract. Creation out of sheer exhaustion, I think. After taping them all back together, he placed them in a neat stack and carried them outside, delicately placing them on the ground in the rain.

That was it. Walter got wet again and changed clothes again but this time to go out to dinner. We took Walter and Edna out to dinner, to the Catfish Haven, 20 miles away, near the hamlet of Pocahontas.

". . . That's colored, that's white, that's white, white, that one's colored, colored . . . that used to be white, now it's colored . . . white on both sides . . . white on both sides . . ." And Edna joined in, his chorus, "One side colored, one side white, all white both sides . . . was colored but died . . . that one's mixed, mixed . . ."

The Catfish Haven had a mixed clientele of white and black diners, which is unusual for restaurants in the area. We all ordered fried catfish, hush puppies and baked potatoes, sweet tea. I had asked for grilled fish but was informed that the grilled fish was also fried so I may as well go with the breaded kind. "It tastes better," Edna said. Sitting behind the Heinz 57, Tabasco, ketchup, sour cream, 55% vegetable butter, salt, pepper, Walter told us he was born in Yazoo City in 1907. Was adopted when he was a year and six months by some colored folks. That his dad was a white man. And that a strange black woman would follow him around when he was young, and he had no idea who she was until one day she turned out to be his mother.

He and Edna both ate well at the restaurant, an unusual and special event, I

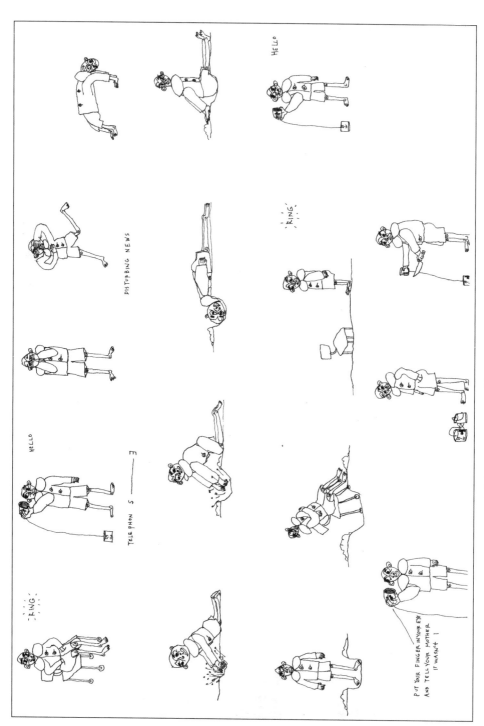

FIGURE 8. Ralph Lemon, *Young Baldwin Drawings*, 2004. © Ralph Lemon.

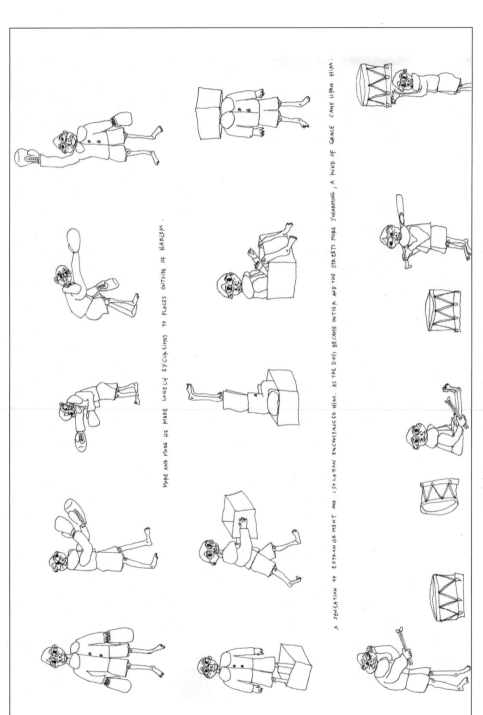

FIGURE 9. Ralph Lemon, *Young Baldwin Drawings*, 2004. © Ralph Lemon.

assumed. Are you ready to go home? I said. It was still raining and dark. And even in the dark and rain, "That's colored, that's white, that's white, white, that one's colored, colored . . . that used to be white, now it's colored . . . white on both sides . . . white on both sides . . ."

Back home, we gathered in Walter's bedroom. Edna kept watch, standing right outside his door, as though beyond the door, inside his private bedroom was off limits to her. Walter showed us photographs of his nine kids; he had 10 but one died. Showed us his ostrich-skin cowboy boots, a birthday present his kids bought him 13 years ago. And his bedside Geri-Vite liquid vitamin supplement. "The doctors gave me this to help my appetite, but it don't do shit," shaking his head. I told him it's not for appetite, that it's vitamins. This is probably keeping you alive, I said.

"Well, I may see you again and I may not, but I sure enjoyed you all," Walter said, cheerfully, as we got back in the car. And then continued, "Yessir, maybe, maybe not, don't think I want to be around at 100, uh-uh, can't sleep as it is." He waved.

We waved and drove away and then the next work of iteration and editing began. What was it, what is it still? I don't know. "I still don't know," quoting Walter. Most of what it shall become, publicly, is in the editing. But one thing's for sure: none of what happened will translate completely. It is, now, simply interesting. There will be a trace of Walter's past, but is it archival? The work we did is also modern, may stay modern, unpreservable and elusive, messy like that. At the moment I cannot code it in genre, culture, or time, as specific as he and I and Mississippi are. Who that I know, have known, does what we just did? Really . . . here or there, except me, Chelsea and Walter? Who would want to? There's one other thing that I know, that really matters, that Walter knows really matters: that if his body invokes one thing, only one thing, it is the crescendo of dying. He's that wildly alive.

At dinner I had asked Walter what he had done that day, "I can't remember," he answered. And then, "a man and his chores, something like that."

> *Part of a work of art is its time and place [. . .] and even though a work can*
> *be reproduced, once transported, its presence may not be recoverable.*
> —Walter Benjamin

*Afterward*

Down South and up here the question of meaning continues to provoke.

Two weeks ago I thought this: I'll know what it all means once the narrative is reworked, illuminating its present (inner) possibilities . . . I will not completely trust my original score, the failure of it, although as I begin to edit I will try to leave it intact, my original thinking, to clash with what is, because I'm stubborn.

I showed some raw footage to my Practice of Form class at Temple University, a few weeks after I returned from Mississippi. One student asked, "What does any of this mean?" I rambled through some memorized conceptions, handed out this list:

Event elements

Hare/Rabbit/*mythology creature storyteller fertility broken fragments*

Sardine can with screwdriver and Crisco/*ritual sacred object tool lubrication crystallized cotton seed oil*

Chair/*empty space negative space form formlessness rest response*

Hole/*earth burial death history recover resurrection*

Broken 78 records/*memory recovered container?*

Wire cable/*vehicle passage umbilical*

Vase/*antiquity the past precious object*

Tin tub and water pitcher/*cleanse water baptism*

Brick/*weapon destruction protection*

But I had no real answer to the student's perfect question.

At this precise moment, I think that it doesn't really matter what it all means. On the surface, Walter's actions represent attempts at translating a prescribed rigor of tasks, actions that then become an event. And the items: rabbit, hose, green water pitcher, vase, Crisco . . . ? Each item holds its own force, history, representation, and possibilities of an alchemic experiment. Maybe there's something remarkable in the raw footage, "unseen," and with a precise mixture, temperature, edit, voila!

But most likely it's something more mundane. I frame it, I frame it again and again and it becomes something curious to look at for a few minutes. Certainly something interesting to think about.

Was Walter's presence archival, is it archival? He will be "enshrined." But as what, and as when? These become important questions.

# DEBORAH HAY'S *O, O*

DANIELLE GOLDMAN

*Stepping Aside, with Eyes Askance*

In January 2006, the choreographer Deborah Hay presented a new piece titled *O, O* at St Mark's Church in New York City. Based on her recent solo, *Room* (2005), the ensemble version brought together five phenomenal performers: Jeanine Durning, Neil Greenberg, Miguel Gutierrez, Juliette Mapp and Vicky Shick. These performers would be well known to anyone who follows contemporary dance in New York. But their presence in *O, O* contained seldom seen fervency and concentration, uniting the dancers as an ensemble despite their age differences and varied performance histories. This was surely a result of Hay's performance practice. Performed in the round, the 55-minute piece engages the cast in a score of several koan-like questions, designed to challenge the dancers' perceptual awareness.

The New York version of *O, O* concludes with rare poignancy, intensified by the dancers' vocalizations.[1] After 50 minutes of scored ensemble work, danced attentively with large pockets of silence, the lights briefly dim. When they rise, they reveal the five dancers in a cluster, grasping each other while facing outwards. The silence is palpable. Then, poised like a masthead facing a storm, Gutierrez begins to sing, unleashing a soulful lament whose deep tones reverberate through St Mark's Church (Figure 1). As Gutierrez repeats his wailing melody, the other dancers mouth the tune in sympathy. With protruding veins and sweating brows, it's as if they sing the wordless dirge together. As the lament fades, the dancers loosen their grip on one another to stand momentarily side by side.

After this brief period of calm, the pitch of the dance shifts dramatically. First, Gutierrez breaks from the group in a short but explosive series of flailing turns and stumbles, while the others slowly step away from each other. Then, Mapp voices her own urgent lament while carving a circular pathway through the space. Gesticulating wildly and repeatedly pitching her torso forwards, she unfurls high-pitched screams and ululations. Hers are the wartime sounds of too much grief: the bone-raking sounds of mothers losing their children. Meanwhile, the others continue their hesitant steps. During this time, almost without notice and entirely without ceremony, Durning takes a black scarf (which had been wrapped around her neck) and places it over her head. Mapp concludes her lament and stands still with the others. Then, in stark silence, the others slowly step aside from the veiled figure, with their gazes turned outwards as the lights gradually fade.

What's at stake in collectively stepping away, eyes askance, from a veiled woman who stands both silent and still? And what do the dancers' vocal laments have to do with this choreographic denouement? Although Hay resists talking about her work in political terms, the final minutes of choreography jut into worldly political contexts, namely the US 'War on Terror'. This context was apparent before the piece even began. Upon entering St Mark's Church, audience members found a visor on each seat, emblazoned with the letters 'O, O' as well as imagery of the Twin Towers and the fateful numbers '9/11'. Given these visors, it's hard to see the veiled woman at the end of *O, O* without at least considering the conflicts of our historical moment.[2]

The day I began to write this essay, *The New York Times* reported that veiled Muslim women in London protested against the leader of the House of Commons, Jack Straw, who said that full-face veils (*niqabs*) hinder communication. The accompanying photograph shows a veiled protestor peering out through a series of frames: her brown eyes gaze outward, first through thickly applied black eyeliner, then through her veil's narrow slits (Cowell 2006). This photograph animates my reading of *O, O*'s final steps, documenting a particular historical conflict, but also raising important questions for dance studies about the ethics of seeing and being seen. The protestor's gaze

FIGURE 1. (*From left*): Vicky Shick, Neil Greenberg, Jeanine Durning, Juliette Mapp and Miguel Gutierrez in Deborah Hay's *0, 0*, St Mark's Church, New York City, January 2006. From the video by Peter Richards.

FIGURE 2. (*From left*): Jeanine Durning, Neil Greenberg, Miguel Gutierrez, Juliette Mapp and Vicky Shick in Deborah Hay's *0, 0*, St Mark's Church, New York City, January 2006. Photograph by Jason Akira Somma.

(like that of a modern-day Olympia, despite being pious and fully clad) demands a discussion of objecthood and visuality.³ Considered in relation to the
end of *0, 0*, it also suggests a critical discussion of Hay's physical practice. Resistant to a visual reduction of the body, while still committed to being seen,
Hay's performance practice is indeed filled with political implications.

*Experimentalism: Inviting Being Seen*

Hay has taken an unusual path. Born in Brooklyn to a mother who taught her
to dance from an early age, Hay moved to Manhattan in the early 1960s to
study dance professionally. Her success came quick and early. Hay toured for
six months with the Merce Cunningham Dance Company in 1964, and was a
dancer in the famous Judson Dance Theater, where she began to experiment
with what would become a lasting fascination: challenging distinctions between trained and untrained dancers. In 1970, Hay left New York City's downtown dance scene, moving first to Vermont and then to Austin, Texas, in 1976.
For the past 30 years, Hay has made work in Texas, developing a rigorous
physical practice—presenting choreography, conducting workshops and publishing beautiful books about her movement explorations, most recently *Lamb
at the Altar: The Story of a Dance* (1994) and *My Body, The Buddhist* (2000).
Throughout this time, and despite what some might consider her remote location, Hay's work has remained absolutely contemporary, and is of great
interest to the current generation of emerging downtown New York choreographers, who have had several opportunities to see Hay of late. In addition
to the January 2006 premiere of *0, 0*, Hay spoke in September 2006 to the
artists-in-residence at Movement Research, a dance service organization in
New York City, and performed *Room* the same month at the Opening Celebration for the newly renovated Judson Memorial Church.

The week before her Judson performance, I attended a workshop with
Hay, which helped to explain the dancers' high degree of concentration in *0,
0*, and their full-bodied commitment to a seemingly mysterious practice. Each
day, from 12.30 to 4.30 p.m., a motley group of dancers and actors assembled
at the Janet Panetta Studio in midtown Manhattan. The title of Hay's workshop was 'Experimentalism', and she frequently referred to the studio as 'our
laboratory'. Over the years, Hay has developed a distinct way of working.
Rather than strictly choreographing a series of 'moves', Hay constructs scores

for each of her dances, which performers interpret while engaging in a practice of perpetual questioning, designed to decentralize the dancer and stimulate his/her curiosity and physical responsiveness. Hay's scores are not written down and given to the dancers to read as notes. Rather, she gives a series of oral directives with varying degrees of specificity, which she refines throughout the rehearsal process based on choices the dancers make when practising. As seen in the score for *0, 0*, some directives indicate timing and spatial patterns ('Enter separately from backstage and pause before you reach the outside edge of the circle'), while others are more abstract, emphasizing the dancer's engagement rather than his or her appearance ('Once you are in place, begin the practice of choosing to surrender the pattern of facing a single direction. There is no way this looks.').

To introduce this way of working, Hay began the workshop with the following question: 'What if every cell in the body (currently estimated at 100 trillion) had the potential to get what it needs?' Hay acknowledges that it would be impossible to keep track of trillions of cells, and she explains that the goal is not to arrive at an answer. Instead, Hay poses questions to activate a practice of perceptual awareness, in which one continually notices bodily feedback and then lets these observations go (2006a). As Hay explains in her essay 'Performance as Practice':

> [T]he inclusion of a performance practice could help loosen the tyranny of the myth of the dancer as a single coherent being—a basic element in dance training in the West. The effects of this idea can best be observed in the photographs in New York's *Dance Magazine*, where images of erectile dancers follow one another, page after page. My vision of the dancer, through the intervention of performance as practice, is as a conscious flow of multiple perceptual occurrences unfolding continuously (2001).

Over the first days of the workshop, Hay added to her initial question. Before long, we were working with the following: 'What if every cell in the body had the potential to get what it needs, while surrendering the habit of a singular facing, and inviting being seen?' Each day, we began class with an extended movement exploration, investigating this question for as long as 45 minutes at a time. On a few occasions, Hay put on music. But mostly we danced in silence without any set choreography or preordained score. As we

FIGURE 3. (*From left*): Neil Greenberg, Miguel Gutierrez, Jeanine Durning and Juliette Mapp in Deborah Hay's *0, 0*, St Mark's Church, New York City, January 2006. Photograph by Jason Akira Somma.

FIGURE 4. (*From left*): Jeanine Durning, Neil Greenberg, Miguel Gutierrez, Juliette Mapp and Vicky Shick in Deborah Hay's *0, 0*, St Mark's Church, New York City, January 2006. From the video by Peter Richards.

stretched our limbs, rolled about, or stood still in our explorations, Hay would casually ask, 'What if?' Her speaking enlivened the questioning in our practice. With her calm, deep voice, she gently reminded us to 'Notice the feedback and let it go . . . The body as teacher.' As the week went on, we tried to maintain this practice while performing the score for a new dance that Hay was developing.

In practice, my body was able to reorganize itself quickly by surrendering to the notion (even if only a trick of the imagination) that every cell has the potential to get what it needs. Rather than working to find space between my shoulder blades and rib cage, or to locate a connection between my heels and sit bones (common goals in many contemporary dance classes), my body was able to fall into alignment quickly and with ease. The pressure of an organizing ego was temporarily relieved, and it felt good to be dancing.

Things necessarily became more complex as our solo practice moved into a social realm, which of course was always already the case. Acknowledging that we were moving in a room full of people, Hay urged us to imagine that everyone was engaged in the same practice. Nothing needed to be 'fixed' because, ostensibly, bodies could get what they needed. At one point, Hay urged the class to 'view others as the subject of one's experience rather than the object', and she continually urged us to invite being seen, describing the practice as an ongoing act of supreme generosity.

A host of ethical questions emerged from Hay's prompts, pooling around issues of objecthood and visuality. Although she claims to be talking about *feelings* rather than an 'idea' or a 'morality', an additional set of inquiries began to push against the practice-oriented questions posed by Hay: Is a certain level of safety or trust required to allow 'generous' invitations? What if one resists the circle of exchange that giving inevitably entails?[4] What difficulties emerge when the pose is imposed, as is often the case in choreography, as well as in daily life? These questions are foundational to dance studies, and they mark the convergence between Hay's practice, *The New York Times*' photograph and the final minutes of *0, 0*. To quote Fred Moten: 'Beholding is *always* the entrance into a scene, into the context of the other, of the object' (2003: 235). Even when attempting to work at a cellular level, one would be remiss not to recognize this fact.

At one point during the workshop, we stopped dancing in order to talk about our experience of 'inviting being seen'. After several people commented on the difficulty of this practice, I asked Hay whether there might be a relationship between the struggle we felt and her suggestion that we 'view others as the subject rather than the object of our experience'. Although the group was incredibly supportive, I was interested in the moments where a dancer's breath would catch or voice would quiver—moments when, aware of being watched, my pulse began to quicken. I asked whether our difficulty might have had something to do with the power dynamics implicit in being the object of another's gaze. 'That's good,' Hay said. Then, after a long pause, 'It's something I'd like to think about more' (2006a).

*Catalytic Pressure*

In his recent book, *In the Break*: *The Aesthetics of the Black Radical Tradition*, Moten insists that 'objects can and do resist' (2003: 1). Concerned with a black radical tradition emerging out of slavery (where subject, object and commodity converge), Moten analyses shrieks and shouts and moans: 'the irreducible sound of necessarily visual performance at the scene of objection' (ibid.). He's interested in the sounds of resistance. This resistance is important to keep in mind because it challenges the notion (implied in Hay's workshop) that it is easy, or always an unqualified act of generosity, to invite being seen. I don't draw attention to this point in Moten's argument to level a simplified criticism of Hay. Rather, Moten's analysis of resistance opens a discussion of aurality in Hay's performance, and the charged relations between audience and performer that her work allows.

In the final chapter of *In the Break*, Moten discusses the disruptive force of aurality in the work of Adrian Piper, a conceptual artist and Kantian philosopher. During the early 1970s, Piper enacted several performances called the Catalysis Series, where she explored moments of confrontation between audience and performer, self and other. As Piper explains in 'Talking to Myself: The Ongoing Autobiography of an Art Object', this work stemmed from 'a lot of thinking about my position as an artist, a woman, and a black' (1996: 31).

Moten pays particular attention to a 1970 work called *Untitled Catalysis*, performed at Max's Kansas City. Piper went to Max's, a popular hangout for artists in New York's downtown avant-garde art scene, and situated herself as an 'art object' to be observed. A photograph of this performance by Rosemary Mayer shows Piper (a young, thin, light-skinned black woman) standing still, her attentive stance and obstructed senses resembling the veiled dancer at the end of *0, 0* (see ibid.: 27). Although Piper's wavy hair hangs down without a veil to cover it, her ears are plugged, her nose is pinched with what looks like tape, her hands are covered with gloves and her eyes are covered with a shiny black mask.

Piper wrote about this performance several years after the fact, in 1981. She explains:

> I didn't want to be absorbed as a collaborator, because that would mean having my own consciousness co-opted and modified by that of others [. . .] My solution was to privatize my own consciousness as much as possible, by depriving it of sensory input from that environment; to isolate it from all tactile, aural, and visual feedback. In doing so I presented myself as a silent, secret, passive object, seemingly ready to be absorbed into their consciousness as an object. But I learned that complete absorption was impossible, because my voluntary objectlike passivity implied aggressive activity and choice, an independent presence confronting the Art-Conscious environment with its autonomy. My objecthood became my subjecthood (ibid.).

Moten begins his discussion of *Untitled Catalysis* by noting that art critics concerned with minimalism and the avant-garde (people like Rosalind E. Krauss and Michael Fried) seemed entirely uninterested in Piper's work, a dismissal that Piper attributes to unacknowledged, socioculturally determined biases.[5] Moten then argues that, by situating herself as an art object, Piper aggressively forces the beholder (both in Max's Kansas City and within the art world at large) to notice her, and to reckon with her materiality. Moten is particularly interested in the phonic materiality of Piper's performance. Although she's technically silent, Moten claims that Piper's objection has a screaming soundtrack tied to more violent scenes.[6] It is important to listen for these sounds—not because hearing ought to eclipse sight, but because 'sound gives us back the visuality that ocularcentrism had repressed' (Moten 2003: 235).

Returning to the vocal laments at the end of *0, 0*: whatever dramatic content the dancers' wailing might contain, their vocalizations also index the sensual complexity of their bodies, which resist being reduced to mere *choreography*, accessed through vision alone. Having witnessed the dancers in *0, 0*—engaged in a rigorous practice of perceptual awareness, and capable of wailing as well as moving through space—it is all the more gripping to see the dancer don her veil at the end of the piece. As the other dancers step aside with eyes askance, their wailing soundtrack hangs in the air, imploring the audience to reckon with the force of the still, silent figure.

In the programme notes, Hay explains that *0, 0* refers to a circle within a circle, the relationship between performer and audience in the round. She refers to this relationship as the 'Wholegg Theory', wherein 'the audiences are both bound to, and distanced from, the core of the performance (the yolk) by a curved, substantive space which folds upon itself as an organic and pliable matter (the albumen)' (Hay 2006b). Before the workshop, this theory seemed both fanciful and opaque. But, in fact, it posits both dancing and beholding as a venture outside or beyond oneself: performance as a *material* encounter. Throughout *0, 0*, but particularly in the laments that occur toward the end of the piece, the voice plays an important role in bridging the gap between self and other, skidding across the 'albumen' and allowing intensities to pass.[7]

### *Making Room at Judson*

In late September 2006, Movement Research hosted an opening celebration for the newly renovated Judson Memorial Church. The evening also served as a send-off party for Carla Peterson, the beloved executive director of Movement Research, who was leaving the organization to assume her new post as Artistic Director of Dance Theater Workshop. It was a big event in an historic space, and two performances marked the occasion: Mapp presented a dance called *Anna, Ikea, and I* and Hay performed *Room*. Although she had been working on *Room* for years, this would be Hay's first solo performance of the work.

I had the opportunity to speak with Hay a few hours before her performance. She explained that she didn't feel sentimental about Judson, the place of her initial forays into the world of experimental dance. Nevertheless, the evening's performance coincided with a crossroads in Hay's career. She explained that while presenters are excited by her group pieces for beautiful young dancers, they seem less interested in her solo performance. Voicing both honesty and frustration, Hay explained that when watching herself on video, she sees an older woman. Although Hay recognizes a radical side of herself that persists in challenging the field of dance, she quietly asked an unexpected question: 'I don't know whether it *helps* to have me perform' (in Goldman 2007).

When I saw Hay step onto the floor at Judson, wearing black pants and a short-sleeved shirt, it's true, I saw an older woman dancing. Her skin looked soft and somewhat thin. I noticed her lips, darkened with lipstick and emphasized by her jet-black hair. She looked classy. But this was just surface. When she began to move, making her way around the circumference of the seated audience, she made the space. I've never felt Judson so rapt.

The audience was filled with quirky individuals who, for various reasons, have come to New York City, or decided to stay, to pursue a life of dance—to somehow be part of, or brush against, this thing called performance. When Hay began her lament toward the end of the dance (the solo and *0, 0* share a similar score), it was as if she became a vessel, releasing sounds that are important to hear, as well as to make. Nobody seemed able to turn away. Perhaps a practice of ongoing questions is necessary if one is to foster a sensually complex, deep cellular engagement with others, while still holding on to politics and history. In the meantime, one answer becomes evident: Yes, it helps to have Hay perform.

## Notes

1  In February 2006, Deborah Hay travelled to France to produce a similar project, which premiered in Lyon in June and was shown again at the Festival d'Automne in Paris in late October. If all goes well, Hay eventually will present the New York and Lyon versions as two halves of a single programme.

2  Having attended a post-performance discussion of *0, 0*, Joanna Brotman discusses the visors in her article in *PAJ* (2006). In particular, she notes how Hay found the visors, as well as Hay's reaction to the suggestion of political content in *0, 0*:

> When we first entered the St. Mark's performance space, a greeter informed us that the visors on each chair were to be worn to protect our eyes from the in-the-round lighting. Sitting down, I notice the visor was decorated with an image of the Twin Towers and the words 9/11 in fake embroidery, with '0, 0' drawn on in pen by hand. After

the performance, I wonder about the intentionality of the visor and the political content of *0, 0.* In the postperformance discussion with Hay, the question of political content was the last to be broached by the audience. 'Dance is my form of political activity,' Hay had responded. 'That I dance is political.' She confessed to feeling 'inarticulate at expressing rage.' [. . .] She explained that when she had needed visors to protect the audience's eyes from the lights, she scoured Chinatown for the largest bulk for the least money, and the Twin Tower visors were it. And so, the visors became a prop, a found object scouted on location [. . .] (ibid.: 70–1).

3   Here I'm referring to Edouard Manet's *Olympia* (1863), widely discussed as one of the first paintings to depict a female nude who gazes directly and unabashedly out at the viewer, thereby resisting the kind of objectification in which one is simply there-to-be-seen. In the case of the photograph, the protestor's gaze also resists being passed over, not seen.

4   In thinking through what Hay calls the 'generosity' of being seen, it is helpful to consider the gift. In *Given Time: I. Counterfeit Money* (1992), Jacques Derrida asks whether it is possible to give without immediately entering a circle of exchange, where the gift inevitably entails debt to be repaid.

5   Adrian Piper discusses this dismissal in her essay, 'Critical Hegemony and Aesthetic Acculturation' (1985). According to Fred Moten, Piper writes:

> The consequent invisibility of much nonformalist, ethnically diverse art of high quality may explain the remark, made in good faith by a well-established critic [Rosalind E. Krauss, according to Moten], that if such work didn't generate sufficient energy to 'bring itself to one's attention,' then it probably did not exist. It would be wrong to attribute this claim to arrogance or disingenuousness. It is not easy to recognize one's complicity in preserving a state of critical hegemony, for that one's aesthetic interests should be guided by conscious and deliberate reflection, rather than by one's socioculturally determined biases, is a great deal to ask (2003: 300).

6   *In the Break* begins and ends with twin chapters, both called 'Resistance of the Object'. Whereas the concluding chapter discusses Adrian Piper, the first chapter discusses a scene from *Narrative of the Life of Frederick Douglass* (1845), where Douglass witnesses his Aunt Hester being brutally beaten, a violent scene that made Douglass aware of being a slave. Moten analyses the aural force of Piper's

performance in relation to Douglass' account of his Aunt Hester's screams (2003: 241–54).

7   Here, I'm thinking of 'Navigating Movements: An Interview with Brian Massumi' by Mary Zournazi. In the interview, Massumi discusses bodily capacities to affect and be affected in terms of intensity (see Zournazi 2003).

*References*

BROTMAN, Joanna. 2006. 'The Story of "O, O"'. *PAJ: A Journal of Performance and Art* 28(3): 66–71.

COWELL, Alan. 2006. 'Blair Criticizes Full Islamic Veils as "Mark of Separation"', *The New York Times*, 18 October, A3.

DERRIDA, Jacques. 1992. *Given Time: I. Counterfeit Money*. Chicago: University of Chicago Press.

GOLDMAN, Danielle. 2007. 'Interview with Deborah Hay. New York City, 25 September 2006'. *TDR* 51(2) (T194): 158–68.

HAY, Deborah. 2001. 'Performance as Practice'. Available at: www.deborahhay.com/journal.html (accessed 29 October 2001).

———. 2006a. 'Experimentalism'. Workshop with author. 18–22 September. Panetta Movement Center, New York.

———. 2006b. Programme note for *0, 0*. Available at: deborahhay.com/-%22O, 0%22%20program.html (accessed 29 October 2006).

MOTEN, Fred. 2003. *In the Break: The Aesthetics of the Black Radical Tradition*. Minneapolis: University of Minnesota Press.

PIPER, Adrian. 1985. 'Critical Hegemony and Aesthetic Acculturation'. *Nous* 19: 29–40.

———. 1996. *Out of Order, Out of Sight: Volume I, Selected Writings in Meta-Art, 1968–1992*. Cambridge, MA: MIT Press.

ZOURNAZI, Mary. 2003. 'Navigating Movements: An Interview with Brian Massumi'. *21C Magazine*. Available at: www.21cmagazine.com/issue2/massumi.html (accessed 19 January 2007).

RESEARCHING DANCE IN THE WILD:
BRAZILIAN EXPERIENCES

CHRISTINE GREINER

The increasing complexity of artistic experiences in Brazil after 1990 has raised questions regarding our very understanding of the dancing body, which radically changed as dancing crossed genre boundaries and moved closer to performance art. Many artists and scholars have been working along these borderlines, asking how thinking about the body is also thinking by means of the body and challenging written texts to expand that which we understand as embodied knowledge. Around the same period, studies in the cognitive sciences explained that what we are capable of experiencing and how we make sense of what we experience depends on the kind of bodies we have and on the ways we interact with the various environments we inhabit (see, for example, Johnson 1987; Varela et al. 1991).

Some of these theories outside the scope of traditional dance theories (see Hanstein and Fraleigh 1999; Alter 1991) have had an impact on the creation of choreographies. It is important to introduce some of the ideas proposed by scholars who have been studied by those Brazilian choreographers I am discussing—choreographers who are more interested in creative processes than in results. By investigating how the body works and how it can communicate without sending 'expected messages', these artists creatively explore distinct levels of interactions between bodies and environments. To delve more deeply into some of these issues and explore choreographies enacted by radical experiences, it is fundamental to research dance 'in the wild'.

This proposition was inspired by cognitive anthropologist Edwin Hutchins' *Cognition in the Wild*, first published in 1995. Hutchins proposes the breaking of some of the rigid boundaries set in place by previous anthropological paradigms based on classical dualisms such as nature–nurture and body–mind. His aim is to locate cognitive activity *in context*. It is important to clarify that, for Hutchins, context is not a fixed set of surrounding conditions but a wider dynamic process of which the cognition of an individual is only one part. Therefore, 'cognition in the wild' refers to human cognition in its habitat, very different from a laboratory where cognition is studied 'in captivity'.

This may sound a bit bizarre for the field of dance. Nobody actually dances in laboratories except those who are developing very specific experiences, such as the choreographer and media artist Johannes Birringer. Since 1999, he has led the dance and technology programme at Ohio State University and the Environments Lab. In his case, dance actually does occur in a scientific laboratory. But inside or outside a science lab, captivity in dance is a philosophical and political question. An ontological grounding for better understanding this relationship is connected to three of the most common paradigms that have been constructed by philosophers to explain what human nature is: the blank slate, the noble savage and the ghost in the machine. By denying explanations of human nature that claim it is a unitary and unchanging thing, some Brazilian choreographers have reinserted important political issues into the dance field. The most important is the recognition of diversity, which means there is neither *a* human nature nor *a* dancing body, only human natures and dancing bodies. Using the plural, they place a needed emphasis on diversity, which is very often the main subject of the contemporary world in a broad range of discussions.[1] I shall discuss these three paradigms by giving some examples of Brazilian dance experiences.

FIGURE 1. DVD projection in Marta Soares' *O Banho* (The Bath), Sesc Belenzinho, São Paulo, 2004. Photograph by João Caldas.

FIGURE 2. Marcela Reichelt in Alejandro Ahmed's *Skinnerbox*, Sesc Vila Mariana, São Paulo, 2005. Photograph by Cristiano Prim.

*White Paper, Empty Body*

Experimental psychologist and cognitive scientist Steven Pinker (2002) suggested that the above-mentioned paradigms are logically independent but, in practice, often operate together discursively. 'Blank slate' is a kind of loose translation of the mediaeval Latin term *tabula rasa*, which means 'scraped tablet'. It is attributed to the philosopher John Locke, who stated that we are born with a mind that is void of all characters, without any ideas, like a blank sheet of white paper. In terms of dance, for many centuries the dancing body was described exactly like this: a blank slate that should be built carefully through physical training. According to this view, all dancers potentially can dance similarly if they learn the same technique and are subjected to the same disciplinary project.

Since 1994, Alejandro Ahmed, the choreographer of Grupo Cena 11, has been developing in the capital city of Santa Catarina state in Southern Brazil, Florianópolis, a methodology to better understand the task of experimentally analysing many of the most complex and vexing problems of behaviour and transmission of body actions. His performances deny the blank slate paradigm by explicitly showing that even when subjected to the same disciplinary project, dancers are not 'exactly the same'. Ahmed and his group (Adilson Machado, Anderson Gonçalves, Karin Serafim, Cláudia Shimura, Letícia Lamela, Mariana Romagnani, Marcela Reichelt, Gica Allioto, Marcos Klann) are well known for their amazing physical strength and endurance, their original costumes and spectacular scenic elements, and for mixing punk, pop and video-game references. However, most important to Ahmed's research is his starting point, his personal history.

Ahmed was born with osteogenesis imperfecta—a disease that literally means 'bone imperfectly made from the beginning of life'. This genetic disorder is characterized by bones that break easily, often with no apparent cause. To cope with this problem, he developed an extremely violent dance technique called 'physical perception'. The technique is based on the attempt to control the most out-of-control situations, like a violent fall or a crash. The exercises he derived with his company strengthened Ahmed's bones while eliminating the risk of injury. However, the risk was not completely eliminated: through the audience's eyes, the movements still seem very risky and dangerous. They never know, for example, if one of the dancers will have an accident during a violent fall. This ambivalence is an important aspect of Ahmed's technique. The training also includes walking with prostheses and orthopaedic instruments to experience different constraints and their resultant movements. Ahmed has studied classical ballet and jazz but there are no explicit references to this training in his physical perception technique. While he is developing a movement vocabulary, the main objective of the technique is not the systematization of movement patterns but the sensorial process between the instruction and its resultant action. Indeed, this is the physical perception of body movement in the dancer's body. All of Ahmed's pieces— *Respostas sobre Dor* (Answers to Pain, 1994), *O Novo Cangaço* (The New Cangaço, 1996), *In'perfeito* (In'perfect, 1997) and *Violência* (Violence, 2000)—deal with the effect of gravity on the body, the body's limits, and the dynamics of puppets and robots to better understand physical action under control and the transmission of information between animate and inanimate bodies.

In *Skinnerbox* (2005), Ahmed questions whether different dancers with singular bodies—and even a dog onstage with them—can enact similar movement patterns by following the same instructions. The title of the piece refers to Burrhus Frederic Skinner, a famous psychologist whose entire research was based on 'operant conditioning'. According to Skinner, the live organism is always in the process of operating in the environment, and the organism's behaviour is always followed by a consequence. The nature of this consequence modifies the organism's tendency to repeat the behaviour in the future. The Skinnerbox is a cage that has a bar or pedal on one wall, which, when pressed, causes a small mechanism to release a food pellet into the cage. A rat bouncing around the cage eventually learns to press the bar so that a food pellet falls into the cage. What Skinner calls the 'operant' is the behaviour just prior to the stimulus, which in this case is the food pellet. Onstage, for 80 minutes, the dancers simulate games among themselves and with the dog, following movement instructions (to cross the stage several times repeating the same trajectory; to hold a partner until he/she says 'let it go' and the body is released to crash to the ground). These instructions are analogous to a stimulus initiated in order to observe the bodily consequences and how the consequences modify in each dancer the tendency to repeat the action in the future. Sometimes the stimulus is a bar of steel that falls down on the stage; sometimes it is a little remote-controlled four-wheel robot crossing the stage.

As theoretical background, Ahmed and dramaturge Fabiana Dultra Britto studied some of the ideas of Ilya Prigogine, who won the Nobel Prize for Chemistry in 1977, and those of philosopher and cognitive scientist Daniel C. Dennett, who pointed out that automatic processes are also creations of great brilliance and their genius lies in seeing how to create something without having to think about it. Dennett (1995, 2003) and Prigogine and Stengers (1997) explained how the rate of entropy increases with time. Indeed, life is a systematic attempt to reverse entropy, to create structures and energy differentials aimed at counteracting the gradual death of all systems. It is always a question of time because, unlike the phenomena of time-reversible Newtonian mechanics, thermodynamic processes exhibit an irreversible tendency toward increasing disorder.[2]

Therefore, when Ahmed organized fresh patterns of movement in different bodies, like a disarticulated jump or a puppet walking, he was trying to explore the singularity of movement organization in each dancer by including entropic processes and acknowledging rather than denying the disorder. Before the premiere of *Skinnerbox*, Ahmed presented several open procedures. During these experiences, he talked to the audience and asked us to answer some questions about what we saw and felt. The objective was to understand how each individual experience communicated different information, taking into account specific circumstances. He was exploring the dancers' body states at the specific moment, which included the context and connection with the audience's bodies. All communicational systems (including artistic ones) are not just dynamic, but adaptive. They are self-regulated to suit both the external context, which means the conditions of the environment, and the internal context or the circumstances inherent to the system itself. This is a fundamental theme in Ahmed's work that has resulted in the creation of a methodology and several patterns of movement. The way the dancers' bodies crashed against each other and against the floor during the performances is a strong image illustrating his main starting point: the idea of a body as matter, and the inevitable risk of being alive and in motion.

### Born to Be Wild

The second paradigm for understanding body–mind relations that Pinker finds still present in our daily lives (and thus, by extension, we can find it operating also throughout the history of dance), is that of the 'noble savage'. It was elaborated by Jean-Jacques Rousseau and inspired by European colonists' discovery of indigenous peoples in the Americas, Africa and Oceania. It encapsulates the belief that humans have an untroubled and peaceful natural state, and that blights such as anxiety and violence are the by-products of civilization.

The work of choreographer Marta Soares unequivocally denies both the *tabula rasa* and the noble savage paradigms. It is not explicit in her projects but by challenging the assumption that there is a natural body she reinserts a political discussion into her dance experiences. Since 1995, she has developed a dance experience in São Paulo that reveals in-between spaces among several cultures and different ways of thinking.[3] There is no 'natural state' nor 'blank body'—only constructed bodily states and an interesting ambivalence between singularity and universality.

For *Les pouppées* (The Dolls, 1997), Soares was inspired by the corporeal anagrams created in the early 1930s by the German artist Hans Bellmer. Bellmer proposed a rearrangement of the parts of the body through more than a hundred drawings, paintings and photographs of distorted and dismembered female dolls. His work was considered by some art historians (see Lichtenstein 2001) as a protest against Germany's Nazi regime, but mainly an expression of erotic feelings. After studying these images, Soares sought another movement form to further investigate the fragmentation of the body. She received a Japan Foundation grant to train for one year with Butoh master Kazuo Ohno in Yokohama. Just as Bellmer's dolls were transformed through fragmentation, the Butoh work allowed Soares to explore the possibilities of the metamorphosis of the body. In response, Soares started deconstructing patterns of movement that she had been incorporating into her own work throughout her dance studies in São Paulo, London and New York,[4] and this process became an efficient starting point for the re-presentation of Bellmer's dolls in her choreography. The choreographic experience was focused on the possibilities of the articulations and disarticulations of the body. Specifically, she was inspired by Bellmer's *Petite Anatomie de l'inconscient physique ou l'Anatomie de l'Image* (Small Anatomy of the Physical Unconscious or the Anatomy of the Image, 1957) and his very notion of a 'dictionary of the image'. In her choreography, this can be observed when she presents a fragmented dancing body. Sometimes we just see a body upside down with legs moving like arms, or a woman in a 1950s ballroom dress transformed

into a headless man with trousers, wearing shoes on her hands. At the end
of the choreography, Soares sticks her head into an old oven. This complex
metaphor for the acephalous body comprises a flux of voices and images
teased from the work of several authors. One of them was Georges Bataille,
who published the *Acéphale Revue* in Paris from 1936 to 1939 and has discussed
the idea of the formless as evidence of a pervasive insistence on form, itself
a means of imposing limits. For Bataille:

> A dictionary begins when it no longer gives the meaning of words,
> but their tasks. Thus formless is not only an adjective having a given
> meaning, but a term that serves to bring things down in the world,
> generally requiring that each thing have its form. What it designates
> has no rights in any sense and gets itself squashed everywhere, like
> a spider or an earthworm (1985: 31).

Soares was interested in experiencing the forms her body takes as she
moves it by means of external impulses and inner images. By creating this
dangerous and perverse self-portrait (formless and acephalous), she is also
inspired by the photographs of Cindy Sherman (*Untitled #261*, 1992; *Untitled
#342*, 1999; and *Untitled #250*, 1992), who created her own fragmented dolls. In
the work of Sherman and Soares, the female body is always a testimony to a
haunted memory. There is no actual person but rather a self-fabricated fictional one. The archetypal housewife, prostitute and depressed woman are
all there but in a very unique and ambiguous way. This research on visual images of the body continues in Soares' next choreography *Homem de Jasmin*
(Man of Jasmine, 2000). For this piece she explored the poems of Unica Zurn,
who was married to Hans Bellmer. Taking off from Zurn's writings, Soares
choreographically tests the fragile boundary between life and death. Here,
Soares moved with difficulty inside a glass box and sometimes appeared to
be barely able to breathe. It was a fragmented and fragile communication between the internal and the external environment, and the battle was being
waged for her survival. In addition to Zurn's poems, Soares was inspired by
the artist Francesca Woodman and her research on formless bodies and metamorphosis—as Woodman explored in the photograph series *Space and House*
created from 1975 to 1976 in Rhode Island (see Leach 2006: 17, 51 and 133).

Woodman's photographs constitute an empathic identification of her
body with inanimate objects (walls, houses, doors, windows, etc.). In some

FIGURE 3. Marta Soares in *Les pouppées* (The Dolls), Ballet Stagium, São Paulo, 1997. Photograph by Gil Grossi.

works, we cannot perceive the frontiers between her body and the objects or places. It is a successive embracing and enveloping of the external world. Soares gave movement to Woodman's photographs not by copying them but by exploring the potential movement of the body positions in the images, which can be better recognized during the performance in the long moments of apparent pause.

For *O Banho* (The Bath, 2004), Soares researched the life of Dona Yayá, a rich Brazilian woman who, after being declared insane in the early 1920s, was locked in her home until her death in 1960. Based on her previous research on Bellmer, who was very interested in Jean-Martin Charcot's writings on 'hysterical' women, Soares decided to use the metaphor of the bath, referencing the long baths used as therapy at the Salpêtrière to 'calm down' allegedly insane women (see Didi-Huberman 2003). For the premiere of Soares' performance at the Vermelho Gallery in São Paulo, the bath was located on the first floor and the audience could see the dancers slowly rolling over inside the bathtub for one hour, as well as the DVD projection of Dona Yayá's house, which was screened on the second floor. The DVD was a poetic edition of the three months of Soares' creative process at Dona Yayá's house, generated through Soares' empathic sensation of Dona Yayá's history and her house. The projections of Soares' body in a glass solarium both duplicated and juxtaposed with the garden relate to the ephemerality of the body and to the passage of time in the house. According to Soares' description of her piece: 'Inside the bathtub-house the performer moves in limited space and limited time, as if suspended by the point which finds itself between life and death' (2004).

These philosophical and visual references—Bellmer's fragmented body, the Butoh body and the formless body of Bataille—converged in a singular dancing body reinvented in São Paulo, Brazil. The appropriation of foreign information can demonstrate in a complex way an original dance technique as a mediation between body, environment and all sorts of cognitive operations, including unconscious ones. Yet Soares' sense of what is real begins with and depends crucially upon her moving body, and can, in a very particular way, also be understood as a political matter. In her pieces, categorization is not purely an intellectual matter; it always occurs after experience because the formation and use of categories is the very stuff of experience. The recognition of this mutual influence between rational thought (like the capacity of categorization) and bodily experiences denies both the noble savage paradigm—which implies the possibility of a natural and pure state of being outside rational rules—and Rousseau's Social Contract whose terms suggest that when the individual alienates himself totally from the whole community he does this together with all his rights.[5] Therefore, Soares' work, even without being explicitly political, reinserts a kind of revolutionary view of consciousness, memory and life in social groups that resonates with notions of hybridity as a performativity of difference, and consciousness as a communal effect articulated by both postcolonial theorist Homi K. Bhabha[6] and the winner of the 1972 Nobel Prize in Physiology or Medicine, Gerald Edelman.[7] I can conclude by comparing the arguments of these authors that the core of this discussion is that by learning more about how the body–mind–environment connection works it becomes clear that passivity and submission are not innate aspects of human bodies.

### Living Ghosts

To complete this brief description of the three paradigms of human nature, as identified by Pinker, I turn now to the 'ghost in the machine'. This was the name given by philosopher Gilbert Ryle to the doctrine of René Descartes, which explained that every human body is in space and is subject to mechanical laws that govern all other bodies in space; but minds are not in space, nor are their operations subject to mechanical laws. This means, according to Descartes, that there is something inside bodies that has a different nature: a ghost that haunts. Transposing this conception of the 'ghost in the machine' to the field of dance, the dancing body was interpreted as an instrument of the mind or even the soul. Many metaphors have been developed by dance teachers such as the body-house, the body-machine, the body-vehicle. For example, Renée Gumiel, a pioneer of modern dance in Brazil, spoke to a whole generation of Brazilian dancers about the body as a powerful *vehicle* of the soul.

In a very particular way, Lia Rodrigues, from Rio de Janeiro, denied Descartes' statement in three different pieces: *Aquilo de que somos feitos* (That of Which We Are Made, 2000), *Formas Breves* (Brief Forms, 2003) and *Encarnado* (Incarnate, 2005). Through these pieces, she introduced the very nature of our embodied minds (without inner ghosts) as well as the classic nature-versus-nurture dilemma to the discussion of the body–mind relationship. Her performances suggest that an efficient way to avoid the old dualism is to explore simultaneous levels of bodily understandings, which include not only an alliance between biology and culture but also the recognition of non-hierarchical mediations. Once information is internalized by a body, the organism has no possibility of knowing whether the information came from a natural or cultural source, and will certainly never classify it as such. This idea is proposed as an important political posture in Rodrigues' research. In 2005, she moved her company Lia Rodrigues Companhia de Dança, founded in 1990, to the Favela da Maré (one of Rio de Janeiro's largest shantytowns), and since then has conducted important social work there. This community work began with the presence of the dance company at the Casa da Cultura da Maré, which is a kind of warehouse located just beside the Centro de Estudos e Ações Solidárias da Maré (Centre of Studies and Solidarity Actions of Maré [CEASM]), a non-governmental organization. The building has no doors, so people can come in whenever they want. During the rehearsals, three young members of the community asked to participate and were included in Rodrigues' company (Allyson Amaral, who was the first, and has been dancing with Rodrigues for four years; Leonardo Nunes Fonseca; and Gabriele Nascimento Fonseca). Some of the company dancers offer free workshops to the community. While Rodrigues is touring with her company, another choreographer, Paula Nestorov, occupies the space with her own company and continues the work with the community workshops. Funding from Europe[8] to develop *Encarnado* was mostly used to improve the warehouse by creating a set (in this case only flooring) for the performance and making it a proper space for the community, with a good roof, ventilation and a restroom. Several choreographers, including Jerôme Bel with his piece *Isabel Torres* (2006), have premiered their work in the warehouse.

Rodrigues has no official (federal, state or municipal) support in Brazil. If she decided to create a dance school for the poor children of Maré she would probably find a sponsor; however, as an artist, she prefers a different approach, one that does not concern itself either with community service or entertainment. The effort is toward an artistic experience that is politically involved through its reflection on the meaning of being human and the unbearable conditions of precarious lives. Rodrigues is inspired by Brazilian artist Lygia Clark's proposition of the 'collective body'. Clark created several performances between 1964 and 1981, focusing on the dissolution of bound-

FIGURE 4. Marta Soares in *O Banho* (The Bath), Sesc Belenzinho, São Paulo, 2004. Photograph by João Caldas.

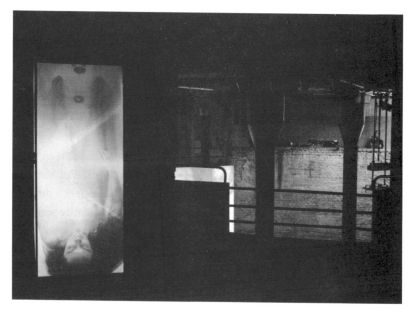

FIGURE 5. Marta Soares in *O Banho* (The Bath), Sesc Belenzinho, São Paulo, 2004. Photograph by João Caldas.

aries between artists and audience. Rodrigues made a connection between Clark's work and Susan Sontag's discussion of the modern understanding of violence and atrocity in *Regarding the Pain of Others* (2004)[9] to consider empathy in relation to the performer/audience connection and the feeling that, for a brief moment, someone can be in the place of another. Testing a collective empathic body in a shantytown like Maré is a huge challenge. How can a well-educated choreographer born into a rich white family empathize with, much less feel like, an inhabitant of Maré? Rodrigues and her dramaturge Silvia Sotter are very aware of this barrier. They don't pretend there are no social differences between the artists and their audience/community. On the contrary, the artistic research starts with the awareness of differences and seeks a possible exchange of singularities. Therefore, it is also important to recognize a political strategy in the way she organizes her dance, a strategy that is inherent in the dance itself—not just in the structure of her organization and its relation to the community and its location.

In *Aquilo de que somos feitos*, for example, words lose their social identity and ordinary sense in order to assume another meaning related to what is corporeal in speech, resisting and confounding the very norms by which speech itself is regulated. This was her first work inspired by Clark, who explored in greater depth the perception of the body and its relationship with objects in works like *Objetos Relacionais* (Relational Objects, created from 1976 to 1981); or the body within a group, as in *Baba Antropofágica* (Antropophagic Drool, 1973). *Baba Antropofágica* was part of Clark's body of work entitled *Arquitetura Orgânica ou Efêmera* (Organic or Ephemeral Architecture, beginning in 1969). Each participant placed in her/his mouth a spool of coloured thread; the end of the unwound thread was in the mouth of another participant who was stretched out on the floor. This event was inspired by Clark's dream of an unknown material endlessly flowing from her mouth, material that was actually her own inner substance. *Objetos Relacionais* attempted to relate therapeutic practice and artistic experience. These were created in the last phase of Clark's work, in which she developed a vocabulary of relational objects for the purposes of emotional healing. She continued to approach art experimentally but made no attempt to establish boundaries between therapeutic practice and artistic experience, and at this point she was no longer interested in preserving her status as an artist. She started using the relational objects on the bodies of audience members/patients by stimulating connections among the senses in order to awaken the body's memories. The objects were made of simple materials such as plastic bags, stones and sand, which acquired meaning only in their relation to the participants. The physical sensations stimulated by the relational objects as Clark used them on a patient's body communicated primarily through touch, stimulating connections among the senses and with the body's traumatic memory.

Rodrigues did not intend to reproduce these experiences but to explore in her own way the breaking of barriers between life and art, artists and audience. To demonstrate this, *Aquilo de que somos feitos* was divided into two parts. The first part explores nudity and different configurations of the body. The audience is asked to move around the performance space to see from different points of view the nine dancers (Micheline Torres, Marcele Sampaio, Amália Lima, Jamil Cardoso, Sandro Amaral, Thiago Granato, Allyson Mendes, Celina Portella and Francini Barros) as they construct living sculptures. They expose their bodies in a radical way, moving very close to the audience, while experiencing a metamorphosis. Two or more dancers will connect their bodies, embracing and arranging their bodies to create new physical forms. A dancer may appear with two heads or without limbs in grotesque and unrecognizable forms. In the second part, Micheline Torres quotes popular phrases from commercials such as 'the Marlboro World' or political slogans like Che Guevara's '*Hay que endurecer sin perder la ternura jamas*' (Let's get tough without ever losing tenderness). The repeated phrases are gradually transformed by the moving bodies of the dancers as they mingle with the audience; the well-known meanings of the words are changed until they are like a foreign substance, a kind of poison in the dancing body. During the 80-minute performance, there is a tension between what we already know—common knowledge and popular imagery—and the way this ordinary information is expressed in a very crude way by the dancing bodies, which allows the movements to offer different meanings for the words. The movements also reorganize traditional dance steps. For example, Torres' body, very well trained in ballet, becomes completely transformed during the performance through different tonus and axes of equilibrium.

In her next piece, *Formas Breves*, Rodrigues was inspired by Oskar Schlemmer's drawings and projects for the *Triadische Ballett* (Triadic Ballet, 1923). Schlemmer was interested in figures in space. His costumes for the Triadische Ballett suggest controlled movements and emphasized the shapes of cones, tubes, hoops and spheres to constrain the possibilities of body actions: one woman wears a bubble, a man appears to be a puppet without strings, and so on. Rodrigues' dancers, of varying body types, begin by testing patterns of movement from yoga, aerobics, gymnastics, classical ballet and Schlemmer's body drawings. In order to demonstrate this, the dancers present small solos. In the very beginning, for example, Marcela Levi replicates fragments of Schlemmer's movements. The choreography is not supposed to be a new version of the original piece—Rodrigues is not concerned with historical reconstitution. Rather, it is an attempt to experience the translation of drawn movement into live movement. In a second solo, Micheline Torres develops a sequence of movements and at the same time she describes (verbally) every detail of what she is doing and feeling. In one moment, for example, she says: 'now I am trying to balance myself on one leg, and now my leg is shaking.' After completing the scene, she repeats the movement sequence without the verbal description. Both duration and skill change in a radical way. The second version is faster and more fluent. It became clear that Rodrigues and her dancers—as Schlemmer proposed years ago—were dealing with the various possibilities of movement (re)presentation in singular bodies and situations.

The other important source of *Formas Breves* was Italo Calvino's book *Six Memos for the Next Millennium* (1988).[10] Following Calvino's non-linear narrative that speaks primarily of invisible and unexpected nexus of different events, there is no linear sequence among the scenes, only fragmented solos. The dancers ask through their movements: how can someone describe embodied action, replicate the trajectory of a movement through muscles, nerves and bones, to create an embodied speech? According to Rodrigues, both Schlemmer and Calvino were thinking about the future and that's why she chose to bring them together. Through his original costumes and scenic objects, Schlemmer anticipated the experience of dancing bodies with technological apparatus. He was looking toward the future of human bodies completely melded with functional objects. Calvino was wondering about the future of literature, and he concluded that there are things that only literature can give us, by means specific to it. In this sense, Rodrigues is working on something unique to corporeal projects; like Calvino, she is reflecting on the singularities of her art. Other authors have explored the idea of corporeal projects. Michel Foucault, for example, is one of the most important thinkers who has reminded us of how the body is constitutively unstable, 'always foreign to itself—an open process of continuous self-estrangement where the

FIGURE 6. Vera Sala in Vera Sala's *Impermanências* (Impermanences), Espaço Ruth Rachou, São Paulo, 2004. Photograph by Cândida Almeida.

most fundamental physiological and sensorial functions endure ongoing oscillations, adjustments, breaks, dysfunctions, and optimizations, as well as
the construction of resistances' (in Banes and Lepecki 2007: 1). By reinventing
body knowledge through dancing, Rodrigues is creating sensorial realms and
alternative modes for a life without false utopias and illusory hopes. This is
her corporeal project, which really seems to be more effective than many
forms of verbal discourses.

*The Sensorimotor Organization of Subjective Experience*

The understanding of knowledge as a corporeal project and a construction
of resistances is also related to the understanding of the self, one of the most
complex subjects of human nature and the core of artistic experience. Choreographer Vera Sala and dramaturge Rosa Hercoles have demonstrated that
the construction and the dissolution of the self can also be a political issue.
They live in São Paulo, the biggest city of Brazil and one of the most violent.
In three solo pieces—*Estudos para Macabéa* (Studies for Macabéa, 1999), *Corpos
Ilhados* (Insulated Bodies, 2002) and *Impermanências* (Impermanences, 2004)—
they were inspired by the work of the neurologist António R. Damásio (2003).
According to Damásio, the self is a collection of images that includes certain
aspects of body structure and body operations, which means that the self is
a repertoire of possible motions within the whole body and its varied parts.
The self also includes identity-defining traits such as family and other personal relationships, activities, places, typical motor and sensory patterns of
response. The images that comprise the self have a high probability of being
evoked repeatedly and continuously by direct signalling, as happens in bodily
states, or by signals arising from stored dispositional representations, as happens with identity and typical response patterns. Therefore, subjectivity
would emerge when the brain is simultaneously producing not just images
of an entity, of the self and of the organism's responses, but also when the
brain is organizing another kind of image, that of an organism in the act of
perceiving and responding to an entity. It seems, for Damásio, that this latter
image is the main source of subjectivity. The neural device that generates
subjectivity serves to connect images with the process of life, and this changing of an organism in the act of perceiving and responding to an entity (an
external object or an imaginary one) is what contemporary dance is most
often about. In Sala's choreography, for example, her subjectivity is the

transformation of her body states in a direct connection with the environment (temperature, audience noise and movement, light, etc.). She is not interested in a collection of symbolic representations or a composition of
patterns of movements with specified meanings (the family, personal history,
a specific event from childhood) to represent her subjectivity. It is, more than
anything else, a complex organization of bodily states—and maybe this will
serve as an acceptable definition not only for Sala's work, but for a whole
new trend in choreography after the 1990s.

Vera Sala is a good example because her pieces are so interconnected as
to be seen as one single work. She enlarges the idea of choreography beyond
visible movement to include invisible movement—thought processes and
other internal actions. Through her performances, there are always the same
questions about body limits, body perception, and the relationships between
self and environment, as well as the radicalization of the same 'movement
cells', as she has precisely stated. She experiences the disappearance of the
body as self-dissolution and the genesis of movement. *Estudos para Macabéa*,
inspired by Clarice Lispector's book *A Hora da Estrela* (The Hour of the Star,
1977), shares a continuity with *Corpos Ilhados*. *Corpos Ilhados* was based on a
different source, not related to Lispector's book but also focused on the subject of the disappearance of the body. In this case, Sala was influenced by a
brief newspaper notice announcing the burning body of an unclaimed child
in the care of Fundação Estadual para o Bem-Estar do Menor (FEBEM, State
Foundation for the Well-being of Minors, Brazil), which is an agency that in-
carcerates minors accused of crimes. In *Estudos para Macabéa*, Sala explored
Lispector's description of a domestic who often feels the dissolution of her
body. This happens when she is lost in the rush-hour crowd on a bus, or doing
housework. She represents the tragic meaning of being poor, unable to adapt
to the big city, like so many migrants in Brazil who came to São Paulo or Rio
de Janeiro looking for a better life. Macabéa feels she is of no value to anybody. This is translated in Sala's performance through the complete absence
of patterns of movement or a priori references. She moves different parts of
her body but the audience cannot identify or recognize her gestures as dance
steps. Lying down during most of the performance, she appears to be unable
to stand on her own legs. In *Corpos Ilhados*, she was moved by the cruelty of
FEBEM, which has been criticized because of the large number of their
charges who have escaped, the rebellion within their institutions, and also

allegations of torture and mistreatment of the minors. In the context of the migrant and of the abandoned child, the disappearance of a body has become so frequent that often now it is not considered a catastrophe or emergency. To represent this situation, once again, Sala does not give any clue or clear reference to the audience. She concentrates on two points: the birth of bodily action in an individual body and the fragility of life. The disappearance of a body seems to be the loss of the primary sign of life: the capacity to move. Therefore, she intercepts, interrupts and reroutes the process of movement in her body. If an action starts in the shoulders and would normally continue in the arm, she displaces the movement to another part of the body, for example, the leg, and improvises different qualities of movement.

In *Impermanências*, Sala radicalizes the non-movements of her body inside a sculpture of wires with no particular form. She presents the first stage of an inanimate body. There is no dislocation, only a tremor and the changing state of a precarious body. The audience is supposed to walk around her, as if they are visiting an art gallery or looking at a homeless person sleeping in the street. This performance has been presented in different cultural centres, as a kind of installation at Sesc Pompéia in 2005 and Itaú Cultural in 2006, but never on a theatre stage.

Clearly, some of the main questions proposed by cognitive scientists, performing artists and philosophers have been changing the dance field in Brazil, especially in the last 15 years. This does not mean that all choreographers are studying the same ideas. Some artists turn to political philosophy, literature, sociology and history. Some are also discussing a recategorization of power and a less hierarchical way of resignifying conventions and rules. This phenomenon enacted by the abandonment of research methods that artificially divorce thought from embodied action-taking is related to a certain understanding of the situation in Brazil through both global and particular contexts. In the past decade, questions proposed by scholars such as scientist Andy Clark (1997) and by Bhabha (1994) have been more useful for the dance field in Brazil than traditional dance theories. Some of the principal questions are: what kind of tools are required to make sense of real-time and embodied cognition? What is the most effective explanatory framework for understanding emergent phenomena, especially those enacted from a system in crisis? Why does the ambivalence of authority repeatedly turn from mimicry to menace?

To create movement in a dancing body, as exemplified by these specific Brazilian artists, is a political posture for surviving in particular communities. These choreographers present history and power embodied in a radical way. To the extent that new theories of the body in the scope of cognitive sciences, politics and philosophy substantially displace the old ones, there is a reconfiguring of what needs to be explained or questioned. This has been explored through dance experiences from different countries all over the world (see note 1). The relevance of the displacement of theoretical paradigms to new understandings of the dancing body in Brazil is that artists like Ahmed, Soares, Rodrigues and Sala no longer attempt to answer questions about the affiliations of stable dance vocabularies or the creation of different aesthetic models in confrontation with past models. They have been moved by other issues to destabilize the already known by exploring the most invariant aspects of our organism and its interactions with different environments. But they do not deny the past. It is more a matter of reorganization. That is why choreographers and dance scholars have become so closely involved with the work being done in the field of performance studies 'where questions of embodiment, action, behavior, and agency are dealt with interculturally' (Schechner 2002: xii).

Some of the new theoretical bridges proposed by these Brazilian choreographers have interested them because, besides creating different artistic languages, they change our understanding of cognitive capacities such as memory and learning (Alejandro Ahmed), communication and empathy (Lia Rodrigues), perception and metaphorical constructions (Marta Soares) and the ambivalent distinction between movement and non-movement (Vera Sala). By dislocating classical paradigms of human nature they offer reflections on some cultural hot-button issues such as violence, gender and power. This is a polemical debate: after all, is it possible to reinsert a political discussion in dance experiences by challenging bodily nature and the construction of movements, even without being explicit about political issues?

Giorgio Agamben, who has extensively discussed the political paradigms of experience as well as Michel Foucault's thesis on how politics become a biopolitics,[11] points out that in the contemporary political debates the very biological concept of life is precisely what deserves to be questioned before anything else: 'What is at stake today is life, and what is decisive is the way in which one understands the sense of transformation' (1996: 152–3).

The recognition of these different levels of political action in the Brazilian dance field is not a simple task. Brazil was a colonized country, and this can be also observed in the dance field. All pioneers from classical ballet to modern dance were immigrants or studied abroad. And even our first university dance programme, the School of Dance at the Federal University of Bahia, was modelled on the ideas and work of the Polish dancer Yanka Rudzka and the German artist Rolf Gelewski. However, all of the above-mentioned artists, among others from all over the country, are trying to recognize dance experiences as possibilities in their own contexts and to avoid considering them as mere samples of global movements. As Bhabha figured out when he started his research on the performative ambivalence of colonial discourse: 'We may have to force the limits of the social as we know it to rediscover a sense of political and personal agency through the unthought within the civic and the psychic realms. This may be no place to end but it may be a place to begin' (1994: 93). In this sense, body studies have become a powerful way of thinking about the relationships among different environments, cultures and subjective experiences.

*Notes*

1  Over the past 10 years, several events, books and projects have been discussing the relationship between dance and cognitive science, for example: the Choreography and Cognition Project, directed by the choreographer Wayne McGregor since 2003, resulting from a partnership with the Cambridge University Department of Neuroscience (www.choreocog.net); the international symposium on 'Dance and the Brain', organized in Frankfurt in 2004, by the choreographers William Forsythe and Ivar Hagendoorn; the Médiadanse Lab directed by Armando Menicacci since 2001, in Paris; the Digital Cultures Lab organized in 2005, in Nottingham (www.digitalcultures.org); and BodyMedia Studies and Its Political Consequences, which is a project I have been developing since 2000 at the Catholic University of São Paulo with Professor Helena Katz.

2  According to Ilya Prigogine in *The End of Certainty*:

Indeed, time, as described by the basic laws of physics, from classical Newtonian dynamics to relativity and quantum physics, does not include any distinction between past and future. Even today, for many physicists it is a matter of faith that as far as the fundamental description of nature is concerned, there is no arrow of time [...] We believe that this is no longer the case because of two recent developments: the spectacular growth of nonequilibrium physics and the dynamics of unstable systems, beginning with the idea of chaos (in Prigogine and Stengers 1997: 1–2).

3   The idea of 'in-between spaces' was proposed by postcolonial critic Homi K. Bhabha: 'Cultural globality is figured in the in-between spaces of double-frames—its historical originality marked by a cognitive obscurity; its decentred "subject" signified in the nervous temporality of the transitional, or the emergent provisionality of the "present"' (1994: 309).

4   Marta Soares completed the one-year course at the Laban Centre for Movement and Dance in the UK, holds a BA from the State University of New York, and has her Movement Analyst certification from the Laban/Bartenieff Institute of Movement Research, Susan Klein School. She also studied and performed with Obie-winning theatre director Lee Nagrin, a former member of Meredith Monk's group, The House.

5   According to Rousseau's Social Contract, the conditions will be the same for everyone only when each individual gives himself totally to society, therefore no one will be tempted to make that condition of shared equality worse for other men. This returns to become one of the starting points of several kinds of nationalism, including the discourse of a political unified body as one national body, and the resulting spectacles of communal identities.

6   As Bhabha writes:

> Terms of cultural engagement, whether antagonistic or affiliative, are produced performatively. The representation of difference must not be hastily read as the reflection of pre-given ethnic or cultural traits set in the fixed tablet or tradition. The social articulation of difference, from the minority perspective, is a complex, on-going negotiation that seeks to authorize cultural hybridities that emerge in moments of historical transformation [...] The borderline engagements of cultural difference may as often be consensual as conflictual; they may confound our definitions of tradition and modernity; realign the customary boundaries between the private and the public, high and low;

and challenge normative expectations of development and progress (1994: 3).

7   As Gerlad M. Edelman writes: 'Consciousness arrives as a result of each individual's brain and bodily functions, there can be no direct or collective sharing of that individual's unique and historical conscious experience' (2004: 6).

8   Lia Rodrigues' funding for *Encarnado* came from Centre National de la Danse, Festival d'Automne, La Ferme du Buisson, Maison de la Danse de Lyon, and Tanzquartier from Vienna.

9   Susan Sontag's book *Regarding the Pain of the Others* reverses the terms she sets out in 1977 in *On Photography*. Arguing instead for an interpretation of images that reveals their ability to inspire violence or create apathy, she evokes a long history of the representation of the pain of others—from Goya's *The Disasters of War* (1810–20) to photographic documents of the American Civil War, the First World War, the Spanish Civil War, the Nazi death camps, and contemporary images from Bosnia, Sierra Leone, Rwanda, Israel and Palestine and New York City on September 11.

10  When Italo Calvino died in 1985, he was working on a series of six essays to be delivered at Harvard University for the Charles Eliot Norton Lecture series. Calvino completed only five of the essays, which have been collected under the title *Six Memos for the Next Millennium*.

11  As Michel Foucault writes: 'By biopolitics I meant the endeavor, begun in the 18th century to rationalize the problems presented to governmental practice by the phenomena characteristic of a group of living human beings constituted as a population: health, sanitation, birthrate, longevity, race' (1997: 73).

*References*

AGAMBEN, Giorgio. 1996. *Mezzi senza fine. Note sulla politica* [Means Without End: Notes on Politics]. Torino: Bollati Boringhieri.

ALTER, Judith B. 1991. *Dance-Based Dance Theory: From Borrowed Models to Dance-Based Experience*. New York: Peter Lang.

BANES, Sally and André Lepecki (eds). 2007. *The Senses in Performance*. New York: Routledge.

BATAILLE, Georges. 1985. *Visions of Excess, Selected Writings, 1927-1939*. Minneapolis: University of Minnesota Press.

BELLMER, Hans. 1957. *Petite Anatomie de l'inconscient physique ou l'anatomie de l'image* [Small Anatomy of the Physical Unconscious or the Anatomy of the Image]. Paris: Allia.

BHABHA, Homi K. 1994. *The Location of Culture*. London: Routledge.

CALVINO, Italo. 1988. *Six Memos for the Next Millennium* (Patrick Creagh trans.). Cambridge, MA: Harvard University Press.

CLARK, Andy. 1997. *Being There: Putting Brain, Body, and World Together Again*. Cambridge, MA: Bradford Books.

DAMÁSIO, António R. 2003. *Looking for Spinoza: Joy, Sorrow, and the Feeling Brain*. New York: Harcourt, Inc.

DENNETT, Daniel C. 1995. *Darwin's Dangerous Idea: Evolution and the Meanings of Life*. New York: Touchstone.

————. 2003. *Freedom Evolves*. New York: Viking Press.

DIDI-HUBERMAN, Georges. 2003 [1982]. *Invention of Hysteria, Charcot and the Photographic Iconography of the Salpêtrière*. Cambridge, MA: MIT Press.

EDELMAN, Gerald M. 2004. *Wider than the Sky: a Revolutionary View of Consciousness*. London: Penguin.

FOUCAULT, Michel. 1997 [1994]. *Dits et écrits* [Complete Works], VOLS I–IV. Paris: Gallimard.

HANSTEIN, Penelope and Sondra H. Fraleigh. 1999. *Researching Dance: Evolving Modes of Inquiry*. Pittsburgh: University of Pittsburgh Press.

HUTCHINS, Edwin. 1996 [1995]. *Cognition in the Wild*. Cambridge, MA: Bradford Books.

JOHNSON, Mark. 1987. *The Body in the Mind: The Bodily Basis of Meaning, Imagination, and Reason*. Chicago: University of Chicago Press.

LEACH, Neil. 2006. *Camouflage*. Cambridge, MA: MIT Press.

LICHTENSTEIN, Therese. 2001. *Behind Closed Doors: The Art of Hans Bellmer*. Berkeley: University of California Press.

LISPECTOR, Clarice. 1977. *A Hora da Estrela* [The Hour of the Star]. Rio de Janeiro: Rocco.

PINKER, Steven. 2002. *The Blank Slate: The Modern Denial of Human Nature*. London: Penguin.

PRIGOGINE, Ilya and Isabelle Stengers. 1997 [1996]. *The End of Certainty: Time's Flow and the Laws of Nature*. New York: The Free Press.

SCHECHNER, Richard. 2002. 'Fundamentals of Performance Studies', in Nathan Stucky and Cynthia Wimmer (eds), *Teaching Performance Studies*. New York: Southern Illinois University Press, pp. ix–xi.

SOARES, Marta. 2004. *Programa do Espetáculo O Banho* [Programme for *The Bath*]. São Paulo: Rumos Dança Itaú.

SONTAG, Susan. 1977. *On Photography*. New York: Picador.

———. 2004. *Regarding the Pain of Others*. New York: Farrar, Straus and Giroux.

VARELA, Francisco J., Evan T. Thompson and Eleanor Rosch. 1991. *The Embodied Mind: Cognitive Science and Human Experience*. Cambridge, MA: MIT Press.

APPARATUS, ATTENTION AND THE BODY:
THE THEATRE MACHINES OF BORIS CHARMATZ

GERALD SIEGMUND

*The Loneliness of a Spectator*

The cellar is a dark and lonely place. On my own I sit on a simple, spartan bench and wait. The old building of the German Library in Frankfurt, Germany, has been deserted since 1997, when the books migrated to the library's new building up the road, leaving behind only their spectral presence. Their absence resonates in the building, which now feels uncannily empty and crowded at the same time. The minutes drag on until an assistant appears from the netherworld to guide me down a flight of stairs into a silent room with a sofa where I am asked to deposit my coat and bags. The door closes behind me. For some time I hover in this in-between space to prepare myself for what is to come. I try to shed some of my impressions of the outside world: the noise of the city, my own thoughts and the thoughts of others that engulfed me once I entered the main door. It would not be the last door. After a while, the assistant asks if I am ready and leads me to the inner sanctum. I step forward. The door clicks shut behind me. I turn around and find that I am alone again.

I had seen the same piece before: *héâtre-élévision* by the French choreographer Boris Charmatz had been shown in 2002 during the Festival d'automne in Paris. A year prior to my Frankfurt experience, my very first journey into the underworld of cultural institutions took place at the Centre Pompidou in Paris, France. In the huge entrance hall the hustle and bustle of people buying tickets and rushing off to see the various exhibitions lay behind me. A female attendant ushered me through a recess of doors into the bowels of the museum where I crossed the threshold into the liminal space of the performance installation. Inside, my role as a spectator—including the way a spectator is supposed to behave and to feel—became unclear. Although going to see a performance is generally a social event, once inside the auditorium everybody is confined to his/her seat and left alone in the dark. In retrospect, my journey up to this point seemed to be some kind of purgatorial ritual, severing any social bonds I might have and highlighting instead the isolation of the spectator. It seemed similar to that which actors or performers undergo, a passage through actual and mental doors until the persona or role he/she is to play can be assumed.

In Frankfurt, memories of my earlier episode in Paris come back to me. They filter my current experience, turning it into its own spectral double. Although I had come to the library as an audience member, I am treated like a performer. It soon becomes clear that I am both: the only spectator and the only performer in the room. The instructions I am given by the assistant include the command to step onto the piano bench and climb onto the big black box that dominates the middle of the room. The shape of the black box that is to become my theatre appears close to that of an actual grand piano. I stretch out on my back, lying on a piece of black dance floor, 'like a patient etherized upon a table', as T. S. Eliot's poem 'The Love Song of J. Alfred Prufrock' describes. My head rests on a cushion. I stare up into mid-air at a television set suspended from the ceiling, its screen invitingly—or is it menacingly—inclined toward me. At the same time I feel powerless lying on my back. My body is open to forces from above and from behind my head where I cannot see. Two loudspeakers are attached to the floor in this inaccessible and uncontrollable space. I remember having passed them on my way in. Will anything happen behind my back, out of my range of vision? Although I am in a relatively comfortable position, the TV set stares down at me like the all-seeing eye of a surveillance camera.

'Etherized' is not a bad metaphor for the state this machine produces. I am surrounded and propped up by machinery that relates to me. I anticipate that it is about to do something to me once the performance has actually started. The assistant has also informed me about an emergency bell that I can ring should anything happen to me during this one-hour performance. A blanket has been provided to keep the cold from crawling up on me. It suddenly strikes me that I voluntarily stepped onto an operating table in a surgical theatre of a hospital. The operating room is not actually a theatre, in the same way that the library building the performance takes place in is not actually a theatre. My body rests on the box, immobilized, almost like a corpse lying in state and open to inspection. I am being operated on. I am being operated on by this seeing and speaking machine that holds and braces my body between the TV set in front of me and the pair of speakers behind, between an authoritative eye above and two mouths below. It is an apparatus that manipulates my body by propping it up and almost literally strapping it down between TV and speakers. The purpose of this machine is to bring my body into a position with regard to images and sounds that will alter the state of my body. It is a hallucinatory dream machine where phantasms pass in front of my eyes and disembodied sounds penetrate my ears and penetrate my body. The apparatus of which I am a part arouses my attention by drawing my attention toward processes in my body. It is an attention-arousing apparatus designed to bring bodies into existence; it produces bodies. As such it has strong sexual and erotic connotations.

During the years 2002–04, *héâtre-élévision* , the performance I am describing above, was shown in several European cities. It is the work of French choreographer and dancer Charmatz, who trained as a classical dancer at the Paris Opera before spending a year at the Conservatoire National Supérieur de Musique et de Danse in Lyon where he familiarized himself with contemporary dance techniques. Born in 1973, he choreographed his first duo together with Dimitri Chamblas, *A bras le corps* (Take [or, With] the Whole Body), in 1993, and it became an immediate success. *Les disparates* (The Disparate) followed a year later, then *Aatt enen tionon* (1996), *herses (une lente introduction)* (harrows [a slow introduction]; 1997), *Con forts fleuve* (1999), *héâtre-élévision* (2002), and his most recent stage production, *régi* (2006), went on to confirm his reputation as one of the most awkward, unusual and interesting contemporary choreographers throughout Europe.[1] All of his pieces ignore any kind

FIGURE 1. (*From left*): Myriam Lebreton, Nuno Bizarro (*image*) and Benoît Lachambre in Boris Charmatz's *héâtre-élévision*, 2002. Photograph by Stéphanie Jayet.

FIGURE 2. Julia Cima and Vincent Druguet in Boris Charmatz's *Aatt enen tionon*, 1996. Photograph by Cathy Peylan.

of established dance technique, instead making use of strange apparatuses like the one I describe above, which give the pieces an installation-like quality.

What function do these machines serve in Charmatz's work? What do they do to the (moving) body? In addition to *héâtre-élévision*, I shall concentrate on two other productions, *Aatt enen tionon* and *régi* as examples of Charmatz's use of machines as structures that organize a confrontation between representational and performative aspects of theatre. As symbolic structures that collide with the bodies of the dancers or performers, they stipulate the rules according to which a particular body may appear to the audience. They are matrices that bring the dancing/performing body into existence by framing and drawing attention to it in a particular way. As a warped and distorted proscenium within the proscenium or, as in the case of *héâtre-élévision*, within another institutional framing, these apparatuses are a reflection of the symbolic order that both supports and excludes the body. The machines become literalized metaphors of the theatre apparatus itself. On the one hand, Charmatz's machines frame the framing. On the other hand, as performative devices, they produce bodies in the here and now of the performance situation. They dissolve common images of the body by providing a space in which its representational structures may collapse, allowing its energies and forces to be unearthed. These forces will, however, be tied to the machine as an instance outside the body itself for their particular presentation.

I will argue that these apparatuses link perception and (re)presentation on the one side and incorporation and *mise en scène* on the other. As an ensemble, perception, (re)presentation, incorporation and staging constitute theatricality and the theatrical situation. By intersecting the conventional bond between these elements the machines take over the function of media. They mediate what we see and feel by capturing and focusing our attention to the point of our complete absorption. Since the nineteenth century, the phenomenon of attention, as Jonathan Crary has argued (1999), plays an important role in creating the idea of a unified subject that would otherwise be dispersed over a field of fleeting impressions and stimuli. According to Crary, the phenomenon of attention rose to prominence as a scientific category in the middle of the nineteenth century. Due to the increase in scientific experiments, consciousness itself was found to be subject to time and therefore to the danger of falling apart into myriad separate impressions. What was thought to bind the subject together under these circumstances was its capacity of focusing, of holding attention for something. Thus attention became the safeguard of the subject's identity. The disciplinary regime of the theatrical situation that excludes, includes demands that we are attentive to the things it presents. Attention binds the subject together. Charmatz's theatrical machines, however, leave the subject in suspense. Although we are bound to see and listen while being part of the installation, the way we are made to do this contradicts the notion of a unified subject. These machines produce a different notion of subjectivity.

In the programme notes, Charmatz describes *héâtre-élévision* as a 'pseudo-spectacle' (see Charmatz 2002). Perhaps this is why the two 't's have been omitted in the title. What we get is an amputated theatre event and an amputated television experience. *héâtre-élévision* is neither theatre nor television and yet, somehow, both. The performance is a 'choreographic piece that takes on the form of a Russian doll', the notes continue, 'a performance reduced to the presentation of a film, which in turn is reduced to the format of a television show which is presented as an installation.' *héâtre-élévision* is 'the suicide of a live performance'. And yet it is live. I experience it in the here and now, locked away behind closed doors in a cold room.

The TV flickers into action screening an empty theatre. It is not just any theatre, but a theatre with red plush seats and a gilded proscenium denoting the very essence of theatricality. On the side of the stage, a piano is being tuned. By the looks of his eyes, I assume the piano tuner is blind. He insistently hammers out one single note—pling, pling, pling—that drones out of the speakers behind me, separating the source of the images from the source of the sound. Suddenly a light goes up: I gather that it must be placed somewhere underneath my berth since it throws its huge shadow on the ceiling. The dark cloud hanging over me looks as if it were the gaping piano lid on the TV screen, turning my resting place on the dance floor into the piano and my body into the strings being tuned. My body becomes an instrument that is made to resonate. While the empty theatre on the TV screen waits for the performance to begin, I realize that my imagined performance has already begun. The performance I create on the basis of the visual, acoustic and sensory fragments is the focal point of the installation (see Müller-Schöll 2004: 342–52).

On the video, the scenes of the empty theatre are harshly interrupted by scenes taking place in a neutral space in which seven dancers dressed in tight, Cunningham-style body suits move in what look like boxes. Some kind of wooden or metallic construction frames them—a box within the (TV) box. The boxes appear in various shapes and sizes and are lit so that the floor reflects the dancers like a mirror. Together, we lose orientation in space. The dancers pull out their tongues, rub against each other, distort their faces and jump up and down as if they are some kind of animals. They produce whimpering, simpering, smacking and clacking noises, which infiltrate my ears from the small speakers next to my head cushion. I have the sensation of being extremely physically close to them, even though they are not present in the flesh. I move among them and they rub against me although I lie on the imaginary piano in a reclined position in a state halfway between waking and dreaming.[2] I share their theatrical space although we are separated by a screen; the video was recorded at another time, and in another space, yet I am there with them. Once, a dancer rolls down his suit and displays his erection. In this erotically charged field of intimate noises and bodies, we are closer than in any kind of traditional theatre.[3]

The images are quick cuts against each other. One second the dancers perform in their boxes and the next they are in the plush proscenium theatre of the first image. An old-fashioned colour-banded TV test screen interrupts any kind of identifiable space by drawing attention to the reality of the flat TV format itself. Like all the other images, the screen-test image looks slightly shaky. After a while, it dawns on me that someone must have filmed, recorded or taped it from the TV screen. Whether the dance scenes underwent a similar transformational process escapes me. The screen-test image is the final image, obliterating any and all of my imaginary projections with its brutal matter-of-factness. A short piano melody is played twice as if the blind man has finally succeeded in tuning the piano and, by extension, me. Drowsy, I get up from my resting place. I remain seated for a short while, not quite understanding what I have experienced. But I have experienced something. The mind is too slow to make sense of this immediately. I have to reconsider and remember what had gone before and what I had apparently missed while *being* there. The assistant opens the door and leads me out of the room.

*Folded Subjects*

What I see from my box in a box are boxed images of images that show images. Charmatz's *heâtre-élévision* is a complex *mise en abyme* of spaces, bodies and sounds. The room I am in is only one room in a line of rooms that are located behind me and in front of me. Some of them I have passed through on my way here and some stretch out on the screen into the future. In this potentially endless repetition of boxes my body becomes a conduit for stimuli. My body is positioned along a trajectory that begins behind and below my head. The trajectory carries me upwards, directing my gaze into the infinity of the TV set on the horizon. The whole set-up of this apparatus is reminiscent of a device for the construction of linear perspective. The illusion of things getting smaller and receding on the horizon is created by a set of lines that merge in one focal point. This vanishing point is connected to the eye of the beholder by one central line, the 'principle of lines', as Leon Battista Alberti (1972) has it, which enables the subject to mirror itself in the distance. Thus linear perspective, as Nelson Goodman (1968) has shown, depends upon a disembodied single eye that remains detached from the field of vision.[4]

In *heâtre-élévision*, I am in line: I am an integral part of this central line moving upwards, thereby meeting images within images that fill up and cover up the fear of the potential void that is at the vanishing point forever out of my reach. Although it carries me into a distance, the line at the same time comes back to me. It works its way out of the screen and into my eyes and ears. It is a recursive structure that, although it progresses, comes back to me at the same time. On its way back, it produces an endless folding of surfaces that creates crevices and cubicles, volumes and hollows as effects of the folding of the exterior.

In his book on Leibniz and the baroque, French philosopher Gilles Deleuze has described this figure or trope as that of the fold: 'The characteristic trait of the baroque is the fold which extends into infinity' (1988: 5; translation mine). This infinite process of folding brings surfaces that are at a distance close to each other to the point of touching. Things touch each other although they are at different points in space. The folding also produces spaces that come into being when surfaces are bent over each other:

> Always a fold within the fold like a hollow within a hollow. The unity
> of matter, the smallest unit of the labyrinth, is the fold, not the point

which is never a qualitative part but only the furthest point in a line. That is why the constitutive elements of matter are mass or various states of density analogous to the compression of an elastic force. Unfolding is thus not the opposite of folding. Instead, it follows the fold to the next fold (ibid.: 9).

The folding of matter is possible because matter is considered to be a muscular thing, connecting things by creating energetic tensions between them (ibid.: 10). These apparently old-fashioned philosophical ideas belonging to a different *epistemé* have, however, a striking relevance for *contemporary* concerns about dance and theatre productions. Exchange between stage and auditorium is not primarily considered to be an exchange of any kind of predefined meaning but a physical and emotional reaction that binds performer and spectator together in the actual performance situation.

Following from this, it is tempting to assume that the standard notion of the disembodied gaze of a singular detached eye, which constitutes the symbolic form of linear perspective, is, in Charmatz's pieces, replaced by a fully embodied subject. This subject is embedded in the sensory field, enabling it to have experiences other than visual ones. Being embedded here also means to give up control, to hand it over to the machine that does something to you. Charmatz's machine does not really show a *mise en abyme* nor does it really create a linear perspective. Both are only approximations. Their constructions are brought into play but are slightly off the mark, which is crucial for *héâtre-élévision*. Although the trajectory in which I assume my place directs my gaze toward a horizon, the gaze is neither disembodied nor is it generated by a subject standing upright and detached, looking from a distance onto the scene surveying it. I am actually lying down, forming an integral part of the machine.[5] The vanishing point is blocked by TV images that shield the infinite recess in the distance. It is already peopled by projections that could be my own but are not entirely my own. Although both the actual arrangement of the rooms in the building and the imaginary ones on the TV screen suggest a *mise en abyme*, the folding of spaces is broken because I do not reappear on the TV screen as 'myself'. Although I am implied in the dancers' activities, I am physically and visually *not* there. If the baroque *mise en abyme* fills up every single spot with space to prevent *horror vacui*, Charmatz's machine forces us to experience the void. Just as the machine plays

FIGURE 3. Vincent Druguet and Boris Charmatz in Boris Charmatz's *Aatt enen tionon*, 1996. Photograph by Cathy Peylan.

with the idea of linear perspective, it literally toys with the 'implications' of the fold. What is implied in the folded, that is to say what is 'folded in' (Latin, *implicere*), is that the subject is separated from itself by the ever continuing and recurring line.

Charmatz's apparatus in *héâtre-élévision* produces out-of-body experiences. The sound behind my head and the images in front of me are both coming toward me from a distance I can never physically travel across. The bodies on the screen are only images, which means that as bodies they are physically absent. The voices close to my ears are disembodied voices, too. They produce a hallucinatory acoustic body where a physical body is lacking. What I am therefore made to see, hear and feel is the absence, the void, the gap that looks back at me from where I am not. Surrounding the machine, the room I am in is empty and cold. The emptiness affects me. This absence is not primarily to be considered as a loss or lack of being, but as the very locus where the subject comes into being by opening up a space for his/her desire. Because there is absence, there is not only a speaking but also a hearing, seeing and feeling subject. In this sense, the TV set and the speakers are spatial extensions of my propped-up body on the would-be piano in the middle of the room. Because there is absence, I can project myself where I am not. The entire room becomes my body. The functions of seeing and hearing become exteriorized. The images and sounds they produce come between me and myself, turning me into my own ghostly double.

My body becomes the theatre. This implies that I am spaced out, like I am spaced out in Charmatz's machine: a force field of conflicting interacting agents coming from different parts of the room. The spatialization of my senses opens me up and questions the place where I am. I am here and yet over there, on the TV screen. I am on the inside of the room I am lying in and yet I am outside of the TV set. My body becomes a reflection of the sound and the images coming toward me from a distance I cannot bridge. I touch myself because I am an/other. If this is the case, then this has serious implications for the concept of embodiment. I perceive myself to be as a fully embodied subject when I am decentred. When I am out of my body I am turned into a hollow cave myself. I am caving in. The body as embodied entity comes into being only at the moment when it is lost. It then haunts the subject and criticism as a phantasm, as an object of desire that forever promises sensual completeness and wholeness. It is an imaginary projection of the body that pretends to seal and heal the gap just like the projected images that close the potentially open space, disguising the emptiness of the vanishing point on the horizon.

What distinguishes Charmatz's machine from this general function of images to shield us is that here absence and loss are embodied in the sense I have just outlined. The moment of loss is played out, remembered, and therefore also recuperated in the theatrical set that suspends my body between the imaginary function of the images and the hold the symbolic machine has on me. My body is the locus of resistance that comes into being when the symbolic and its imaginary representations on the TV screen collide. The images are representations of possibilities of the machine, possibilities to de-centre you and make you see, hear and feel.

How can we describe the subject of this apparatus, then? Deleuze writes that perspective is a device to produce subjects: 'Such is the basis of perspec-tivism, which does not mean a dependance in respect to a pregiven or defined subject: to the contrary, a subject will be what comes to the point of view, or rather what remains in the point of view' (1988: 19; translation mine). One becomes a subject by taking one's place in the symbolic structure of the per-spectival grid of lines. In Charmatz's machine, I become a subject by lying down on its structure. Structure, here, for once can be taken literally. By being 'in' the structure, holding a place in it, I am not an embodied subject in an ontological and phenomenological way, but a subject that is disembodied. I am an eccentric subject, out of myself, a subject that dispenses of itself, that spends itself—not in the sense of physical exhaustion (after all, I am lying more or less still on my piano bed), but in the sense of streaming away and flowing back to the space where I lie. It is an activity that returns to itself, all the while turning away from itself like the Deleuzian fold.

### Crypted Subjects

If embodiment is brought about by the loss of embodiment, then the suppos-edly interior becomes exteriorized. But the exterior space thus created is at the same time an inside reversed. The subject in Charmatz's machine incor-porates its own exterior. Being disembodied, it incorporates the absences of physically present bodies, thus spacing itself out theatrically. The figure that is related to the idea of an inside/outside chiasm is the crypt. Here, my associations from the very beginning of each performance of *héâtre-élévision* raise their spectral heads. The room I was led into by an assistant in both instances resembled a vault that I was locked away in. As a living human being, I was shut away in an interior unused space in some cultural building. It was a room hidden away, almost forgotten, in the heart of a building that was (once) full of cultural activity. The performance plays with the hidden interior of cultural experiences. The heart of darkness was indeed empty until my body assumed its space in it. Stretched out like a corpse and put on display, etherized upon a table, the idea of being buried alive was never far off. What if in the meantime the assistant left the building? What if he forgot me and simply did not return to let me out again? At the same time, my body as a theatrical space became such a vault, a vault within the vault, speechless and immobilized like the locked-away traumatic 'thing' itself. My body is locked away in this crypt and it becomes a crypt for my pleasures. While, however, the room I am in is locked, the room that is my body is open. Charmatz's 'pseudo-performance' unlocks the crypt to let me touch forbidden pleasures. Here, Charmatz's specific way of making use of the moving body gains significance. While any dance technique or style hides the body behind a shield of symbolic codes, thereby transposing it into a certain image of the dancing body, Charmatz's refusal to deal with technique in favour of the physical materiality of the body makes the traumatic body come to the fore. Unprotected, the body appears as the waste or the remains of both the symbolic and the imaginary, a reject that comes back to haunt us like a ghost.

In psychoanalytic thought, the crypt, as conceptualized by Nicolas Abraham and Maria Torok (1986), is an architecture containing and forever hiding a failed introjection. Whereas the 'I' comes into being by a series of introjections of object cathexis—people whose voices, gestures, touch and bodies we remember by making them parts of our own future identity—there is one primary object that resisted introjection. Introjection failed because the first object was never an object but only an imagined object that came into being in retrospect as a memory of a state of completeness that was always already lost. While we are never 'natural' bodies in the first place because we are always already made-up bodies, there is one space—the space of the original object—that remains empty. This lost imagined object is thus put to rest in a crypt as the living dead. Although it is interiorized, becoming part of the

FIGURE 4. Julia Cima and Boris Charmatz in Boris Charmatz's *régi*, 2005. Photograph by Alexander Wulz.

FIGURE 5. Raimund Hoghe and Boris Charmatz in Boris Charmatz's *régi*, 2005. Photograph by Alexander Wulz.

subject's psychological and physical set-up, it is at the very same time refused interiorization because of its traumatic nature. It is therefore designated a special space, which, as Jacques Derrida puts it in his reading of Abraham and Torok's text, is contained within a space: 'The cryptic enclave [. . .] forms, inside the self, inside the general space of the self, a kind of pocket of resistance, the hard cyst of an "artificial unconscious". The interior is partitioned off from the interior. The most inward safe (the crypt as an artificial unconscious, as the Self's artifact) becomes the outcast [. . .] the outside' (1986: xix). The crypt becomes the space that hides its own walls so that it may never be visited again. The crypt, as Derrida describes, 'is a contract with the dead' so that they may stay were they are, living as dead, living as ghosts (see also Siegmund 1996, 2006; Rayner 2006).

The subject Charmatz's machine produces is a crypted subject. We are encrypted, locked away and written upon, during the course of the performance by the machine and its sounds and images, which our body depends upon to come alive and into being. In this respect, Charmatz opens the crypt to let out our individual and subjective ghosts in the shape of sensual pleasures—at least to fill the empty room within the room that functions like a body enveloping our body. In her book on ghosts and the theatre, Alice Rayner put it this way: 'The body/theatre is thus an exterior space that displays, like a hollow vessel or vaulted crypt, the surfaces of its own interiority' (2006: 62). While we are disembodied, we are at the same time incorporated. We incorporate absent bodies, while at the same time we are incorporated ourselves by the vault-like room.

*Apparatus*

Two more aspects follow: the medial aspects of the machine, and its function as an apparatus that produces attention. The machine supplies a structure for our body and our organs to be organized in a certain way. The source of the images and the sounds are separated from each other; they are spatialized to surround us. At the same time, this structure or organizing principle is a form that puts itself on display. It is, in Rayner's words, 'a visible form that shelters an emptiness or a wound'. The wound sheltered here is, of course, the useless, passive and 'wasted' body itself. 'The apparatus shapes a hollow interior whose surfaces keep the secrets of the dead' (ibid.: 65). The apparatus thus comes between the room and my body as a theatrical space to bring my body to attention in this unique way. The apparatus mediates myself by splitting perception from consciousness and (re)presentation.

For some scholars, the theatrical event is not a medium. While it has the power to include all media in its productions and performances in their respective ways of functioning, the theatre itself is a live situation of people coming together. It is not a medium, because it is exchange in and of itself. On the other hand, it is undeniably true that theatre frames events and (re)presents situations that would otherwise remain unseen or unheard of. It produces (spectacular) images. One may, therefore, conceive of the theatre as a medium whose most visible technical device is the proscenium arch that splits the audience from the actors. What I suggest from my argument is therefore to speak of 'medial aspects' of theatre. One such medial aspect, then, is the intervention theatre makes between my perception as a member of the audience and that which is shown onstage. The theatre as a visible apparatus organizes what I see, hear and feel.

If Charmatz's machine in *héâtre-élévision* displays itself, it repeats the framing that is inherent in the theatrical situation. It repeats the frame only to give it an/other disposition. The apparatus therefore is a visible structure that brings about disembodied and incorporated subjects. As such it is equivalent to an extraneous symbolic structure on which the (re)presentation of our bodies depends. It stages our bodies to bring them into existence. In this respect, Charmatz's apparatus is a theatrical device or disposition that functions as a medium representing another medium, i.e. the theatre as such. The *mise en abyme* structure the performance-installation plays with extends to the entire situation. It has become clear that my understanding of the medium as an intervention opening up in-between spaces does not consider a medium (and the theatre) to be merely a channel for the transmission of information, a channel or material carrier that vanishes behind the information carried. Neither is it to be understood as an extension of human faculties such as seeing or remembering that may, eventually with technological progress, be replaced by the media (the camera, the hard drive of your computer) altogether. In the context of artistic production, media in general and Charmatz's apparatus in particular take on a materiality of their own. They become part of the performance, producing a sensual surplus of atmospheres or emotions that exceed their function. As aesthetic features in their own right, they draw attention to themselves and to my experiences while being absorbed in the performance.

It is here that the notion of attention comes into play. Theatre, like Charmatz's apparatuses' doubling of it, is an exteriorization of an interior that speaks of the dead as *living*. The apparatus produces attention. Attention depends on exclusion and focus. I see and hear more when I see and hear less. The cavity the theatre apparatus carves out of the theatre apparatus keeps the noises from the street out when I enter the foyer. In a recess analogous to the one that Charmatz stages and twists around, it keeps the conversations and clinking of glasses out when I enter the auditorium. Once seated, I have to remain more or less silent and immobile. Theatre withdraws in order to give us attention. What we attend to are the objects, bodies, gestures, voices, words, sounds and music that clamour for our attention on the stage or, in a more open performance situation, around us. What we pay attention to is therefore the result of a force field of stimuli, a force field of things vying to be seen, heard and felt. The force field is never only a measuring of quantities against each other. Bigger, brighter and louder may not do the trick for everybody. What we attend to is, as Sigmund Freud (2003) and Henri Bergson (1988) stipulated at the turn of the twentieth century, a qualitative result of things connecting to our memories, desires, expectations, our will and our experience.[6]

Theatre is an attention-arousing apparatus that finds one possible representation or image of itself in Charmatz's machines, and it plays on the split that is constitutive of theatre, the media apparatus and the phenomenon of attention. According to German phenomenologist Bernhard Waldenfels, that which holds our attention withdraws itself at the same time; the moment of estrangement, of otherness, is inherent in the phenomenon of attention. Something catches my attention because it unexpectedly and suddenly falls onto me, something that I can never control completely, because it is always already gone. Waldenfels therefore distinguishes between *Auffallen* and *Aufmerken*, between perceiving and consciously remarking. 'This deferral means that here and now I am somewhere else, where I never was and never will be. That which we perceive happens too early, the remarking happens too late' (2004: 72; translation mine). When I re-mark I turn around; I re-turn to a space where I never was to meet that which comes toward me from that other place. But the moment coming toward me is already gone when I react. That which catches my attention comes from somewhere else and therefore precedes and escapes me.

Attention therefore is an encounter with the ghostly other, which may come forth in the interstices, gaps, rifts and ruptures of consciousness. Theatre as an attention-arousing apparatus opens up these gaps of perception and (re)presentation. Like Charmatz's machines, theatre works on the margins of the intelligible, the visible and the audible, bringing it into play while all the time withdrawing it from us.

## Aatt enen tionon

The apparatus of *héâtre-élévision* is by no means the only machine-like structure in Charmatz's *oeuvre*. It is, however, his most radical production of the wasted and crypted body. *Programme court avec essorage* (Short Cycle with Spin Dry; 1999), a collaboration with visual artist Gilles Touyard, follows the short cycle of a washing machine. The machine's motor spins two huge disks while the bodies of Charmatz and Julia Cima struggle against centrifugal forces to stay on top. They fight against the machine, being allowed to rest only during the short time the programme halts the disks. In *Aatt enen tionon* (1996), a metal scaffold dominates the space, and in *régi* crane-like structures dispose of the dancing bodies. In all of these performances, however, the traditional theatre situation is more or less kept intact. The apparatuses attend only to the dancers' bodies while the audience simply watches. Nonetheless, these performances, like *héâtre-élévision*, use their structures to produce bodies. Although they function differently, they still play on the split between embodiment and incorporation.

The split constitutive of attention implies that the subject is always in danger of losing itself in the gap instead of closing itself. This is what happens in Charmatz's production *Aatt enen tionon*. This time the apparatus is a metal scaffold with three platforms of about four square metres each (Charmatz and Launay 2003: 88–90). Each of the three dancers is assigned one such small dance floor, Charmatz himself taking the lowest one, Vincent Druguet the one in the middle and Julia Cima the one at the top. Whereas the lower two are roofed, forming a kind of cubicle or, again, an open box, the one on the top has no shelter, exposing the dancer high up above our heads. As if to counterbalance the heaviness of the metal, three huge white balloons, which serve as giant lamps or lightbulbs, float in the two corners of the room, variously illuminating the scene or casting it into darkness. This structure stands exposed in the middle of a theatrical space. The audience is asked to stand, sit or walk around it. Although we are not physically part of this machine, it organizes our way of looking at the dancers. Like the much more complex apparatus of *héâtre-élévision*, it intervenes in the chiasmatic continuum of perceiving on the part of the audience and (re)presentation on the part of the dancers. Its staging brings forth a specific kind of body that draws attention to itself.

The dancers are already in their isolated yet open cubicles when we enter the space. When the lights dim, they take off their sweatpants, exposing the naked lower half of their bodies. The upper half is covered by a white T-shirt. Crash. Gathering their energy, the dancers fall to the ground, roll sideways, stick their legs up in the air and their bottoms in our faces. They swing their arms, prance to and fro, jump, fall and get up again—not only crashing on the floors of the platforms but also against the metal that confines them. The structure frames them in an otherwise open and unspecified space. And yet they try to break free from the cadre that both limits their way of moving and enables them to move in this peculiar way. The violence is both audible and visible as flesh mashes against the structure, threatening to bruise. On the upper platforms, Druguet and Cima are in constant danger of falling off the platforms should they accidentally come too close to the edge. The perception of height alters their sense of movement; vertigo dictates a curious mixture of abandon and control.

In a traditional dance performance, the dancers share the same floor. There is physical or visual contact among them to facilitate exchange and energy flow. The structure of *Aatt enen tionon*, however, abandons the horizontal in favour of the vertical. Instead of placing the dancers next to each other on the same horizontal plane, it stacks them on top of each other, assigning each his/her own space. Although both physical and visual contact is blocked, the dancers try to establish a flow of movement that runs up and down the metal construction. They have to establish contact by hearing and sensing the vibrations of the metal structure when their colleagues collapse. Often they wait, hovering on their platforms until they pick up movement that stopped on the platform above or below. In this respect, the piece is a reflection of one of the paradigms of modern dance: the imperative of flow. The flow of movement created in this piece, however, is only established by its interruptions. The sense of it is rendered by its failure, its not (quite) making it. And in the end, even the interruptions are interrupted: Charmatz uses music to blot them out. The performance is framed by two songs by the female British rock singer PJ Harvey. The second song, which is played toward the end, is so loud that any kind of attention to the sounds of bodies falling is drowned by the music.

The vertical orientation creates another flow: my gaze as it glides and slides up and down the structure. 'The eye finds no fixed point on which to rest' (Pontbriand 1982: 154).[7] It is set in motion, trying to see everything while all the time aware that it is missing something. We cannot get the whole picture, because the verticality of the structure is bigger than the eye can take in; resolution is stymied, closure is prevented. I can never get as far away from the scaffold as I would need to in order to frame a fixed image. The all-seeing eye/I is replaced by an eye/I that is moving with the dancers—embedded in the scene and yet at a distance from it. André Lepecki has described this as 'a play with sexual desire and optical tactility'. The tactile gaze slides over the opaque bodies that draw attention to their own materiality 'by means of a constant insistence on the body's presentness' (1999: 136, 137). The up-and-down movement along the scaffold is doubled by an up-and-down movement of a slightly more erotic nature. My eyes also find no fixed place to rest because I waver between the dressed upper part of the dancers' bodies and their naked lower region. Should I concentrate on their faces and T-shirts because it is the socially acceptable thing to do? Or am I allowed to rest on their private parts? Do I feel at ease when I do because there are other members of the audience surrounding and judging me in this act of the private made public?

All these contradicting forces are wonderfully summed up in the title of the piece. The three distinct parts of the word compound *Aatt enen tionon* mirror the three tiers the dancers perform on. The doubling of vowels and consonants, beginning with a wide open 'A' before the word itself like a dancer stumbling and falling down, onomatopoeically creates moments of hesitation, of a drawn-out action that is brutally brought to an inconclusive conclusion indicated by the gap between the first and second part. The doubling of the syllables 'en' and, in the last section, 'on' marks a continued stumbling, a skipping forward without really getting on toward the end. The 'on' preceding the final 'on' gives the whole word the status of a noun as if it were a 'theatron', where people are given things to see. The two blanks cut the word into three sections like the performers' platforms. Their edges cut the vertical horizontally like the hems of the T-shirts dividing the bodies into two parts. They mark the interruption of the energy flow, the stuttering, which is taken up in the batting of my eyelids, which cuts and intersects my field of vision horizontally and fills it with absences and blind spots.

All this taken together spells out implications of the meaning of the word 'attention'. The title implies that it is a continued waiting for something to happen which is still present in the French verb *attendre*. When I am attentive, I project my senses toward the things surrounding me. I am therefore in an alert state anticipating something that might happen—the dancers hurting themselves or really falling off and out of the structure, that something dangerous might occur, something that will interrupt the natural flow of things. Attention implies an unforeseen event that restructures experience. Attention builds into the gap of perceiving and re-acting. Charmatz's theatrical machine of the vertical scaffold produces the rift; it makes it visible by insisting on it. In the act, it produces bodies at risk that we are attentive to. We care about them with our attention.

## régi

Sssssttt. Low, almost inaudible, a strange noise whirs and buzzes through the space. The air shimmers and vibrates. Somewhere on the dark stage something is torn apart. Something creaks under pressure. A black carpet runs from the back of the stage to the front like a little river. A small crane winds its arm across the stage like a kraken searching for intruders or seeking easy prey. Gradually, our eyes adjust to the low lighting. Two winches holding two ropes glow like eyes in the dark. A motor winds up one of the ropes, pulling it tighter and tighter until it breaks free from one of the numerous loops fastening it to the walls of the theatre. Plingggg. Rittsssssshhhhh. Another loop is torn off and jumps across the floor. More and more loops are ripped from the wall. It sounds as if the whole theatre building is being torn apart and about to collapse and bury us alive. Like two nerves the ropes zigzag across the stage, turning it into a living organism that reacts to pressure and energy flow by changing its shape. Our eyes try to follow the ropes whipping through the air. They are guided by the noise travelling and moving across the stage without finding anything to hold on to for very long. No identifiable object comes into view; we have only the sound of a theatre falling apart. The beginning of *régi* holds our attention for a very long time even though nothing happens.

Finally, we are given a piece of information. A dark lump lies on the floor. Slowly it is dragged centre stage by the winch. Just what exactly it is, I cannot determine: a body, a bundle of clothes, a sack full of something heavy? What do we see when we see? What do we project onto the 'thing' to make it come alive for us? The arm of the crane lifts the lifeless bundle up in the air, holding onto its midriff, bending it over in the middle. It is a body indeed, yet no head, face or hands can be discerned. Suspended on a hook, the figure sways in the air. The machine shakes it a little before lowering it to the floor again. Suddenly, the second rope is being pulled tight. This time its nervous movement guides us directly to a second body that is being pulled centre stage on one of its legs. The two motionless bodies are being moved by the machine. They are lifted up in the air where they touch each other by chance, gently swaying and turning around each other as in a *pas de deux*. From the dark depths of the stage a third figure emerges, making its way to the front. Dressed in black like the two others, he whirls their bodies around like children on the swings.

The scene ends. The bodies are lowered as the carpet is suddenly pulled back. The unidentifiable flying objects, the two dancing UFOs, loosen their hooks and pull off their masks. We can identify them as Charmatz and Cima now, a belated act of recognition that does not put to rest the feeling of uncertainty. The third dancer is the German choreographer and performer Raimund Hoghe. While Cima moves to the back of the stage, still wearing her black uniform, Charmatz and Hoghe strip naked down front. The back is brightly lit; the front is left in the dark. Another machine goes into action. Cima climbs onto a kind of conveyor belt installed along the back wall, way up over her head. She tries to walk, but with every step the machine pulls the carpet out from under her, making her fall down. To a stripped-down vocal version of Michael Jackson's 1983 dance-floor classic 'Billie Jean', she tries again and again to 'dance'.

During this time, the two men at the front climb over each other. They touch each other's limbs by accident until Charmatz takes Hoghe's hand and strokes himself with it. Suddenly the word '*insulte*', insult, blares out of the speakers. '*Insulte, insulte, insulte.*' In response to the rhythmic repetition of that one word, Cima jumps up and down on her moving belt like a jumping jack. The words fall down on Charmatz's body like arrows piercing him; he tenses his muscles and twitches. The word penetrates the bodies—it almost stigmatizes them—directing our attention to their failings and their failures: to dance, to signify and to be their own masters. The voice is hoarse, the word is expulsed, expulsing the bodies in return. Just what exactly the insult is remains unclear. Is the insult to Cima's body, kept from dancing and forced to fall down? Or is the audience to be insulted by the two naked men engaged in some kind of homoerotic exploration? Or is it directed at Cima by leaving her out of the fun? Or is *régi* an insult to the audience who has come to see a dance performance but gets (almost) nothing of the kind? Or is the insult to be found in Michael Jackson's lyrics, 'the kid is not my son'—the supposed father insulting the mother?

The French word *régi*, neither exactly *régie* nor the verb *régir*, yet somehow both of them, implies the imposition of some kind of rule, law or discipline onto something or someone. There is a certain kind of determination in its rule, imposing a function onto someone. This is exactly what the two machines in *régi* do. Both the crane and the running belt determine what the bodies can do. They thwart their ambitions to break free by imposing their structure onto the bodies, thus producing subjected bodies, 'wasted' bodies thrown up like remains for the audience to see and hear. In this respect it is important to note that Hoghe's deformed body—he is hunchbacked—is a body that defies the norm both socially and artistically. The theme of being run or 'directed' by something or somebody continues during the second half of the performance: Hoghe, alone now, repeats, in French, words we all hear broadcast in English from the loudspeakers. The recorded words are spoken by Charmatz, and they blare from the loudspeakers like the master's voice, commanding a response. Taking the lyrics of Michael Jackson's song into account, the scene could be read as a family situation. After all, whose influence on us could be greater than that of one's family?

As with the three-tiered apparatus of *Aatt enen tionon*, Charmatz again splits our gaze and the focus of our attention. Both oscillate between the lit background and the dark foreground, traversing the emptiness and the rift between the two centres of activity. Where are we to look? What are we allowed to look at? At the female Sisyphus in the back or at the two naked men in the front touching each other? At Hoghe's hunchback or at Charmatz's Adonis-like figure? The performance is structured around a series of oppositions: background–foreground, light–dark, man–woman, dressed–naked, young–old, a trained dancer's body–a body with a hunchback defying norms, heterosexual–homosexual, solo–duo. But as our gaze travels across them, the distinctions become confused and blurred in the process. In this force-field of attention I have to find my own place from which to look, and to determine for myself what to look at.

### Tender Attention to Bodies

Charmatz's machines narrow and widen the focus at the same time. Our attention is suspended between two or three centres of activity. Assuming one's place and thereby assuming an identity as a spectator, for instance, is made much more difficult. Just as attention is suspended, so is the subject who constitutes him/herself by being attentive to some thing. We withdraw from ourselves. We escape ourselves, becoming ghosts of our former selves in the process.

The medial aspect of theatre understood to be an intervention between perception and (re)presentation is mirrored in the machine. The machine functions as a visible and materialized structure in which the subject to be is to assume its place. Having done so, however, it produces a complex set of sensual and mental reactions, opening up both the performer's and the audience's body. The body, on the one hand, depends upon the machine because it is brought about by the machine. It hangs onto it for dear life, literally dragged behind as in *régi* or threatening to fall off the scaffolding as in *Aatt enen tionon*. On the other hand, however, it is not identical to the machine. The machine as an apparatus arranges and forms these bodies, standing or lying in it and yet remaining apart from it. It arranges specific constellations of sight and sound that lead to a spacing out of the body, opening it up and producing absences between the registers of the senses. The machine reverses inside and outside. It folds outside over outside, creating a subject whose interior consists entirely of folded surfaces. Thus the body itself is spatialized, folded into space as a space and turned into the site of theatre itself. The bodies in Charmatz's machines are disembodied and incorporated at the same time. By interiorizing the absent bodies and the empty spaces they leave between the senses, the body in a crypt-like architecture becomes a body within a body whose limits are nowhere and therefore constantly redrawn and renegotiated. After they have divested themselves of any kind of symbolic dance technique and their respective imaginary bodies, Charmatz's bodies are 'wasted' bodies, remains that remain because they resist disappearance. They resist the machines that subject them and limit their range of activities. Like the theatre, these machines exclude possibilities in order to increase (and not to reduce) complexities between bodies and voices by drawing attention to the bodies' opaque crypt-like density.

## Notes

1  For more on his work, see Boris Charmatz and Isabelle Launay (2003).

2  Nikolaus Müller-Schöll uses the image of an opium den to describe the situation of the performer/spectator (2004: 348).

3  For a review of the performance that comes to a similar conclusion, see Thomas Hahn (2003).

4  I have explored the role of perception and perspective in dance in a previous essay (Siegmund 2003).

5  André Lepecki writes about the horizontal position in relation to the work of La Ribot and Trisha Brown (see Lepecki 2005: 65–86).

6  For Henri Bergson, our whole past coexists with our present experiences, a past that could be accessed once motion is suspended. To Sigmund Freud, human consciousness is a protecting shield against the permanent influx of information and stimuli. What is actually allowed to pass in order to become a conscious perception must be tied to some kind of previous experience.

7  Chantal Pontbriand used this phrase by Walter Benjamin in an essay from 1982 to describe the effects of the multiple framings of Richard Foreman's theatre productions.

*References*

ABRAHAM, Nicolas and Maria Torok. 1986. *The Wolf Man's Magic Word: A Cryptonomy*. Minneapolis: University of Minnesota Press.

ALBERTI, Leon Battista. 1972. *On Painting and on Sculpture. The Latin Texts of De Pictura and De Statua* (Cecil Grayson trans. and ed.). New York: Phaidon.

BERGSON, Henri. 1988 [1896]. *Matter and Memory* (W. Scott Palmer and Nancy Margaret Paul trans.). New York: Zone Books.

CHARMATZ, Boris. 2002. 'Pseudo-spectacle'. Programme notes for *héâtre-élévision*. Paris: Festival d'automne, Centre Pompidou, 13 September–20 December.

—— and Isabelle Launay. 2003. *Entretenir: À propos d'une danse contemporaine* [Conversing: About a Contemporary Dance]. Dijon/Pantin: Les Presses du Réel/Centre national de la danse.

CRARY, Jonathan. 1999. *Suspensions of Perception: Attention, Spectacle, and Modern Culture*. Cambridge, MA: MIT Press.

DELEUZE, Gilles. 1988. *Le Pli: Leibniz et le Baroque* [The Fold: Leibniz and the Baroque]. Paris: Les editions de Minuit.

DERRIDA, Jacques. 1986. 'Foreword: FORS: The Anglish Words of Nicolas Abraham and Maria Torok', in Nicolas Abraham and Maria Torok, *The Wolf Man's Magic Word: A Cryptonomy*. Minneapolis: University of Minnesota Press, pp. xi–xlviii.

FREUD, Sigmund. 2003. *Beyond the Pleasure Principle and Other Writings*. Harmondsworth: Penguin.

GOODMAN, Nelson. 1968. *Languages of Art: An Approach to a Theory of Symbols*. Indianapolis: Bobbs-Merrill.

HAHN, Thomas. 2003. 'anz'. *Ballettanz* 10(10): 60–3.

LEPECKI, André. 1999. 'Skin, Body, and Presence in Contemporary European Choreography'. *TDR* 43(4) (T164): 129–40.

——. 2005. *Exhausting Dance: Performance and the Politics of Movement*. London: Routledge.

MÜLLER-SCHÖLL, Nikolaus. 2004. 'Theater ausser sich' [Theatre Beside Itself], in Annemarie Matzke and Hajo Kurzenberger (eds), *Theater Theorie Praxis* [Theatre Theory Praxis]. Berlin: Verlag Theater der Zeit, pp. 342–52.

PONTBRIAND, Chantal. 1982. 'The eye finds no fixed point on which to rest . . .'. *Modern Drama* 25: 154–62.

Rayner, Alice. 2006. *Ghosts: Death's Double and the Phenomenon of Theatre*. Minneapolis: University of Minnesota Press.

Siegmund, Gerald. 1996. *Theater als Gedächtnis* [Theatre as Memory]. Tübingen: Gunter Narr Verlag.

———. 2003. 'Tanz im Blick. Die Wiederentdeckung des verkörperten Zuschauers' [Dance in View: The Rediscovery of the Embodied Spectator], in Erika Fischer-Lichte, Christopher Balme and Stephan Grätzel (eds), *Theater als Paradigma der Moderne? Positionen zwischen historischer Avantgarde und Medienzeitalter* [Theatre as Paradigm of the Modern? Positions between the Historical Avantgarde and the Age of Media]. Tübingen: Francke Verlag, pp. 417–28.

———. 2006. *Abwesenheit. Eine performative Ästhetik des Tanzes* [Absence: A Performative Aesthetics of Dance]. Bielefeld: Transcript Verlag.

Waldenfels, Bernhard. 2004. *Phänomenologie der Aufmerksamkeit* [Phenomenology of Attention]. Frankfurt am Main: Suhrkamp.

PARATOPIAS OF PERFORMANCE:
THE CHOREOGRAPHIC PRACTICES OF CHANDRALEKHA[1]

ANURIMA BANERJI

I'm giving up on land to light on, slowly, it isn't land

[. . .] Look. What I know is this. I'm giving up.

No offence. I was never committed. Not ever, to offices

or islands, continents, graphs, whole cloth, these sequences,
not even footsteps (Brand 1997).

**para-**

Main Entry: 1 para-
Variant(s): *or* par-
Function: *prefix*
Etymology: Middle English, from Middle French, from Latin, from Greek, from *para*; akin to Greek *pro* before—more at FOR
1: beside: alongside of: beyond: aside from <*parathyroid*> <*parenteral*>
2a: closely related to <*paraldehyde*> b: involving substitution at or characterized by two opposite positions in the benzene ring that are separated by two carbon atoms <*paradichlorobenzene*>
3a: faulty: abnormal <*paresthesia*> b: associated in a subsidiary or accessory capacity<*paramedical*> c: closely resembling: almost <*paratyphoid*>

**topia**

Main Entry: **to·pos**
Pronunciation: 'tO-'päs, 'tä-
Function: *noun*
Inflected Form(s): plural **to·poi**/-'poi/
Etymology: Greek, short for *koinos topos*, literally, common place: a traditional or conventional literary or rhetorical theme or topic[2]

**Paratopia:** A space of alterity. That which exists alongside, beside, aside from the dominant (but does not necessarily reference it). That which is closely related to, closely resembling or almost the dominant (and so necessarily references it). That which is faulty, abnormal, associated in a subsidiary or accessory capacity to the dominant (and so necessarily is defined and subjugated by it). All of these associations of the paratopia can coexist and be put to imaginative use, but, in coining this term, I became mostly intrigued by the first meaning that can be generated under the auspices of the dictionary and my political imagination: *namely, the paratopia as a space of performance which exists parallel to dominant culture, without necessarily referencing its terms, productively or reactively, at its constitutive core.* The other two possible allusions seem too close to the ideas of hegemonic or counter-hegemonic places and performative modes. What interests me here is an elaboration and thinking through of a theory of paratopia that is committed to this notion of alterity—

not 'alternative', but 'alter', as in literally, the other. Or, another. Another ontology, another time, another way of being, another zone, another ethic.

*Paratopia and Performance*

How does the paratopia compare to prevailing theories about performance, and what does it offer in terms of redefining or reimagining its terms and limits? Perhaps this question is best answered by presenting a series of exclusions and negations—contrasting the concept with what it is *not*—to arrive at what its substantive core *is*. I am not proposing an idea of 'alternative', 'residual' or 'emergent' cultures that imprint society with their 'structures of feeling' (Williams 1977); nor am I suggesting a substitute for the ideas of 'counter-culture' or 'subculture' (Hebdige 1979). The paratopia is not just a site of 'disidentification' (or, for that matter, identification or counter-identification, as José Esteban Muñoz maps out [1999]), as its concerns are not only animated by a desire to negotiate reigning discourses. Neither is the paratopia a place that totally anchors the ideological agenda of 'counter-hegemony' (Gramsci 1971). Equally, it cannot be conceived as a 'hybrid' milieu (in the tenor of Homi K. Bhabha's 'third space' [1994]) or a site of 'intracultural/intercultural' encounters (Bharucha 2000) because it is not exclusively diasporic, nor is it about reconciling differential or antithetical discourses, whether linked to the colony or metropole, periphery or mainstream. The paratopia is not an equivalent for the 'liminal', as it does not exist in between, interstitially, on the threshold, boundary or border (Turner 1977). These are all spaces that are shaped, in some way, as responses, redefinitions or refinements of dominant cultural domains.

In critical theory in general, the rhetoric of 'resistance' is clearly valorized; the reason for its appeal is not difficult to discern, since the posture of defiance signals and affirms a political will or consciousness that serves as the catalyst for social change (Gramsci 1971; Williams 1977). This model of 'resistance' is arguably politically limited, in that it is condemned to contend with prevailing systems of value and representation; however, critiquing the mainstream is not sufficient for imagining a different field of existence. The paratopia does not mark the event of resistance in this vein; it is not automatically subversive, even though it is a site of agency.[3]

What interests me are those agentive acts that are not wholly incorporated within the central circuits of power—acts that somehow escape, or exist in a zone totally separate from, the call of the dominant. There are no spaces free of political signification, pristine and uncontaminated, of course; I am speaking of performances that generate their own ideologies outside of dominant discourses, but not just as rebellious gesture: rather, I am drawn to those artists who are genuinely seeking to create new social grounds and orders, meanings and visions; those who are engaged in inventing and instituting their own practices (whether in a solitary or collective capacity); and those who are creating settings and situations in which to enact these practices, in a communitarian environment. Beyond critiquing the mainstream alone, the paratopia is defined by innovation. The intention motivating its production is creative and experimental, rather than purely interrogative— though contest may be its inevitable consequence.

The paratopic performance is akin to what Muñoz (1999) calls 'world-making', but again, the creation of a world that explicitly subverts or opposes the dominant culture is not its aim; instead, paratopic culture lies adjacent to it. Dislocation, deconstruction and disruption are not its principal aims (though it may implicitly or inadvertently register them). But the paratopic idea is also not designed to protect or insulate the dominant locus from its effects, or vice versa; rather, my specific interest is in those who have renounced the dominant milieu, and exited into zones that escape the penetration of governing hegemonies and their coercive powers. This is a search for a new economy of the body. There is even an ascetic ideal, perhaps, one that is inspirational and imaginative. There is more to this than the simple abandonment of the dominant, or defying ideological interpellation. Something else is implied here—an ethical performative impulse that is sought out by the subject, despite the rewards of staying within the limits of the known, despite the overwhelming force that power exerts on the body and psyche under converging regimes of discipline and surveillance. These are some of the lures, rationales and investments—ideological, moral, aesthetic and affective—for exploring the possibilities of the paratopia.

I also deliberately evoke the terms of utopia, dystopia and heterotopia as comparative sites: the paratopia is not positioned as a surrogate for either of these notions, but acts as their adjunct, as a materially grounded conception of space that is neither idealized, nor framed through a cynical politics of nihilism located in an imaginary immanence. The paratopia is about the present, but contains the lineages of the past, and presages some future. It is not about exalting eradication, and so does not address itself to Jacques Derrida's 'atopia' (1992), which signals 'no-place' at all and as such, situates itself against these other valences. The paratopia shares some resonance with the 'heterotopia', conceived by Michel Foucault (1986) as a kind of 'other space', with the critical difference that the former is a temporal realm that materializes specifically *through embodied movement*—it is not a defined architectural zone that the body enters, in which corporeal experiences are structured and shaped. The site of the paratopia, then, extends as far as the body's peregrinations and exists for the duration of the embodied act. As such, the paratopia is a highly grounded idea of performance, and can be deployed specifically to theorize a spectrum of territorialized acts—among them, dance.

The practices and philosophies of the radical South Asian choreographer, Chandralekha, serve as prisms for reflecting on ideations of paratopic performance. While Chandralekha's persona and work has been read in terms of resistance to the structures of South Asian classical dance and patriarchal politics by noted scholars such as Rustom Bharucha (1995) and Ananya Chatterjea (2004),[4] I suggest her choreographic practice can also be affiliated with the paratopic concept. Powerful works such as *Angika* (1985), *Prana* (1990), *Sri* (1991), *Yantra–Dance Diagrams* (1994), *Raga: In Search of Femininity* (1998) and *Sharira: Fire and Desire* (2000)—to cite only a sample of important pieces in her repertoire—illuminate this affinity.[5] I focus on three elements here that link together the theory of paratopia with Chandralekha's dance praxis: morphologies of movement, space and time.

### Chandralekha, Classical Dance and Contemporary Movement

There are live concepts in our culture still capable of activating the people. The tragedy is that progressive movements have failed to go to our own sources of culture to tap all those areas charged with energy and harness them to build up vitality in people, which obviously, is important for changing conditions in life like any other revolutionary theory. This becomes all the more important when we see that cultural levels, at times, have the possibility of being far ahead of political levels and thus have the potential for initiating social change (Chandralekha 1980).

Speaking of civic and artistic spaces as sites for producing dissent, for producing mutinous bodies that transform existing relations of power so new
social orders can be imagined, Chandralekha articulates a vision that dove-
tails with that of the paratopia. Culture, for her, isn't equated with the dead
weight of tradition, but stands for an active and vital force—a source of 'live
concepts' animating protest, an oppositional consciousness toward the struggle for a different world. 'I am not talking here of revival or preservation but
of the need for a *holistic creative vision for our times*,' she writes (2001: 68; italics
mine). Critically then, for her, dance becomes a paratopic cultural practice
in which revolutionary politics are not only symbolized, but concretized and
realized in the present.

Chandralekha is both an icon and an iconoclast of South Asian dance.
Her works eclipse the dance categories of 'modern' or 'classical'; 'contemporary' is the most nebulous and ambiguous, but closest descriptor.[6] Yet it is
precisely this inability to fully fix or essentialize her practice that makes
Chandralekha's corpus an ideal exemplar of paratopic enactments.

Born in 1929, during the reign of the British Raj, Chandralekha was raised
in a middle-class family and came of age in the era of Independence in India.
She became interested in developing a totally new dance aesthetic after being
confronted by the 'stunning paradox' that 'art and life seemed to be in conflict' (Chandralekha 1984: 60), a revelation that indelibly marked her initial
experience of performance.[7] Dramatically, she completely abdicated her successful solo career as an exponent of Bharatanatyam, one of the dances from
India constructed as 'classical'. Bharatanatyam owes its classical status to its
divine themes, and a movement vocabulary based on the expressive codes
prescribed in the ancient Hindu treatise, the *Natyashastra*, which serves as a
philosophical and practical guide to performance, and is the foundational
text for many of the self-consciously 'traditional' dance and theatre practices
of India.

Absent from the scene for over a decade, Chandralekha finally returned
to dance and proceeded to regenerate its meanings, inaugurating a new paradigm. Chandralekha's philosophy lifts classical dance out of the purely de-
votional sphere, which served as its originary alibi, and permeates it with a
strong political consciousness (Bharucha 1995). Her style is stark in comparison to the conventions of classicism; she takes the idiom of Bharatanatyam[8]

FIGURE 1. Chandralekha at the Nritya Natika Festival, New Delhi, in
*Angika*. Performed by the Cultural Centre of Madras, November 1995.
Photograph courtesy of Sangeet Natak Akademi, New Delhi.

and distils it to its barest elements, then fuses it with quotidian gestures (taken primarily from South Asian women's movement repertoires), and adds stylistic elements from yoga, martial arts (such as the South Indian form, *Kalaripayattu*), and other body-based practices. Through the development of a novel choreographic language, she shatters and splinters the space demarcating 'dance' to leap into the more exploratory realm of 'movement'. She also does away with the elaborate production elements that have accompanied the rise of classical dance as international spectacle and symbol of Indian aesthetic; any elaborate costuming, jewellery or ritual prayer is abandoned in favour of minimalist and organic representations of the body. Minimalism, in her perspective, is 'not a style or a trend, or a theatrical statement. It is a value' (in Kolmes 1998: 40).

Falling outside the edges of any kind of established dance, uniquely and insistently its own eclectic form, Chandralekha's choreography is moored in an original aesthetic philosophy devised through deep engagement with a range of performance texts and practices. She reinterprets and recontextualizes canonical literature, or mines marginalized histories of Indian thought, often Hindu in origin.[9] For example, her theorization of choreography draws on Hindu precepts of spatialization, such as the *mandala*, 'a multidimensional principle of space–space that is rooted as well as radiating' (Chandralekha 2001: 67). This polycentrism is manifested in her group compositions, as in *Sri* and *Prana*, where she arranges bodies in ways that alternate between the depiction of singular images that centre the gaze (a pair of dancers mirroring each other's movements in the middle of the performance space; a cluster of dancers moving together as a single entity, in unison across the stage) and multiple points of focus (dancers arranged in a diagonal formation from downstage to the back); dancers sporadically coming on and off stage in the background, as the principal actors continue their movement in the foreground; bodies dispersed across the space, each absorbed in their own gestures. The body merges with space to become a *mandala* itself (Coorlawala 1999: 7). The linearity, geometry and austerity of her style frame the body as an instrument for exploring abstract movement and relationality, transforming it into an infinite field of energies (Chandralekha 1997: 47).

Her creative work emanates from the distinct set of artistic and ideological commitments that have come to define her worldview. In each of her pieces, she travels outside orthodox notions of time, space and the dancing

subject, and deals with themes that are often proscribed, prohibited, dangerous, taboo, extreme (Bharucha 1995; Chatterjea 1998, 2004). Questions of gender, queer desire and the secular elisions of the divine appear as major motifs
in her work.[10] She also exhibits an interest in the concepts that organize
everyday life, departing from narratives of myth and religiosity, focusing exclusively on the dimension of somatic subjectivity, discarding narrative as
the purpose and alibi of classical dance, instead using the body to trace lines,
concepts and politics that speak to contemporary concerns.[11] Her principle
of 'movement' bridges conceptions of the individual body and its repertoires
with the larger conception of social movements: 'I'm a believer in a kind of
politics that should be equal with aesthetics. For me, the two should be together in order to change our world. I believe that this is the real problem,
that we emphasize one and neglect the other. We make compartments between politics and aesthetics, life and art' (in Cash 1998).

A strongly feminist conviction shapes, for instance, *Raga: In Search of Femininity*, in which the principal duet is unexpectedly and provocatively composed of two men and their erotic engagement. The sentiment anchoring this
performance is invoked in a tenth-century poem, authored by the South Indian saint Devara Dasimayya: If they see/breasts and long hair coming/they
call it a woman,/if beard and whiskers/they call it a man/but look, the self
that hovers/in between/is neither man nor woman.'[12] Chandralekha proposes
a unique archaeology of gender in *Raga*—a non-dualistic view in which masculine and feminine elements reside in a single body; the true self cannot
claim an absolute and social identity as male or female. This revelation also
liberates the body from patriarchal ideologies that reify binaries of gender,
and allows for a revival of self outside oppressive ideologies. Corporeal expression becomes a site for the practice of freedom: 'I believe dance is a "project" that would enable a recovery of the body, of our spine, which for me, is
a metaphor of freedom,' Chandralekha states. '[I]t is all about evoking hu-
manising energy and dignity in an increasingly brutalising environment'
(1997: 46).

Refuting 'a modernist search for origins or for a unitary notion of truth'
(Chatterjea 1998: 28), Chandralekha rejects the idea of imbuing her choreographies with the mystique of ancient auras—calling the archival materials
she uses as a basis of her dance 'modern texts' (i.e. even the *Natyashastra*) and
refuses to appropriate and reinforce typical notions of 'modernity' and 'tra-

dition' to redeem her practice in terms of the currency of a globalized world clearly committed to sustaining these reductive categories of difference.

In a stunning example of this tendency, dance critic Deborah Jowitt makes the following (misguided) claim in her review of *Raga*:

> Like all Asian artists keen to experiment or to bring new stories to the stage, she has had to labor to come to terms with powerful classical dance and theater forms—querying and probing their strictures rather than abandoning them. If artists of her caliber borrow from the West, they borrow primarily the credo of freedom and personal expression (1998: n.p.).

Here Jowitt, like many other critics, traffics in pernicious ideas of cultural difference: that Asia is a bastion of tradition to be contrasted with, and liberated by, the West—which in turn is defined by the values of freedom, unshackled by the burdens of custom and tradition.[13] The notion that freedom could be a value indigenous to Asian philosophies is effectively precluded in Jowitt's rhetorical gesture. And although she is influenced by various sources of tradition, Chandralekha rejects the idea that an encounter with the West is necessary to arrange her choreographic project as avant-garde or progressive; she recasts and mobilizes the aesthetic resources available to her in her immediate cultural environment, deploying a new articulation of dance—both in form and content—that cannot be misapprehended as 'Western' or 'modern', but is produced instead as 'South Asian' and 'contemporary'. Chandralekha has said she is 'constantly relating, refining the reality of the in-between area; to enable tradition to flow free in our contemporary life' (1997: 47). In this regard, it is Chandralekha's commitment to a distinct morphology of dance, built on indigenous praxis, making a new body outside of the domains of classical strictures, outside the reductive discursive sites of Orientalism—and her desire to disengage and delink from these over-determining systems of signification—that seal the status of her artistic work as paratopic.

## Paratopic Time

The time of paratopia stretches across past, present and future, to create a zone of coeval time/shared time (Fabian 1983)—a duration that stretches across each of these partitioned temporal structures to create an encounter with the contemporary. This is not the idea of performance as marked by the

FIGURE 2. Sumitra Gautam (*standing*) facing another performer in Chandralekha's *Angika*. Performed by the Cultural Centre of Madras at the Nritya Natika Festival, New Delhi, November 1995. Photograph courtesy of Sangeet Natak Akademi, New Delhi.

FIGURE 3. (*Front, left to right*) Sumitra Gautam and Sujatha Ramalingam, with Raghunath Manet (*back*), in Chandralekha's *Angika*. Performed by the Cultural Centre of Madras at the Nritya Natika Festival, New Delhi, November 1995. Photograph courtesy of Sangeet Natak Akademi, New Delhi.

temporality of the 'now', as Peggy Phelan has famously asserted (1993). It lies outside the frames of 'traditional', 'modern' and 'postmodern', 'precolonial', 'colonial' or 'postcolonial'; it engages with multiple temporal schemas that are not defined primarily by these prevailing constructs (Chandralekha 1997). Rather, the temporal structure of the paratopia resonates and reverberates with elements of many kinds of times, depending on what the performer, medium and audience together bring to the space.

Phelan suggests that the definitive temporality of performance is indeed the moment of the radical present, ever elusive, always threatening to disappear; this fragility, this eternal risk of vanishing is not the hallmark of the paratopia, which creates and leaves behind evidence that is not at all ephemeral—tangible traces and real remains, ideological imprints and material marks. The paratopia is not marked by transience, nor is its definitive moment the radical present. Its definitive ontology is not even 'liveness', because within its contours, the dead or otherwise immobile body—mortified, maimed, tortured, imprisoned, bound—is still able to perform, if only through its very existence, as it is used in service of ideology, to illuminate a political condition or catalyse a form of ethics. *The paratopia illustrates the ways in which performance most radically speaks to presence across time, but not liveness.* It complicates and undermines the premises that subtend the reading of performance as an entity perpetually out of grasp, perpetually at risk of vanishing.

The paratopia can temporarily disappear, but it is constantly repeating, reappearing and reasserting itself. And it animates gestures outside of its space. Its alterity is not expressed in terms of the classical 'other' that is inextricably linked to and definitive of the 'self' as its negation, as its state of the exception. This is alterity in its simplest, most basic and literal sense: 'Otherness' not as alternative to the dominant, not as the marginal 'otherness' that marks the locus of the centre. This is alterity in terms of 'another', as in, another ontology and epistemology—ways of being and knowing that exist beside what is offered as the centre or the ideal.

The conception of 'another' time and the disruption of dominant categories attached to it is accomplished in Chandralekha's work: she perfectly executes a paratopic performance by fabricating her own time. This is primarily because the dominant schemas governing notions of time in present political discourse are inadequate for describing the chronotypes proposed and constructed in her work (Coorlawala 1999). Chandralekha's idea of time is more localized, layered and contextual, deriving its power from a particular Indian ethos that amalgamates the temporalities of myriad Indian practices while absorbing perspectives from other cultural systems.[14] Her 1995 piece *Mahakal*, for example, expressly uses Indian concepts of cyclical time as its signature and motif. In her dance, 'where the most radical, the most avant-garde, is based on a recycling and revisioning of root, past history and present creation coalesce and comment upon each other' (Chatterjea 1998: 29).

*Sri*, for instance, opens with Chandralekha alone in a halo of white light on the dark stage. She is in a yogic *asana*, in a shoulder-stand, legs braided together, suspended in the air. You can see the muscle and the sinew of her body in the sharp light. Slowly, she brings her legs, still joined together, down over her head, then opens them. She holds this position, with the crown of her head between the open legs, as if giving birth to herself. A startling pose. She then closes her legs and lifts them back up, twisting them together again. Then in a single movement, her legs descend and she pulls herself up into a sitting position, revealing her back with the waves of white hair, her silver-bangled hands behind her. Only the darkness sees her face. She refuses the kind of affinity that might be constructed if the audience could see her face. In this set of strangely compelling movements, Chandralekha fuses yogic time with the time of performance, creating a paratopia composed of a floating temporality that stretches between past and present. This temporality challenges notions of dance as virtuosity or exotic spectacle, and forces instead a concentration on dance as an evocative public exercise, a true bodily discipline.

In a later sequence of *Sri*, time is deployed ideologically to critique both patriarchy and the exoticizing gaze. As the melancholic music begins, a group of women in identical body positions enter the stage in profile: knees bent, feet sliding forward as if they are incapable of lifting them off the ground, spines sloped, as if some invisible weight is pressing down on their backs. But they look straight ahead, their heads never moving down. They refuse the spectatorial gaze, seemingly oblivious to the presence of onlookers. Finally, as they reach the other side of the stage, the women start moving backwards, feet dragging, as if in retreat from what they had found. This fragment of the piece openly depicts the subjugation of women and their survival in a patriarchal world, but it does so specifically through the manipulation of time in the body. In their excruciating slowness, the gestures are simultaneously mesmerizing, alienating and unbearable, placing an intense focus on the struggles of the body—a feat that would have been rendered impossible if the speed were accelerated. For the audience witnessing this laborious performance, there is little possibility of catharsis, identification or escape.

This deliberate slowness in Chandralekha's choreography is exceptional, when juxtaposed against the landscape of the globalized postmodern—the dominant formation of space/time, as conceived in current political discourse —which compresses time and confers movement with extraordinary speed and meaning.

'Movement' here implies a much broader terrain than 'the body that moves', of course. Movement, in Chandralekha's work, is less an index of speed, mobility or virtuosity; her paratopia is conceived in a time that is slow and luxurious, but disciplined and rigorous, never indulgent.

The ideation of the subject produced in Chandralekha's dance is never stable or seamless; she is not abstracted as a rational agent, but exalted as a somatic subject dedicated to constructing herself through nuanced movements of the body. What is normally invisible as the body executes a phrase —the pauses, the slow stretch of a limb, the lingering gesture, the eye moving from one focal point to the next, the waves of the body reverberating, even as it stands still—are exhibited in a temporal structure that is lengthy, prolonged, decelerated. If rapid mobilizations, and 'freely mobile energies' (Brennan 2000: 62) are symptoms of both modernity and postmodernity, then there is something profoundly disturbing and jarring in Chandralekha's dedication to an aesthetic of immobility—her arrest of time through the arrest of movement in the body's slowed-down tempos and rhythms. She collapses different temporal structures into each other, to produce an original kind of blurred zone. Her feat lies in renouncing categories of received time and producing new temporal sensations that reside alongside inherited categories. Hers is not a restless body, but a corporeality that stays in its stillness, its presence, the poetics of atrophy.

### Territorialized Acts

The paratopia inaugurates an 'ethics of the ground'. In an exquisite meditation on *The Lie of the Land* (1996), theorist Paul Carter describes dance as an imperialist enterprise that inaugurates a 'politics of the ground' as it is predicated on the colonization, claiming and clearing of space; the land is razed, its natural elements destroyed to make way for a social performance to take place within a newly pristine sanctuary, emptied of meaning and content:

> If the man dancing can enjoy a certain state of mind, an absorption in his own movement, it is because of the prior activities of the explorer and the surveyor. After all, without their labours in discovering or creating a clearing, levelling its irregularities and removing its obstacles, the figures of the dancer could hardly be performed. Logically, and perhaps historically, the colonizing explorer precedes the pirouetting dancer (ibid.: 291).

Indeed, it is striking to realize that the formal origins of the Western choreographic project, with its narratives of authority, mastery and spatialized subjecthood, coincide with the origins of colonialism and is metonymically aligned with it; the first written treatise on the subject in the West is the 1589 text *L'Orchesographie* by Thoinot Arbeau.[15] The dancing master and the docile body of the pupil he controls symbolize that attainment of a subjectivity configured through civility, grace and ideality while it indelibly transforms the surrounding space. In this context, dance reveals itself to be a genre of power that captures space and empties and eviscerates it in order to fill it with the bodies of the privileged dancing subject. There is a strong parallel with the colonial project here: in that it too annexes the territory of the colonized, expressing its dominion over the bodies of its subjects, and controlling native space with its foreign bodies. The seizing of land, and its occupation by the dominant body, is a colonial gesture mirrored in dance. In this way, dance performs the politics of hegemony and subjugation, becoming an aesthetic of domination. And 'these modalities within the Western tradition of representation are not emptily formal or structural; they imply different ways of occupying land and governing its peoples,' says Carter (1996: 301). Dance not only acts as an *allegory* of domination, but actually *enacts* this domination by marking and tracing the boundaries of its property through movement. Suzerainty and sovereignty are central thematics embedded in dance as performance.

In contrast to this politics of the ground, can the paratopia crystallize an ethics of the ground? Such an affinity with the earth is a motif of most classical styles of Indian dance (expressed in its opening prayer of *bhumi pranam*, where reverential salutations are offered to mother earth, as a gesture of gratitude for letting the dancer step on her complicit body)—but in Chandralekha's choreographic practice, this intimacy with the ground is even more pronounced. 'In terms of the body, *mandala* is a holistic concept integrating the human body with itself, the community, and the environment. It generates a centered, tensile and complex visual form,' she writes. 'It is a principle of power, stability, balance, *of holding the earth*' (Chandralekha 2001: 68; italics mine).

Consider the movements in *Raga*. The beginning: Three bodies roll and turn on the floor to enter the stage, their skin suffused with the blue hue of the pool of light interrupting the black stage. Then the colour changes, and blue bodies radiate red. Lined up in a single row, each body successively goes into a shoulder stand. As they stretch their hands and torsos, legs slicing the air, the bodies make indecipherable shapes, layered with light. Their bodies do not leave the ground in this opening segment. Later: a woman holds fire in a long, curved lamp. She moves in such a slow tempo that we can see the smoke rising from the flame. Underneath, two men start dancing together. With their supine bodies, they stretch out side to side, then face each other, moving toward the other body in sinuous, liquid moves. They move around in a circle, bodies fully extended, coming close, moving apart, torsos rising and falling, but always on the ground, supporting their weight on their hands. They gaze at each other, and then turn their heads in unison to face the audience, as if to say, they know they are being seen, they know they are not in their own private world. We do not know yet if this is passion or penance.

With this proximity of the dancing body to the ground that it holds—and which holds it—the element of lightness and aerialization that situate many kinds of Western concert dance are absolutely rare if not absent in her choreographies. Often, seemingly impossible poses are executed against the topos in painstakingly slow and excruciating manoeuvres intended to test the bodies of the dancers and illustrate the effects of submission and subjection. The choreography in *Sri* is a vivid testament to this. At the same time, while embracing an anti-oppressive stance, Chandralekha is expressing the new potential for a subjectivity that eludes the dominant gaze and is produced through the prism of eros. Her choreographies produce a ground for creating new types of bodies, representations and relations that remain unsanctified in public spheres.

In *Raga*, the dancers stand on the unstable ground of queer desire, as the male performers search for the feminine element that resides within them and in each other; the theme of *Ardhanarisvara* (a divine body composed as half-man, half-woman) is openly offered as a construct that offers a reimagining of male and female embodiment alongside the binaries of masculine and feminine that manage sexual and gender identities in mainstream discourse. She has said that her intent is to make 'a piece about sexuality, sensuality, spirituality and the female principles of our culture', as well as to explore the femininity residing 'deep down in the bodies of men, waiting to be evoked, waiting to be invoked' (in Jowitt 1998: n.p.). This kind of thematic vexes many critics, including Western ones, who fail to comprehend the queer tropes Chandralekha uses, which are not alien, but actually *indigenous* to Indian models of gender. For example, Jowitt writes of *Raga*:

> Two men smooth their hands over each other's bodies. They slide into an embrace, interlocking as formally as the twin halves of a yin/yang symbol. What makes their actions startling on the stage of the BAM Majestic—a stamping ground, after all, of avant-garde theater—is that these are men of India, a country where the provinces of male and female are defined along very traditional lines, and masculinity doesn't usually involve public displays of interdependency and sensual tenderness (ibid.).

Against this reductive claim that essentializes Indian sexualities, Chandralekha frames the body as a mass, sensate entity that holds weight and acts in concordance with gravity, almost sinking into it. The cultivation of beauty per se is not a concern; the rendering of a destabilized body that examines its own transgressive potencies, and self-consciously merges with space, is her object of inquiry: choreography 'is almost like sculpting space with movement [...] While choreographing, one is conscious to sculpt space as precisely as one sculpts the form' (Chandralekha 2001: 66).

Chandralekha's philosophy of choreography, and the phenomenological relationship proposed between the body and the surrounding space, aligns itself with a paratopic ideal. Literally, it clears out space not for the purposes of domination, but for the creation of a domain that exhibits new types of bodies. This is not a deterritorialized ontology, but a subject position linked to a constant cycle of reterritorialization—one which situates movement as a territorialized act, and frames the body as a highly territorialized entity—rooted and moored to the ground, integrated with the dancer to produce an ontology of synthesis.

Space is created in Chandralekha's paratopia through choreography as abstracted movement—there is no pre-existing field for this kind of representation. Space is literally carved out and shaped. The gestures that create the paratopia are not solely affiliated to dance, but to quotidian techniques of the body as well, and special movement vocabularies generated in other systems of practice: labour, politics, indigenous precepts (Chandralekha in Jung 1984). But the union of these gestures borrowed from different fields that discipline the body in distinct ways do not create a totalized, monolithic system of movement with stable signs: rather, new paradigms of gesture are always being generated, new systems of hermeneutics and signification are always being produced. There is no fixity or stability; only the shifting site of meaning that nevertheless refuses to close in on itself, but is expansive, and incorporates a full spectrum of progressive significations, denotations, implications, effects, consequences.

This is space as a shared place, where bodies coexist with each other and their surrounds; Chandralekha's paratopia creates a different ethics of the ground, where it is not land waiting to be conquered or cleared but a space of difference where pervasive ideologies of sexuality and nation are cleared away, and the codes and constraints imposed by dominant discourses are abdicated, only tangentially indexed as a parallel system subject to change, parody or destruction. Chandralekha's ethics of alterity prevails and proliferates, her paratopia travelling and traversing across time, across space, multiplying and manifesting itself, choreographing new terrains, to propagate its liberating imaginaries.

*Notes*

1   This essay won the 2007 Outstanding Graduate Research Award from the Congress on Research on Dance (CORD), and I am grateful to them for this honour.

2   Definitions taken from the *Merriam-Webster Dictionary*.

3   Here, I would like to avoid a conception of agency that unilaterally conflates it with an oppositional consciousness—recognizing that agency can also be expressed through the acts of deliberately conforming to or engaging critically with the demands of power.

4   This emphasis is evident in the very title of each book—respectively, *Chandralekha: Woman Dance Resistance* (by Rustom Bharucha) and *Butting Out: Reading Resistive Choreographies Through Works by Jawole Willa Jo Zollar and Chandralekha* (by Ananya Chatterjea).

5   In addition to the above, Chandralekha's major works include: *Devadasi* (1961), *Navagraha* (1972), *Request Concert-Solo* (1989), *Lilavati* (1989), *Bhinna Pravaha* (1993), *Mahakal* (1995) and *Sloka: Self and Renewal* (1999). She also collaborated with American artists Kristen Jones and Andrew Ginzel on the 1995 installation/performance piece *Interim: After the End and Before the Beginning*.

6   'Contemporary' cannot be considered coeval to 'postmodern' either, since the latter term bears little relevance to the concepts embraced by Chandralekha in her artistic practice. I elaborate on the relationship between these terms later in the text. For now, it is important to note that contemporary dance is a politically charged field in India, since it is both vilified and celebrated—depending on the spectator—for its alleged attachments to 'Western' modernity, its aesthetic and thematic sensibilities that defy those of conventional classical and folk forms, and its experimental ethos. Contemporary dance therefore contends with the predictable dilemma of reconciling 'tradition' and 'modernity'. Chandralekha's work has escaped this burden in some ways, as she deploys and critiques both notions to her advantage. For more on the debates surrounding contemporary Indian dance, see Sunil Kothari (2003).

7   Chandralekha discovered the partition between dance and everyday life in her first Bharatanatyam performance, as she was presenting a piece on the theme of the abundance of water, while an actual drought was taking place in the locale where she was dancing. This moment of disjuncture prompted her to rethink the role of dance in relation to the social, and led her to

envision a new aesthetic practice capable of addressing pressing political concerns (see Chatterjea 2004; Chandralekha 1984).

8   The movement lexicon of the dance is based on the elaborate codes of the *Natyashastra*, attributed to the sage Bharatamuni. In fact, the dance was deliberately named Bharatanatyam (literally, the dance of Bharata) in the twentieth century, to underline its adherence to the codes contained in this work. The oldest known text on stagecraft (dated between the 2nd century BCE and 2nd century CE), the *Natyashastra* provides an elaborate taxonomy, specifying different kinds of movements for the head, neck, eyes, hands and feet. In addition to naming and delineating the technical body positions and gestures to be used in dance (known as *angika abhinaya*), the treatise describes the emotions to be represented in performance (*sattvik abhinaya*), explicating the theories of rasa and bhava—modes of depicting and communicating sentiment—which are designed to generate affective responses from the audience. Chandralekha borrows from Bharatanatyam's interpretations of *angika abhinaya*, especially the *ardha-manda* position, which resembles a *plié*. For more on Chandralekha's dance vocabulary, see Shanta Serbjeet Singh (2001), Uttara Asha Coorlawala (1999), and Ananya Chatterjea (1998, 2004); for in-depth discussions of key elements of the *Natyashastra*, the history of its origin and authorship, and its rescensions, see Kapila Vatsyayan (1996) and Manmohan Ghosh's translation of Bharatamuni's text (1967).

9   Indeed, one of the most intriguing aspects of Chandralekha's work is her recontextualization of Hindu philosophy and Indian aesthetics. Coorlawala alleges this tendency to embrace Indian sources while downplaying the effects of Western thought on her work implicates Chandralekha in a 'nationalist agenda' (1999: 10). I disagree with this claim. The phrase invokes a particular reality in post-Independence India, where right-wing fundamentalists have hijacked and ideologically redefined the 'nationalist agenda' to propagate an idea of a rabidly Hindu India in which minority identities are violently suppressed. While Hindu nationalists are a heterogeneous group, they find common ground in a stance largely defined by cultural conservatism, sexism, anti-Muslim/anti-Christian sentiments, and belief in the hierarchy of the caste system (see Sen 2005: 49–72). There is a wide gulf between this 'nationalist agenda' and Chandralekha's orientation; in fact, seen in this context, her perspective is deeply antithetical to it. While she undoubtedly draws on a rich and robust Indian history—of which Hinduism is undeniably an integral part—

I would argue that her work is not nationalist in scope, as her intent is neither sectarian nor exclusionary, nor does she purport to prop up the political projects articulated by self-professed nationalists. In the logic expressed by Hindu fundamentalist and Western metanarratives, where the 'modern' is viewed as incompatible with 'Indianness', Chandralekha's insistence on making 'contemporary Indian' dance is a radical move. But nowhere in her work does she suggest collapsing Indianness and Hinduism into each other as an exclusive definition of what these mean. Instead of shoring up fundamentalist claims, I would suggest that she offers visions of *another Hinduism and another Indianness* that rely on making visible the alternative knowledges in these histories that are open and inclusive, often signalling heterodoxy. I agree then with Coorlawala's later assertion that instead of rejecting tradition wholesale, Chandralekha 'shifts her focus in her dances to mythic spaces still within traditional thought but outside conventional representation' (in Singh 2001: 70). Singh sums it up well when she points out, 'Chandra's is quintessentially a Hindu mind, though of a variety and conviction' that no fundamentalist could accept (ibid.).

10 *Sri* and *Raga* especially encompass these themes, and my analysis will focus on these two works.

11 *Angika, Yantra-Dance Diagrams* and *Sharira: Fire and Desire* perfectly illustrate her interest in material conceptions of the body, her attention to a specifically corporeal expressivity.

12 Chandralekha recites this poem at the beginning of the performance of *Raga: In Search of Femininity* (see Chandralekha 1998; also published in the Programme Notes for the performance at the BAM).

13 Here, I do not mean to single out Deborah Jowitt; however, her statements are representative of a type of thinking that commonly defines mainstream Western writing on Chandralekha's work. For other commentaries that exemplify similarly problematic positions, see Anna Kisselgoff (1998), Jochen Schmidt (1990, 1994), Jennifer Fisher (1993) and Thea Singer (1998). For treatments that are considerably more interesting and complex, see Niyatee Shinde (1990), Susanna Sloat (1999), Simon Dove (1990), Jacqueline Kolmes (1994) and Sarah Rubidge (1992).

14 By an 'Indian ethos', I mean the sense conveyed by Amartya Sen (2005), where he speaks of the plural histories and influences that define India today. Sen

argues (in opposition to nationalists) that far from being a Hindu empire, throughout its history India has absorbed multiple perspectives—including colonial ones—in shaping its culture. In this sense, my conception of the 'Indian ethos' is inclusive of a history of difference and cultural hybridization, and also contains some elements of Western European thought. However, according to Coorlawala (1999), and the choreographer's own writings, Chandralekha strategically disavows the role of non-Indian influences in her work, despite having worked on several intercultural projects with Western artists (and very prominent ones, like Pina Bausch). I speculate that Chandralekha may have embraced this position precisely to dislodge persistent assumptions and accusations (within and outside India) that her work cannot be contemporary and Indian simultaneously, as I note above. Or, she may have genuinely taken her practice for granted as 'Indian', without any need for explanation, permission or apology, and without framing her work within Western dance paradigms just to legitimize her work internationally.

15  For commentaries on this text, see Thoinot Arbeau (1967). On the theoretical implications of Arbeau's principles, see Mark Franko (1986) and André Lepecki (2006).

*References*

ARBEAU, Thoinot. 1589. *L'Orchesographie. Et traicte en forme de dialogue, par lequel toutes personnes peuvent facilement apprendre & practiquer l'honneste exercice des dances* [Orchesography. A Treatise in the Form of a Dialogue. Whereby all manner of persons may easily acquire and practise the honourable excercise of dancing]. Langres: Jehan des Preyz. Facsimile available from Dance Instruction Manuals collection, US Library of Congress, Washington, DC, at: memory.loc.gov/cgi-bin/ampage?collIdmusdi&fileName219/musdi219.db&re-Num.0 (accessed 20 April 2008).

———. 1967 [1589]. *Orchesography* (Mary Stewart Evans trans. and Julia Sutton ed.). New York: Dover Publications, Inc.

BHABHA, Homi K. 1994. *The Location of Culture*. London: Routledge.

BHARATAMUNI. 1967. *The Natya Shastra*: Ascribed to Bharata-Muni. (Manmohan Ghosh trans. and ed.). Calcutta: Manisha Granthalaya.

BHARUCHA, Rustom. 1995. *Chandralekha: Woman Dance Resistance*. New Delhi: Harper-Collins.

BRAND, Dionne. 1997. *Land to Light On*. Toronto: McClelland & Stewart Ltd.

———. 2000. *The Politics of Cultural Practice: Thinking Through Theatre in an Age of Globalization*. Hanover: University Press of New England.

BRENNAN, Teresa. 2000. *Exhausting Modernity: Grounds for a New Economy*. New York: Routledge.

BROOKLYN ACADEMY OF MUSIC (BAM). 1998. Programme Notes for *Raga: In Search of Femininity*. New York: Brooklyn Academy of Music.

CARTER, Paul. 1996. *The Lie of the Land*. London: Faber and Faber.

CASH, Debra. 1998. 'Introducing the Indian Isadora Duncan'. *Boston Sunday Globe*, 8 November.

CHANDRALEKHA. 1980. 'Militant Origins of Indian Dance'. *Social Science* 9(2/3) (September): 80–5.

———. 1984. 'Contemporary Relevance in Classical Dance—A Personal Note'. *National Centre for the Performing Arts Quarterly Journal* (East–West Dance Encounter Special Issue) 13(2) (June): 60–4.

———. 1990. *Prana*. Dance videotaped in performance at the Cultural Centre, Madras, as part of India International Dance Festival, 21 December. VHS videocassette, colour, 80 minutes, India.

———. 1992. *Sri*. Dance videotaped in performance at The Place, London, as part of the Vivarta Festival of South Asian Dance, 3 October. 2 VHS videocassettes, colour, 109 minutes, UK.

———. 1997. 'The Backbone of Freedom: A Statement by Chandralekha'. *Ballett International/Tanz Aktuell 7* (July): 46–7.

———. 1998. *Raga: In Search of Femininity*. Dance videotaped in performance at Brooklyn Academy of Music (BAM) Majestic Theater, New York, as part of the 1998 Next Wave Festival, 22 November. Co-presented by Asia Society. 2 videodiscs, 95 minutes, colour, USA.

———. 2001 [1989]. 'Choreography in the Indian Context', in Ashish Mohan Khokar (ed.), *Attendance 2001: The Dance Annual of India*. Uday Shankar and Choreography Special, pp. 66–8. Originally presented at Sahitya Kala Parishad, 2nd National Ballet Festival, New Delhi, 2 December 1989.

CHATTERJEA, Ananya. 1998. 'Chandralekha: Negotiating the Female Body and Movement in Cultural/Political Signification'. *Dance Research Journal* 30(1) (Spring): 25–33.

———. 2004. *Butting Out: Reading Resistive Choreographies Through Works by Jawole Willa Jo Zollar and Chandralekha*. Middletown, CT: Wesleyan University Press.

COORLAWALA, Uttara Asha. 1999. 'Ananya and Chandralekha: A Response to Chandralekha: Negotiating the Female Body and Movement in Cultural/Political Signification'. *Dance Research Journal* 31(1) (Spring): 7–12.

DERRIDA, Jacques. 1992. 'Choreographies'. *Diacritics* 12: 66–76.

DOVE, Simon. 1990. 'India: "Navanritya"—New Dance'. *Ballett International/Tanz Aktuell* 13(11) (November): 24–7.

FABIAN, Johannes. 1983. *Time and the Other: How Anthropology Makes Its Object*. New York: Columbia University Press.

FISHER, Jennifer. 1993. 'New Directions in South Asian Dance'. *Vandance International* 21(1) (Spring): 4–7.

FOUCAULT, Michel. 1986 [1967]. 'Of Other Spaces' (Jay Miskowiec trans.). *Diacritics* 16 (Spring): 22–7.

FRANKO, Mark. 1986. *The Dancing Body in Renaissance Choreography*. Birmingham: Summa.

GRAMSCI, Antonio. 1971. *Selections from the Prison Notebooks of Antonio Gramsci* (Quintin Hoare and Geoffrey Nowell Smith trans. and eds). London: Lawrence and Wishart.

HEBDIGE, Dick. 1979. *Subculture: The Meaning of Style*. London: Methuen.

JOWITT, Deborah. 1998. 'Rich and Strange: Three Women Ignite Asian Traditions'. *Village Voice*, 1 December. Available at: www.villagevoice.com/dance/-9848,jowitt,1707,14.html (accessed 20 April 2008).

JUNG, Anees. 1984. 'The Search is One'. *National Centre for the Performing Arts Quarterly Journal* (East–West Dance Encounter Special Issue) 13(2) (June): 52–5.

KISSELGOFF, Anna. 1998. 'A Hovering Self, Not Man or Woman'. *The New York Times*, 20 November, E6.

KOLMES, Jacqueline. 1994. 'Chandralekha Forges Feminist Abstractions'. *Dance Magazine* (December): 34–6.

———. 1998. 'Chandralekha Brings Raga to U.S.'. *Dance Magazine* (November): 35, 40.

KOTHARI, Sunil (ed.). 2003. *New Directions in Indian Dance.* Mumbai: Marg Publications.

LEPECKI, André. 2006. *Exhausting Dance: Performance and the Politics of Movement.* London: Routledge.

MUÑOZ, José Esteban. 1999. *Disidentifications: Queers of Color and the Performance of Politics.* Minneapolis: University of Minnesota Press.

PHELAN, Peggy. 1993. 'The Ontology of Performance: Representation Without Reproduction', in *Unmarked: The Politics of Performance.* New York: Routledge, pp. 146–66.

RUBIDGE, Sarah. 1992. 'Review: Shobana Jeyasingh and Chandralekha at The Place'. *Dance Theatre Journal* 9(3) (Spring): 40–1.

SCHMIDT, Jochen. 1990. 'Dancing One's Way to Freedom? Modern Dance in Asia: The Example of China and India'. *Ballett International* 13(11) (November): 8–11.

———. 1994. 'Divine Law Versus the Body'. *Ballett International/Tanz Aktuell* 8(9): 70–5.

SEN, Amartya. 2005. *The Argumentative Indian: Writings on Indian Culture, History and Identity.* London: Penguin Books.

SHINDE, Niyatee. 1990. 'Prana'. *The India Magazine of Her People and Culture* (November): 86–7, 89. MGZR, Chandralekha clippings folder, Jerome Robbins Dance Division, New York Public Library for the Performing Arts, Lincoln Center, New York.

SINGER, Thea. 1998. 'Chandralekha's Misstep in Translation'. *Boston Globe,* 16 October, D15.

SINGH, Shanta Serbjeet. 2001. 'Chandralekha: Walking Towards Herself', in Ashish Mohan Khokar (ed.), *Attendance 2001: The Dance Annual of India.* Uday Shankar and Choreography Special, pp. 69–76.

SLOAT, Susanna. 1999. 'Chandralekha's Raga'. *Attitude* 14(1) (Spring): 26–7.

TURNER, Victor. 1977. *The Ritual Process: Structure and Anti-Structure.* Ithaca: Cornell Paperbacks.

VATSYAYAN, Kapila. 1996. *Bharata: The Natyasastra.* New Delhi: Sahitya Akademi.

WILLIAMS, Raymond. 1977. *Marxism and Literature.* Oxford: Oxford University Press.

GESTURING HOOMAN SHARIFI:
ON GESTURE, MASS AND RESISTANCE

MYRIAM VAN IMSCHOOT

*For a friend lost*

For over a thousand years, he had been waiting to happen. When finally the
moment had come, he rocked as a comet cut loose from its orbit. His ID was
OD: abundant, perennially on the move, all over the place. He was a dynamite
store, the explosion only a match strike away.

She was the opposite. Her chronic condition was to feel exhausted. Perhaps she was not just tired, but things seemed tiresome to her. In the light of
her own deficiency other people's outbursts became intolerable. Not that she
was jealous or had energy envy. Hers was more suspicion, a deeper recognition. Call it faith: all were citizens of a culture of exhaustion. Sooner or later,
they would end deflated. Insatiability was just the prelude to sedation. Opposites lost their significance once you realized they were the shades of the
same spectrum, only removed by time, by degree, by stamina. Things get out
of hand, either way. Call it fate.

In anticipation of the inevitable clash, he practised crashing. Scream your
guts out, if you will. Run in circles, jump aside, feel the rage, enjoy the stage.

Welcome to the delirium of eruptions. Taste the fear. Banging on metal, head banging, falling on the floor. Tear it apart. Rip the skein. Call it bombastic or pathetic minimalism. Biopolitics in miniature version: I will bomb you with my body, crush you with the bare flesh of my soul. Suddenly, of course.

How would she relate to him? By having tea and cookies. They talked and listened to music. It was all very sweet. After all, they were relatives.

*I*

In the essay 'Kommerell, or On Gesture', Giorgio Agamben says, 'Criticism has three levels: philologico-hermeneutic, physiognomic, and gestic. Of these three levels, which can be described as three concentric spheres, the first is dedicated to the work's interpretation; the second situates the work (in both historical and natural orders); the third resolves the work's intention into a gesture (or into a constellation of gestures)' (1999: 77).[1] According to Agamben, all criticism traverses these three levels, and, depending on a critic's temperament, one will spend more or less time on one of these levels in particular, yet rare are those that make the third level their major dwelling. Gestic criticism reduces 'works to the sphere of pure gestures. This sphere lies beyond psychology and, in a certain sense, beyond all interpretation. It opens not onto literary history or a theory of genres but onto a stage such as the Oklahoma theater or Calderón's Great Theater of the World [. . .]' (ibid.: 80).

This text also conjures a stage—not the stage of Kafka or Calderón, not of the *commedia dell'arte* either, which is another reference dear to Agamben, but the stage of Hooman Sharifi's body of work. Rather than offering an interpretation, it seeks to delineate the underlying gesture of a choreographer who himself has been working *with* gestures, for let us equate the movements, video fragments, texts, light cues and projections that Sharifi is compiling into a piece for the time being with 'gesture'. Gestic criticism would then be, as Agamben would have it, the description of the *overall* gesture that holds all of these gestures together.

*II*

The dancers in Sharifi's pieces generally don't move in a fluent way. Nearly all the time one is reminded that their movements belong to a matrix. They never start drifting; they do not wander or meander. Each movement remains a unit, delineated and designated, contained within the confinement of the larger sequence or phrase. Sharifi is not crafting states, but *stanzas*: he crafts a frame of slots.[2] The slots can be filled or remain empty, yet the frame always departs from a zero point. Someone is standing, sitting or lying, waiting, and then Tsjjaak/Tjak/Tjaks/ Pumdum/Takaam//. A sentence of stabs and slashes until the end of the line is reached. Full stop, before returning to zero. Zero, always zero. Ready to deliver the next line.

Gesture, says Agamben, is 'not an absolutely non-linguistic element, but, rather, something closely tied to language. It is first of all a forceful presence in language itself, one that is older and more originary than conceptual expression' (ibid.: 77). Yet, if this is true, Agamben continues, 'then what is at issue in gesture is not so much a prelinguistic content as, so to speak, the other side of language, the muteness inherent in humankind's very capacity of language, its *speechless* dwelling in language' (ibid.: 78). Picture this: there has been way too much explanation, 'the making of references and signs is worn out, and something harsh is born—violence toward speech' (ibid.).

Sharifi's movements are essentially discursive. Not only because they resemble a phrase (sequencing, punctuation, etc.) as was just pointed out, but also because they seek to argue, to speak, to declare, to deny, to claim. Similarly, Sharifi does not craft states but statements. Yet, these statements transmit no content. More than full of meaning, they are *heavy* with effort. Lost in translation, the only language that is left to them is the lingua franca of energy. Phatic: with stress, emphasis. The force and urgency of enunciation strike more than the ingredients of declaration.

Sharifi says: 'The dancers don't ask why they do such and such movement, because there is nothing to know, there is no meaning behind it.'[3]

And:

I resist movements that are cluttered with meaning, lyricism or pretense of any kind. Such movements are not full of themselves, they have a lack and need filling to be fulfilling or compelling. In contrast, I like movements that are fully empty. These movements do not need anything besides themselves: they are so full that they can remain empty.

And also:

In *Hopefully* we take actions from televised war scenes, you know, the stuff that bulldozes into our living rooms day after day, like for example protest demonstrations or this scene of 'throwing stones'. The dancers take on these actions, but in a way that voids them of their meaning. I want the dancers to deliver things blank, precise, task-like, as if mute to the meanings in the slipstream of the action.[4]

Again and again Sharifi reminds us in his comments that there is nothing to say, that there is 'no meaning' behind his movements, and that he is looking for emptiness in movement. The ideal is to find a void that does not need any additional filling because it is already full of itself. If we did not know better, we could mistake him for a Merce Cunningham adept or an abstract dance maker. Yet, although there are affinities with the formalist or modernist strands of postmodern dance, Sharifi stands apart from it where he adds one more component: there may be nothing to say, *but there is everything to tell*.[5]

But then, what story is it Sharifi is delivering, since the building stones of the story in his performances—the words, the components—are void of meaning? What is there to be heard in the fullness of the emptiness that Sharifi is referring to?

Let us return to Agamben for a minute. Late modernist echoes resonate too in Agamben's recurrent definitions of gesture, like his predilection for autonomy of the medium, for 'pure' gesture, and his fascination with emptiness and meaninglessness. Ideally, gesture does not only exist for the other (the recipient), but 'only insofar as it exists for itself can it be compelling for the Other'. Agamben quotes approvingly the words of the German critic Kommerell, who was exemplary for his gestic criticism applied to authors like Goethe, Jean Paul and Heinrich von Kleist (1999: 78). The aesthetic Kantian motive of 'purposiveness without purpose' is thus never far away, but in 'Notes on Gesture', published a year later in *Means Without End*, Agamben hastens to point out that this is not a call for 'movement that has an end in itself (for example, dance seen as an aesthetic dimension)', but for a dance as gesture, where means are cut off from finality but keep every quality of their being means (2000: 57).

Only then, he believes, 'a gesture felicitously establishes itself in *this emptiness of language, without filling it*, makes it into humankind's most proper dwelling. Confusion turns to dance' (1999: 78–9).[6]

The title essay in Agamben's *Profanations* (2006) gives some clues as to how such transformation ('confusion turns to dance') takes place and can have a political purport. Agamben calls those processes 'profanations' whenever there is a transference of an element from one sphere to another separate sphere of use. The example he gives is of a cat that plays with a mouse for the sake of playing. Although the gestures resemble those of the 'real hunt', this play, as cruel as it may seem, is cut off from its finality and thus a sheer means without an end. Yet, in this process of emptying out the originary gestures, they do not dissolve completely. The conduct of the cat (the hunt), for example, is not completely erased but *substituted* in the realm of play, deactivated so as to open a new possibility of use. In fact, Agamben speaks sometimes of gestures as 'excretions' that could not be exhausted completely but survived on the ruins of previous uses: 'the ruin of their formal garment and their conceptual meaning' (1999: 80). Gestures have a spectral quality; they are relicts whose discharged load keeps haunting the sites of emptiness.[7]

Although Agamben does not state it explicitly, theatre is an excellent place for profanation: a separate sphere from outside reality, it allows the transference of elements from the latter into the isolated sphere of theatrical (dis)play, where meanings have been emptied and/or transfigured and new potentialities can arise.

It should now not be too hard to capture some resonances between Agamben's concept of gesture and the movements/gestures in the dance pieces of Sharifi. Sharifi does not look for mimetic illusionism, but practises the art of metonymy and profanation, dragging previously 'loaded' actions into the sphere of theatre and draining them to give rise to new possibilities. *Hopefully* is full of examples (political marches, demagogic mass agitation, throwing stones, etc.), but also other choreographies tap regularly into the iconic. Although the delivery is blank, something has not been erased altogether. Remember that Sharifi said that he wants the delivery of his dancers to be task-like, '*as if* mute to the meanings in the slipstream of that action' (italics mine). In this 'as if' all is said, since all paradoxes of speech and speechlessness, of emptiness and fullness, of meaning and non-meaning operate in the space of sublimation. In the space opened up by the 'as if' linger the after-images, resonances and echoes that populate the void of Sharifi's theatrical hunt-raid. The *extraction* of meaning from an action, such as throwing a stone, makes that very gesture into a relict, a shell. They 'establish themselves on the ruins of communication in the emptiness of language, without filling it'.

They remain to remind.

*III*

It is at first sight quite astonishing that Agamben cultivates the extraction of meaning from actions and statements. Isn't the problem of our times precisely this: in the 'society of spectacle' (Debord 1967), meanings are continuously voided and evaporating?[8] The result is not so much that 'confusion turns into dance', but that confusion nowadays *is* the dance, a dance *of* confusion. In the rift between meaning and sign arises an endless drift of floating gestures.

Agamben seems to be aware of this quandary since in *Profanations* he points to the fact that the profaning act has lost its significance and potentiality in a culture where profanation has become the absolute cultural mode. Instead of being a 'practice of the relict', it has become a relentless consummation that swallows everything without remainder. The consequence of this absolutization of profanation is not only that the displacement of one element to another sphere is no longer tinged with reminiscence (premise) but also—and far more problematic—that the possibility for new usage (promise) is rendered obsolete. The devouring machinery of total consummation is no longer engaged with transference nor with substitution but with a far more devastating annihilation.

In somewhat different terms, but with a related diagnostic viewpoint, Jean Baudrillard analyses contemporary society as having entered a global 'etherealization' (1992). When lifted from every anchorage in a sphere (or historical reality), actions and events evaporate. Baudrillard finds a prophetic anticipation of 'etherealization' in the work of the French writer Alfred Jarry and more specifically in his novel (unpublished until after his death) *Gestes et Opinions du docteur Faustroll, pataphysicien* (1980). Faustroll is the inventor of 'pataphysics', a subverted science that critiques the theory and methods of modern Western science by turning the 'universal laws' as we know them into their farcical antidotes—and gravity, one of the most central laws in Western scientific thought (since it offers a dominant explicatory framework as well as an ontological base to our definitions of 'reality'), is a case in point. In the topsy-turvy world of 'pataphysics', things are no longer drawn to a gravitational centre; the axiom of mass is turned inside out: things want to fly away to the periphery where they finally dissolve in emptiness. With Dr Faustroll, Baudrillard believes we have entered eternal weightlessness, the impasse of anti-mass.

It is at this point that Sharifi's description of his movements as *fully empty* becomes significant. If the hollowing out of actions, in the age of absolute profanation, is taking 'pataphysical' dimensions to the point of complete evaporation, Sharifi reverses once more this reversal—not to restore the Newtonian world, as we knew it before weightlessness started to implode molecular structures, but to arrive at an intensified hyper-Newtonism, that is to say, at the hypertrophy of mass. Sharifi's own physiognomy—he is a big man—is exemplary in that manner. He moves as if his weight is a fifth limb, the lever to catapult him into space. Yet the slimmer dancers in the company also move as if weighed down by an invisible cargo or as if they are colossal, with even more bound and monolithic effort than Sharifi's own dancing makes apparent. Often they look as if they are tearing themselves away from an invisible strain, as if the air has thickened with viscosity through which they wade. Whereas in the Newtonian world dancers abide in the aesthetics of flow and let themselves be steered along the paths of least resistance with gravity as a compass, the dancers in the Sharifian, neo-Newtonian world of hypermass choose the paths of *most* resistance. Mass does not clear the way, but gets in the way, or is the way.

Mass and resistance: in Sharifi's work these entities are clearly interlocked. In a conversation he says that he wants to give back a body to the ethereal images from television. 'We have grown indifferent to the images, they are sucked out by the vampirism of mass media.' His choreographic work therefore does not stop at extracting meaning from actions, for one could say that the 'image sucking' of mass media has already successfully done so, and turned them already into gestures, anorexic gestures so light that they float in the atmosphere of simulacra. No, to resist such flaccid vampirism the labour of choreography needs to become bulimic with physicalization. Ingredients should not lend themselves to easy swallowing, but instead make us choke. Only then, when the intake is too big and disorders such as reflux (vomit) or constipation (the hardened excretion) disturb relentless assimilation, is there a chance that acts are not exhausted totally.[9] Only by being fully re-embodied can gestures become excremental tokens of resistance on the ruins of communication.

Gesture, says Agamben with his reputed love of etymology, may be inscribed into the sphere of action, but it must be distinguished from 'acting' and 'making'. It is of the order of 'gerere' (as in 'gestus') or 'carrying' (2000: 55).[10] We might as well accommodate the full array of connotations of the word 'carry'. *Carrying across*: in gesture something is carried across the threshold that separates two spheres. In this passage, the original load is emptied out. *Carrying over*: yet, the separation cannot eliminate fully the spillover between one sphere and the other, which takes the form of a relict. More literally, those who gesture *carry* something, a weight. Burden weighs the gesture down, anchors it, gives it body; it calls for endurance and persistence, so that something *carries on*. 'What characterizes gestures is that in it nothing is being produced or acted, but rather something is being endured and supported' (ibid.: 56). Endurance . . . the word comes back when Agamben explicitly refers to dance: 'If dance is gesture, it is so, rather, because it is nothing more than the endurance and the exhibition of the media character of corporal movements. *The gesture is the exhibition of a mediality: it is the process of making a means visible as such*' (ibid.: 57; italics in original).

Sharifi and his dancers expose the mediality of their dance in its most dense form, in the thickness of the body, the opaqueness of its flesh and matter. It is corporeality taken as critical mass. Such is his answer to the lightness of our society and its mass media: the heaviness of *massive* media. To exhibit not meanings, but bodily means: Sharifi's massive attack. Enduringly.

*IV*

Admittedly, Sharifi hardly ever speaks about gestures. He prefers to speak of actions. With a wink to political militancy, he has even been branding his work on occasion as 'art activism'.

Action suggests something of a directness. It is concrete and factual. One does not *act* an action: one *takes* action and in doing so something is done. Action is alteration on the level of no nonsense, *right*?

Such attachment to immediate action aligns Sharifi to a different theory of agency than the 'performativity' heralded over the last decades by the advocates of performance theory. By underscoring some active 'doing' in 'acts' of all kinds—i. e. the performative dimension—performance theories predicate some sort of intrinsic 'operationality', whereas Sharifi seems not to content himself with this implicated, too general agency as belonging to all kinds of performative *acts*. He calls for a more direct, clear and cutting act*ion* so as to increase performance's impact beyond sheer performativity.

On a technical dance level this urge to radicalize the scope of performance's repercussion led to a particular performance style that is executed with razor-blade rigour. Dancers in Sharifi's work usually don't show the preparations it takes to do such or such movement, but instead cut out the preliminary steps so that their movements erupt like sudden outbursts. Rather than remind one of pedestrian actions typical of daily behaviour, they breach emergency states, instant rupture. Dancers are like human bombs ticking off. Suspense and surprise merge into a theatre of maximal impact/ion. Such seems to be Sharifi's licence.

Sharifi is, however, not a late echo of La La La Human Steps, Wim Vandekeybus and other 'Eurotrash' variants of hyper-energetic 1980s choreography, with its appetite for fearless bodies, throwing themselves around. Hardly ever does the energetic boost convey a sense of kinetic pleasure. The self-abandon, if there is such, comes closer to impersonal drill and sacrifice. When one cares to look more closely, it becomes clear that the volatile action is in fact quite problematic since it is fractured with a deep sense of catatonic paralysis on the one hand and the characteristics of an epileptic fit on the other. It is a recurrent image everywhere in the work of Sharifi: dancers stand seemingly apathetic, until they snap and propel into high-voltage activity before retreating into immobility. They may resemble guerrilla bodies during sudden attack before retreat (the militant art 'activist' style), but the far less heroic interpretation is that they portray bodies under extreme stress.

Sharifi's choreographies present not some glorified heroism of action, but an overall dissection of its crisis. More than any other work, *as if your death was your longest sneeze ever* (2002) brings this to the surface. At the festival Amperdans in Antwerp, where I attended the piece, the opening scene occurred in a courtyard in open air within the sonic range of street noise. Two men (Sharifi himself and Peder Horgen) were bashing a pile of metal plates with bats, *as if* vandals in the street were releasing their anger on a car. The spectators gathered in a circle around the scene, *as if* witnesses were registering a crime without intervening. The matter-of-fact style of the 'heavy metal' beating reminds us of the way Sharifi tends to empty out iconic actions of anger, revolt and turmoil, that is, how he *gesturalizes* and exposes them as sheer physical *mediality*. The crux of the scene, however, was that a third person, Kristine N. Slettevold, was filming one by one all the faces of the spectators from a close angle. Later, this film was projected on a large screen once the spectacle moved to the main performance hall; there, the audience could 'freely' circulate among choreographic sections. Interestingly, the spectators who had mostly posed during the filming in cool postures (with slightly amused or bored or 'so what?' detachment) were revealed in the close-ups in an entirely different manner. The faces were now anything but detached: they were vibrating sites of involuntary eye twitches, better known by psychologists as the 'startle reflex'. Trembling micro-motions, contractions of the facial muscles, small frowns on the forehead, narrowing pupils—these were the cracks through which the agitated nervous system disturbed the faces. If at first the spectators had seemed self-contained and unaffected by the drilling loudness of the metallic sounds and the suppressed violence of the image, they were now shown as porous containers pervaded by what they had been seeing and hearing.

The minute exposure of the spectators' demeanour in *as if your death was your longest sneeze ever* is just one instance of Sharifi's prevailing interest in the figure of the spectator, a figure that is not just a role *in the theatre* but also an overall modality of being *in society*. This interest should therefore be understood in its most extended scope, beyond the obvious ploys of working with spectators in participatory ways (for example, beyond the fact that the spectators could move about, or were exposed in their act of looking). For sure, in theatre there is a schism that divides performers and spectators—within its most caricatured form: the overactive component and the consumerist passivity as two sides of the same coin—but the point is that this cleavage is not superseded in *as if your death was your longest sneeze ever*, since the piece does not subscribe to 'participatory theater'; even less so does it 'break' with the classical conventional role division between players and lookers. Every time, free circulation is shown as a more advanced and perverse mock-up that tempts us to believe in greater agency, while in fact we run the pre-set options of a carefully orchestrated programme.

The piece, which was announced as a critique of democracy and its fallacy of freedom, may as well be considered as a manifesto for all of Sharifi's work: an ongoing inquiry into the impasse of agency in the spectacular democracies of our times, when we all have become primarily cast as spectators and 'hardly believe any longer that a global situation can give rise to an action which is capable of modifying it—no more than we believe that an action can force a situation to disclose itself, even partially. The most "healthy" illusions fall' (Deleuze 1986: 206).

The quote comes from Gilles Deleuze in his phenomenal study on cinema.[11] Deleuze describes how the catastrophe of modern times manifests itself as a falling apart of action's former tripartite sensory-motor scheme into unrelated 'templates' of perception, affect and reactions. Whereas formerly these components were wired and one component would lead to the other, in a sort of cause-and-effect logic, these components now stand apart as isolated parts. It is precisely this isolation that Sharifi exposes in his work and that characterizes the behavioural patterns of his dancers in his work at large. Perceptions, affections and actions occur in total isolation, as if purified—not to their essence but to their excess.

For example, the excess of perception as a pure and insular mode can be traced back to moments when dancers in many of Sharifi's works stand as if they are sheer monitoring devices, human cameras or flesh antennas that, seemingly unaffected (not unlike the spectators in the opening scene around the metal bashing), capture the seismic energies of the earthquakes around them but without any visible sign of impact or expressive translation. The spectatorial *phase* is here pushed to the limit of a spectatorial *aphasia* and inertia.

The most recent piece by Sharifi, *God exists, the Mother is present, but they no longer care* (2008), is then again rich in examples of 'pure affect' moments, like in the scene when the dancers utter hurling sounds, cry and grunt and moan beyond the expressivity of emotions: they have become abstracted sound gestures or sound gestalts. Or, in the same piece, the dancer whose face turns into a grimace, mouth wide open—horror solidified into an iconographic facial.

Yet, perhaps the most obvious isolation is the one where the cutting out of any visible preparation or build-up (the hiding of pre-motor movements, which are a prerequisite for the execution of movement) render actions in such a way that they become energetic capsular outbursts, broken down to sheer directness (without direction), efficacy (without efficiency), function (without finality), means (without an end). In other words, if action is taken it seems out of proportion and out of context—a slice of 'hyper-activity' lifted from the hinges of cause and effect, of psychological motivation and sensorial embedment. There are no organic linkages, no developments.

It may be clear even from a rough sketch such as this that many of Sharifi's choreographic choices should not only be understood aesthetically, as crafting a certain style, but also 'diagnostically', as confronting us with a type of action when, as Deleuze described it, most '"healthy" illusions haven fallen' (ibid.) and firm grounding in the sensorial and affective strata is lost.

*VI*

We need new signs (Deleuze 1986).

*VII*

They observe, they erupt, they are pure crying.

No smooth transitions in between, only thresholds. On these thresholds gesture is born. For gesture emerges from the fracture of action. It *is* the shard, the broken fragment, lifted up from the hinges of causality and finality.

That's how Agamben could pick up Deleuze's analysis of cinema and propose an extended cinematic theory that would revolve around gesture instead of the moving image. With Deleuze, he believes that the political 'seems to be going through a protracted eclipse' (Agamben 2000: ix). But rather than looking for 'new signs', Agamben looks for the 'the transformations that gradually have emptied out its categories and concepts' as if the same phenomena that caused political eclipse can now hold a remedy for its resurrection (ibid.). Thus, he looks for genuinely political paradigms in usually not considered spheres. And gesture precisely offers such a sphere: 'Politics is the sphere of pure means, that is, of the absolute and complete gesturality of human beings' (ibid.: 60). Gesture may not exactly be a 'new sign', but it is the closest one gets to something that at least signals 'a passage, an opening' (ibid.: 55–6).

The political does not end at the threshold. The political lives as we take thresholds, as we live them. When the linkages that assure a smooth transition from situation to action have turned from conveyors into blockages in the circuitry of behaviour, gestures are the clumsy effects of stumbling over these obstacles. That's how they speak of immobility even as they move on, of muteness even as they shout, of passivity even as they act upon their surroundings.

Bringing politics face to face with its own failures and its lack of consequence, Agamben advocates thus a politics of gesture—stumbling 'between desire and fulfilment, perpetration and its recollection', tainted with the incurable defects of human beings and their aspirations (ibid.: 58).

It may then come as no surprise that near the end of 'Notes on Gesture' Agamben relates gesture back to communication, but not in terms of conceptual content or message. Rather, what is communicated is communicability itself. Communicability does not stop when one is unable to figure something out in language; it underscores all the more one's sheer being-in-language, as pure mediality. If we have nothing to say, we may still have a need to tell, and to keep trying to figure something out with whatever means is left. Means, indeed. And a whole bunch of paradoxes.

Agamben likes to refer to mime, *commedia dell'arte* or other theatrical figures who are bound by speechlessness. He does so because, so it seems, he sees a fundamental 'mute' figure in these practices that exemplifies some of the daunting paradoxes of our tragic-comical 'condition humaine' in its linguistic limbo, 'only a "gag" destined to hide an incurable speechlessness' (1999: 80) In one sense of the word, Agamben explains, the gag is an instrument of torture, which impedes the 'gagged' person from speech, and—in another sense of the word—the 'actor's improvisation meant to compensate a loss of memory or an inability to speak' (ibid.). This actor's compensation is bound to be full of exaggeration, too big or grand (who will tell?). Too loud in all of its silence, trying to overcome, carry on, seek with whatever means to express something, if not a content, then still one's unyielding desire.[12]

*VIII*

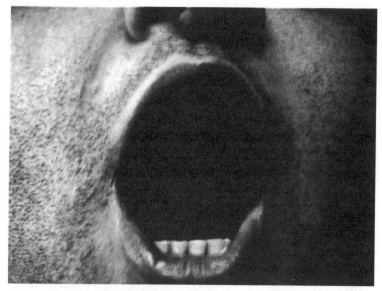

FIGURE 1. Video still from *When day followed hard on night and night on day*. Video by Hooman Sharifi with Kristine N. Slettevold, 2002.

*IX*

So, what is this overall gesture that could summarize the work of Sharifi, comprise it, condense it?

An image appears. It is a still from *When day followed hard on night and night on day* (2002), a video Sharifi made with Kristine Slettevold during a residence in Monty in Antwerp. It shows him with his mouth open wide so that the face nearly becomes one big dark abyss, framed by a white row of teeth. Other scenes in the video evoke torture, bondage, humiliation and restrained movement. One might think therefore that this mouth might relate to torture too and could be thought of as being forced open by, say, an invisible gag.

Next to the meanings of gag that Agamben already pointed out—'something put in someone's mouth to keep him from speaking and, then, the actor's improvisation to make up for an impossibility of speaking' (ibid.)—a third, more physical meaning of the word 'gag' seems to come to light in the video image: to gag as in the gag-reflex, a reflex contraction of the back of the throat that prevents objects from entering the throat except as part of normal swallowing. Gagging is the act of vomiting without vomit; it is an obstruction device that blocks further intake, or initiates return when overdose is near. Openness and closure at the same time—without this defence mechanism we would choke.

What the system cannot tolerate becomes bodily resistance, a physical return. Add a finger to the picture of Sharifi and you get the obscene gesture of someone who says: this makes me gag, I am about to vomit. The picture does not only show a mouth (symbol of speech) but also a throat (symbol of digestion) as a tunnel leading into the opaqueness of the body. Thus, speaking and digesting, language and metabolism conflate so that metaphors are literalized: *spit it out* (say it like it is), *I am (not) swallowing this.*

According to Jacques Rancière (2005), it is the intolerable that instigates the political moment of action. Michel de Certeau (1998) would have described this moment ideally as the moment that prompts the oppressed to seize the word. According to his analysis of the political movement of 1968, the importance was not to be found so much in the statements of the protesters as such, but in the symbolic transgressive instant of coming into speech, the gesture of taking the word. But in Sharifi's case the taking does not lead to much wording. Instead, the instant of symbolic capture or seizure of speech (*prise de la parole*) has been literalized to the second meaning of the word 'seizure' (*crise de la parole*)—a bodily fit, a physical attack, on the threshold of inside and outside, intake and outpour, language and mere slime.

The indi*gesti*bale is what makes gesture come into existence. Gesture is the in-di-gestus, that which resists consummation and absorption. It is the reflux after too much, too many, too much to handle. It is excess, (over)compensation, on top of the violence of speech(lessness), since we can take it no longer.

Could the overall gesture be this, yes: a silent scream, an outcry? But then in its most physical form, its raw flesh nudity. Whereas Agamben speaks of the pure mediality of speech(lessness), Sharifi adds to this the pure mediality of the speech *organ*, which is also an organism of digesting and excretion, a sphincter, an orbicular muscular ring.

To be in language at the other side of language where muteness underlies all that can be said, however hard one yells: Sharifi's dances are tragicomical pantomimes of this gesturality. To communicate with all one's force—not a communication but communicability. To speak without substantial speech—yet to gesture, to signal, to show oneself as being-in-language, being-in-existence and being-in-the-body; the sheer attempt to exist and reveal one's existence as being that which is formulating with no formula. In this relentless exhibition of a pure medial and physical gesturality, politics operates, but most of all a deep sense of humanity.

Just that, but always that.

## Postscript

Far from intending a close reading of Agamben's or of Sharifi's work, or from offering an explicatory framework that reduces one to the sole benefit of the other, this text offers a sample of close writing, with Agamben and Sharifi as mutually reinforcing strains of thoughts, a textual rubbing or frottage, looking more for static electricity than solid theory. A splinter that chipped off in the process of writing is included here as a remainder of past stages and a re-beginning of more writing to come.

## Remainder: Equations

The story goes like this: in 1987 or 1988, at the young age of 15, Sharifi fled his country of birth, Iran, to start a new life in Norway. His first experiences in dance were with hip-hop and street-jazz. Not the regimented codes of hip-hop; dancing was what mattered, movement invention and developing one's own style with whatever means available.[13] Less well known is that Sharifi shifted to community work with youngsters, with whom he made group dances and took part in contests. This means that at an early stage of his dance development, the making of dance was wired into the fabric of street credibility and 'gang' dynamics, street work/dance and youth work/culture.

The story continues like this: Sharifi exchanged the street for a future in contemporary dance when he enrolled in 1997 at the National College of Ballet and Dance in Oslo for a three-year course in choreography. Hardly out of school, Oktoberdans 2000 (Bergen) commissioned *Suddenly, anyway, why all this? While I . . .* , a solo piece that intertwined texts of Beckett with Sharifi's

own story of a relationship of a son to a father. In the same year, he established Impure Company and started to tour an increasingly international cir-
cuit. Presenters called him a trailblazer for a 'return of the political in dance'
and praised it on precisely these terms.

The physiognomy of Sharifi, his Persian ethnicity and the life-story of
the refugee definitely fuelled the construction of a strong political profile. In
statements like 'Art Equals Politics', Sharifi professed that social awareness
and commitment are a prerequisite for making art. Art should connect first
to a personal level before further processing takes place. Only a personal
approach can endow work with genuine appeal, Sharifi claimed in some of
the first texts circulating around his work.[14] In the solo, he mixed slides of
his childhood with the themes of being a 'stranger' in want of intimacy, wandering among the audience, who sat in sections on the stage, and who Sharifi
got to play musical chairs with so that they, too, might have a taste of what
it feels like to be displaced. Gerald Siegmund writes in a review (2001) that
although actions like these risk being naive and one-dimensional, they do
not miss their target. Sharifi's energy and physical presence succeed in making the scattered scenes gel.

The choice of the word 'equals' in Sharifi's slogan 'Art Equals Politics' is
an interesting one, because it reminds us of another equation that became
the adagio of the political movement in the 1970s, and that is the underlying
assumption at work here: the personal is the political. It is as if a syllogistic
operation is involved, that jumps from (a) 'if art is personal', and (b) 'if the
personal is political' then ergo, (c) 'art equals politics'. But the more pertinent
question to ask here is whether the biographical ingredients have not produced a billowing cloud of 'politicalness' that surrounds even the more formal
operations of Sharifi's work and obscures a comprehensive understanding of
far more intricate political underpinnings. In fact, I like to defend a whole
different approach, which I could paraphrase in an opposite slogan that says:
'the impersonal is political,' or, more precisely, 'the political resides where
one fails to become impersonal.'

Sharifi has made two solos since he established Impure Company, which
must be set apart from the group choreographies.[15] Solo work and group work
generally are of different orders but in this case the differences are stunning,
albeit they point to the same problematic. If in the solo work Sharifi inclines

toward an 'artistic creed of the personal', he looks in the group work 'for a certain "unspecificity"'. He says, for instance, that 'in contrast to choreographers like Alain Platel and Meg Stuart', he does not 'recruit dancers for their personal baggage' and does 'not encourage them to "act out" their distinctive traits'. 'I want my dancers to be plain, to represent "everybody", "anybody", the "average".' 'Neutrality' also underlies the choice of costume, which 'should be generic, just usual fashionable clothes, the contemporary uniform'. The movement vocabulary is not 'socially' or 'psychologically' distinguished by difference in detail, idiosyncratic vernacular or tics (those token signatures in 'style' that must underscore individual characterization). The task-like quality of the dancers' performance makes them look more like 'functionaries'. Whereas in solo work Sharifi stays closer to himself, with a direct address, personal dress and natural poise, the dancers in the group pieces portray the functions of people in general, whatever people.

The 'function-approach' calls to mind Michel Foucault, who in his famous essay 'Qu'est-ce qu'un auteur?' (What is an author?; 1994) described the function as something that can operate only with a certain degree of success if it involves a death, that is to say, the surrender of personal biography into the more impersonal mechanisms that govern functions. To die, even if such a death is understood symbolically, is the prerequisite of becoming function.[16]

It is this symbolic death that his dancers die to become 'cadres of the common' that is denied to Sharifi himself. Sharifi expressed this very pertinently when he said: 'whenever I am on stage, even when I do nothing at all, just standing still, I am already a political statement.' Especially since the aftermath of 9/11, the media have endowed the representation of Middle Eastern-looking men with fear-laden associations of terrorism and fundamentalism—Sharifi came to notice that he cannot not be political. 'That's what happens when your face is everyday on the front page of the newspaper.'[17]

Here we see a different sort of equation: an equation that is in fact the reduction of a human being to his face. When the face holds the verdict of always already being politicized as 'other', one becomes, paradoxically enough, 'faceless', because any link with exteriority constituting the face ideally as a site for the common and the private is kept at bay.[18] Pushed to its extremes, this exile to racialized 'otherness' is not unlike the reduction that

Agamben spoke of in relation to the refugee. The inhabitants in the camps had not entered 'as a result from a political choice but rather of what was most private and incommunicable in oneself, that is, one's blood, one's biological body' (2000: 122). Agamben calls the 'camp' the 'inaugural site of modernity' because 'it is the first place in which public and private events, political life and biological life, become rigorously indistinguishable' (ibid.). To equate a person not only to biography, but also to biology, is to reduce him or her to the 'absolutely private person', without ever allowing him or her 'shelter in the realm of the private'.

Rather than having all distinctions implode, one must resist such 'absolutization' of the private (and I would add 'of the personal') if we are not to enter the logic of the camp. The right to remain private is a necessary condition of being part of a political community. To have a political choice presupposes that one is able to exercise and negotiate the terms of privacy and public functioning.

Agamben believes with Foucault that in order to acquire a public function, like for instance the author function, one must be able to dissolve and surrender one's personal identity and specific biography/biology to the more impersonal mechanisms that operate in the function. However, if Agamben calls authorship a process of gesturalization in the illuminating essay 'L'auteur comme geste' [The Author as a Gesture] in *Profanations* (2006), it is because the same procedures that characterize gestures of all kinds can be said to be active in authorship: the 'voiding' of 'previous charge' or content to the end of the emergence of a more 'empty' form that allows other uses. Just as gestural traces of former meanings linger on—as relicts—the elimination of the individual story is never achieved completely in the 'function'. Even in the empty functioning of authorship identity issues remain—that is, they protract into the picture.

Let us therefore rephrase the stakes: the political in Sharifi's work flares up not in the personal per se, but in the impossibility of becoming impersonal or transcending the specificity of one's own features. As a consequence, the political is never a one-to-one relationship with the personal per se, nor does it allow its complete erasure. The political is precisely what escapes any equation to the absolute personal or to the absolute impersonal. The political is always the result of the specifics of the meeting between the personal with the given impersonal 'dispositif'.

*Notes*

1  These are also the opening lines of Giorgio Agamben's seminal essay on gestures, 'Kommerell, or On Gesture' (first published in 1991). Agamben has foregrounded his ideas on gesture since the early 1990s in this essay, as well as in his collection of writings *Means without End: Notes on Politics* (2000), with, in particular, the 'Notes on Gesture' (1992) and 'Marginal Notes on *Commentaries on the Society of the Spectacle*' (1990). Not aiming at a full-grown theory, Agamben presents here a string of inspiring and—taken together—remarkably coherent theses. English translations of these writings were made available around the turn of the millennium, which accounts for the rather recent career of Agamben's notion of gesture as a critical concept in the English-speaking world. In the more recently published *Profanations* (2006), the insightful essay 'L'auteur comme geste' [The Author as a Gesture] should be noted as yet another development in the literature on gesture. Besides, in this collection of essays 'gesture' has pervaded the fabric of most of the collected texts. More than a metaphor, it has become a poetic concept. I will draw from all of these sources as if they constitute one weave, one para-text.

2  The word 'stanzas' alludes to *Stanzas: Word and Phantasm in Western Culture*, which Agamben published in 1993.

3  All quotes by Hooman Sharifi come from a series of preparatory conversations in the spring of 2005, unless otherwise stated. For additional material on Sharifi and Impure Company, see Sarma, the digital archive for dance and performance criticism, which harbours several texts, transcriptions and audio-records of Sharifi (www.sarma.be). Publications by Impure Company include three magazines that were released on the occasion of the premieres of *as if your death was your longest sneeze ever*, *Hopefully someone will carry out great vengeance on me* and *We failed to hold this reality in mind*.

4  *Hopefully* is the abbreviation of *Hopefully someone will carry out great vengeance on me* (2004).

5  In the conversations we had, Sharifi warmly credits his teachers at the National College for Choreography, Annegrete Eriksen and Leif Harnas, for passing on Cunningham values to him.

6  Agamben is referring here to Max Kommerell.

7  This spectral quality is also apparent in the following description Agamben gives: 'Consigned to their supreme gesture, works live on, like creatures bathed in the light of the Last Day' (1999: 80).

8   Agamben on Guy Debord in 'Marginal Notes on *Commentaries on the Society of the Spectacle*': 'Guy Debord's books constitute the clearest and most severe analysis of the miseries and slavery of a society that by now has extended its dominion over the whole planet—that is to say, the society of spectacle in which we live' (2000: 73).

9   I will come back to the 'choking' later, at the end of the text.

10  For the etymological understanding of gestus, Agamben draws from Varro (1987).

11  Gilles Deleuze focuses in *Cinema 1. The Movement-Image* and *Cinema 2. The Time-Image* on the change that occurred after the Second World War—a change from movement-image-based cinema to a time-image-based cinema. But the study should not be understood in cinematic terms only, as it offers also a cultural–societal analysis in the trail of Debord's prophetic critiques on the society of spectacle. To penetrate into the core of the society of 'integrated spectacle' is not only to seize the dominion of the image but also to capture the way it has been rearticulating the relations among Western subjectivities. The prevalence of the image thus finds its correlate in the protraction of the spectator into all domains and, with this telescoping, comes the gradual decline of action.

12  The nexus between the tragicomical and parody is still to be explored. In 'Parodie', Agamben has a whole specific understanding of parody which is to him another form of profanation (2006: 39–59). As for world politics: 'in fact, we could say that world politics is nothing more than a hasty and parodic mise-en-scène of the script contained in [Guy Debord's] book' (2000: 80).

13  Sharifi did not choose to integrate hip-hop vernacular into his choreographies, although it would have been consonant with the wave of interest in hip-hop by the European contemporary dance scene since the 1990s. In a conversation with André Lepecki at Springdance (Utrecht, 2005), Sharifi—on a panel with Bruno Beltrao and Rosemary Lee—speaks about his relationship to hip-hop. The talk also encompasses other topics like identity politics, the difference between solo work, and group work and the relationship with the audience (the talk is available as an audio-file at www.sarma.be).

14  Sharifi in an announcement for Junge Hunde Festival in 2001: 'Art Equals Politics'. This statement, where social awareness and commitment define the word 'politics', marks the outset for Impure Company. It signifies what art is

and should be. When producing a piece, the theme is approached and reassigned to a personal level, before it is processed from the point of view of the individual. By work with this structure, you arrive at the essential: society consisting of individuals. A closeness to the theme is created in a captivating but confronting form. The result is a personal appeal to the theme. For similar descriptions of his work, see 'Artistic Objective', an artistic statement published on Sarma on the occasion of the colloquium 'Unfolding the Critical' (March 2003).

15 The other solo is *We failed to hold this reality in mind* (2005).

16 A wonderfully insightful essay on Michel Foucault's proclamation of the death of the author (as individual subject) is by Agamben, 'L'auteur comme geste' [The Author as a Gesture] in *Profanations* (2006). Two conferences by Foucault are at the centre of his discussion: 'Qu'est-ce qu'un auteur', a speech for the members of the Société française de Philosophie on 22 February 1969, and two years later, the same speech in a modified version for the university at Buffalo. Although the lectures deal with literary authorship, most thoughts can be applied to a wide array of functions that revolve around a similar tension between individual and 'function'.

17 In *We failed to hold this reality in mind*, Sharifi finally decided to confront the fact of his 'difference' full on, by suggesting that 'the oriental' as well the perception of him a priori as a political subject is not an intrinsic given, but an effect of a way of being looked at. In the piece he integrates for the first time Persian music (next to Missy Eliott) and a Persian carpet. Yet the piece hovered somewhere between invocation of ethnicity as a theme and the suspension of the very same theme, between explicit references and oblique comments, between identity issues and a resistance to be placed solely under the interpretative lens of identity politics.

18 For Agamben on the face as a site and threshold for community and the political, see 'The Face' in *Means Without End: Notes on Politics* (2000).

*References*

AGAMBEN, Giorgio. 1993 [1977]. *Stanzas: Word and Phantasm in Western Culture. Theory and History of Literature Series*, VOL. 69 (Ronald L. Martinez trans.). University of Minnesota Press: Minneapolis.

————. 1999. *Collected Essays in Philosophy* (Daniel Heller-Roazen trans. and ed.). Stanford, CA: Stanford University Press.

————. 2000 [1996]. *Means Without End: Notes on Politics* (Vincenzo Binetti and Cesare Casarino trans.). Minneapolis: University of Minnesota Press.

————. 2006. *Profanations* (Martin Rueff trans.). Paris: Editions Payot and Bibliothèque Rivages.

BAUDRILLARD, Jean. 1992. *L'illusion de la fin ou la grève des événements* [The Illusion of the End or Strike of Events]. Paris: Galilee.

DEBORD, Guy. 1967. *Societé du Spectacle* [Society of the Spectacle]. Paris: Buchet-Chastel.

DE CERTEAU, Michel. 1998. *The Capture of Speech and Other Political Writings* (Tom Conley trans.). Minneapolis: University of Minnesota Press.

DELEUZE, Gilles. 1986 [1983]. *Cinema 1. The Movement-Image* (Hugh Tomlinson and Barbara Habberjam trans.). London: Athlone Press.

————. 1989 [1985]. *Cinema 2. The Time-Image* (Hugh Tomlinson and Robert Galeta trans.). London: Athlone.

FOUCAULT, Michel. 1994 [1969]. 'Qu'est qu'un auteur?' [What is an Author?], in *Dits et écrits 1954-1988* [Sayings and Writings 1954–1988]. Paris: Gallimard, pp. 789–820.

JARRY, Alfred. 1980 [1911]. *Gestes et opinions du Docteur Faustroll, pataphysicien* [Gestures and Opinions of Doctor Faustrool, Pataphysician]. Paris: Gallimard.

RANCIÈRE, Jacques. 2005. *Chroniques des temps consensuels* [Chronicles of Consensual Times]. Paris: Seuil.

SIEGMUND, Gerald. 2001.'Im Rahmen von "Springdance/Dialogue" zeigen Hooman Sharifi "Suddenly. Anyway. Why all this? While I . . ." und Benoit Izard "Scanning" im Mousoturm' [Within the Frame of Springdance/Dialogue showings of Hooman Sharifi 'Suddenly. Anyway. Why all this? While I . . .' and Benoit Izard 'Scanning' in Mousoturm]. *Frankfurter Allgemeine Zeitung/Rhein-Main*, 19 November.

VARRO. 1987. *On the Latin Language* (Roland G. Kent trans.). Cambridge, MA: Harvard University Press.

NOTES ON CONTRIBUTORS

ANURIMA BANERJI is Assistant Professor in the Department of World Arts and Cultures, UCLA. Her current project traces the history of Odissi, a South Asian classical dance form, from its role as ritual practice to transnational spectacle, with a focus on the state's regulation of the form and its performances of gender. Her essays, articles and reviews have been published in journals such as *Economic and Political Weekly*, *e-misferica*, *Manushi* and *Women and Performance*. Anurima is also a poet and dancer. She has received several honours and fellowships for both her creative and scholarly work.

PAULA CASPÃO is a Portuguese writer/researcher on choreographic performance based in Paris, particularly interested in exploring dramaturgy and the production and representation of theoretical modes. She is currently a PhD candidate researching theories of sensation, choreographic agencies and politics at University Paris-10. The author of *Amphi-biografias de Contagio* (Amphi-biographies of contagion, 2002/2003) which won the Literary Award IPLB/Fiction (2005), Caspão developed several writing experiments in Berlin and in Vienna (1995–99). As a researcher, dramaturge and documentarist, she has collaborated with choreographers João Fiadeiro (Lisbon, since 1999), Petra Sabisch (Berlin/London, 2002/2005) and Alix Eynaudi (Brussels, 2007).

VICTORIA ANDERSON DAVIES is a PhD candidate in the Department of Performance Studies at Tisch School of the Arts, NYU, where she also teaches in the Expository Writing Program. She has performed as a dancer in New York with Fiona Marcotty-Dolenga, Mark Jarecke, Gina Gibney and many others. In 2005, she created and performed an evening-length piece titled *Debbie's Debbie* with collaborator Elizabeth DeMent. The creative team is currently working on a series of choreographic photos entitled *The One*.

JOSÉ GIL was born in Mozambique, a former Portuguese colony. He obtained his undergraduate and Master's degrees in Philosophy at the Sorbonne, and his doctoral degree at Paris VIII. He was Directeur de Programme of the Collège International de Philosophie de Paris, and is currently Full Professor of Philosophy at Lisbon's Universidade Nova. He has published books on the body (*Métamorsoses do corpo* [Metamorphoses of the Body, 1980], *Os Monstros* [Monsters, 1994]), on aesthetics (*A Imagem-nua e as Pequenas Percepções* [The Naked-Image and the Small Perceptions, 1996]), on dance (*Movimento Total— O Corpo e a Dança* [Total Movement—the Body and the Dance, 2001]) and on the poetics of Fernando Pessoa. Some of his books have been translated into French, Italian and English. In December 2004, the French magazine *Nouvel Observateur* chose Gil as one of the 25 most significant contemporary intellectuals in Europe.

DANIELLE GOLDMAN is Assistant Professor of Dance at Eugene Lang College, The New School for Liberal Arts. She recently edited a special issue of *Women & Performance: A Journal of Feminist Theory*, exploring gendered relations between music and dance, and was a guest co-editor for the *Movement Research Performance Journal* 33. She has published articles in *Dance Research*, *Dance Research Journal*, *Etcetera* and *TDR*. She is writing a book about the politics of improvised dance, to be published by the University of Michigan Press. In addition to her academic endeavours, Goldman is performing in the work of Beth Gill and DD Dorvillier.

CHRISTINE GREINER is Professor in the Department of Body Languages, Graduate Program of Communication and Semiotics and the Undergraduate Course of Communication and Body Arts at the Catholic University of São Paulo, Brazil. She is the author of *Butô, pensamento em evolução* (Butoh, A Thought in Evolution; 1998), *Teatro Nô e o Ocidente* (Noh Theatre and the West; 2000), *O Corpo, pistas para estudos indisciplinares* (The Body: Clues for Indisciplinary Studies; 2005), and several articles published in Brazil, France and Japan. She was a visiting scholar at the Department of Performance Studies at Tisch School of the Arts, NYU, from January to March 2007.

JENN JOY is a PhD candidate in Performance Studies at Tisch School of the Arts, NYU, and teaches at Pratt Institute and Rhode Island School of Design. Her writing has been published in *Movement Research Performance Journal*, *Studies in Gender and Sexuality*, *Dance Theatre Journal*, *TDR*, *Women and Performance*, *Contemporary*, and *NYC: Das vermessene Paradies Positionen zu New York* (Haus der Kulturen Welt/Theater der Zeit). She has collaborated as a dramaturge with Chase Granoff and Jeremy Wade. From 1997–2000, she founded and directed jennjoygallery in San Francisco.

SANSAN KWAN has a PhD from New York University and is Assistant Professor in the Department of Theatre Arts and Dance at California State University, Los Angeles. Her work can be found in *Performance Research*, *Tessera*, *Thresholds*, an anthology titled *Intersections: Dance, Place, Identity* (2007) and elsewhere. She is also a co-editor of the essay collection *Mixing It Up: Multiracial Subjects* (2004). She is working on a book titled *Kinesthetic Ethnicity: Dance, Movement, and City Space in the Chinese Diaspora*.

RALPH LEMON formed Cross Performance/Ralph Lemon Company in 1985. As Artistic Director, he conceives, choreographs and directs the cross-cultural and cross-disciplinary performance and presentations of the company. His artistic work also includes drawing, painting, video/film and digital media. Since 2005, Lemon has been engaged in The Walter Project, a series of works in various art forms developed in collaboration with Walter Carter, a 100-year-old African American man who has lived his entire life in Bentonia, Mississippi. Their collaboration is the basis for the mixed-media installation, *(The Efflorescence of) Walter*, exhibited at the Walker Art Center, The Kitchen and the Contemporary Art Center in New Orleans. The eventual inclusion of other Bentonia residents in The Walter Project has led to creation of The Mississippi Institute, a formal structure through which local residents can participate in the development and production of new interdisciplinary and experimental work. In 2005 Ralph concluded The Geography Trilogy, a decade-long international research and performance project that included three evening-length dance/theatre performances: *Geography* (1997); *Tree* (2000); and *Come Home Charley Patton* (2004); two Internet art projects; and the books *geography: art/race/exile* (2000) and *Tree: belief/culture/balance* (2004) published by Wesleyan University Press. He has received numerous fellowships including the United States Artists Fellowship in 2006, a 2005 Bessie (NY Dance and Performance), a 2004 NYFA Choreography Fellowship, a 2004 Fellowship with the Bellagio Study and Conference Center. His many teaching positions include artist-in-residence at Temple University in 2005–06, George A. Miller Endowment Visiting Artist at the Krannert Center in 2004, a Fellow of the Humanities Council and Program in Theater and Dance at Princeton University in 2002, Associate Artist at Yale Repertory Theatre in 1996–2000.

ANDRÉ LEPECKI is Associate Professor in the Department of Performance Studies at New York University. He is the curator of the 2008 and 2009 editions of the performance Festival IN TRANSIT, at House of World Cultures, Berlin. In the 1990s, he was the dramaturge for Meg Stuart and her company Damaged Goods. He co-created video installations with Bruce Mau (*Stress*, for the MAK in Vienna) and with Rachel Swain (*Proxy*, for the Australian New Media Arts Council). In 2004, he co-created (with Brazilian performance artist Eleonora Fabião) the performance series *Wording* (*I*, *II*, *III* and *IV*, presented in Berlin, Paris and Rio). He is the author of *Exhausting Dance: Performance and the Politics of Movement*; the editor of *Of the Presence of the Body*; and co-editor (with Sally Banes) of *The Senses in Performance*. His most recent projects include the redoing of Allan Kaprow's *18 Happenings in 6 Parts* (Haus der Kunst, Munich and PERFORMA 07) and the curatorship of the 'Nomadic New York' performance festival for Haus der Kulturen (2007). He is currently working on a book on dance and sculpture.

ERIN MANNING is Assistant Professor in Studio Art and Film Studies at Concordia University (Montreal, Canada) as well as Director of *The Sense Lab*, a laboratory that explores the intersections between art practice and philosophy through the matrix of the sensing body in movement. Her artwork is primarily devoted to painting and sculpture. She dances Argentine tango professionally and writes about it as relational movement. Her dance background includes · classical ballet and contemporary dance. Publications include *Politics of Touch: Sense, Movement, Sovereignty* (2006) and *Ephemeral Territories: Representing Nation, Home and Identity in Canada* (2003). Her current book project is called *Mov-*

*ing the Relation: Force Taking Form* and deals with movement, art and techniques of relation (2008).

ROYONA MITRA is a trained Indian classical dancer and a UK-based dance-theatre practitioner. She is Senior Lecturer in Drama andPerformance at the University of Wolverhampton, UK, and is also enrolled in a PhD programme at Royal Holloway College, University of London, where she graduated with an MA in Physical Theatre. Her research interrogates the corporeal, aesthetic and sociological interplay between Indian classical dance and European dance-theatre practice.

JEROEN PEETERS was trained in art history and philosophy. He is currently living and working in Brussels as a writer, dramaturge and curator in the field of dance and performance. He publishes various specialized media, including *Contact Quarterly, corpus, Dance Theatre Journal* and *Etcetera*, and has co-edited books on the aesthetics of Jean-François Lyotard and on queer theory. Recent publications include *Bodies as Filters* (on Boris Charmatz, Benoît Lachambre and Meg Stuart; 2004) and *Shadow Bodies* (on Philipp Gehmacher and Raimund Hoghe; 2006). (An extended bibliography and selection of writings are available at www.sarma.be/nieuw/critics/peeters.htm.) Since 2002, Peeters has directed Sarma together with Myriam Van Imschoot. Sarma is both an online platform for dance and performance criticism (www.sarma.be) and a workplace for discourse, dramaturgy and artistic research. As dramaturge, artistic collaborator and performer, Peeters has contributed to performances and research projects of (amongst others) Milli Bitterli, Paul Deschanel Movement Research Group, Frankfurter Kueche, Anne Juren, Thomas Lehmen, Vera Mantero, Martin Nachbar, Lisa Nelson, Meg Stuart and Superamas.

FRÉDÉRIC POUILLAUDE has studied philosophy at the Ecole normale supérieure in Paris and holds a PhD in philosophy. His dissertation, 'Le désoeuvrement chorégraphique: Etude sur la notion d'oeuvre en danse' [Choreographic Inoperativity: Study of the Concept of *Oeuvre* in Dance], was published by Vrin in 2009. He teaches philosophy at the University Paris IV Sorbonne.

GERALD SIEGMUND is Professor of Theatre Studies at the University of Berne, Switzerland. He has studied theatre, English, and French literature in Frankfurt am Main, Germany, and taught at the Institute of Applied Theatre Studies in Giessen, Germany. In addition to publishing widely on contemporary dance and theatre performances, his most recent book—which focuses on the work of William Forsythe, Meg Stuart, Jérôme Bel and Xavier Le Roy—is *Abwesenheit. Eine performative Ästhetik des Tanzes* (Absence: A Performative Aesthetics of Dance; 2006).

PETER SLOTERDIJK is one of Germany's most well-known public intellectuals and received the Sigmund-Freud-Award for Scientific Prose in 2005. He is currently the director of the Staatliche Hochschule für Gestaltung (HfG center for new media in Karlsruhe, Germany). His seminal books *Critique of Cynical Reason* (1988) and *Thinker on Stage: Nietzsche's Materialism* (1989) are his only works to be translated into English. His most recent books comprise a trilogy entitled *Sphären* [Spheres], including: *Sphären I-Blasen, Mikrosphärologie* (Spheres I: Bubbles, Microspherology, 1998); *Sphären II-Globen, Makrosphärologie* (Spheres II: Globes, Microspherology, 1999); *Sphären III-Schäume, Plurale Sphärologie* (Spheres III: Foam, Plural Spherologies, 2004), all published by Suhrkamp.

NOÉMIE SOLOMON is a dancer, choreographer and writer working in and around contemporary performance practices. She worked as choreographer and assistant director for the re-doing of Allan Kaprow's *18 Happenings in 6 parts* at the Haus der Kunst, Munich and PERFORMA, New York. Solomon holds an MA in Dance Studies from Université Paris-8, and is currently completing her PhD in the Department of Performance Studies, Tisch School of the Arts, NYU.

MYRIAM VAN IMSCHOOT, based in Brussels, works as a dramaturge, curator, performer, writer and teacher in the field of dance and performance. Trained as a dance historian, she became an independent researcher after being affiliated for many years with the Institute of Cultural Studies at the Catholic University of Leuven. She founded Sarma, a workplace for dance research and critique (www.sarma.be). Her dramaturgical work relates to her numerous collaborations (Meg Stuart, Hahn Rowe, Benoît Lachambre, Philipp Gehmacher, etc.). Currently she is preparing a book on Jérôme Bel, with Christophe Wavelet and Jérôme Bel.